Making Social Welfare Policy in America

Making Social Welfare Policy in America

Three Case Studies since 1950

EDWARD D. BERKOWITZ

THE UNIVERSITY OF CHICAGO PRESS CHICAGO AND LONDON

The University of Chicago Press, Chicago 60637
The University of Chicago Press, Ltd., London

Published 2020
Printed in the United States of America

29 28 27 26 25 24 23 22 21 20   1 2 3 4 5

ISBN-13: 978-0-226-69206-7 (cloth)
ISBN-13: 978-0-226-69223-4 (paper)
ISBN-13: 978-0-226-69237-1 (e-book)
DOI: https://doi.org/10.7208/chicago/9780226692371.001.0001

Library of Congress Cataloging-in-Publication Data

Names: Berkowitz, Edward D., author.
Title: Making social welfare policy in America : three case studies since 1950 / Edward D. Berkowitz.
Description: Chicago : University of Chicago Press, 2020. | Includes bibliographical references and index.
Identifiers: LCCN 2019035397 | ISBN 9780226692067 (cloth) | ISBN 9780226692234 (paperback) | ISBN 9780226692371 (ebook)
Subjects: LCSH: Public welfare—United States—History—20th century. | Disability insurance—United States—History—20th century. | Medicare—History—20th century. | Aid to families with dependent children programs—United States—History—20th century.
Classification: LCC HV91 .B395 2020 | DDC 361.6/10973—dc23
LC record available at https://lccn.loc.gov/2019035397

♾ This paper meets the requirements of ANSI/NISO Z39.48-1992 (Permanence of Paper).

Contents

Preface vii

Introduction 1

CHAPTER 1 Congress Passes a Law, the Labor Movement Unites, and Walter George Retires 15

CHAPTER 2 What Happened to the Disability Program and How Policy Makers Tried to Respond 47

CHAPTER 3 Wilbur Mills, Wilbur Cohen, and Nelson Cruikshank Curate Medicare 77

CHAPTER 4 The Consequences of Medicare from Accommodation to Regulation 122

CHAPTER 5 The Continuing Consequences of Medicare: Choice and Prescription Drugs 158

CHAPTER 6 The Welfare Reform Debate from JFK to Reagan 190

CHAPTER 7 Clinton, Gingrich, and Welfare Reform in 1996 221

Conclusion 262

Notes 281

Index 325

Preface

For much of my adult life I have studied the history of social welfare programs, and this book marks, so far as I know, my final effort in the field. Since this book depends so heavily on what I have written before, it might be worthwhile to describe briefly my past projects that have informed this one. My interest in the field of social welfare policy probably comes from my father, who spent his long academic career studying workers' compensation and other disability programs. When it came time for me to write a dissertation in my chosen field of history, I picked the topic of the vocational rehabilitation program, a little-studied federal-state program that offers counseling and other services to people with disabilities. As if to bring things full circle, the vocational rehabilitation program figures in this book as well.

Nothing about this circular path reflects conscious planning on my part. As a member of a cohort of historians who have always worked in an uncertain academic market, I have drifted from one project to another—mostly in response to someone asking me to write something. This book contains three case studies that concern programs I have considered over the course of my career. This book, in other words, derives from my previous ones and uses research I have done in the course of writing those books. If there is something new here, it consists of my desire not only to chronicle the passage of legislation but also to figure out what happened to the programs after they were launched. Each of the programs developed in a different way that perhaps illustrates something about the expansion of America's welfare state after the founding eras of the New Deal and the Great Society.

I began my academic career by writing a book with a friend from graduate school. Sympathetic advisors advised us against the project and counseled that published versions of our respective dissertations should come first. We persisted, in my case because I had nothing better to do. When an editor for a prestigious academic press approached us at an academic conference and asked whether we had a book manuscript, it was as close to a commission as we were likely to get. The resulting book had the usual travails. The prestigious press rejected it after receiving what I remember as three negative reports. Part of the problem might have been that, in our ignorance of the rules of academic publishing, we sent the manuscript to the publisher without including footnotes. The readers could not find themselves in the text. We remedied the problem, and in 1980 a marginal press published the book. Within the very small realm of social welfare history, the book acquired a niche because it fit into the literature being developed by Harvard professor Theda Skocpol and her associates on the development of America's welfare state.

That began an academic career that included stints at the University of Massachusetts Boston where white working-class students interested in accounting met Marxist professors and other harbingers of a radical change that never quite reached the students in South Boston and Dorchester. I next worked on the staff of a presidential commission in Washington, increasing my interest in public policy, then in an office at Brandeis University devoted to fundraising, where I got to pitch Brandeis to bored executives at the Gillette Company in Boston and the Chemical Bank on Wall Street, before landing at George Washington University, where I spent the rest of my career.

In these various locations, I encountered the three social welfare programs that form the case studies in this book. My first choice was a program that Congress legislated in 1956 that contemporaries referred to most often as SSDI (Social Security Disability Insurance). It extended the Social Security program, created in 1935, so that people with disabilities could receive retirement benefits before reaching the normal retirement age. I first encountered the program when I wrote my doctoral dissertation on the history of disability programs, and it became a recurring interest. When I came to George Washington University, I needed a scholarly project, and a grant from the Twentieth Century

Fund allowed me to pursue my research on disability programs in conditions of relative comfort. *Disabled Policy* (1987) marked one of my first self-conscious attempts to use history to illuminate contemporary developments in public policy.

Medicare, created in 1965 at the height of the Great Society, serves as my second case study. This program is another that has come up repeatedly in the course of my career. I first seriously encountered it when I wrote a biography of Social Security bureaucrat Wilbur Cohen, *Mr. Social Security* (1987). Writing that book brought me into contact with Wilbur Joseph Cohen, one of the frontline bureaucrats who worked on Social Security, increasing my respect for the competence of these government employees and my appreciation of their influence. I also dug into Medicare archives in places like the Wisconsin Historical Society and the Lyndon Baines Johnson Presidential Library. Somewhere along the way I met Martha Derthick, whose book *Policymaking for Social Security* (1979) is the most perfect blend of history and public policy I have ever encountered. Both Martha Derthick and Wilbur Cohen reinforced the importance of considering public administration in the study of social welfare programs. So did Robert Ball, the Social Security administrator who implemented the Medicare program, whose biography I published in 2003.

I had other opportunities to study Medicare as a Robert Wood Johnson Foundation Faculty Fellow in Health Care Finance at Johns Hopkins (1987–1988) and as a commissioned author of histories of the Group Health Association in Washington, DC (1988), and of the National Academy of Science's Institute of Medicine (1998). Later I had a chance to do interviews for the Health Care Financing Administration, the National Libraries of Medicine, and the National Academy of Social Insurance with many of the key administrators and researchers in Medicare and health care services (all of which are available on the internet). Each of these oral history projects came to me over the transom, so to speak, and not as part of a conscious plan to learn about the history of Medicare.

My third case study concerns Aid to Families with Dependent Children and the more general process of welfare reform. When I served on the staff of the President's Commission for a National Agenda for the Eighties, welfare reform remained a hot issue, and I was assigned the task of designing a welfare reform program for the commission to recommend. That experience brought me into contact with some members of the policy-making establishment for welfare. Part of the experience worked its way into *America's Welfare State* (1995) and into pieces I wrote on my commission experience.

As I hope this preface makes clear, this book recapitulates and with luck synthesizes what I have written over the course of my academic career.

Most academic books begin with acknowledgments, but in this case I have to acknowledge all of the people who have helped me with my research and writing over the course of many years. Before I embark on the more formal and academic parts of the book, let me list at least some of the people to whom I owe major debts of gratitude: Andy Achenbaum, Brian Balogh, Howie Baum, Bill Becker, Daniel Beland, Monroe Berkowitz, Shalvo Berkowitz, Christine Bogdanovich, Richard Burkhauser, Blanche Coll, Donald Critchlow, Gareth Davies, David Dean, Peter and Dale Demy, Martha Derthick, Larry DeWitt (who also graciously did the charts for this book), Jennifer Erkulwater, Dan Fox, Frank Hubbard, Hugh Graham, Brian Grattan, Chris Howard, Jonathan Hughes, Amy Kahn, Robert Kelley, Alice Kessler Harris, Eric Kingson, Michael Katz, Pamela Larson, Mark Leff, Rick Mayes, Kim McQuaid, Ida Merriam, Thomas Murphy, Robert Myers, Kathy Newcomer, John H. Noble Jr., Peter Ochshorn, Jim Patterson, Roger Prouty, Jill Quadagno, Leo Ribuffo, Jeff Rice, Jeff Rubin, Mark Santangelo, Richard Scotch, Theda Skocpol, Jim Smith, Deborah Stone, Richard Stott, Robert Wiebe, Wendy Wolf, and Julian Zelizer

Introduction

This book chronicles three key moments in America's welfare state and traces their consequences. For two of the three programs under discussion, the book includes a long chronological narrative of the process that led to their enactment, followed by shorter histories that detail what happened to the programs over time. The third case study culminates in the passage of a major new law, with the preceding chapters trying to explain why such a change was possible. This introduction provides an overview of the programs and makes some initial conjectures about how such programs come into existence and how they develop over time. This book leaves grand theories of public policy formation and modification to the social scientists and others with a more formal methodology. Instead, this book, like most histories, tells stories in detail—in this case three of them—and describes the long-term consequences of those stories.

The first case study, presented in the next two chapters, covers a program legislated in 1956 that contemporaries referred to most often as SSDI (Social Security Disability Insurance). It extended the Social Security program, created in 1935 and launched in 1940, so that working-age people could retire from the labor force if they could prove to the satisfaction of government authorities that they were unable to work because of a physical or mental impairment. In an indirect way, the law lowered the legal retirement age. The 1956 passage of the law was a near thing:

one vote here or there could have changed the outcome. With varying degrees of conviction, insurance executives, medical doctors, the Eisenhower administration, Republicans, and some southern Democrats in Congress lobbied against the bill. They pushed a counternarrative to the one promulgated by the Democratic leadership, social workers, labor unions, and federal bureaucrats who argued that disability created economic hardships best remedied by making cash payments to people with disabilities. The opponents emphasized the theme of rehabilitation. In a world of advancing medical treatments and new technologies of all sorts, the process of rehabilitation allowed people with disabilities to be restored to a condition that made them fit for work. Both sides saw tragic consequences if their opponents' proposals were adopted. Supporters of the legislation warned that failure to pass it would consign a group of individuals who had worked all their lives and encountered hardships not of their own making to a life of poverty and, quite possibly, early death. Opponents of the legislation feared that its passage would relegate a sizable group of people to a life of enforced inactivity at considerable government expense.

On one level, then, the battle for disability insurance was a contest over ideas, but historical contingencies and institutional realities affected the outcome of that contest. The very shape of the bill came from the Social Security program. It would, for example, be financed through payroll taxes and award benefits that were similar in form to old-age insurance retirement benefits. Although the robust economy at the time made it easier to pass the measure, the divided nature of the government, with Democrats in charge of Congress and Republicans in charge of the White House, made it harder. At a more structural level, the committee in charge of the legislation in the Senate contained a group of southern Democrats who blocked the bill in committee, greatly complicating the passage of the bill through the Senate. Two almost serendipitous events produced the final outcome. The labor movement had just acquired more political clout because of a merger between the two largest labor organizations that extended its reach. A powerful and in some quarters beloved Senator from Georgia announced his retirement and decided that disability insurance might become one of his legacies.

The 1956 passage of disability insurance was not inevitable, and the outcome could have gone either way. Seemingly incidental details—just the sorts of things that close historical study can uncover—mattered to the outcome. No automatic process as, for example, the expansion of the

American welfare state led to its passage. Because of explicit political bargains that took place when the measure was under legislative consideration, disability insurance had its own trust fund, separate from the fund for old-age and survivors' benefits, and an unlikely administrative arrangement that allowed individual states to make disability determinations under contract to the federal government. One could create an intellectual rationale for each of these things, but that rationale comes after the fact. It follows from an event that had already taken place rather than being the reason for that event.

Insights from political scientists and economists, in particular path dependency and policy feedback, help to explain what happened next. A law is very malleable during the legislative process because of all the political bargains being made. Once a bill becomes law, however, its structure gets locked down and put into permanent form. That constrains what becomes possible after that because, in effect, the choices have already been made and many of the alternatives foreclosed. That rigidity sets the law down a particular path, which illustrates the notion of path dependency. Past decisions limit present decisions. To apply the concept to the program under discussion, the future of the disability insurance program was determined by its past.[1]

An example further developed in chapters 1 and 2 suggests why that might be so. Disability insurance operated by having people apply for benefits to the federal government, in this case the Social Security Administration. The application initiated an arduous process of trying to determine if the applicant was truly disabled and hence deserving of benefits. Because of the way the law was written in 1956, the procedure involved sending the applicant's file to state disability determination offices, which were working under contract to the federal government. When inconsistencies from state to state became a political problem, legislators found they could not remedy the problem by converting disability determination from a state to a federal operation. Institutional rigidity or path dependency blocked that route. Some things about the disability insurance program, such as limiting benefits to those fifty or older, proved amenable to change—a process that Martha Derthick calls "invisible incremental change"—but the program's basic structure hampered future efforts to change the program.[2]

This example also introduces the second of the social science concepts that are useful in understanding the process of policy change over time. Structures that are locked in place create what political scientists call policy feedbacks. According to political scientist Andrea Louise Campbell, the policy feedback approach "incorporates existing policies as inputs into the policymaking process." In other words, policy creates politics. Hence legislation like the disability insurance law contained many idiosyncratic features—such as the disability determination process—that became the object of future policy battles. Or as Campbell puts it, "Scholars interested in policy feedback study aspects of policy designs to illuminate what kinds of effects policies have on subsequent politics." That idea invites scholars to examine the administrative structures that policies put in place, a practice that this book will follow.[3]

Medicare, created in 1965 at the height of the Great Society, serves as the book's second case study, presented in chapters 3, 4, and 5. Legislative bargains made in 1965 have influenced not just the future development of Medicare but also the future course of American medicine itself. Hence reformers labeled a 2019 health care reform proposal "Medicare for All." The idea capitalized on Medicare's popularity to suggest that its health insurance program for people over sixty-five and people with disabilities be extended to people of all ages. The proposal recognized the fact that Medicare had become the largest single health insurance program in America because it covered a wide swath of people and the private health insurance market consisted of thousands of health insurance plans for private companies and individuals. At the same time, the proposal also almost willfully ignored the administrative structure of the Medicare program.[4]

Medicare resulted from a period of congressional consideration that lasted from 1961 to 1965. The fact that doctors who practiced in every congressional district in America opposed it made it controversial and hence difficult to pass. Passage required intense political bargaining of the sort that preceded passage of disability insurance in 1956. The congressional apparatus that legislated Medicare in 1965 differed from the one that prevailed in 1956. In that year the Senate Committee on Finance blocked passage of disability insurance. In 1965 the House Committee on Ways and Means and its Chairman Wilbur Mills (D-AR) proved more of a problem. Much of the legislative maneuvering involved finding a proposal that Mills could endorse, a process that reached a conclusion only at the end of 1964. Between 1961 and 1965, all sorts of suggestions for the Medicare program arose. Many of them emphasized that the elderly should have a choice rather than having Medicare foisted upon them and that general revenues might be a better way of financing health insurance rather than the Social Security payroll taxes. As always, the details of the law remained fluid right up to the moment of congressional passage in the summer of 1965, despite a huge Democratic majority in Congress after a Democratic landslide in 1964.

The resulting structure sent the program down the road of path dependency, as described in chapters 4 and 5. Part A of the program most closely resembled the administration's proposals from 1961 to 1965. It initiated a program that paid the hospital bills of people over sixty-five. In deference to Representative Mills and the desire to extend the program so that it also covered doctors' bills, the law also contained Part B. It was a different program than Part A, with voluntary enrollment, premiums that users were required to pay, and general revenue financing. Congress negotiated the boundary between Parts A and B—what about X-rays that patients routinely received in the hospital, for example?—with the benefit of the doubt going to Part B. Although the program could be expanded so that, for example, it covered people with disabilities and people with end stage renal disease, the basic structures of Parts A and B remained in place.

Then the process of policy feedback began. The financing of Part A developed problems related to rising costs that took the distinctive form of impending bankruptcy of the Part A trust fund. Efforts to reduce costs ran into the structural barriers that stemmed from the way in which the 1965 legislation provided for the reimbursement of doctors and hospitals. Policy makers tried to adjust those reimbursements in ways that resembled the invisible incremental expansions of the past—the more invisible, the better. In the end, legislators realized that the desired changes could not be made in Parts A and B but rather required a new Part C, which offered Medicare recipients the voluntary choice of plans that used the techniques of managed care to contain expenses. The prosperity of the 1990s and early years of the twenty-first century combined with the political ambitions of President George W. Bush to put a Republican stamp on the Medicare program led to still another Medicare program, labeled Part D, to cover the costs of prescription drugs. Part D operated in a different way than Parts A and B. Private pharmaceutical companies sold plans to Medicare beneficiaries that were subsidized and lightly supervised by the federal government. The expansion of Medicare therefore differed from the expansion of disability insurance. Disability insurance simply incorporated new groups into the program. Medicare added new programs within the existing program and expanded the scope of the Medicare law.

The modern proposal of Medicare for All begs the question of which of the Medicare programs everyone should receive. Would the new program most closely resemble Parts A, B, C, or D, or would it be completely different and become Medicare Part E? In other words, Medicare, as something more than a metaphor for national health insurance, requires policy makers to make choices about financing, the services to be covered, and the integration of the nation's hospitals and doctors into the new program. Historical myopia and deliberate obfuscation of program details cloud public understanding of the Medicare program. Perhaps a historical narrative of the program's development, as presented here, can help to clarify the situation.

The third and final case study in the book concerns Aid to Families with Dependent Children (AFDC). Chapter 6 provides a general background on welfare reform and the various efforts of Congressman Wilbur Mills and Presidents Kennedy, Nixon, and Reagan to change the AFDC program. Chapter 7 deals with welfare reform in the era of Bill Clinton and Newt Gingrich and explores the passage of a major welfare reform bill in 1996. The new law marked a conscious attempt to end welfare as we knew it and represented a more fundamental break with the past than occurred in either disability insurance or Medicare. One might argue that the traditional welfare system had fewer defenders than did social insurance programs such as SSDI and Medicare and was therefore more vulnerable not just to change but to being eliminated altogether.

All social welfare laws, no matter how strong the influence of path dependency, reflect the conventional wisdom of the era of their founding. In the case of welfare, the conventional wisdom shifted in a much more decisive way than it did for Medicare and disability insurance. AFDC started as a relatively minor part of America's state that generated far less controversy than did the old-age insurance program that we now call Social Security. The program alleviated the financial stress of widows raising children and enabled them to stay at home and care for them. The beneficiaries of the program passed the bar of the deserving poor with ease. Over time, however, the situation changed. The program served dependent children and their mothers (and in a very few cases fathers) because of the welfare categories embedded in the 1935 Social Security Act. Path dependency meant that those categories could be expanded to embrace new groups, such as the permanently disabled in 1950, but not eliminated. Old programs had to cope with new social conditions, such as the mass entrance of women into the labor force and a falling marriage rate that raised the number of "illegitimate" children. Because AFDC was a much more flexible category than the others, such as blindness, and because Social Security soon served as the main social welfare benefit for widows with dependent children as a result of the 1939 Social Security Amendments, AFDC became America's largest welfare program devoted to income maintenance. Even as that happened, its beneficiaries—children living in single-parent families—became stigmatized and lost many of their congressional defenders, a process reinforced by the entrance of many black and Hispanic families to the rolls. The program never developed, as many people hoped, into some sort of more general income maintenance law. Although policy makers tried to change the program's identity from a means of providing a safe haven for dependent children to a way of moving welfare mothers into the labor force, the program's basic structure and the process of path dependency made that a difficult objective to achieve. Instead AFDC remained in place until 1996, when a conservative consensus reached critical mass and the window for fundamental reform reopened.

The resulting legislative process featured the usual twists and turns as President Bill Clinton and Speaker of the House Newt Gingrich bargained over the terms of the law. As always, the contents of the law remained fluid until Congress locked those terms into place with the final passage of the law. The new law abolished the old AFDC program and replaced it with something called Temporary Aid to Needy Families (TANF). The name of the new program reinforced the notion that people could receive its benefits only on a temporary, time-limited basis, and only the truly needy need apply. Although the new program inherited its basic structure from the old program, it represented a new administrative arrangement. In the new program, the federal government made what were called block grants to the states. Block grants consolidated a group of previously separate grants into a single grant with a unitary purpose, and block grants came in limited amounts. In other words, a state received a certain amount of money and no more at the same time that it received more discretionary power to spend the money as it wished. In the policy parlance, the block grants ended the practice of making AFDC an entitlement in which anyone who qualified received a welfare payment.

Although the new law shut the door on the past and launched the program on a new path, there remained avenues to expand the program in the usual invisible incremental manner. In this case the expansions involved restoring the rights of particular groups that had been removed by the 1996 legislation so that they qualified for benefits. Capitalizing on the popular mood of the times, Congress excluded legal aliens from receiving TANF benefits. Subsequent laws removed some of the prohibitions. This sort of reform was analogous to opening up the disability rolls to people younger than fifty or expanding Medicare to cover people with kidney disease. In each case the basic structure of the program remained in place, even as the program expanded.

The fact remained, however, that Congress abolished the AFDC program and replaced it with something new or at least different. Even in the face of withering criticism, disability insurance and Medicare remained in place. Furthermore, the criticisms were similar in all three cases and took the line that the programs were out of step with the times. Critics charged that disability insurance failed to meet the modern objective of rehabilitation or recognize the civil rights of people with disabilities. Medicare failed to reflect the best practices of the management of modern medicine. The AFDC program used 1930s methods to solve the problems of the twenty-first century. The responses to these criticisms differed across the programs. Policy makers added new laws, such as the Americans with Disabilities Act of 1990, in order to reach modern objectives but left disability insurance in place, ensuring that retirement rather than rehabilitation would be America's main response to the "problem" of disability. Responding to the problems of Medicare, policy makers added new titles to the program to accomplish new purposes such as expanding the choices available to Medicare recipients and bringing prescription drugs into the program but left the 1965 program, or as it became known, traditional Medicare, largely intact. House Speaker Newt Gingrich put AFDC out of existence but failed to modernize the other programs in the way he would have liked.

A Note on Method

The implicit hypothesis behind this book is that history matters to policy outcomes and that chronicling a program's history helps to illuminate policy problems. Historians have few methodological tricks to offer in this process. Instead they tell stories about change over time that honor the complexity of the process and respect the confusion and uncertainty faced by policy makers at points of decision. At the same time, creating a historical narrative is not a clinical process like x-raying a broken arm. Embedded in the narrative are many decisions that remain hidden from the reader. In the first place, histories are products of their sources, and those sources always temper the narrative. If one spends a month examining the Wilbur Cohen Papers at the Wisconsin Historical Society, it is not unlikely that Wilbur Cohen will become a central character in the story. The danger in that is the author might miss the contributions of other significant individuals in shaping the narrative or, worse, the author might get captured by Wilbur Cohen's point of view.

In the second place, asking what happened always raises the question of what happened next. Any ending to a story, or beginning for that matter, is arbitrary and artificial. In this book, the problem gets compounded because it emphasizes both what happed during the creation of a program and also what happened next. It marks an attempt to capture the long-range effects of a particular policy and the durability of the policy over time. This general subject has captured the interest of political scientists, such as Eric Patashnik, and produced elegant work that is of some use here.[5]

In the third place, histories have to have some coherence or meaning rather than being mere recitations of facts in which one thing simply follows another. Stories have morals or at least some sort of point, and the historian is not immune from having to answer the question of what a particular narrative means. Not only can there be problems in the construction of a narrative that prevent it from being in some sense "correct," the historian must also make a case for the narrative's significance.

Historians argue about the past in part because both the present and the past keep changing. Current contexts almost always distract the historian from viewing the past on its own terms and understanding conditions on the ground, so to speak, at a particular moment. Modern developments can make it hard to see the past clearly. Take the sensitive case of race for example. Things with obvious racial implications or outcomes might or might not have had different meanings in the past. A classic case relevant to the case studies in this book concerns the 1935 Social Security Act. Were farmers and self-employed people excluded from coverage in the old-age insurance program because of a conscious desire to exclude blacks from the program or for some other reason?[6]

A Look at the Literature

Unlike a novelist, a historian does not write on a blank slate. Instead, historians need to confront the scholarship that already exists, or "the literature," as academics call it. Each of the three programs discussed in this book have their own histories written by academics who, in an effort to give their narratives meaning, often find themselves in the role of social critics. In the case of disability insurance, books that examine the program's history remain relatively few, although economists have shown great interest in how disability benefits create work disincentives and lower the labor supply. Each discipline, it seems, finds a lens through which to view a particular program. Among historians disability programs have caught a different methodological wave and become the history of disability rights. A growing literature describes the emergence of people with disabilities as a minority group who have mobilized for their rights. Political scientist Jennifer Erkulwater titles her book about the Supplemental Security Income program *Disability Rights and the American Social Safety Net*, and she has since written about the origins of political identity among people with disabilities. Historian Felicia Kornbluh has published an important article in the lead American history journal titled "Disability, Antiprofessionalism and Civil Rights." These efforts follow from the pioneering work of sociologist Richard Scotch, and they make important contributions, as the academics like to say.[7]

Nonetheless, SSDI remains the most important of all of America's disability programs whether measured by money, enrollments, or influence. Although it has civil rights implications, such as by defining disability as the inability to work, civil rights, at least as understood as minority rights rather than due process, has very little to do with its creation or subsequent development. Because of the program's importance, it deserves its own history, one that concentrates on the program itself rather than on a related and significant topic that has caught the historians' attention.

Medicare, the second of the book's programs, presents a classic case of a legislative triumph becoming a contemporary failure in the eyes of many historians. Most of the books on the subject come from the realm of health care practitioners and health care services researchers who must cope with the program's complicated features, such as the way the program attempts to control the quality of care.[8] When historians and historically minded social scientists write about the program, they tend to criticize Medicare because it is a central part of a flawed medical system. As Christy Ford Chapin has pointed out, it relies on an insurance model that fails to provide "patients with integrated medical care in one location" and leads to incorrect diagnoses because of its fragmented nature. Chapin recognizes that after Medicare's passage path dependency set in with the result that "it has become almost impossible to dislodge the insurance company model from the health care system." It cannot be disputed that private insurers play key roles in the public Medicare program. They are the principal players in the program's prescription drug program, and they administer the program's daily operations in many places.[9]

A similar trend is visible in the more general literature that offers a more panoramic view of American history. The initial historical accounts of Medicare had a gee-whiz quality that celebrated the way that Medicare's passage ended a long impasse over federally supported health care for the nation's elderly population. By the time Allen Matusow published his influential overview of the 1960s in 1984, Medicare, with its rising costs that proved difficult for policy makers to control, had become "a ruinous accommodation between reformers and vested interests."[10]

The subject specialists tended to confirm this judgment. Beatrix Hoffman reported that "in the mad dash to political compromise, Medicare's framers deliberately kept mechanisms for cost control out." Hoffman bemoaned a health system dominated by private interests that "make a great deal of money from health care and have a vested interest in the status quo." This analysis suggested that change would be slow and the United States might never acquire an equitable and affordable system of national health insurance. The question of why the United States lacked national health insurance figured heavily in historical inquiries into the American health care system and, by extension, into Medicare.[11]

Critiquing the US health care system and its largest health insurance program makes plenty of sense, given such things as rising health care costs, high numbers of people without health insurance, and poor performance on measures such as infant mortality and life expectancy compared to other developed nations. It does, however, tend to flatten out the arc of Medicare's history: its fluid nature at its founding in 1965, its expansion to cover people with disabilities and people with end stage renal disease in 1972, the shift from accommodation to regulation in Medicare's payments to doctors and hospitals in 1982 and 1983, its extension into the realm of prescription drugs in 2003, and its gradual shift from a single payer to a program incorporating the notion of consumer choice. Medicare, in other words, has its own history that can be separated from the more general woes of the American health care system. If for no other reasons than the size of the program and its influence over American medicine, that story deserves to be told, but to do so requires a tight focus on the program itself, rather than beginning with American health care problems or some other general concern, such as racism, and working back from there.

In writing about Aid to Families with Dependent Children, the third of the programs under study in this book, one simply cannot avoid dealing with race and gender, because they are in fact central to the program's history. As one might expect, academics who write about the history of welfare tend to emphasize its racial and gender aspects, and they have produced a raft of studies, some them quite brilliant and nearly all of them informative. One of the more suggestive is Martin Gilens's book *Why Americans Hate Welfare*.[12]

As these studies make abundantly clear, AFDC was a welfare program, a product of progressive-era changes in the state and local poor laws that gave needy widows a special entitlement to public aid. After AFDC (or as it was originally called, Aid to Dependent Children) was incorporated into the 1935 Social Security Act, it differed from the social insurance programs for old age and unemployment that were also included in the omnibus act. The social insurance programs paid benefits to regular labor-force participants who, through their payroll tax contributions or, if participants were unemployed, their employers' contributions, had "earned" their benefits. One might argue therefore that AFDC, with its demeaning means tests, was a second-class program from the start that unlike Social Security served mainly poor (and white) women (and their children of both sexes). That line of argument suggests that welfare was a stigmatized program from the get-go.

A closer look at the development of welfare programs from 1935 to 1950, however, suggests otherwise. Between 1935 and 1950 welfare was more popular than Social Security and paid higher benefits. To be sure, most of the welfare recipients were elderly individuals, not widows and their children. After 1950 these elderly people found their way into the Social Security program, leaving the blind, who were always a small group, the permanently and totally disabled, and dependent children behind. Many widows received assistance from the survivors' provisions of the Social Security program. In 1972 Congress federalized the so-called adult welfare programs, leaving only single mothers in the traditional welfare program. By the late 1950s, the welfare caseload consisted mainly of AFDC recipients who were single mothers who had never married rather than widows. In the past, as welfare scholar Jennifer Mittelstadt has noted, some local welfare agencies used their discretionary powers to "distinguish among poor mothers, often on the basis of race, forcing some to work and allowing others to become eligible for welfare."[13] Just at the time that AFDC became a prominent welfare program, local welfare workers, particularly in urban centers that were destinations for African Americans migrating from the South, lost some of these discretionary powers. The courts emphasized that no one could lose his or her welfare benefits without due process of law. The welfare rolls became blacker, and welfare became more of an entitlement and less a gratuity.

Once people believed that the welfare rolls contained a disproportionate number of illegitimate black children who lived elsewhere, as happened during the 1960s, all of the usual reactions, well captured by political scientists, set in. Welfare recipients became stigmatized and suffered much rougher handling from Congress in 1996 than did other social welfare benefit recipients. When political scientist Joe Soss of the University of Minnesota and two of his colleagues made a systematic study of the 1996 welfare reforms, they discovered that over the course of the debate "beliefs about African Americans and welfare programs turned sharply more negative." Stereotypes of "black laziness and sexual irresponsibility" aided in the passage of the 1996 Temporary Aid to Needy Families law.[14] Taking a long look at the development of the AFDC program shows that these antiblack features took time to develop and that the original 1935 welfare categories that followed from earlier state programs and the development of other programs after 1935 created policy feedbacks that resulted in the arguably racist 1996 law.

* * *

This book, then, keeps its narrative focus on three social welfare programs. It examines the creation of these programs with an appreciation of how political bargaining affects the legislative outcome but in no certain direction or way. Once the programs are created, they set off on a course of path dependency and arrive at crises often exacerbated by their internal structures. Weaknesses and inconsistencies of this structure stem from the fluid way in which the programs were originally constructed and the way the legislative process privileges political accommodations, passing a law, above administrative design. Neglected in the program's creation, the administrative design exercises a great deal of influence over the program's subsequent development. This book examines public policy through the lens of public administration. The reference point is the work of Martha Derthick.[15]

Programs have different reactions to crises. Some of the crises that a program encounters are strong enough to induce legislative changes, but the form those changes take stems in part from the program's popularity. Some programs like disability insurance resist change, and policy makers seeking a change in an approach to a particular problem must look elsewhere and, for example, pass the Americans with Disabilities Act in 1990. Other programs like Medicare remain durable, with the result that the core of the program survives through time. New policy initiatives get added to the legislation, as in Medicare Part D. Finally, programs with little political popularity, such as AFDC, face the risk of going out of business altogether, as happened to that program in 1996.

Historians resist generalizations and want to see the particulars. It is time, then, to turn to the three case studies and learn about the programs in detail.

CHAPTER ONE

Congress Passes a Law, the Labor Movement Unites, and Walter George Retires

In 1956 the United States broadened the scope of its welfare state by removing the age limits on the receipt of retirement benefits. Instead of waiting until age sixty-five to claim benefits, a worker could take early retirement in the form of a disability pension. Once declared disabled—no longer able to work—by state authorities, a person would receive benefits similar to those he or she would have gotten had he or she waited until age sixty-five. To gain congressional passage, the legislation underwent an intense period of political bargaining, which left the outcome and the content of the final law in doubt until the very last minute. Casual decisions acquired permanent consequences. Understanding the rudiments of modern social policy in the important area of disability therefore becomes a matter of tracing the 1956 law through the political process. In other words one needs to tell its history, leaving lots of room for the role of contingency in shaping the final outcome.

At the same time, passage of disability insurance involved more than serendipitous political bargaining. All sorts of factors figured into the outcome. Institutions mattered, such as the fact that the House Ways and Means Committee and the Senate Finance Committee occupied a prominent place in the policy-making process. Interest-group politics also mattered, and here one needs to be aware that these interest groups themselves have histories that shaped their political outlook. In the case of disability insurance, the role of the labor movement was crucial, and developments within the labor movement figured prominently in the outcome. Ideas shaped the scripts of both proponents and opponents. Conservatives argued that a job for people of working age should be the ultimate objective of social policy, anticipating in some ways arguments that would later be made by liberals in favor of regarding disability as a matter of civil rights—as in the notion that people with disabilities should not be excluded from the labor market on that basis alone—and by conservatives in favor of workfare as the solution to welfare. Liberals believed that some people were simply too impaired to hold a job on a regular basis. Those people deserved the dignity of a disability pension, and an affluent country could afford to give it to them, particularly because they had "earned" those benefits through the taxes that they and their employers had paid during their working lifetimes.[1]

One way of uniting the serendipitous and structural explanations for the passage of disability insurance is to focus on 1956, the year of passage. In that year, the Social Security program, the legislative vehicle from which disability insurance was launched, had achieved a popular status among social welfare programs. Continuing expansion of Social Security benefits and Social Security coverage since 1950 testified to that.[2] By 1956 rehabilitation had become at least an arguable alternative to cash benefits as a social policy strategy, as the development of rehabilitation medicine during and after the Second World War indicated.[3] Finally, Democrats regained control of Congress in the 1954 elections, bringing the Congress that would pass disability insurance to Washington, and in 1956, a presidential and congressional election year, disability insurance served as a good wedge issue between the political parties.[4]

This chapter provides a narrative history of the passage of disability insurance in 1956. It sets up a discussion in the next chapter of how the 1956 law affected the nation's approach to social policy in the area of disability. Together the two chapters provide the first of the book's three case studies of the formation of social policy.

Passage of Disability Insurance in the House, 1955: The Rise of Rehabilitation

Like most important social reforms, disability insurance did not arise spontaneously in the year of its passage. Instead, a long "prehistory" shaped the legislation. In 1938, only three years after the passage of the original Social Security Act, an advisory council gave serious consideration to recommending that disability benefits be added to the law. Conservatives, including an influential insurance executive, countered that the old-age insurance program, which dated from 1935 and had not even begun to pay regular retirement benefits, was simply not ready to initiate a disability insurance program. These benefits had proved tricky for private insurance companies to manage in the group policies they offered to employers in the 1920s. The problem was that a period of mass unemployment, such as the Depression, occasioned something like a run on the bank. People regarded disability benefits as an appropriate means of exit from an uncertain labor market, and neither the insurance companies nor the courts could control the stampede. That experience argued against the creation of disability benefits because they were too volatile. But advocates of an expanded Social Security system persisted, arguing that social needs mattered more than potential administrative problems, and a Social Security advisory council that met in 1947 and 1948 once again considered the matter and this time recommended that Congress create a disability insurance program. Although the House of Representatives acquiesced to this request in 1949, the Senate failed to concur. The matter extended into the 1950s and the end of twenty years of a Democrat in the White House.[5]

Congress changed hands after the 1952 election, and that tended to slow down but not derail the movement toward disability benefits. Here the technical arcana of Social Security took over in developments that were important in Social Security policy-making circles but relatively invisible to the general public. In 1954 the Republican Congress took a tentative step toward disability benefits by agreeing that a worker's wage record could be closed or "frozen" should he become disabled. That meant, at least in theory, that once the disabled worker got to be sixty-five, he or she could claim his regular retirement benefits, despite having been out of the labor force for many years. Significantly, the administrative structure that congressional conference committee members negotiated to make disability determinations under the disability freeze first in 1952 (when they legislated a disability freeze that never went into effect) and then in 1954 prevailed in all subsequent discussions of disability insurance. The arrangement created in 1952 and 1954 allowed state authorities, acting under contract to the federal government, to make disability determinations. It represented a concession on the part of welfare state expansionists to conservatives who believed that the state would take a more cautious approach to disability benefits than would the federal government. The same arrangement governs disability policy today—a key example of how casual decisions made in the heat of political negotiations created permanent institutions of the American welfare state.[6]

The 1954 election restored a slim Democratic majority in both houses of Congress and reinvigorated the drive to pass disability insurance in 1955. At this point the issue reentered the realm of partisan politics, with many Democrats in favor of disability insurance and many Republicans opposed.

By the summer of 1955, the Eisenhower administration first passively and then actively opposed disability benefits that were under consideration in the House of Representatives. According to the popular press, the issue now involved "a clear challenge by the Democratic Congress to the President's leadership." Eisenhower's Secretary of Health, Education, and Welfare advised the Ways and Means Committee—the key committee in Social Security legislation—to give the matter further study before recommending disability benefits, and Republicans urged Democrats to conduct hearings on the matter in public rather than in closed private sessions. These delaying tactics only increased the desire of Democratic leaders, such as Ways and Means Chairman Jere Cooper (D-TN) and House Speaker Sam Rayburn (D-TX), to pass the measure.[7]

No clear consensus existed in favor or against the measure. Speaking through their national trade associations, both the life insurance companies and the doctors raised objections. The life insurance industry saw disability benefits as a government encroachment on its turf, and other sectors of the business community tended to agree. If nothing else, disability benefits, financed by payroll deductions, would increase the tax load for many employers. The business community was hardly united on this matter, however. Large employers in the automobile and steel industries already paid for a broad range of fringe benefits, and having the government pay for disability benefits might decrease rather than increase their costs.[8]

The American Medical Association (AMA) had a more particular objection to disability benefits. The leaders of this umbrella organization for health care practitioners worried that disability benefits were actually a form of government regulation of the medical industry. Doctors would, for example, be recruited to make determinations of whether a particular worker was impaired enough to qualify as disabled. AMA leaders were not eager to have doctors take on this responsibility for fear it might lead to what some doctors regarded as the ultimate horror of national health insurance. If that happened, doctors might become government employees as they were in England. That might put a lid on doctors' salaries and substitute bureaucratic for medical expertise in diagnosing and treating diseases.[9]

In the absence of an effective countervailing force to the doctors, disability benefits would never have passed in 1956. Organized labor became that countervailing force. In the mid-1950s, unions were nearly as ubiquitous as hospitals, which meant that local union leaders, just like local doctors, could lobby congressmen.

The resulting maneuvering led to the July 1955 passage of disability insurance in the House of Representatives. It would take more than a year for the Senate to consider and vote on the measure, and in that year arguments for and against disability insurance took hold. Proponents believed that disability insurance would close an important gap in social protection. Opponents, such as the American Medical Association, believed that the disability provision was "the stealthy hand which would socialize medicine." They argued that it was a difficult matter to distinguish between people who were disabled and people who were unemployed. Rather than trying to parse that difference, policy makers should strengthen the public and private programs that restored impaired workers to employment. A related line of argument held that it was difficult to estimate the future costs of disability insurance with the likelihood that the addition of this feature would bankrupt the entire Social Security system, "perhaps causing today's worker to wake up some bleak tomorrow to find his stake in the fund to vanish."[10]

The Ways and Means Committee had already evaluated many of these arguments and come out on the side of the proponents. The absence of disability insurance in the Social Security system presented a gap that needed to be closed. To be sure, the committee wanted to move cautiously by initiating disability benefits only for those aged fifty or older, presumably the most serious cases. Younger people would have to fend for themselves, possibly by going to a state vocational rehabilitation agency and undertaking a course of training and medical treatment that would restore an impaired person to an employable condition.[11] The problem was that these state rehabilitation programs, around since 1920, had an indifferent record of placing their handicapped clients in jobs, despite an uptick in the postwar years as the rehabilitation of veterans became a matter of national concern and as a dynamic administrator took over the program.[12]

Promotion of the state vocational rehabilitation program and of the closely related cause of rehabilitation medicine became important pieces of baggage in President Eisenhower's social welfare program. The President wanted to extend Social Security coverage to previously excluded groups such as self-employed lawyers and regular, as opposed to itinerant, farm workers. But he did not favor broadening the scope of the program to include disability benefits. Instead, he sponsored a major expansion of the vocational rehabilitation program in 1954.[13]

Liberal Democrats went along with the initial phases of Eisenhower's program but believed, as the Ways and Means Committee reported, that many "disabled persons cannot be rehabilitated and even those who can will need benefits during rehabilitation." Besides, most of the suitable rehabilitation candidates were under the age of fifty and hence not covered in the disability insurance legislation. In short, "Important as rehabilitation is, it cannot be a substitute for disability benefits."[14]

Republicans on the Ways and Means Committee believed that the committee's measure did not go far enough in its encouragement of rehabilitation. This argument provided them with what they hoped was a positive response to the growth of dependency brought about by the expansion of America's welfare state. The primary goal of a disability program should be "to encourage disabled persons to regain their position as useful, self-supporting members of society." Every disabled worker had the potential for a rehabilitation process that emphasized "individual effort and incentive."[15] Representative Noah Mason (R-IA) put his objections to disability insurance in succinct form. He cited the bad experience of life insurance companies with disability benefits. He asserted that disability benefits would discourage rehabilitation. He emphasized that benefits for total disability would encourage malingering. He preferred a program that operated at the state rather than the federal level. He believed that the costs of cash disability benefits were unpredictable and would soon "get out of hand."[16]

Such arguments failed to sway a majority of congressmen, and the measure, tied to the increasingly popular Social Security program, passed easily by a 372–31 vote.[17] During the House debate, Herman Eberharter (D-PA) argued that the true alternative to a Social Security disability program was not rehabilitation but rather reliance on welfare in the form of means-tested, state-run public assistance programs. Enacted in 1950, these Aid to the Permanently and Totally Disabled programs turned handicapped individuals into paupers, in Eberharter's stylized view of public policy, because they demanded that people prove they were poor—lacking in money or assets—in order to claim the benefits. With the enactment of disability insurance, "it will no longer be necessary for a disabled insured worker to sacrifice his self-respect and the well-being of his family in order to obtain some regular monthly income during the period of disability."[18]

Secretary Folsom

Most observers believed that the real showdown over disability insurance would occur in the Senate, not the House. Because Congress adjourned at the end of July, the Senate could not take up the measure until the second congressional session, which began in January 1956. That meant that the Senate would consider disability insurance during an election year and, because of the apparent differences between Democrats and Republicans that had arisen in the House debate, it might become an issue in those elections.

As the action shifted from the House to the Senate, a key change occurred at the cabinet level that had the potential to influence the debate over disability insurance. Eisenhower appointed a new Secretary of Health, Education, and Welfare in the summer of 1955 to replace the woman who had been named as the first secretary of that department in 1953, Oveta Culp Hobby. Hobby knew little about Social Security and depended upon federal bureaucrats and outside consultants to bring her up to speed. The new secretary, Marion Folsom, a prominent Eastman Kodak executive, had a pedigree in the field of Social Security. He had served on important Social Security advisory councils in 1934, 1938, and 1947. He was perhaps the leading expert on Social Security in the business community, with many contacts among Social Security administrators and other experts. Unlike many of his business colleagues, Folsom defended the existing Social Security program and even argued for its expansion. He believed, based on his long experience in the field, that public social welfare benefits could coexist with and even strengthen

Kodak's private social welfare programs. Social Security was compatible with the type of welfare capitalism in which Folsom and his company had been so influential.[19]

The appointment of Folsom encouraged the proponents of disability insurance, even though in the past he had exercised considerable caution over the matter. It might be a step too far for the public sector, and as many conservatives believed, it might inhibit the more positive rehabilitation approach. In the advisory council that met at the end of the 1940s, Folsom joined his insurance company business colleague and signed a minority report against the council's endorsement of disability insurance. His opposition was by no means total. He regarded disability insurance as something that the Social Security program might tackle down the road with the proper hedges against abuse.[20]

When Marion Folsom came to the Department of Health, Education, and Welfare from his earlier post as Undersecretary of the Treasury, Social Security Administration officials of that department greeted him with enthusiasm. Robert Ball, the Assistant Director of the Bureau of Old Age and Survivors Benefits who was regarded as the top bureaucrat in charge, sent Folsom a note to the effect that those who had worked with him in past, as Ball had on the 1947 advisory council, "are looking forward particularly to working under your leadership in the department."[21] Perhaps Folsom could push the discussion within the administration in favor of disability insurance or at least temper some of the opposition.

Folsom's innate caution and the administration's record as opposing disability insurance made such a development unlikely. Roswell Perkins, a lawyer and an associate of Health, Education, and Welfare Undersecretary Nelson Rockefeller, with the title of Assistant Secretary for Legislation, became the chief advocate of the rehabilitation approach to disability. He had shepherded the 1954 legislation that expanded the vocational rehabilitation program and established the procedure that allowed disabled beneficiaries to freeze their Social Security records so that they could collect retirement benefits at age sixty-five. Perkins envisioned this procedure not as an expansion of Social Security or a step toward disability insurance so much as a recruiting tool for rehabilitation. Congressional Democrats and the Social Security Administration wanted to take the next step and create a formal disability insurance program. Folsom wavered. Perkins urged him to remain firm.[22]

On March 22, at the very end of the Senate hearings, Folsom testified against disability insurance. He objected to adding the cost of these benefits to the Social Security payroll tax burden. He also repeated the mantra that "the most constructive approach to problems of disabled workers is through vocational rehabilitation."[23]

The Labor Movement Merges and Becomes a Key Interest Group

When Marion Folsom testified before the Senate Finance Committee, George Meany, the President of the American Federation of Labor–Congress of Industrial Organizations (AFL-CIO), issued a statement to newsmen in attendance at the hearing. He called Folsom's testimony "extremely disappointing."[24] Meany's statement came on behalf of a newly created labor organization some fifteen million workers strong that was the product of the merger of the American Federation of Labor and the Congress of Industrial Organizations.[25] Similar to the other institutional components of the policy-making process, interest groups like organized labor had their own complicated histories, which made a difference in policy outcomes.

Organized labor unambiguously favored disability insurance in 1956 and provided support that was vital in the midcentury expansion of Social Security. Labor occupied a central place in the policy apparatus that created America's welfare state. Before that happened, however, a transformation had to take place. Just as Marion Folsom and other welfare capitalists needed to be persuaded that government-mandated benefits had a legitimate place in the labor market, so Samuel Gompers and other leaders of the early trade union movement needed to believe that such benefits did more good than harm. At the beginning of the century, labor unions tended to look upon the activities of the federal government with suspicion. Many labor leaders assumed that government was a servant of capital and could not be trusted to carry on the fight for higher wages or improved working conditions. The government was a threat to the very existence of unions, as likely to destroy them as to come to their aid.[26]

As the Democrats became the majority party in the 1930s and as the identity of that party changed from conservative (think Grover Cleveland) to its modern liberal identity, unions were better able to enter into a partnership with the federal government. New Deal legislation, particularly the National Industrial Recovery Act of 1933 and the Wagner Act of 1935, helped to create the sense that the government wanted workers to join unions. At the same time, organized labor became a major patron of the Democratic Party. When Roosevelt proposed and Congress passed the Social Security Act in 1935, labor acquiesced in its passage and supported the old-age insurance and unemployment compensation programs that were contained in the legislation.

Internal divisions in the labor movement limited its effectiveness as a political force to defend Social Security and advocate its expansion. In 1938, for example, labor leaders served on the advisory council that created a blueprint for the creation of survivors and family benefits but, caught up in union business, they often missed meetings. Business representatives, such as Marion Folsom and insurance executive Albert Linton, were far more influential in the council's deliberations.[27]

The issue that preoccupied organized labor in the 1930s concerned the proper approach to organizing American workers so that unions could bargain on their behalf with management over wages, hours, and the other terms of the labor contract. Samuel Gompers, the founder of the American Federation of Labor, practiced what might be called a bread-and-butter form of unionism that centered on wage gains for skilled workers such as carpenters, who were descendants of artisans in earlier forms of labor organization. William Green, Gompers's less charismatic successor, tended to follow Gompers's example and advocate union organization by the skill or job, so as to avoid a situation in which two rival unions competed for the loyalty of particular workers.

In the 1930s, the decade of favorable labor legislation, some labor leaders, and in particular the ambitious and influential John L. Lewis of the United Mine Workers, saw the possibility of organizing not just skilled workers but the labor force of entire industries. They set their sights on the auto and steel industries, the two largest in America. Green and the American Federation of Labor leaders reacted defensively to this effort to reorient American unionism. It led to a bitter squabble between Green and Lewis, both former coal miners, and a major rupture in the American Federation of Labor. By the Second World War, a rival Congress of Industrial Organizations had succeeded in creating the United Auto Workers and the United Steelworkers. The American labor movement now contained a major fissure between the AFL and the CIO, which, despite the tremendous gains in labor organization made during the New Deal and Second World War, complicated organized labor's ability to mobilize on social issues.

During the 1950s, the AFL and the CIO reunited to form a large umbrella organization that became a strong lobbying arm in the passage of disability insurance.[28] In November 1952, three events occurred in quick succession that paved the way for the creation of the AFL-CIO. On November 4, Dwight Eisenhower, the hero of World War II in charge of the invasion of Normandy, won the presidential election against former Illinois Governor Adlai Stevenson. He carried every state except for those in the solid South, Kentucky, and West Virginia. In January 1953 he would become the first Republican president since Herbert Hoover left office in March 1933 and bring the first Republican Congress since Hoover's era with him. On November 9, CIO head Philip Murray died unexpectedly in San Francisco of a heart attack. On November 20 William Green died in his Ohio home, also of a heart attack. The personalities who had presided over the departure of the CIO from the AFL in 1936 and shared a long and tangled history were gone at a time of political vulnerability for the American labor movement.[29] The end of personal antagonism in the top ranks of organized labor and the perceived need to advance labor's legislative agenda contributed to the possibility of merging the two organizations.

Each of the organizations selected new leaders who were more amenable to a merger than their predecessors had been. The AFL executive council named George Meany, a fifty-eight-year-old plumber, as the president of the eight-million-member organization. Even as Meany was being considered, the *New York Times* reported on the talk "in labor circles that it was the proper—and dramatic—moment to reunite the two major wings of American labor after seventeen years of divorce."[30] On December 1, 1952, it became apparent that Walter Reuther would become the next president of the CIO, despite differences between the United Auto Workers and the United Steelworkers. Reuther's supporters noted that Reuther was on good terms with George Meany and that the two leaders would work together to effect a merger.[31]

Although Reuther and Meany made an odd couple, they shared social goals. Reuther, younger and more charismatic than his rather doughty, cigar-smoking AFL counterpart, looked "more like a stand-in for Van

Johnson or some other movie prototype of clean-cut young American manhood than he does a labor leader."[32] Reuther was clearly more of a visionary reformer and Meany closer to the bread-and-butter tradition of Samuel Gompers. They nonetheless could make common cause over the issues of the 1950s and put organized labor in closer alignment with the liberals in Congress.

On December 4, 1952, Walter Reuther became the President of the Congress of Industrial Organizations in what was then the heavily utilized convention site of Atlantic City. The convention unanimously passed a resolution authorizing the CIO leaders to meet with their AFL counterparts in the cause of "honorable labor unity that will advance the welfare of all labor."[33] Two nights after the CIO convention, Meany and Reuther shared a platform at a banquet in a New York City hotel. "I extend the hand of friendship and solidarity to the AFL. I will do everything in my power to work together for unity," Reuther said in introducing Meany. "There is no trade union reason for division in American labor ranks, and I know of no trade union reasons for the continuance of that division," Meany replied. The two labor leaders soon announced that they would meet in the new year.[34]

Like most complicated negotiations, the merger took time to effect, with the resolution taking place in late 1954 and early 1955. As it happened, therefore, the AFL and CIO merged just at the time that disability insurance had risen to the top of the social policy agenda, nicely illustrating the role of historical contingencies in the creation of social welfare policy.[35] On February 9, 1955, the labor leaders announced that George Meany would lead the new organization, with Reuther in a subsidiary but important role as the head of a Council of Industrial Organizations. Meany touted the benefits of the merger. He looked forward "to improving labor legislation and to adding new laws when they are necessary." One of those new laws and the subject of the moment in Congress was disability insurance.[36] The final details of the merger fell in place in July 1955, when disability insurance had passed the House but awaited action in the Senate. The AFL made room for the CIO in the new headquarters it was building on Sixteenth Street almost within sight of the White House. The imposing structure announced the permanent presence of organized labor within the confines of the American state.[37]

The Staff Connection

The merger entailed complicated organizational maneuvers and was highly dependent on the personalities of the labor leaders and the course of current events. At a staff level, however, organized labor already enjoyed a close working relationship with the federal bureaucrats who made Social Security policy; the merger only made it closer. This collaboration was an important building block of the American welfare state.[38]

In the 1930s, the decade of the dramatic creation of the CIO, many of the future Social Security bureaucrats were either administering state labor legislation laws or learning about them in academic settings. Economists at the University of Wisconsin, such as Selig Perlman and John R. Commons, studied labor unions and trained many future leaders in the fields of labor relations and Social Security. Wilbur Cohen entered the University of Wisconsin as an undergraduate in 1930 and found his way to the economics department and John R. Commons. He wrote his senior thesis, which was much influenced by his mentor, Selig Perlman, about the history of the International Association of Machinists. He wanted to stay for graduate study with Perlman, but before he could do so he received a compelling offer to work in Washington. In the summer of 1934, Cohen traveled to Washington to work for Edwin Witte, one of his Wisconsin professors, who was helping to write what became the Social Security Act. After working for Witte as a junior staff member, Cohen stayed in Washington for the next twenty-two years and became an important Social Security official. Under different circumstances Cohen could as easily have worked for the National Labor Relations Board, but he saw the work of the Social Security Board as related to that of the labor movement. Both organizations were in the business of reforming the labor market.[39]

Robert Ball, another important Social Security bureaucrat, never attended the University of Wisconsin. Instead, he majored in English at Wesleyan. He graduated in 1935, a year after Cohen's matriculation at Wisconsin. With the economy becalmed, Ball decided to take a year of graduate study at Wesleyan, where he studied with Norman Ware, who was an institutional economist in the Commons tradition. Ball wrote his master's thesis about the split between the AFL and the CIO. He then became an active member of the labor movement as an assistant editor of the *People's Press*, a labor newspaper. Although like Cohen he hoped for a permanent career at the National Labor Relations Board, he settled for the Social Security Board instead and entered federal service at the beginning of 1939. In 1962 he became the Social Security Commissioner.[40]

Cohen and Ball shared a strong interest in the labor movement and regarded labor as a natural ally in the fight to establish and expand Social Security. Nelson Cruikshank became their chief contact in the AFL. Like Robert Ball, Cruikshank was the son of a Methodist minister who became a labor organizer. In 1944 he took a job in the AFL main office, knowing little about Social Security, which would become his major responsibility. His friends advised him that the thing to do was to get in touch with Wilbur Cohen. He and Cohen, and later Ball, entered into a working relationship and a close collaboration on Social Security legislation.[41]

Even as the AFL and the CIO continued their quarrels and tended to duplicate their work in Washington, therefore, the labor movement already enjoyed a tight connection with the Social Security bureaucracy. There was a strong affinity and an intellectual continuity between the two groups. Once created, the AFL-CIO, with its fifteen million members, lobbied for the expansion of Social Security. In 1956 disability insurance became the first test of the united labor movement's strength.

The Senate Finance Committee, Harry Byrd, and LBJ

Since the measure had already cleared the House, the task became getting disability insurance through the Senate. The Senate had not been a supporter of disability insurance in the past and had failed to pass the measure in 1950. The same formidable forces arrayed against the measure—the insurance industry, the doctors, and fiscally conservative senators—remained in place in 1956. The situation facing disability insurance showed how hard it was to pass liberal legislation at the time, even though Social Security itself, considered as old-age and survivors insurance, was an increasingly popular cause. As a result of amendments that had been passed in the 1950s, more workers participated in the program, and many of the original coverage restrictions in agriculture and among small businesses were lifted. Broader coverage meant more interest in Congress and more of a willingness to raise benefits, particularly considering the healthy state of the American economy.[42] Raising benefits for retired workers, however, was not the same thing as ending the age restrictions and creating a new class of benefits. These represented new territory.

In the House, the Ways and Means Committee had proceeded on disability insurance without even holding public hearings and conducting all of its business in executive session. That was not the Senate's style. The Finance Committee, the committee with undisputed jurisdiction over the matter, planned to hold extensive hearings. The agenda was to put all of the evidence against disability insurance on the record and to make a case for reporting out a bill that expanded the conventional Social Security program but omitted disability insurance.

The complicated politics of this initiative involved more than the usual split between the Democrats and the Republicans. The 1954 congressional election had restored the thinnest of Democratic margins, with the result that the Finance Committee had eight Democrats and seven Republicans. This party division, however, could not neatly be aligned with the dichotomy between conservatives and liberals. Of the eight Democrats on the Finance Committee, for example, five came from the Deep South, and many were wary of disability insurance. Beyond the committee level, which had a tight lock on social policy politics, particularly in the House, a more fluid situation prevailed. Senate Majority Leader Lyndon Johnson (D-TX) was determined to enlarge his party's majority in the Senate and to produce distinctive legislation that differentiated his party from the Republicans and showed the Democrats off to best advantage. The problem was that he could not count on the Democrats on the Finance Committee to advance the party's agenda.

Harry F. Byrd (D-VA), the committee chair who had taken over from another senior southern senator in 1955, maintained his distance from the party leadership. Byrd's Senate career stretched from 1933, when a vacancy in the Virginia delegation occurred, to 1965. In this time of expanding federal power, Byrd remained a voice of fiscal conservatism, wary of new and costly programs that raised tax rates and added to deficits. For him this principle of fiscal prudence overshadowed party politics and made him particularly skeptical of new social ventures like disability insurance. He had, in any case, been an unreliable Democratic Party supporter in presidential elections, opposing Truman in the year of the Dixiecrat rebellion and Stevenson in 1952. In 1956, he began and ended as an opponent of disability insurance.[43]

With the one-person Democratic majority- and with first the ambivalence and then the opposition of the Eisenhower administration, there was every reason to believe that Byrd could carry a majority of the committee membership with him, even though the Democratic leadership favored it and it had already passed the House by a substantial margin. If he reported out a bill without disability insurance, it would be very difficult to get that measure through a conference committee.

The split between northern and southern Democrats such as Byrd became an indirect factor in the politics of disability insurance. The southerners, with only a few exceptions, defended racial segregation, which made them popular among their nearly all-white constituents. (Blacks were blocked from voting in places with high concentrations of black population such as Mississippi and South Carolina.) Leaders of the southern delegation issued a manifesto in 1956 that elevated their defense of racial segregation to a matter of deep principle.[44] On the surface the involvement of the Chairman and other key members of the Finance Committee in the segregation movement mattered little in the consideration of disability insurance. Still, just as doctors saw many federal measures as the leading edge of national health insurance—and for that reason opposed disability insurance—so southerners regarded social programs, such as federal aid to education, that would have showered money on the region, as the leading edge of racial integration. Government would force private southern employers to pay disability pensions, a possibly dangerous intervention in the market and, just maybe, the beginning of new racial rules regarding hiring. In a more tangible sense, the uncertainty of the measure's cost made Byrd and other fiscal conservatives uneasy.

One way around the problem was to put more liberals on the Finance Committee in the hope of creating a majority in favor of disability insurance. That happened over time but could not be achieved in 1956, despite the leadership's desire to pass disability insurance. Rules of seniority and the amassed power of the southern delegation blocked this path. Johnson and the Democratic leadership did what they could. When Alben Barkley (D-KY) died toward the end of the committee's disability deliberations, his replacement was Paul Douglas (D-IL), who was perhaps the Senate's most liberal member. Although the pro-union, pro–civil rights, pro–Social Security Douglas worked very actively in favor of disability insurance, his presence made little difference in the outcome of the committee's 1956 deliberations. Johnson's decision to step down from the Finance Committee permitted Clinton Anderson (D-NM), a future leader of the drive to expand Social Security, to be a member, but it was not enough to create a majority for disability insurance.

Senator Byrd convened his committee at the end of January. The first speaker was Robert J. Myers, the Social Security's chief actuary and an important player in the Social Security politics of the era. Public policy, in this field and many others, was a continuing discussion of the future consequences of present actions. Myers functioned as the official scorekeeper who estimated what a particular proposal would cost. In most fields, economists or accountants would do this sort of work. In Social Security, an actuary, someone trained to do cost estimates for insurance companies, performed this function. That reflected the carefully maintained fiction that Social Security was not a typical government program but rather an insurance program for which workers received benefits from the premiums that they and their employers paid. In theory at least, a benefit, once promised, remained a continuing obligation of the government, unlike, say, a measure to fund government research to fight cancer. Myers and his actuarial colleagues faced a great deal of pressure because so much was riding on their predictions.[45] In the future, Congress would generate its own cost estimates. In 1956 Robert Myers was the only game in town.

Myers handled the pressure by sequestering himself with the Finance and Ways and Means Committees and maintaining his distance from his own agency during the times when Congress was considering sensitive legislation. He knew that his agency had a stake in the outcome and wanted the cost estimate to be as low as possible. Opponents like Senator Byrd were instinctively suspicious of the figures from the agency and hoped for estimates that were as high as possible. Myers himself was a nonpartisan civil servant but a Republican by political preference. His standing in the actuarial profession meant as much to him as his reputation in the agency. If things had turned out differently in the Depression-era labor market, Myers might well have gone from his actuarial training into the employ of an insurance company rather than the Social Security Board.

Myers and his fellow actuaries had to play by the established rules of his agency. When someone proposed to lower the retirement age to sixty-two or pay disability benefits to those aged fifty or higher, Myers needed to estimate the costs of that specific proposal. He was not allowed to speculate on future developments that might cause costs to balloon. He kept things constant. A casual observer might speculate that, once enacted for people aged fifty or older, disability insurance would be expanded to cover workers of all ages. Sticking to the task at hand, Myers dismissed future political developments as he went about his work.

Appearing before Byrd, Myers put the cost of lowering the retirement age for women and initiating disability benefits at age fifty at $600 million a year to start. This high number could be made to look small when translated into Social Security parlance. A boost of 1 percent, shared between employers and employees, in the contribution rate would more than cover the costs. Since Marion Folsom had not yet testified, Myers needed to be circumspect in his testimony and try not to answer policy questions. Senators were nonetheless skeptical about the disability estimates and wondered just how a fifty-year-old would be judged to be permanently and totally disabled. Myers described but did not critique how the disability determination system would work.[46]

Myers's testimony mattered, but the Finance Committee also needed to touch base with a wide array of groups with a stake in the legislation.[47] Representatives of the medical profession, including the American Academy of General Practice, the National Veterans Medical Society, the American Academy for the Study of Alcoholism, the American Academy of Physical Medicine (which represented the interest of rehabilitation doctors), the American Academy of Orthopedic Surgeons (another group closely associated with the treatment of handicapped individuals), and the medical societies of Georgia, Vermont, Nevada, Minnesota, California, Texas, and Arkansas, pleaded their case before Byrd on February 9. They testified that certifying disability would place "an intolerable burden" on them and keep them from seeing their regular patients. Disputed disability cases would clog the courts. The costs of the disability program would mount much more rapidly than the Social Security actuaries predicted. The program might ultimately take up 30 to 40 percent of the taxable payroll and throw the entire Social Security system out of kilter.[48]

As expected, insurance industry spokesmen and other businessmen sided with the doctors. The disability provisions brought the Social Security program into a new area in which costs were uncontrollable and fraudulent claims would be difficult to police. Businessmen added that disability insurance might discourage recipients from taking advantage of the "constantly improving" rehabilitation services.[49] Not so, countered Walter Reuther. Insurers may have had a bad experience with disability claims in the 1920s. More recently his union had successfully put disability benefits into the contracts of more than a million workers. He urged the Senate to close "the most conspicuous gap in the American social security system."[50]

The doctors and the businessmen made an encore appearance before the Senate Finance Committee on February 21. This time spokesmen for the state medical associations of North Carolina, Kentucky, and Utah and the dean of the insurance industry on Social Security testified. Once again, the doctors emphasized how disability benefits would nullify the great progress in rehabilitation. The head of the Kentucky medical association, a constituent of ailing committee member Alben Barkley, advised the committee to drop the disability provisions in the House bill and expand the vocational rehabilitation program instead. A new disability law would bring forth a vast army of "medical care malingerers" and impose a heavy burden on the doctors. Speaking in particular to Utah Senator Wallace Bennett, the head of the Utah medical association pointed to a host of conditions that would make disability determination difficult. These included nervous conditions, alcoholism, rheumatism, headache, and female pelvic disorders. Albert Linton, the insurance company executive who had consistently argued against disability insurance in Social Security circles since 1934, warned that his experience told him that the program would begin modestly but soon expand. "Irresistible pressures will build up to expand coverage to all ages," he said.[51]

As the hearings wound down at the end of February, it appeared that the committee would delete the disability features from the House bill. A majority on the committee feared that the disability provisions would throw the entire Social Security system into chaos. The *Washington Post* reported, on the one hand, that some Democrats and most Republicans on the committee would oppose the measures. On the other hand, Senator Johnson put the Social Security legislation, as defined by the contents of the House bill, at the top of his program for the session.[52] The press speculated that between ten and twelve Republican senators might vote for the measure on the Senate floor.[53]

When Byrd called the committee together at the end of April to make a final decision on disability insurance, Secretary Folsom had already delivered his March 22 testimony against disability coverage. Republican committee members who voted to strip this provision from the House bill could do so with the apparent blessing of the administration. Of course, even if disability insurance died in the committee, the measure could still be restored on the floor of the Senate. Senator Johnson's partisan interest in the measure and the favorable climate in the Senate made that a very real possibility.

Before there was any sort of Senate floor fight, the committee process needed to play itself out. On May 10 Harry Byrd announced that a substantial majority of committee members had voted against disability insurance. The committee conducted its business by means of voice vote, so no official vote tally existed. Speculation centered on Senator Allen Frear (DE) as a Democratic senator who had joined Byrd and the Republicans. Because of Senator Barkley's recent death, the committee conducted its business with an equal number of Republicans and Democrats. By May 25, the Senate Finance Committee had completed its action on the Social Security bill and sent it along to the Senate.[54]

The committee issued its formal report on June 5, 1956. The committee said that, although it recognized prolonged and severe disability as a serious problem to the worker, his or her family, and the community, the preponderance of evidence (such legal expressions were common in what was in essence a community of lawyers) collected in the hearings argued against the measure. The committee cited the many witnesses who said that the payment of cash benefits retarded rehabilitation. Disability presented insurmountable problems of public administration, as it was easier to claim and harder to deny than other Social Security benefits. Because it was difficult to determine disability, it was also difficult to predict and hence to control costs.[55]

The Conversion of Senator George

Byrd failed to take all of the committee members with him. The report contained a dissent from Senators Walter George (D-GA), Russell Long (D-LA), and the newly appointed Paul Douglas. The fact that three of the committee's seven Democrats, two of whom were from the Deep South, dissented indicated that opinion on the issue was far from unanimous. It boded well for a possible floor fight. Long had already publicly announced he would work to restore the liberal provisions on the Senate floor. Douglas's support in the effort was assured. Senator George's participation in the dissent and in the floor fight that followed came as a true surprise.[56] It showed the results of behind the scene maneuvers of the liberal coalition of staff workers in the labor unions and the federal bureaucracy.

The dissenters claimed that disability determinations were already being made successfully every day. "Stringent eligibility requirements, limited benefits and positive stress on rehabilitation" guaranteed that the benefits would not discourage rehabilitation. "A great deal of emphasis must rightly be placed on rehabilitation. However, the fact must be recognized that a great many older disabled workers cannot be rehabilitated successfully." Nor could rehabilitation "be a substitute for income for the disabled worker." The only solution for the problems of permanently and totally disabled workers was a carefully managed program of cash benefits.[57]

The conversion of Walter George to the cause of disability benefits changed the whole debate. George, every bit as much as Byrd or his senatorial colleague Richard Russell (D-GA), was a solid member of the southern congressional delegation. The death of Senator Tom Watson in 1922 first encouraged George to leave the practice of law, having already served as a prosecuting attorney and an associate justice of the Georgia Supreme Court, and seek the open Senate seat. After being appointed to the seat, he won the ensuing election and succeeding elections through 1950. He gained credentials among his fellow senators for his victory in 1938 after Roosevelt tried to purge him, despite his support of the Social Security and Agricultural Adjustment Acts, and replace him with a candidate who was more sympathetic to the President's court-packing plan.[58] As his seniority mounted, so did his influence. He chaired the Finance Committee between 1941 and 1947 and again between 1949 and 1953. Like his successor Byrd, he tried to hold the line on government expenditures and greeted many liberal measures rudely. He took the usual southern hard line on civil rights.

George could have resumed his chairmanship of Finance after the Democratic victory in the 1954 elections. President Eisenhower and Secretary of State John Foster Dulles persuaded him to chair the Foreign Relations Committee instead. They recognized what the *New York Times* described as his "natural gifts of physical presence and oratorical power." Columnist Jimmy Reston wrote that "he has a voice like an organ and combines it with quiet personal majesty that makes the Senate pay attention."[59]

In 1956 Senator George faced a tough reelection fight against Georgia Governor Herman E. Talmadge. His chances uncertain, he announced on May 9 that he would retire rather than take on a bruising primary fight. The Eisenhower administration showed its respect by offering him an appointment as special ambassador to the North Atlantic Treaty Organization. People hailed Walter George as the Dean of the Senate.[60]

These developments occurred during the Senate Finance Committee's consideration of disability insurance and early retirement. The proponents of the measure sought a strategy to counter Senator Byrd, whom they recognized as an unmovable force set against disability insurance. At first Wilbur Cohen, who had quit his job at Social Security and become a professor in the University of Michigan's School of Social Work at the beginning of 1956, pinned his hopes on persuading Secretary Folsom not to oppose the measure. That might increase Republican support inside the Finance Committee and on the Senate floor. When that effort ended in disappointment, he sought someone else who might lead the fight against Byrd.[61]

Both Cohen and AFL-CIO staffer Nelson Cruikshank approached Walter George, who, at the time, either needed an issue he could use against Herman Talmadge (D-GA) or, if he decided to retire, might want to add disability insurance to his legislative legacy. No one doubted George's clout but wondered how the conservative senator might be persuaded to lead the fight for a very liberal measure. Cohen and Cruikshank were like the indefatigable salesmen who sold things door to door: rejection was part of the job. Elizabeth Springer, the clerk of the Finance Committee, gave Cohen and Loula Dunn, the Director the American Public Welfare Association, access to Senator George. Dunn had the advantage of her Alabama background and her courtly southern manner. Cohen asked George to introduce an amendment in the Finance Committee to strike out the age fifty limitation in the House bill and substitute a program to pay disability benefits to workers of all ages. To Cohen's surprise, George agreed to the request and asked him to draft a bill and an accompanying statement. This was standard Washington procedure: congressmen often used outsiders to do necessary staff work in the legislative process. Although George's motives were unclear, his decision meant that he would take the initiative in the fight for disability benefits, improving the odds of their ultimate passage. Cohen confided to a friend, "I feel we did a very essential job because nobody was organizing the fight against Byrd," who Cohen said was "trying to prevent any bill from being reported out. I think this is fantastic but it indicates what a strange world Washington is now." Cohen also received an invitation from Lloyd Rader, an influential state welfare director from Oklahoma, to see Senator Robert Kerr (D-OK), another powerful senator on the Finance Committee. These developments encouraged Cohen as the Finance Committee prepared to go into executive session.[62]

The fight for disability now involved complex calculations. As Cohen handicapped the matter, "Lyndon Johnson is likely to help George and it seems difficult to imagine how if George and Johnson, the Majority Leader, push disability they can lose because they should be able to get the southerners plus the Democratic liberals plus a few Republicans." Cohen realized that all sorts of compromises might be necessary in the bargaining over disability insurance. Disability benefits did not have to begin at age fifty; they might instead start at age fifty-five or sixty. The key point was to establish the basic principle; then one could be confident that, once enacted, the measure could be liberalized in future congressional sessions.[63]

Nelson Cruikshank operated in tandem with Cohen. He later remarked that the leaders of the AFL-CIO "consciously made the decision that [disability insurance] would be the first thing on which the organized labor movement would work." He realized, as had Cohen, that trying to persuade Harry Byrd was a nonstarter. Cruikshank groused that Byrd caucused with the Republicans, which not only served "to carry on the negative legislative activity of the administration but gives it a Democratic coloration." Senator George might be a more promising target. The CIO, according to Cruikshank, was "unable to get near him." The AFL-CIO might fare better because the AFL had supported George, even in the 1938 election in which President Roosevelt had intervened. That opened the door, and Cruikshank and fellow labor lobbyist Andrew Biemiller, who had the added credential of having served two terms in Congress, managed to get an appointment with Senator George. By the time they got to see him, he had already announced his retirement. They pitched disability insurance to him as his "parting gift to the American people." Cruikshank then drafted a letter for Meany's signature that predicted George would enjoy "no greater satisfaction from his Senate career" than he would get from leading the disability fight.[64]

Writing his memoirs at the end of his career, Senator Paul Douglas claimed that he became interested in disability benefits around 1955 when he began to see the possibility of expanding the Social Security program to include disability benefits, and he made common cause with the labor movement in the effort. "We were making some progress," Douglas wrote in his autobiography, "when we were joined by an unexpected and welcome ally, none other than Walter George, the leader, with Dick Russell, of the Southern conservatives." Douglas and George were not natural allies. Douglas regarded his colleague as "a safe defender of the interests of the planter and moneyed Establishment." Douglas claimed that George's retirement motivated him to break character and "do something for the class he had neglected for so long." That way he could "go out as a humanitarian, rather than a crusty conservative." Social Security bureaucrats were more than happy to make changes in the legislation to accommodate George's fiscal conservatism, such as creating a new trust fund for the disability program that would, at least in theory, separate its finances from those of the rest of Social Security. In Douglas's optimistic opinion, southern conservatives might deplore "George's new attitude but they could not deny him his wish." The fact that the Republican leadership "was receiving so many favors from him" muted its opposition.[65]

All the Way with LBJ

Douglas recalled that the "bill sailed through Congress," but that was not exactly true. On June 22 the senator gave a press conference in Chicago and predicted passage of the measure. At a minimum, most observers expected lively debate on what was widely regarded as one of the most important items on the legislative calendar. Senators George, Kerr, and Johnson were at the center of the legislative action. George would introduce an amendment to the Finance Committee bill that added disability benefits and created a separate disability trust fund. Johnson would direct the action on the floor and turn out as many Democrats as he could. George, like Douglas, expressed his confidence that the amendments would pass. Still, George, aware that the American Medical Association and the administration would work hard against the measure, predicted a close vote.[66]

The Senate debate on the Social Security bill, which began on July 13 and concluded on July 17, reprised the themes of earlier policy discussions. Herbert Lehman (D-NY), who like George was at the end of his Senate career, said that the rehabilitation program was inadequate to handle the problem of disability-related income insecurity. Some people were too old or too impaired to profit from vocational rehabilitation, even if that program's resources could be stretched to accommodate all of the people in need of its services.[67] Henry "Scoop" Jackson (D-WA) assured his fellow senators that disability determination was well within the federal government's wheelhouse. The 1954 amendments creating a disability freeze had already put three-quarters of the states in the disability determination business. Jackson invoked the political mantra that Social Security benefits were "earned benefits" and that the disability payments would go only to those "who have made substantial contributions to the social security system, those who have demonstrated a capacity and a will to work." Disability payments, added Senator Albert Gore (D-TN) would support "not an itinerant worker, not a spasmodic job holder" but rather reliable steady workers who had achieved longevity in the labor force.[68]

A key moment in the Senate debate came in a July 17 exchange between Wallace Bennett of Utah and Russell Long of Louisiana. Bennett believed that 90 percent of disabled workers could be returned to active employment. Cash disability payments were little more than a "semi-floatable milestone" that would drag workers down to dependency. Long questioned whether Bennett's optimistic prediction of disabled workers returning to work applied to heart attack victims. He urged the Senate to see that manual laborers who became disabled faced a harder readjustment than company presidents. "Every Senator," emphasized Senator George, "knows individual cases where prolonged sickness and disability have reduced a proud and self-supporting person to a helpless, dependent individual."[69]

Heart attacks had a special relevance to the discussion. Senator Bennett mentioned that his brother had suffered three heart attacks and still worked as a supermarket manager. In that respect he resembled another prominent person. On September 24, 1955, President Dwight Eisenhower had a heart attack while on vacation in Colorado. His health status came to preoccupy the nation, with people concerned first about his survival and then about whether he had the stamina to resume his presidential duties. He did not return to the Oval Office until Christmas. Coming at the point of the political cycle that it did, the heart attack affected the 1956 presidential race, as people wondered whether Ike would run for a second term. As it turned out, he did, and he survived his second term intact, although with periodic health problems that might have been related to his heart attack.[70] Senator Bennett said that his brother the supermarket manager had done the same thing as the President and readjusted his lifestyle to embrace a better diet and more exercise. Lyndon Johnson, the man who orchestrated the Senate's debate over disability, was, like Eisenhower, a heart attack survivor. His coronary occurred on July 2, 1955, in rural Virginia, and it took until the end of August before he was well enough to fly back to Texas, with months of recuperation ahead of him. Like his colleague Robert Kerr, who also was a heart attack patient, Johnson eventually died of a heart attack.[71]

Heart disease served as a subtext of the disability debate. People with ample resources, good access to medical care, and secure jobs that did not involve heavy labor might well survive a heart attack. After an often lengthy period of recuperation or rehabilitation, they might even return to their secure jobs that were being held for them. A worker on an assembly line who had a heart attack might survive but find it impossible to resume his job, which, in all likelihood, was now filled by another person. Within the disability discourse, these outcomes were applications of the Roosevelt rule. For many people polio, which caused a previously healthy person to become a paraplegic, would end their labor-force participation. Franklin Roosevelt, who spent years trying to regain the use of his legs, became, through force of will and considerable family resources, Governor of New York and President of the United States. His executive jobs required special accommodations that were not available to ordinary workers. For the Roosevelts, Eisenhowers, Johnsons, Kerrs, and even Bennetts of the world, rehabilitation was sufficient, and cash disability benefits were not necessary. Yet Johnson and Kerr, perhaps remembering their working-class roots or perhaps caught up in a partisan political battle, advanced the cause of disability benefits. Similarly, Douglas, an enthusiastic advocate of disability benefits, did not let the loss of the use of his left arm in the Second World War prevent him from taking his Senate seat in 1949.

Harry Byrd, who led the Senate fight against cash disability benefits, took solace in the views of noted rehabilitation advocate Henry Viscardi. Born with withered stumps in place of legs, Viscardi mastered the activities of daily living and embarked on a successful career. At age twenty-six he received his first pair of prosthetic legs in time for military service in the Second World War. After the war, he met Howard Rusk, the charismatic and politically connected rehabilitation doctor, and became involved in rehabilitation activities. In 1953 he founded Abilities, Inc., a nonprofit enterprise dedicated to finding private labor force jobs, away from the sheltered workshops, for people with disabilities. Byrd invited him to testify at the Senate hearings and invoked his name in the Senate debate. Viscardi believed that the disability legislation would "stigmatize" the disabled and "condone the ignorance and misunderstanding that exists." Byrd, Viscardi, Folsom, Eisenhower, and Bennett favored jobs over cash benefits.[72]

The climactic moment in the Senate debate came on July 17 when Majority Leader Johnson brought up the George amendment for a vote. Over the course of the four days preceding the final vote, Johnson's tallies fluctuated like stock prices on the stock exchange. "We'd wake up in the morning with about a ten vote margin," said Johnson aide George Reedy, "and by two or three in the afternoon it would have dropped to about three and then it would shrink to one."[73] The frenetic activities of doctors and labor union members, not to mention the Democratic and Republican leadership applying pressure on the senators, accounted for the variance.

Johnson, for his part, negotiated with individual senators looking for the political favor he could trade for their vote, all the while conferring with his ally Nelson Cruikshank on his progress. Johnson had the advantage over his Republican and Southern Democratic opponents of controlling the pace of the proceedings. At one point Johnson gave Cruikshank an hour to come up with six votes. At this stage of the debate, the wavering senators included a number of Republicans who might be peeled off from the rest of their party members. Their votes were necessary because nominal Democrats like Senator Byrd were sure to vote against the amendment. Both Cruikshank and Johnson worked on George "Molly" Malone, whose hold on his Nevada seat was tenuous. Johnson traded a favorable vote on the federal government's tungsten purchases for Malone's vote on disability benefits. Robert Caro paints the incident in dramatic terms. Malone "stayed in the cloak room, appearing only momentarily to call his 'aye' vote for the disability amendment and ran out of the Chamber before (the Republican leader) could get a crack at him." On the Democratic side, Johnson put pressure on Earle Clements of Kentucky to vote in favor the measure.[74]

In the end forty-one Democrats and six Republicans voted for the George amendment, which carried by a final margin of 47 to 45. If Clement or Malone or any of the other senators who wished to duck the vote had shifted to the other side, it would have created a tie that Vice President Richard Nixon would have broken to defeat the measure. George's conversion obviously played a large part in the result, as the favorable votes of Senators Ellender (LA), Ervin (NC), Fulbright (AR), Johnston (SC), Russell (GA), and Wofford (SC) indicated. Cruikshank's work with Republican Senators Young (SD) and Wiley (WI) also paid dividends. Byrd managed to carry only Senators Frear (DE), Eastland (MI), Holland (FL), Robertson (VA), Smathers (FL) and Stennis (MS). The large block of thirty-eight Republicans voting against disability benefits could not offset the larger block of forty-one Democrats voting in favor.[75]

Endgame

The result showed that, with the right sort of maneuvering and a popular enough cause, the liberals in the Senate could defeat the conservatives of both parties, despite the structural barriers posed by the committee system. On a close measure like disability insurance, the key was to attract at least some votes from the southern Democratic delegation. The 1956 vote marked a victory for Senator Johnson and a defeat for the Eisenhower administration. It also paved the way for passage of the entire bill. After the close vote on disability insurance and a less close vote on lowering the retirement age for women (86–7), the Senate proceeded to pass its version of the House bill by a unanimous roll call vote. On the record, then, the bill passed unanimously, but that masked the inner conflicts over key parts of the bill.[76]

The slight differences in the House and Senate bills created the need for a conference committee. The Senate bill, for example, contained the separate trust fund for disability. At this point in July, with the party conventions close at hand and the session about to end, no one wanted to string out the process. The conferees met promptly, at least by congressional standards, with the Senate version of the bill expected to prevail over the House version. On July 20, only four days after the Senate had acted on the bill, the conferees had reached agreement. A week later the measure had cleared both houses and Congress adjourned.[77]

The final question in the legislative process centered on whether President Eisenhower would sign the measure. It contained some things, like broader Social Security coverage and new grants to the states for welfare, that he supported but also the disability provision that the administration had worked hard to defeat. The omnibus nature of Social Security legislation always made it hard for a president to veto. Some in his party urged him to do so. Senator Carl Curtis (R-NE), a conservative and an outspoken critic of Social Security who had hoped that the end of Democratic rule in 1953 would radically reform the program, said that signing the bill would be "a very bad mistake." Curtis feared, as had the doctors in the AMA and Senator Byrd, that the program "will be expanded to cover all sorts of disability and sickness. We will have compulsory government health insurance as a result."[78]

Ignoring Curtis, President Eisenhower, campaigning for a second term, signed the Social Security bill into law on August 1, 1956. He cited his strong support of the Social Security program and noted that the Senate had improved the House bill, even though the administration had "serious reservations" about disability insurance. "We will, of course, endeavor to administer the disability provisions efficiently and effectively," he said. Nor would the administration lose sight of its emphasis "on efforts to help rehabilitate the disabled so that they may return to useful employment." On the whole, the President believed that the new law would "advance the economic security of the American people."[79]

Although some Republicans, like Senator Curtis, did not agree with the President's decision to sign the bill, the President had long since come to terms with the Social Security program, even as he fought its extension to new areas like health and disability coverage. He thought it worthless to continue the battle against Social Security that some employers had been conducting since 1935. In October 1953 President Eisenhower had advised the stock broker E. F. Hutton that "it would appear logical to build upon the system that has been in effect for almost twenty years rather than embark upon the radical course of turning it completely upside down and running the very real danger that we would end up with no system at all." Despite this attitude on the part of the first Republican president in twenty years, the Manufacturers Association of Connecticut still found it worthwhile in 1956 to hand out a booklet called *More Social Security, Less Take Home Pay.* "There are few things in life that are free," the pamphlet advised, "and Social Security is not one of them."[80]

Whatever the President might have thought of it, the 1956 law marked a major expansion of America's welfare state.[81] The 1956 law gave the welfare state a new flexibility to cover workers of all ages. One did not have to wait until age sixty-five for Social Security benefits to begin. Disabled workers had license to drop out of the labor force before the official retirement age of sixty-five. Women could exercise the special privilege of taking early retirement at age sixty-two.

Although a consensus governed the need for the expansion of the Social Security program, the 1956 law was a partisan measure. Most

Democrats favored it, and most Republicans opposed it. Those positions stemmed from cues that congressmen received from their constituents: unionized workers favored the measure and the medical profession, and many business leaders opposed it. The Democratic leadership in Congress supported the measure, and the Republican leadership in the White House opposed it. Eisenhower had to sign a law with which he was not totally happy. Lyndon Johnson created a wedge issue for his party by demonstrating differences between the Republicans and the Democrats on a matter on which there was otherwise broad agreement. Democrats could claim credit for disability benefits. Republicans had to be more reticent. Democrats tried to press their advantage in the 1956 campaign, both on the congressional and presidential levels. Secretary Folsom defended the administration by calling attention to the fact that "in the past four years more resources have been summoned to the cause of better health, education and economic security than ever before." Adlai Stevenson could counter that the Republicans "drag their feet on every proposal" to improve Social Security.[82]

Eisenhower overcame doubts that he was not healthy enough to be president and won the election in a landslide.[83] Adlai Stevenson carried only seven states and lost otherwise Democratic states including Louisiana, Florida, Oklahoma, and Texas. Johnson fared better. The Democrats emerged from the 1956 elections with a two-vote majority in the Senate and picked up two seats in the House to expand their margin to thirty-three. The results meant that Eisenhower did not carry too many Republicans with him, and Majority Leader Johnson gained slightly more room to operate in the Senate. The results did not provide a mandate for the passage of liberal legislation; the southerners remained too entrenched and too powerful for that. The 1958 congressional elections would be a much more decisive liberal victory.

With his handling of the disability amendments, Johnson had already shown his ability to pass legislation in difficult circumstances. Louisiana went Republican in the 1956 election but both of its Democratic senators voted for disability insurance in the summer preceding the election. The situation was similar in Oklahoma, Texas, Tennessee, and Kentucky. It showed that the Democrats could govern even with a Republican in the White House and many undependable southerners in Congress, including some, like Harry Byrd, in positions of major responsibility.

The situation with disability insurance was fluid—its passage was by a small margin —and depended on historical contingencies. The Social

Security Administration conducted a sub rosa campaign on behalf of disability, despite the change in political party in the White House. The AFL and CIO merged to form a more powerful organization, which decided to push for disability insurance despite the political risks of failure. The AFL-CIO bureaucracy formed what was almost a partnership with the Social Security Administration and the Democratic leadership and became an important institution in the creation of the American welfare state. The merger itself was the result, at least in part, of the deaths, at almost exactly the same date, of the two prominent leaders who had helped to perpetuate the feud between the two organizations. The AFL-CIO and the Social Security Administration, or at least its recent alumnus Wilbur Cohen, lobbied Walter George, who provided important leverage in the Senate. His favorable response reflected his personal circumstances as much as anything else. His impending retirement left him with a desire to leave behind a memorial, and Lyndon Johnson and Nelson Cruikshank were more than willing to supply it. Johnson traded favors with Senator Malone to get his vote and pressured an otherwise reluctant Earle Clements to vote for the measure. He did his best to prepare for the legislative battle, but he improvised his final moves. Marion Folsom opposed the measure, but President Eisenhower signed it, at least in part because it was a presidential election year and his heart attack did not leave him too weak to run.

It went almost without saying that practical politics mattered more than the rudiments of public administration, even though the arguments for and against disability insurance involved predictions about the program's future performance. The policy-making system permitted broad ideological discussion about dependence on welfare and the promise of rehabilitation. It allowed people to speculate on the inevitability of a disability program to expand and to ruminate on how costs would rise over time. There was even discussion of the need for a separate trust fund for the disability program, so as to keep the finances of old-age retirement and disability benefits separate. No one thought to look into the system's design—by what process public administrators would determine if someone was disabled—because that seemed irrelevant to the fundamental question of whether the system should contain disability benefits at all. That matter was settled as a result of political bargains that had been struck in 1952 and 1954. Practical politics predominated over considerations related to public administration, with political contingencies such as the merger of the AFL-CIO or the retirement of Walter George shaping the final outcome. The people who would administer the program had to take what the legislators gave them.

The situation was in doubt until nearly the last minute. Then the fluid political situation hardened into the new disability insurance program. So malleable in the legislative stage, disability insurance became a permanent fixture of the American welfare state. So distracted with the political battle, the proponents could not possibly have anticipated all of the future consequences.

CHAPTER TWO

What Happened to the Disability Program and How Policy Makers Tried to Respond

When Senator Harry Byrd warned his colleagues of the danger inherent in disability benefits, he drew upon his long tenure in office, claiming that in the course of twenty-four years he had seen many a program start at the size of a mouse "and rapidly grow to the proportion of an elephant."[1] SSDI was the elephant at the gates, and the senators should not invite it inside. His colleagues failed to heed his advice, and the program became a permanent part of the American welfare state.

In July 2015 the Obama White House issued a report on the program that described it as a "lifeline for American workers and families." The report seemed almost a point-by-point rebuttal of the issues raised by Senator Byrd and the other opponents of disability insurance. Disability insurance protected the middle class from the threat of serious disabilities. It paid only modest benefits that nonetheless helped to reduce poverty. Each of these things indicated that Senator Byrd's fears of a runaway program had never materialized. The White House report even included sketches of disability insurance recipients, one more worthy and upstanding than the next. "Charlotte" worked three part-time jobs until she suffered two debilitating strokes that put her out of commission. SSDI came to her rescue, and the money she received helped her "to pay bills, keep a roof over her head, and pay for her medication."[2]

The examples all featured women workers who had entered the labor force after the days of Senator Byrd but otherwise showed a program that worked exactly as its founders had intended in 1956. Disability recipients were people who had had jobs all of their adult lives and paid into the program until they became disabled. Because of the careful way in which the program was managed, the United States spent a smaller percentage of its gross national product on disability than did France, Italy, the United Kingdom, and the Netherlands. As for fraud, or malingering as Senator Byrd might have put it, it was "rare" and "taken very seriously" when it did occur. There had been a period of growth in the disability rolls but that had "slowed and is projected to remain steady over the next decade."[3]

As for Senator Byrd's and Secretary Folsom's worry that cash disability benefits retarded rehabilitation, there was the example of Angela. She worked as a part-time teacher until multiple sclerosis made it difficult for her to continue her duties in the classroom. She received disability benefits, but she began to miss teaching. Resourceful and determined, she seized upon the opportunities presented by new technology that were not available to people in 1956. She took a job teaching online for a large online university. She worked when she could, but disability insurance stood ready to help her in the months when her medical condition prevented her from working.[4]

As was often the case in the disability debate, the White House presented a very stylized portrait of SSDI that largely ignored its history. Much about that history spoke to the points raised by Senator Byrd. For one thing, disability insurance began small and became much larger. That fact became apparent when one looked, as many conservative analysts did, at total spending for the program. It rose steeply from 1960 to 1980. Then it leveled off until 1989 before beginning a precipitous rise that lasted until 2015 (see figure 2.1). In the year 2000 the program cost on the order of $56 billion, and in the year 2013 costs reached $144 billion (see figure 2.2). Of course the number of workers who were potential disability recipients also rose during those years. One measure that took that rise into account was the number of disability recipients per one thousand US workers. Instead of remaining static, the measure rose during the 1970s, declined from the late 1970s until 1989, and then rose again after that. The ratio of disabled workers to all workers doubled from the early 1990s to 2011.[5]

If one took a snapshot of the program, one would discover that in 2015, as the Congressional Budget Office reported, SSDI paid a total of $143 billion, or about 0.8 percent of the gross domestic product, in

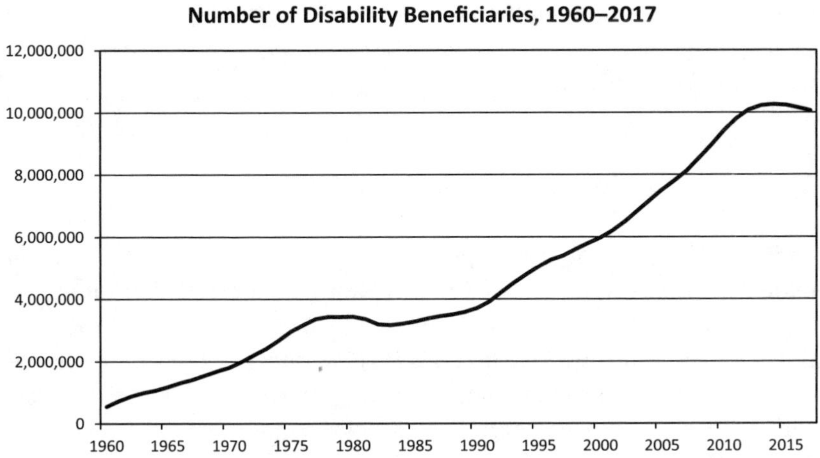

FIGURE 2.1. Number of Disability Beneficiaries, 1960–2017.
Note: Chart includes disabled workers and dependents who receive benefits on the accounts of the disabled workers.
Source: *Annual Statistical Report on the Social Security Disability Insurance Program, 2017*, Table 3. "Number, average, and total monthly benefits, December 1960–2017." US Social Security Administration, 2018. Available online at https://www.ssa.gov/policy/docs/statcomps/di_asr/2017/sect01b.html.

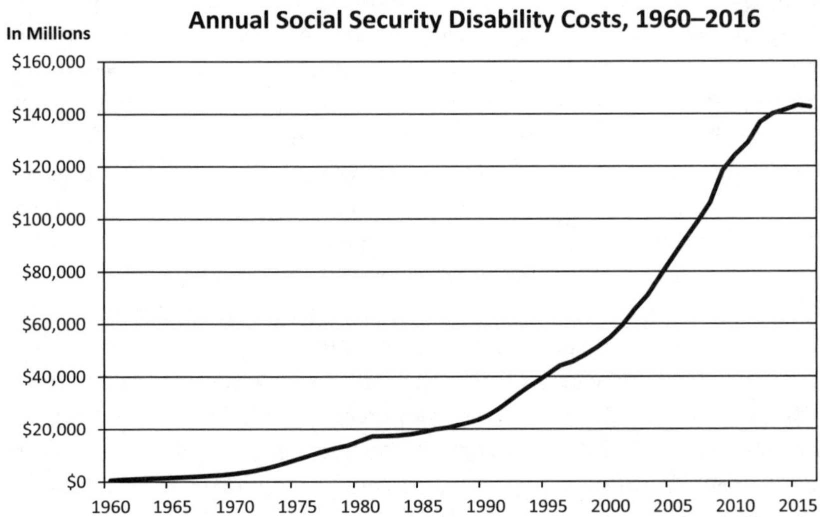

FIGURE 2.2. Annual Social Security Disability Costs, 1960–2016.
Note: Chart includes disabled workers and dependents who receive benefits on the accounts of the disabled workers.
Source: *Social Security Bulletin, Annual Statistical Supplement, 2017*, Table 4A6. "Total annual benefits paid from DI trust fund, by type of benefit, 1957–2016." US Social Security Administration, 2018. Available online at https://www.ssa.gov/policy/docs/statcomps/supplement/2017/4a.html#table4.a6.

benefits to almost nine million disabled beneficiaries and two million of their spouses and children. Whether those proportions were elephantine was in the eye of the beholder.

Toward Expansion: Initial Considerations

To illustrate the history of the program's growth required a movie rather than a snapshot. In the movie the program was not static but rather dynamic and growing. Approximately 789,000 beneficiaries in 1960 became nearly 3,000,000 beneficiaries in 1970 and 5,223,311 beneficiaries in 1980. The number fell to 4,934,350 in 1990, rose to 7,550,930 in 2000, and reached 11,280,792 in 2010.The plot of the movie involved changes in the law, the disease environment, and the economy.[6]

As the Obama White House suggested, the benefits remained relatively modest. The average benefit for disabled beneficiaries was $1,166 a month in May 2016 and benefits for the worker's dependents were lower.[7] As government benefits went, however, these were relatively desirable. Social Security paid its beneficiaries in cash, not coupons or funds redeemable only for food as in the Food Stamp Program. People were free to spend the money as they wished. No one checked to see if they were buying vegetables at the grocery store or stocking up on alcohol and cigarettes. Checks entered the recipient's bank account each month by automatic deposit. Once initiated, the benefits kept coming.

Despite the nearly constant growth, people did leave the program, not so much because they were rehabilitated and ready for a new job, as Senator Byrd and Secretary Folsom might have hoped, but rather because they had reached the normal or full retirement age. At that age (sixty-six in recent years) disability benefits switched over to old-age benefits. Some of the beneficiaries died, and only a very few others reentered the labor force and left the program. In 2014, for example, of those who went off the disability rolls, 58 percent reached the full retirement age and 32 percent died. In 2015 there were 8,909,430 disabled workers on the rolls, of whom 39,103 or 0.4 percent left the rolls because they had gone to work.[8]

As Senator Byrd feared, one engine driving the disability program was the unemployment rate.[9] In the rational-behavior world of the economist, hard times made more people turn toward disability insurance. When the labor force was unsteady, a worker with a physical impairment might well decide to cash in his chips and go on the disability rolls. It cost nothing to apply, and the benefits (or pay) were certainly better than a worker could receive from being unemployed. For older workers, who faced a labor market stacked against them, the disability option was particularly tempting. Not everyone reacted in this way, but the unemployment rate and the rate of applications for disability insurance appeared to move together. The economic doldrums of the 1970s produced a spike in disability applications. So did the great recession that began at the end of the George W. Bush administration and the start of the Obama administration.

The policy makers who governed the SSDI program had no more control over the unemployment rate or the general state of the economy than did the airplane pilot buffeted by headwinds. In both cases, however, those in control submitted a flight plan that indicated the general route they would follow. An airplane pilot, anticipating thunderstorms, could choose to fly away from them. Although large social programs were difficult to steer, policy makers constantly monitored their path and if the situation warranted it, altered their course through legislation and administrative actions.

Although some of the SSDI program's growth came about through the direct intervention of Congress, not all features of the program were equally amenable to change. Incremental expansion came easier than did reforms that altered the program's structure. Whatever the political costs of creating the program—such as alienating the medical profession—they had been paid in 1956. The political battle over whether there should be a disability insurance program was over. It now made sense for members of Congress to reap as many benefits for their constituents as possible. The result was less conflict over program expansion than over the initial creation of the program. As benefits began to be paid, it was only natural for policy makers to question why some people, who seemed equally impaired, equally needy, and equally worthy, were not eligible to receive benefits.[10] The 1956 law contained features designed to decrease the initial cost estimates but that were in fact quite arbitrary. A person fifty or older could receive benefits but not someone aged forty-nine. The Social Security program had long recognized that workers lived in families and as early as 1939 made provisions for extra benefits to be paid to the dependents of a Social Security recipient. Disability benefits contained no such features. Someone raising a family of ten received the same benefit as a bachelor who had the same earnings record. Each of these things provided incremental paths to program expansion: lower the age barrier and make disability benefits compatible with regular Social Security benefits.

All it required to expand the program in this manner was assurances by public authorities that the program could afford it. These assurances came not only from expectations of economic growth but also from the balances in the Social Security trust funds. A growing labor force and a rising wage rate all meant that more people were paying Social Security payroll taxes.[11] That in turn boosted the finances of the Social Security trust fund and provided incentives for policy makers to remove the arbitrary limits—such as the age fifty restriction—from the law.

More fundamental reform was more difficult to bring about. The administrative arrangements for determining that someone was unable to work for an extended period of time because of a mental or physical impairment remained in place. Each liberalization of the program or extension into a new area such as disability benefits for welfare beneficiaries only carried that arrangement forward. It was also difficult for policy makers to adjust the system's basic imbalance between paying monetary benefits through disability pensions and providing rehabilitation services, despite nearly constant efforts to do so. These policy makers intended disability benefits only for people who could prove to state authorities that they were unable to work. Effective rehabilitation therefore required people who had already demonstrated their inability to work to engage in a process designed to make them able to join the labor force. As often happened in policy history, it was difficult to change a system designed for one thing, in this case facilitating the retirement of people with disabilities, to accomplish something else—providing the necessary medical and vocational services to bring people back into the labor force. Existing policies shaped subsequent policy outcomes—a good example of what the political scientists called policy feedbacks.[12]

Incremental Expansions

The expansion of the program began almost as soon as the program was created. As the program started to accept applications for disability benefits, members of Congress worried that too many of their constituents were being turned down. Representative Carl Perkins (D-KY) took to the House floor to complain about the "thousands and thousands of applications" that had been denied.[13] The 1957 Congress could not do much about that because the previous Congress, composed of many of the same people who sat in the 1957 Congress, had legislated a very tough disability standard. As fully elaborated in 1967, the standard held that a disabled worker needed to have an impairment "of such severity that he is not only unable to do his previous work but cannot, considering his age, education, and work experience, engage in any kind of substantial gainful work which exists in the national economy."[14] It was not supposed to matter that coal mining jobs in Kentucky were drying up or that there was no specific job vacancy for a particular applicant.

Nonetheless, the program's slow start rankled. One thing Congress could do was make sure that disability benefits were every bit as generous as old-age benefits. Old-age benefits included extra payments for a worker's spouse or dependent children. In the same summer that Congressman Perkins complained about the Social Security Administration's miserly attitude, Congress created benefits for the dependents of disabled workers. To be sure, the actuaries needed to examine the changes to determine their future costs. In the still prosperous 1950s, wages and employment continued to rise, despite the 1957 recession. That meant there was plenty of money on hand to fund the changes. The 1958 amendments passed relatively easily. The hard political costs of creating the program had been paid. Now it was time to reap the benefits.[15]

The age limitation on benefits presented the greatest barrier to an expanded program. One had to be at least fifty years old to qualify for benefits. That left out all of the younger workers who might well have suffered debilitating impairments that knocked them out of the labor force. In 1956 the age fifty rule had been one of the program's safeguards to mollify wary doctors, life insurance agents, and other opponents. In 1960 Congress swept that safeguard away. It took a little more work than did the 1958 expansion, but the measure passed easily. In particular, Bureau of Budget officials in the Eisenhower White House worried about the costs of the expanded law. Robert Ball and other Social Security officials assured them they had no cause for concern. In one internal Social Security Administration (SSA) memo describing a meeting with the Bureau of the Budget, an SSA bureaucrat wrote his commissioner that Ball "snowed them under with lengthy answers to short questions."[16] The SSA also used a Ways and Means hearing on the administration of the disability insurance program to press the case for removing the age limit. Social Security Commissioner William L. Mitchell testified that there were "no administrative obstacles in the way of improving the protection afforded by eliminating the age requirement." Health, Education, and Welfare (HEW) Secretary Arthur Flemming added his assent. He was much more eager to expand disability insurance than his predecessor Folsom had been to initiate it. The measure passed overwhelmingly in the House and the Senate.[17]

In 1965 a change in the disability definition made it easier to get benefits. One no longer had to have an impairment that was likely to last for an indefinite duration or result in death. Instead, the impairment needed only to last for more than a year.

The expansion process reached a climax in 1972. In that year, Congress passed an omnibus Social Security law that, among many other things, permitted disability beneficiaries to receive Medicare coverage. The change followed the rationale of making disability benefits similar to old-age benefits. Another key change legislated in 1972 applied to all Social Security benefits, not just disability benefits. Congress changed the old ad hoc system of raising benefit levels. The 1958 amendments, for example, raised benefits by 7 percent. In 1972 Congress created *automatic* benefit increases that were keyed to the inflation rate. Once fully in place in 1975, the new system became an important spur to program growth. Old-age benefits were the main focus of the debate, but the changes applied to disability benefits as well. Another 1972 change, particular to disability insurance, extended coverage to people with end stage renal disease.[18]

The Program's Structure as a Source of Growth

Not all of the growth in the disability insurance program came from conscious legislative intent or design. Some of it resulted from the program's administrative structure, which was much less amenable to change than were benefit levels or self-conscious program expansions such as giving disability beneficiaries health insurance. The administrative setup that came from earlier disability and Social Security legislation produced results that were not so much unintended as they were unanticipated. In 1956 congressional leaders, so intent on passing disability insurance, failed to notice program attributes already in place that posed far greater problems for disability than they did for old-age insurance.

The disability determination system legislated in 1956 was cumbersome, but few advocates wanted to make an issue of it. As a result of legislation first passed in 1952, disability determinations were made by the states acting under contract to the federal government. If someone were denied disability benefits, the decision as often as not came from the applicant's state government as it did from the federal government. At a time of great concern over the elusiveness and imprecision of the very concept of disability, Congress allowed each state to make disability determinations. This decision created the potential for differences in the disability rolls not just over time but also across space.

States had different rates of approving the applications they received. In 1974, for example, Alaska denied eligibility to 63 percent of the cases its examiners saw. Meanwhile, in the state of Iowa, examiners denied only 36.6 percent of the cases they handled.[19] To be sure, the two states were very different in their geography, their occupational structure, and the ethnicities of their work forces. But the wide disparity in the acceptance rate suggested that something more was at play than variation in the local populations. Perhaps the Iowa officials were simply more lenient than were their Alaskan counterparts. Perhaps the two states applied the same rules differently.

Why did Congress not put a stop to the system and substitute something different? In 1956 congressmen cheered the fact that state examiners would make disability declarations because state employees were closer to the ground and enjoyed close relationships with local doctors and rehabilitation officials. It meant that remote bureaucrats, of the sort so feared by doctors, would not have total change of the disability program. And once in place, the system tended to stay in place, despite periodic interest in Washington in changing it. It was hard for congressmen to take jobs away from their local constituents, and state disability examiners soon became a vested political interest that blocked more fundamental reform.

The tangible political costs of change outweighed the hypothetical administrative advantages. Bringing benefits to the dependents of disabled workers and workers under fifty were relatively benign expansions of an existing program that closed the gaps that the program had exposed. The economic boom that made it possible to expand the program without raising payroll taxes made the changes irresistible. The same considerations failed to apply to overt efforts to expand the size of the federal government at the expense of the state governments.

States made the initial decisions on disability benefits and rejected quite a few cases. The rejection rate, like nearly everything else about the program, varied by year, sometimes in surprising ways. Connecticut denied 41 percent of disability cases in 1974. Six years later the state rejected 63.6 percent of the cases, even though the law had not changed. In calendar year 2015 the states approved only about 30 percent of the cases they saw.[20]

The system provided many avenues of appeal for people who had been denied benefits. The appeals process altered the outcome of the disability determination system significantly. Rejected applicants appealed their decisions in 40 percent of the cases in calendar year 2011. These appeals were anything but pro forma. In calendar year 2011, 60 percent of the applicants who appealed won their cases.[21]

The disability insurance program inherited the appeals process from the Social Security system. Early administrators believed it was very important for beneficiaries not to have their benefits tampered with by political officials as was often the case before the Social Security Act. To avoid that fate, the system included a way for applicants to appeal the administrative decisions of the Social Security Administration to what were called administrative law judges (ALJs). These judges were qualified lawyers who specialized in Social Security law, reinforcing due process for disability applications and freeing the program from the formal court system in which the judges were generalists who often knew little about Social Security.

When disability insurance was created in 1956, policy makers gave no thought to the differences between disability benefits and old-age and survivors' benefits. They failed to realize, at least in this technical detail of the legislation, that disability was a much more subjective concept than old age. The inability to engage in substantial gainful activity was a more difficult matter to determine than whether a person was sixty-five years old or the wife of a retired worker. They also failed to anticipate that it would be easier for state authorities to reject an applicant on the basis of a paper file than it would be for an administrative law judge who saw the applicant in person. In a formal hearing the person could show signs of mental confusion, limited mobility, and pain that did not show up in the paper file. The state disability examiners worked in relative isolation. The ALJs presided over an open hearing in which the plaintiffs were often represented by lawyers. Some of these lawyers worked for firms that made a business of representing disability applicants.

The creation of this disability bar happened relatively quickly in the history of SSDI. Between 1955 and 1958, requests for hearings in the Social Security system increased by more than 500 percent. By 1959 requests for hearings reached 1,300 per month. By 1965 the Social Security Administration received 23,323 requests for hearings, and by 1980 the number had reached 252,023. As a direct result, administrative law judges came to play a more prominent role in the program. By the 1980s more than one out of every five people admitted to the disability rolls used the appeals process to get there.[22]

Hearings before administrative law judges took time to schedule. Like trials in regular courts, each hearing consumed a great deal of time, and there was no way, short of the hearing, for applicants to reach a settlement with the Social Security Administration. ALJs, like their counterparts in the rest of the legal system, could hear only a limited number of cases in a single day and needed time to prepare their decisions. All of these factors contributed to the backlogs that developed. In 2015 the average interval between a hearing request and a final decision was 480 days. During this lengthy period, an applicant might hesitate to engage in a rehabilitation program or even take a job for fear of injuring his case. Just as an unlucky defendant in a criminal case might draw a hanging judge, so applicants could have their hearing before an ALJ who was less lenient than his colleagues.[23] A recent analyst reported that one hearing office in the Chicago region had an allowance rate of 83 percent for cases with disorders of the back. But another hearing office in the Chicago region had an allowance rate of 45 percent for cases with the same impairment. One judge approved 97 percent of cases with back disorders, while another judge only allowed 15 percent of back disorder cases.[24] It was like two major league umpires with different strike zones.

Lawyers participated in the system because it was lucrative for them to do so. In theory applying for Social Security benefits was supposed to cost nothing; the program was a public amenity like the National Zoo and cost nothing to enter. Disability applicants who used lawyers had to pay for the privilege. As in automobile accident cases, the loser in this contingency payment system owed the lawyer nothing. A winner received benefits that went back to the onset of the disability. Lawyers were entitled to a quarter or up to $6,000 of this back pay. The bounty amounted to $425 million in 2001 and $1.4 billion in 2011.[25] In search of these payments, lawyers fueled the growth the system and added to its costs.

The system contained levels of appeal beyond an administrative law judge hearing. By the time a case reached an ALJ, the state disability determination office had made an initial decision and reconsidered it. If an applicant were still dissatisfied after an ALJ hearing, he could take the case to the Social Security Appeals Council. The persistent applicant could then push his case into the federal courts. That meant that a Social Security disability case could, under the right circumstances, end up in the Supreme Court.

The Elusive Nature of Reform: 1980 and 1984

Senator Byrd might not have predicted the persistence of litigation, even though its preconditions already existed in the Social Security system by 1956. He understood the difficulties of trying to define disability and administer a program that paid cash benefits based on disability and anticipated that such a program might be plagued with rising costs. The events of the 1970s and 1980s added something new and unanticipated to the process. In the 1970s an adverse economy and an administrative system burdened by new responsibilities and perplexing changes in the disease environment all combined to produce a spike in the number of people on the disability rolls. For the first time, policy makers needed to use legislation not to expand the program but to restrain its growth. To the surprise of many, this effort ended up achieving the exact opposite of what policy makers intended.

The 1970s witnessed something like a run on the disability rolls. At the end of 1972 there were 3.1 million disability insurance beneficiaries and by 1976 4.6 million.[26] This rise induced a sense of panic among policy makers, not unlike the way in which the rise in the welfare rolls during the 1960s troubled the people in charge. Welfare rolls were supposed to move with the state of the economy. Good times should have reduced the rolls. In the 1960s, the nation experienced an unprecedented economic boom, and still the welfare rolls continued to rise. In the case of disability, the 1970s rise occurred when people were living longer and, at least on the surface, healthier lives. It was a time of celebrated medical advances such as antibiotics, polio shots, and heart transplants. In this golden age of American medicine, a growing percentage of the labor force claimed to be disabled. Among older male workers aged forty-five to sixty-four the number who reported they were unable to work rose from 72 per thousand in 1969 to 101 per thousand in 1978.[27]

People began to suspect that something was wrong with the SSDI program. One problem was that the disability determination system was overburdened, leading to hasty and perhaps incorrect decisions. In the 1970s Congress loaded two new responsibilities on this system. In 1972 policy makers put the SSA and the state disability determination offices in charge of certifying welfare recipients who were either disabled or blind for benefits. Supplemental Security Income (SSI) was a new federal welfare program for the elderly and the disabled that replaced the old state programs. As was often the case, Congress gave little thought to the administrative details of the new program, instead accepting the SSA's assurances that it could run the program effectively. Another new program of the era allowed coal miners who had "black lung" to receive compensation. These cases too went to the state offices. By 1974 1.4 million people applied for the disability (and blindness) welfare benefits, 1.2 million for SSDI, and another half a million for black lung.[28] It was like a kitchen in a restaurant getting slammed during the dinner rush.

Another problem was that the "general state of disarray in disability programs," as the Senate Finance Committee put it, escaped from the obscure confines of bureaucratic offices and landed on the front page of the *New York Times* and the cover of *Time*. The lead story in a June 1978 issue reported that the number of people receiving disability benefits had tripled in thirteen years to become larger than the population of Norway or Virginia. The magazine, with its usual mixture of straight reporting and editorializing, expressed a sense of outrage and declared that the SSDI program had lost sight of its original purpose. Far from serving as a leading edge of rehabilitation, the program encouraged people "to remain prostate, permanent wards of society." The conservative nightmare of 1956 had been realized.

The *New York Times*, in its more restrained manner, reported on the disability paradox. Medical science rendered many diseases less disabling, but the disability rates rose anyway. The evidence cited included the fact that the rate at which federal employees had taken disability retirement had tripled in twenty years. Particularly vexing were mental disorders, cirrhosis of the liver, and loss of hearing. In 1965, 4.8 of 1,000 persons paying into the Social Security trust fund received disability benefits. In 1974 the figure reached 6.2. "It's hard to believe that the incidence of disability is actually rising that fast," an HEW official said.[29]

Congressional hearings followed. The Carter administration proved less sympathetic to disability insurance and Social Security more generally than had its predecessors. Joseph Califano, the savvy lawyer and former LBJ domestic aide whom Carter had appointed as Secretary of Health, Education, and Welfare, testified before a Ways and Means subcommittee on February 22, 1979. He brought the usual statistics with him, as had been reported in the *New York Times*. Something needed to be done or disability benefits would get completely out of hand.[30]

In a sense one of the safeguards put in place in 1956 had worked. Falling balances in the disability trust fund had alerted policy makers to an impending problem. Despite its virtues as an early warning system, however, the trust fund provided only the thinnest barrier against the disability program overspending the money available to it. The disability trust fund was always smaller than the one for old-age and survivors insurance, and interfund borrowing got SSDI through a number of crises.[31]

The congressional hearings of 1979 led to corrective legislation in 1980, with the House debating the issue in September 1979 and the full Senate taking up the measure in December. The congressional debates of 1979 treated the SSDI program much less gingerly than previous debates. Congressman Jake Pickle (D-TX) argued that disability insurance replaced too much of a worker's income and created too much of a temptation to seek disability benefits. His critique illustrated how economic principles had entered public policy discourse. Those on the disability rolls were rational consumers, just like their counterparts in the labor force. Pickle proposed a fix that included better policing of the disability rolls to make sure that those on the rolls deserved to be there. In the future, a nonpermanently disabled beneficiary on the rolls would be reviewed at least once every three years. He also advocated changes in the disability benefits formula to make them smaller for some disability applicants. In other words, he proposed that the incremental engine of Social Security expansion be slowed—a watershed moment.[32]

The way in which policy makers worked out the problem of making benefits smaller illustrated the techniques they would use in the future. None of the cuts was direct, such as removing the 1958 addition of family benefits or the 1960 change in the age limitation. Instead, the changes took technical forms that disguised their purpose and gave them a protective cover. One was a cap on family benefits. A family, no matter how large or how poor, could not receive benefits that were greater than 150 percent of the disabled worker's benefit. Another was a change in the formula by which the amount of a benefit was computed. To get around bad years, the SSA permitted a number of low-income years to be dropped from the calculation of average wages (like a teacher who allowed his students to have one bad test). Average wages mattered because benefits were directly based on them, with a few statistical manipulations to bring older wages more in line with more recent, and presumably higher inflation-induced wages. In the new formula, the number of years a worker could drop out would vary by age. Someone twenty-eight years old or younger would not be allowed to drop out any years.[33]

With so many close observers, it was impossible to sneak these changes through Congress without notice. In the spirit of past disability legislation, proponents tried to temper the changes by adding features to the program that would make it easier for beneficiaries to walk off the rolls and into the labor market. It marked a return to the old spirit of rehabilitation. These measures included letting people deduct more work-related or disability-related expenses from their incomes, thus increasing work incentives (once again the image of a beneficiary as a rational consumer prevailed). With more deductions, a worker could earn more than the "substantial gainful activity amount" and still get disability benefits. Other changes included making it easier for someone who had left the rolls and gone to work to go back on the rolls in the case of a relapse, without having to go back through the cumbersome disability determination process. Another provision allowed disability beneficiaries to retain their Medicare benefits for a number of years after they had begun working.

Opponents dismissed these rehabilitation components of the legislation and urged people to see that the proposals were in fact ways of cutting disability benefits. To many liberals, such as Senator Edward Kennedy (D-MA) or Representative Claude Pepper (D-FL), it was the wrong path for the Social Security program to follow. Unions remained faithful to the Social Security cause. "If anything disability benefits should be raised, not lowered," said one AFL-CIO official. Unlike in 1956, this time the worries about the program's solvency outweighed the fear of putting a hole in the nation's safety net. The measure carried, and President Carter signed it on June 9, 1980.[34]

If the story had ended there, it could be used as an example of responsible policy making in the sense that policy makers correctly diagnosed a problem and took steps to remedy it, while preserving the basic structure of the program and keeping its social protections intact. The implementation of the program changed the picture completely. A triumph morphed into a disaster.

When Jimmy Carter signed the legislation, he was well into the 1980 campaign against Ronald Reagan. He had already faced a direct challenge from Senator Edward Kennedy, based in part on Kennedy's fear that Carter was dismantling the liberal legacy of the New Deal and of his brothers. The disability legislation was a case in point. Carter survived that challenge, but Ronald Reagan made a more formidable opponent, particularly during a severe recession and a more general feeling that America was not living up to its potential. Reagan, of course, went on to a sweeping victory in the 1980 election. His victory meant that the disability legislation signed by President Carter would be implemented by President Reagan.[35]

Not too much changed too quickly in the bureaucracy. There would be plenty of old Social Security hands available to institute things like the continuing disability reviews that Congress had mandated. The Reagan administration examined the entire government, with the exception of the military, with an eye toward cutting expenditures. Social Security was a tempting target, but it was still a very popular program that contained iron-clad promises to workers that they would receive benefits in the future. David Stockman, Reagan's budget guru, referred to it as the "inner fortress of the welfare state."[36]

During the transition period, Reagan officials received word that there were savings to be realized in the Social Security program, primarily from the disability insurance program. Reagan officials learned that the General Accounting Office (GAO) had made a study that suggested that an estimated 20 percent of the disability caseload did not meet the eligibility standards. The GAO did not release a study until the affected agency had a chance to respond to the findings. This particular disability study did not become public until March 1981, but the Reagan transition team had already seen it. The study suggested that the cheaters, malingerers, and others receiving benefits to which they were not entitled could be removed from the rolls. Since disability benefits were essentially lifetime benefits, the savings from removing someone from the rolls were substantial. Furthermore, the GAO was a nonpartisan source whose integrity could not be attacked by the Democrats. New studies seemed to agree with the GAO study. Analysts working for the SSA reported that 26 percent of the people on the disability caseload between July and September 1980 did not belong there.[37]

The 1980 disability legislation provided a perfect rationale for the Reagan administration to investigate individual cases on the disability rolls and, in the event the investigation showed that a person was no longer disabled or had never been disabled, then the SSA could suspend the person's benefits. The 1980 law had suggested that someone not permanently disabled be investigated at least once every three years. In fact, however, no one expected a great deal of this provision. It would take time and manpower, and those removed from the rolls could still appeal the decision. Reagan administration officials, new on the Social Security scene, had no such hesitations. Instead of waiting until 1982, as the legislation suggested, they decided to begin the disability reviews immediately and increase the number of people under review. The administration became increasingly optimistic that it could save a great deal of money.

If saving money were the object of the exercise, then it made sense to target younger workers and the workers who were most likely to have recovered. Decisions made in 1974, when Congress dumped all of the new cases on the disability determination system, were particularly suspect. The disability determination services, sent as many as 500,000 cases to review in 1983, scurried to keep up with the increasing workload. They examined a person's paper file rather than the person himself and used new medical examinations as evidence. They then judged whether a person remained disabled. A person could be removed from the rolls even if his condition had not improved. The SSA sent the person a letter saying his disability benefits would be discontinued and that the person owed the government for all of the benefits he had received in error. By the fall of 1984 the administration had reviewed about 1.2 million disability beneficiaries and suspended 400,000 of them.[38]

It was impossible to carry out such a large project outside the public's view. Legal aid attorneys began to feed the cases that appeared to strip worthy beneficiaries of their benefits to the newspapers and the Congress. The tenor of disability stories turned from exposés of malingerers to criticisms of callous bureaucrats who were conducting a purge on the disability rolls. As the story changed, policy makers largely abandoned their defense of the 1980 amendments and suggested remedial action was in order. The *New York Times* picked up the story as early as September 1981, and the *Los Angeles Times* and *Philadelphia Inquirer* were not far behind. The fact that 40 percent of the people being reviewed were removed from the rolls appeared to be a miscarriage of justice.[39]

Congressmen, who read the *New York Times* and their local newspapers, itched to expose the problem. Democrats, in considerable disarray as Republicans passed the Reagan budget, appreciated the chance to be on the winning side of an issue, and liberal Republicans, such as Senator John Heinz of Pennsylvania and William Cohen of Maine, followed suit. Heinz got his information from the Philadelphia legal aid office that became a national leader in contesting disability cases and took one case, which substantially changed the way disability benefits were awarded to children, all the way to the Supreme Court. Cohen faced reelection and saw the issue as a good one for him. He got his information from his home offices in Maine and worked closely with Kathleen Grover, a lawyer in Portland, Maine.[40]

The new crisis in the disability program expanded the range of congressional committees probing the case. In other words, it temporarily changed the institutional structure for disability policy making. In times of perceived scandal, committees with jurisdiction over a problem or a program often found themselves shunted aside by a congressman who wanted to claim something like a finder's fee and sought available forums to pursue the case. Senator Heinz worked through the Joint Committee on Aging, and Senators Levin and Cohen operated through a subcommittee of the Government Affairs Committee. Members of the Ways and Means Committee, particularly Congressman Pickle, who had a certain pride of authorship in the 1980 amendments, abandoned them only reluctantly and resented the interference of other committees.[41]

Senator Heinz showed particular interest in the problems of the mentally ill, who, he claimed, presented the "clearest example of abuse and catastrophe." In an age of psychotropic drugs that helped to stabilize the condition of mentally ill people, figuring out the relationship between mental illness and disability was particularly difficult. If someone were bipolar, he might appear before a disability examiner just when his behavior was going through the normal phase. Judged not disabled, he might then find it impossible to hold down a job. The very nature of the illness might prevent a person from giving an accurate personal history. The medical standards for determining the disability of a mentally ill person were both demanding and vague. A schizophrenic needed to demonstrate "marked restriction of daily activities and constriction of interest." Heinz helped to bring many of the problematic cases to public attention.[42]

Mental illness was an impairment that showed up much better in administrative law judge hearings than it did in the paper reviews performed by state disability examiners. State examiners who read the files for the continuing disability reviews had terminated 31,700 mentally ill people by August 1992. The states had a termination rate of 76 percent of the mental illness cases they received. About 13,400 of these people requested reconsiderations, and administrative law judges reversed 91 percent of the mental impairment cases that reached their hearing rooms. In fact, many of the people who were on the rolls had only gotten there in the first place after an ALJ hearing. The Reagan administration, despite the advice it received from Social Security bureaucrats, lost sight of that fact.[43]

The congressional hearings on the disability reviews produced dramatic testimony. Ethel Kage of Reed City, Michigan, testified before Senator Carl Levin (D-MI) and a subcommittee of the Government Affairs Committee on May 25, 1982. She told the story of her husband, who had worked on a survey crew, even after he lost sight in his left eye. Then he had a stroke, which left him with tunnel vision in his other eye and made it impossible for him to work. He entered the disability rolls at the age of forty-two. His case got selected for review, and when word reached him that he had been terminated, "it was quite a shocking affair," his wife said. He began to despair and questioned whether his family could make it without the monthly checks from the SSA. "We were on for seven years and never any indication," Ethel Kage testified. On Thanksgiving evening, her husband took sick and died the next day, the victim of two massive coronaries. Such cases became known as horror stories and generated a great deal of negative publicity.[44]

During the course of the Reagan era disability reviews, the system nearly came apart. Congress held more hearings than ever before. The state disability examiners began to rebel against the task of throwing people off the rolls, and some governors declared a moratorium on continuing disability reviews. Administrative law judges found themselves in the center of controversy for reversing so many of the state decisions and accused the Reagan administration of imposing a quota on favorable decisions. The courts took up controversial cases with the result that different circuits followed different procedures in disability cases.

The result of a very tortuous process was that President Reagan ended up signing the Disability Benefits Reform Act on October 9, 1994. The law made it harder to remove someone from the rolls and loosened what program insiders called the "adjudicative climate." To remove someone from the rolls now required "substantial evidence" that demonstrated medical improvements had occurred and that showed the person was able to engage in substantial gainful activity. For all applicants, disability examiners also needed to consider the combined effects of several impairments, each of which might not have been disabling in and of itself. The new law also required examiners to pay more attention to an individual's statements about pain.[45]

The disability program had become a rubber band that snapped, negating the effects of the 1980 reforms and demonstrating the limits of legislative action to discipline the program. The results were quite visible in the program statistics, which show disability payments plateauing and even declining in the first half of the 1980s before rising precipitously in the late 1980s. These developments occurred even in the face of a severe recession at the end of the 1970s and the beginning of the Reagan years. By 1991 disability expenditures were well above where they had been in the 1970s and continuing to rise. Applications for disability benefits declined sharply during the years of the review—again contrary to what one might expect during a recession—but then rebounded. Although the 1980 changes in the benefit formula remained on the books, the 1984 law permanently altered the shape of the disability program. For example, the share of disabled beneficiaries with mental or musculoskeletal disorders (think lower back pain) increased from 30 percent of new awards in 1983 to more than 50 percent in 2014.[46]

Disability and the Disease Environment

The mental illness category showed how the very nature of disability or at least the categories that clinicians used to classify it could change over time. Medicine did an effective job in combating infectious and parasitic diseases. The number of disabled beneficiaries in these categories started at 10,903 in 1960 and by 1988 was down to 2,802, despite the significant increases in the total disability caseload. In 2015 the number was still significantly lower than it had been in 1960. Mental disorders presented a much different picture. The number of disability beneficiaries classified as having mental disorders stood at 17,287 in 1960. By 1967 it had doubled, and it doubled again by 1977 and again by 2000. It reached a peak of 218,862 in 2010. As the numbers increased, so did the categories within the larger mental disorder category. Like chemists expanding the periodic table, psychiatrists increased the number of mental illnesses. In December 2015 the caseload of disabled workers included 17,816 people with autistic disorders, 357,219 with intellectual disability (mental retardation in the old terminology and a very large percentage of the disabled children), 1,290,603 with mood disorders (the largest single category), and 412,977 with schizophrenic and other psychotic disorders.[47]

As medicine combated individual diseases, it seemed to discover new ones. The very growth in the number of diseases served as a factor in the expansion of the disability rolls. It joined the changing state of the economy, the changing demographics of the labor force, and the changing age structure of the population as factors in the growth of the rolls. The recessions of the 1970s and the 2010s, the mass entrance of women in to the labor force, and the aging of the baby boom generation all contributed to the growth of the disability rolls. Each of these things was either inevitable or beyond the immediate control of policy makers and, with the exception of the recessions, none was a particularly bad thing. In the face of these forces, the plateaus, like the one in the 1980s and the one that appeared to be forming in 2015, lasted for only a few years before the relentless pattern of growth continued. When policy makers tried to intervene and clamp down on admissions to the program and remove people from the rolls, as they did in 1980, the results were often counterproductive.

The Continuing Search for the Rehabilitation Remedy

Always, though, there remained the appeal of rehabilitation as a benevolent means of controlling the growth of the disability rolls. Rehabilitation has been part of the policy conversation from the beginning of the program to the present day. The problem was that policy makers never figured out how to deploy it effectively. The goal of rehabilitation remained elusive, like the Northwest Passage in the early days of North American exploration.

The natural affinity between cash disability benefits and rehabilitation existed well before the 1956 passage of SSDI. Federal bureaucrats who worked on proposed disability legislation for the Social Security Administration included rehabilitation in their plans. As a practical matter, rehabilitation meant the state-federal vocational rehabilitation program that had been created in 1920, rather than, say, physical medicine or, as it would be called after the Second World War, rehabilitation medicine. Accordingly prominent SSA bureaucrat I. S. Falk argued in 1938 that a program of social insurance against disability should include occupational training for persons with chronic impairments. He cited vocational rehabilitation as a program that could provide such services.[48]

By the end of the 1930s the Office of Vocational Rehabilitation and the SSA were housed in the same federal agency. The Federal Security Agency, a sprawling new bureaucratic entity that would become the Department of Health, Education, and Welfare in 1953, contained the SSA, the Public Health Service, and the Office of Vocational Rehabilitation. This new alignment, a demotion for the previously independent SSA and a promotion for the rehabilitation program previously housed in the Department of the Interior, brought vocational rehabilitation and Social Security into closer contact with one another.

During the 1940s, despite the great boost in employment provided by the Second World War, the vocational rehabilitation program was in something of a lull. The program measured its success by the number of clients who received its services and achieved gainful employment. This number declined after the war. For example, the program rehabilitated 44,000 people in 1944 and 36,106 in 1946.[49]

During World War II and its immediate aftermath, public interest in rehabilitation quickened. Press reports on the heroic ways in which medical doctors saved the lives of wounded soldiers, sailors, marines, and fliers contributed to this new burst of enthusiasm. The war launched a new medical specialty. The medical practitioners who restored the quality of injured veterans' lives began to call themselves rehabilitation doctors instead of internists or orthopedic surgeons. In the wartime year of 1943, Congress reacted to the new interest by passing a major new rehabilitation bill for veterans. At the same time it amended the civilian rehabilitation program to allow civilian state rehabilitation agencies to use their grants from the federal government to purchase medical services that worked toward the removal of a static disability for people unable to purchase such care themselves.[50]

Rehabilitation medicine became the first in a series of plausible interventions that failed to develop into an effective means of removing disability recipients from the rolls. The vocational rehabilitation programs failed to take much advantage of the new feature in the law because rehabilitation medicine cost a great deal compared to the other services that the agency purchased, and the outcome was far from certain in any particular case. A person might be rehabilitated by the doctors and able to transport himself by means of a wheelchair but not necessarily be able to hold down a steady job. The SSDI program had even less reason to utilize rehabilitation medicine, since Social Security officials, with their eye on Medicare, did not want to do anything that might link them to socialized medicine.

Despite vocational rehabilitation's lackluster record, it remained in the SSA's plans in the years heading toward the passage of SSDI in 1956. In the planning stages, SSA bureaucrats tinkered with putting an appropriation into their disability insurance bill for a program of "medical, surgical, rehabilitation and other services to disability beneficiaries." The lure of rehabilitation remained strong. Rehabilitation, according to the SSA, was "almost as important as the payment of cash benefits." It sounded good, but whether SSA officials, who put the need for cash benefits far above the need for rehabilitation, ever believed in it remained an open question. When disability insurance was finally passed in 1956, a former SSA administrator wrote to his former assistant Wilbur Cohen that it was time to ignore rehabilitation proponents and "press our advantage."[51]

As late as 1949 and the successful House passage of a disability insurance measure, the rehabilitation provisions remained in the bill until Ways and Means Committee Chairman Robert Doughton (D-MS) removed them. The congressman said that policy makers would have to choose between cash disability benefits and rehabilitation. When the Senate failed to pass the House bill, the issue became academic.[52]

The 1950 Social Security Amendments that were the product of this congressional skirmish added a new public assistance program for the permanently disabled and the blind to the Social Security Act. The implementation of this law provided dynamic rehabilitation administrator Mary Switzer, appointed in 1950, with a chance to show policy makers that welfare recipients could be rehabilitated. Switzer, who did more than anyone else to effect the vocational rehabilitation program's escape from its 1940s doldrums, tried to persuade state welfare administrators to make a vocational rehabilitation counselor part of a team that certified someone for the new welfare benefits. She touted the program's success in rehabilitating welfare beneficiaries, mentioning in Congress and elsewhere that in 1952, for example, her program successfully rehabilitated seventy-eight hundred individuals who had previously been on public assistance. In this way and others, she kept vocational rehabilitation in the policy conversation between 1950 and 1956. When the Republicans arrived in 1953, they found vocational rehabilitation (VR) a refreshing alternative to a costly cash benefit program that, in their minds, would produce dependency.[53]

As the critical battle of 1956 approached, even strong proponents of SSDI, like Senator Paul Douglas, knew that rehabilitation would have to receive prominent mention in the debate. HEW and SSA bureaucrats convinced the Republican officials who headed the agency that SSDI would be nothing more than a "great huge recruiting program for rehabilitation." When someone came to a local Social Security office and asked to be put on the disability rolls, he would be put in touch with a rehabilitation counselor.[54]

That hope faded almost as soon as the SSDI program went into operation. So many people flooding the small VR agencies overwhelmed the state agencies and made it appear as though they could not handle the problem, as indeed they could not. All of the people in the initial caseload were fifty years or older and had a disabling condition that would probably keep them out of the labor force for the rest of their lives. Such people were not motivated to seek rehabilitation, particularly when one factored in the lag between applying for benefits and actually receiving them. The VR agencies and the SSA reached an agreement in which the VR programs were excused from interviewing SSDI applicants who were over fifty-five, bedridden, institutionalized, or mentally ill with a negative prognosis or who had impairments that were worsening. Of 456,000 disability applicants who were referred for rehabilitation between 1956 and 1959, only 48,800 were accepted by the program.[55]

Vocational rehabilitation was a nonstarter in the Social Security Disability Insurance program. Congress could not simply mandate a relationship between SSDI and VR. It did not help that each side was wary of the other. VR officials worried that the Social Security Administration, which was so much larger, would take over their small program. SSA officials were concerned that the VR officials would block the expansion of their disability program to cover people under fifty and pay benefits to the families of their beneficiaries.

Maybe money could lubricate the system. The SSDI program had a lot of money at its disposal. Rehabilitation, if it were successful, was much cheaper than paying someone cash benefits for life. Using the disability trust fund to pay for rehabilitation represented, at least in theory, an investment that would return much more to the trust fund than it would cost. If the SSA gave the rehabilitation programs money without asking the states to match the money, as they had to do in the regular VR program, states would find it attractive to accept people from the SSDI rolls into their programs. Mary Switzer, the dynamic administrator, remained wary and continued to see SSA as an imperialist bureaucratic power that would occupy the VR program. She gained more influence in the HEW bureaucracy in 1963 and the vote of confidence made her more comfortable assenting to what became known as the Beneficiary Rehabilitation Program in 1965. The state rehabilitation agencies received 1 percent of the cost of disability payments, distributed based on the percentage of the disability caseload in each state. It was extra money without a great deal of accountability—a stipend from the affluent Social Security program to the deserving but underfunded VR program.[56]

The Office of Vocational Rehabilitation and the Social Security Administration had common goals but different incentives to pursue those goals. The larger the disability caseload, the more money the state rehabilitation agencies received. A natural process of incremental expansion also affected the Beneficiary Rehabilitation Program (BRP). One percent of the disability payments became 1.2 percent in 1973 and 1.5 percent in 1974. When the SSI program began operations in 1974, Congress said that welfare beneficiaries should also be rehabilitated and provided funds for that purpose. That would seem to indicate congressional approval of rehabilitating disability beneficiaries. The trouble was that, once accepted by the rehabilitation program, SSDI clients became just like all of the rest of the VR clients and received the same services. SSDI recipients remained poor rehabilitation candidates.[57]

The returns on the program were not as robust as policy makers had envisioned. In fiscal year 1978 the BRP served 154,541 SSDI and SSI clients. It rehabilitated 12,268 people at an average cost of $7,904. Of this number only 6,346 people left the rolls. Either they failed to hold on to their jobs or their earnings were below what the program called the "substantial gainful activity" level. One fundamental problem was that, to qualify for the BRP, a person needed to be on the disability rolls. Such a person would already have proven to federal authorities that he or she had a significant impairment that prevented him or her from working. The program did not catch people who applied to the program but were weeded out by the disability determination process. Those people might have made good BRP beneficiaries, but Congress could not spend trust fund dollars, contributed by employers and employees, on them.[58]

When the Reagan administration arrived, Congress pulled the plug on the BRP. It was exactly the sort of loosely administered social service program of which Budget Director David Stockman disapproved. Congress did not abolish the program. Instead, VR agencies could receive reimbursements from the SSA for people who, as a result of VR services, engaged in substantial gainful activity for nine continuous months. Retrospective payment replaced the prospective payment system, another feature common to the era that emphasized economic incentives, in the design of social welfare programs. Social agencies, along with hospitals and defense contractors, preferred their money to be guaranteed. The effect on the BRP was immediate. SSA payments to VR agencies promptly fell from $86 million to $3 million.[59]

The BRP failed to exhaust the search for the intervention that would keep the disability rolls under control. Neither rehabilitation medicine in the 1950s nor mandating rehabilitation for disability insurance beneficiaries in 1956 nor even direct payments from the SSA to the vocational rehabilitation program in the 1960s appeared to work. The search continued. A new program called "Ticket to Work" arrived in 1999. It became the last legislation of the millennium that President Clinton signed in an impressive ceremony at the FDR Memorial in Washington. It enabled a public or private rehabilitation provider to guide a person from the disability rolls to a job, with considerable financial rewards for successful providers. Few people took up the tickets, and the program foundered during the great recession of 2008 and 2009.[60]

A more prominent development occurred in 1990 when Congress passed the Americans with Disabilities Act (ADA). The ADA was a sweeping civil rights law that brought civil rights protection for people with disabilities to parity with protection enjoyed by blacks and other minority groups. The act prohibited an employer of an enterprise with fifteen employees or more from discriminating against an applicant on the basis of his handicap. There were of course exceptions: the bill did not condone that a blind person receive a job as a bus driver. The law nonetheless had a grand sweep. Public transportation, telephone communications, grocery stores, hotels, and other places of public accommodation all needed to be accessible to people with disabilities. The ADA was a liberal civil rights measure but unlike other such laws it had a strong Republican backing.[61]

Once again the rehabilitation rationale entered public discourse. Society had a choice. On the one hand, it could give people disability benefits for life. On the other hand, it could give people a job that would be facilitated by some relatively simple adjustments in the physical and mental environments. An employee in a wheelchair who hesitated to take a job because the workplace had steps, narrow toilet stalls, and other barriers would now be able to take the job after the employer made a "reasonable accommodation" to the workplace that did not cause the employer "undue hardship." The employer would approach the hiring process with a new mind-set, aware of the productive capabilities of people with disabilities and not ruling out a person for his disability alone. Best of all from policy makers' point of view, the ADA did not represent a new item on the federal budget. Executive agencies already existed to administer the law, and the changes the law required were to be carried out by the private sector rather than the public sector.

The ADA had its origins in the vocational rehabilitation program. In 1973 Congress amended the program to prohibit recipients of federal funds, such as schools, hospitals, and transit systems, from discriminating against people with disabilities. Few people noticed the 1973 amendments at first because policy insiders concentrated on such things as the level of federal reimbursements for rehabilitation rather than on grandiose visions of the future. In time Section 504, as it was called, began to receive wide notice as the affected entities pondered the cost of making facilities, such as subway systems designed at the turn of the century or universities whose physical plants dated from colonial times, accessible to people with disabilities. It took until President Carter's arrival to put the regulations in place and to work out some of the hard problems of implementation. The regulations provided that a university, for example, did not have to make each and every one of its dorm rooms, offices, and classrooms accessible to people with disabilities; it just had to provide enough accessible dorm rooms, offices, and classrooms to accommodate the students and faculty members who attended (or wanted to attend) or worked at the university.[62]

At the time of the ADA concerns about the costs of creating a barrier-free environment remained current. The President of the Greyhound Bus Company worried that he could not afford to make his fleet of buses accessible to people with disabilities. Others grew concerned that the new law would be the cause of much costly and time-consuming litigation. Proponents of the ADA used the rehabilitation rationale as a form of rebuttal. The ADA, by making so many jobs accessible to people with disabilities, would reduce the nation's expenditures on such costly programs as SSDI and SSI. President George Herbert Walker Bush could argue that the ADA was a respectable Republican measure in the tradition of the vocational rehabilitation program.

James Brady, President Reagan's former press secretary and a member of the disability community by virtue of the assassination attempt on Reagan's life, contributed an op-ed piece to the *New York Times* that made the Republican case for the ADA. Brady identified himself as a Republican and a fiscal conservative. He expressed his pride that the legislation had been developed by "15 Republicans appointed to the National Council on Disability by President Reagan." He pointed to the historical tradition of Republican support for disability rights, explaining that President Eisenhower had urged that people with disabilities "become taxpayers and consumers instead of being dependent upon costly Federal benefits." He concluded that the ADA was an outgrowth of Eisenhower's philosophy. It would "save taxpayers billions of dollars by outlawing discrimination, putting disabled people on the job rolls and thereby reducing Government disability payments."[63]

Similar rhetoric came from Richard Thornburgh, George H. W. Bush's Attorney General. "Certainly," the Attorney General said, "the elimination of employment discrimination and the mainstreaming of people with disabilities will result in more persons with disabilities working, in increased earnings, in less dependence on the Social Security System for financial support, in increased spending on consumer goods and increased tax revenues."[64]

The only problem was that the ADA, once enacted, had little or no effect on the disability rolls. The older people on disability, all of whom had severe impairments that led to functional limitations, did not see themselves as disabled in the same way as did younger people, often with good educations because of new mainstreaming initiatives, who regarded themselves as members of a minority group that was the victim of discrimination at the hands of the majority. The ADA caused school systems to move teachers with respiratory problems into rooms with better ventilation. It made employers more aware of job applicants with disabilities. It did little to discourage older workers from applying for disability benefits and almost nothing to stem the growth of the rolls. It was another intervention that failed to deliver on its promise.

Conclusion

The continued growth of the disability rolls showed that the conservatives had gotten the better of the argument in 1956. Disability was a difficult concept to define, and disability benefits were hard for policy makers to control. Liberals who argued that the creation of disability benefits met a real social need and would not retard rehabilitation efforts probably won their side of the argument as well. In the years after 1956, the vocational rehabilitation program, like the Social Security Disability Insurance program, continued to grow. New rehabilitation methods, such as paying rehabilitation agencies to rehabilitate people on the disability rolls or to ensure the civil rights of people with disabilities, continued to arise on a regular basis. None of them appeared to have much relevance or to work effectively for disability beneficiaries. In some sense, though, the creation of SSDI strengthened rather than retarded the interest in rehabilitation. Contrary to the argument of conservatives, rehabilitation did not appear to be an effective substitute for cash disability benefits.

The history of SSDI showed the ways in which demography, the disease environment, and the state of the economy influenced the development of the program. Furthermore, things to which policy makers in 1956 had devoted little attention, such as the bureaucratic structure of the disability determination system and the appeals system, played a large role in the program's subsequent development. Immediate political concerns nearly always trumped worries that a program, once enacted, would prove hard to administer.

Congress expanded the program in an incremental manner between 1956 and 1972 and then tried to slow its rate of growth in the period after that. The 1980 amendments, which tightened the program, resulted in legislation four years later that loosened the program. Significantly, these amendments made few overt changes in the program but rather changed the rules by which benefits were computed. The basic structure of the program as enacted in 1956 endured, even as its approach to disability policy appeared to become outdated. The Americans with Disabilities Act reflected the rise of the disability rights movement and marked an attempt to cast disability policy in terms of civil rights. It had no appreciable effect on the disability insurance program.

The Social Security Disability Insurance program proved to be one of the nation's most enduring social welfare programs. Created in 1956, it remains in place, on much the same terms, in 2020. Many things happened in the intervening years but none of those things disturbed the program's basic structure. The program became a permanent memorial to the policy-making environment of 1956. The process of incremental reform might have ended in 1972, but by then most of the program's obvious limitations, such as the age fifty limitation on benefits, had been removed. Even as incremental reform stalled, the program continued to grow, reflecting the increasing demand for disability benefits in the modern economy. Nor did the benefit levels get out of date. Cost of living adjustments and other program features common to all the Social Security programs helped to sustain the disability insurance program, and these automatic adjustments required little action by Congress.

Social Security Disability Insurance established the precedent that many important social problems could be handled through the Social Security program. Still in its state of incremental improvement in 1965, the program's presence reassured policy makers that the nation could enact an even more ambitious program to cover the medical expenses of Social Security beneficiaries. Medicare, as that program would come to be known, had its own complicated history that will be chronicled in the following chapters.

CHAPTER THREE

Wilbur Mills, Wilbur Cohen, and Nelson Cruikshank Curate Medicare

In 1965 Congress expanded America's welfare state to include Social Security benefits in kind rather than in cash. In the past the program had made monthly cash payments to people who were retired, disabled, or the survivor or dependent of an insured worker. Beginning in July 1966, the program reimbursed doctors, hospitals, nursing homes, and other health care providers for services they provided to Social Security beneficiaries. It meant that an elderly person could go into the hospital knowing that the federal government would pick up some of the tab. From the program's very beginning, Medicare became the largest health insurance program in America. A plethora of private companies and nonprofit enterprises participated in the health insurance market and in so doing divided it up into lots of little pieces. Medicare, by way of contrast, served nearly all of the nation's elderly and, in time, many of the nation's disabled workers.

Because of Medicare's prominence in the health insurance market, it exerted a large influence over American health care practice. The way it reimbursed doctors and hospitals affected both the private health insurance market and how doctors organized their practices and hospitals organized their services. Medicare's original design, legislated in 1965 after the usual process of intense political bargaining, exerted a strong influence over subsequent developments in American medical care. As usual, short-term deals and political developments in 1965 produced long-term consequences.

This chapter takes an extended look at the passage of Medicare in 1965. Subsequent chapters will examine what happened to the program after 1965 and how those developments changed social welfare policy in America.

Disability and Medicare

As a general proposition, Medicare benefits raised more policy questions than did the disability benefits that had been created in 1956. With disability benefits one could argue over whether cash payments impeded recovery and slowed rehabilitation and thus over whether the benefit should take the form of medical and rehabilitation services rather than cash. The 1956 legislation disposed of that question. Regular cash payments would predominate over rehabilitation services. With Medicare the open questions covered a much broader range of concerns. The legislation necessarily required the government to determine the priorities of the health care system. Politicians might talk about providing senior citizens with medical care—a vague commitment—but the legislative process required them to be more specific. Legislative consideration of Medicare thus raised a host of questions. How many days in the hospital should the program reimburse and who made the decision about how long a patient needed to stay in the hospital? What about doctor's visits outside of the hospital? Should the government reimburse all hospitals and nursing homes, or should these facilities be required to meet some test of their adequacy? Did, for example, an adequate hospital have to maintain a particular ratio of nurses to patients? Each of these questions and many more arose in the debate over the establishment of Medicare and persisted through the program's history.

Medicare, like all pieces of social legislation, reflected the conventional wisdom of the era of its creation.[1] This wisdom limited the range of policy options. Few people suggested in 1965, for example, that every senior be given a cash voucher and then be left to his or her own to make health care arrangements. Health costs were too variable and the private health insurance industry too fragmented for that. Nor did many people suggest that American health care be socialized, with doctors becoming government employees and hospitals becoming public property and opening up clinics that provided health care for all. The existing health care system was too established and too successful for that. Instead, the push was to get people who might have lacked the means to pay for their health care into the highly regarded private health care system.

The politically popular Social Security program became the administrative and legislative vehicle for Medicare, although that decision was neither natural nor inevitable. After all, there was a vast difference between cash and in-kind benefits and, before 1965, the Social Security program had little or no experience with medical benefits. The policy action in health insurance traditionally occurred at the state rather than the federal level, because private insurers were regulated at that level.[2] If one conceded that the Social Security program was the appropriate location for health insurance, however, then that decision implied a federal law rather than a series of state laws, and coverage of Social Security beneficiaries as a primary concern.

The 1956 passage of disability insurance therefore became an important precedent for Medicare in 1965, even though the political circumstances of one year were not the same as the other. For one thing, the two measures followed different political paths in Congress. In 1956 disability insurance passed through a relatively compliant House of Representatives and got hung up in the Senate. The 1965 pattern was more traditional. First the House and then the Senate, following the favorable recommendations of first the House Committee on Ways and Means and then the Senate Committee on Finance, approved the measure, and it became the law of the land. In 1956 Senator Walter George needed to be brought in from the wings as a surprise guest of the liberals who staged a floor fight to pass disability insurance. The 1965 situation required no such tricks.

In a second difference between Medicare and disability insurance, their passages came at different points of the electoral cycle. Disability insurance passed in an election year and provided campaign fodder for the Democrats in 1956. They could argue that they had expanded the Social Security program over the opposition of the Republicans and could deliver even more goodies if they occupied the White House and increased their congressional majorities. Although the Democrats achieved no success at the presidential level, disability turned out to be a resonant issue in the campaign, with the Republicans running a candidate who had recently suffered a heart attack.

Medicare passed in the year after a presidential election, which meant that the Democrats' success in the 1964 election contributed to the passage of Medicare in 1965. The landslide victory of Lyndon Johnson (61.0 percent versus 38.5 percent for Barry Goldwater in the popular vote) put a strong proponent of Medicare in the White House. The pattern of the electoral vote placed a premium on Medicare supporters. The Democrats gained seats in the House and the Senate, and their victories came in northern and midwestern locations, such as New York, New Jersey, and Michigan, where candidates tended to favor Medicare, rather than in the South, which had never strongly supported the measure. What gains the Republicans made tended to be concentrated in the formerly solidly Democratic South, such as in South Carolina and Mississippi.[3]

Beyond these differences related to the mechanics of electoral politics, disability insurance paved the way for Medicare in the sense that both laws followed a similar policy format. In both cases, the federal government ceded a sensitive policy operation to state or local intermediaries. The 1956 legislation permitted state governments to make crucial eligibility decisions, although with federal oversight and a federal appeals system. In 1965 private or quasi-public organizations, like Blue Cross and Blue Shield, which provided hospital insurance and coverage of doctors' services respectively, received the crucial responsibilities of administering payments to hospitals and doctors, and explaining the payments to the beneficiaries. The fact that Congress entrusted public responsibilities to private agencies in 1965 showed the limits of its tolerance for expanding the power of the federal government even at the high tide of liberalism and the Great Society.

The Interest Group Structure around Medicare

The structure of interest groups around Medicare resembled the one around disability insurance. Doctors played a more prominent role in the fight against Medicare because their interests were the most directly affected by the legislation. Insurers also had a stake in the fight because the new legislation threatened one of their profitable products, but the policy debate allowed a continuing role for private health insurers in the medical market. In 1965, therefore, the doctors and insurers changed places, with the doctors now taking the lead. Opposing the doctors in 1965 as in 1956 were the labor unions. By this time labor union representatives in Washington, Social Security bureaucrats, and liberal members of Congress were practically joined at the hip. Furthermore, the labor unions nurtured a different sort of interest group that was based on age rather than occupation. The National Senior Citizens Council testified frequently on Medicare.

The archival record of Medicare shows the near constant appearance of AFL-CIO staffer Nelson Cruikshank at important meetings and strategy sessions. In June 1964, with the politics of Medicare in a particularly precarious state, Cruikshank and labor lobbyist Andrew Biemiller spent an hour and a half with key legislator Wilbur Mills.[4] They immediately reported the contents of their meeting to Wilbur Cohen, who now served in an official capacity in the Department of Health, Education, and Welfare as the Assistant Secretary for Legislation appointed by Kennedy and promoted by Johnson after Medicare's passage first to Undersecretary (1965) and then Secretary (1968). If Cruikshank was labor's major authority on Medicare, Cohen was the departmental official who held the Medicare portfolio. He in turn worked closely with Robert Ball, who had been promoted to Social Security Commissioner in the Kennedy years and played close attention to the administrative details of Medicare.

Toward the end of 1964, Cohen, in the Department of Health, Education, and Welfare, stayed in touch with Clinton Anderson in the Senate. The New Mexico Senator was a member of the Senate Committee on Finance and a strong Medicare proponent. On November 18, 1964, Assistant Secretary Wilbur Cohen reported to Senator Anderson that he had just spent a number of days working with Robert Ball on the latest iteration of the Medicare legislation. Cohen mentioned a recent conversation with President Johnson, who asked that work on the bill be accelerated and that Cohen touch base with the AFL-CIO. Cohen and his HEW boss had just met with Nelson Cruikshank to go over a general outline of the bill. Cohen reassured Anderson that "I am checking very closely with Nelson Cruikshank on these matters."[5]

Cruikshank acquired near veto power over the Medicare legislation as it was being written in November and December 1964. Meetings between Cruikshank and Cohen dealt with critical matters such as whether the legislation should include a provision that encouraged Social Security beneficiaries to buy private health insurance policies to cover their doctors' bills. Cruikshank weighed in on this matter on equal terms with Senator Anderson, Senator and soon to be Vice President Hubert Humphrey (D-MN), Speaker John McCormack (D-MA), and Majority

Leader Carl Albert (D-OK). Cruikshank remained a vital member of the team all the way through to its final passage. At a sticky point in May 1965, Cohen told Larry O'Brien in the White House that he had asked Cruikshank and Andrew Biemiller "to go see Senator Long and urge him to cut down on his amendments."[6]

Congressional Players

Senator Russell Long, first elected to the Senate in 1948, became an important player on Medicare by virtue of his senior position on the Senate Finance Committee. His decision to support the measure in 1965 helped in the measure's passage. His prominence on the Finance Committee made him first in line to chair the committee after Senator Harry Byrd, who was ailing, announced his resignation from the Senate on November 10, 1965. To the very end of his Senate career, Senator Byrd refused to bend with the political winds. He remained a staunch opponent of increased federal government spending. Hence he not only voted against disability insurance and kept it bottled up in his committee in 1956 but led the floor fight against it. In 1965, even after Johnson's landslide victory, all of the participants in the debate knew that Senator Byrd, who had managed to retain his position as Finance Committee chair, would not support Medicare. The only question was how obstructive he would be.

In fact his grip over the committee was weakening. When disability insurance was passed in 1956, the balance between Democrats and Republicans on the committee remained tight, with a margin of one. The members of the sizable Republican minority were natural allies of Byrd. With each Congress, as the congressional strength of the Democrats increased, another liberal senator joined the committee. The margin and size of the committee expanded so that in 1964, the year Medicare received serious consideration, the balance of Democrats and Republicans stood at 11–6. Anderson, Paul Douglas, and Albert Gore held committee seats in 1957, when Medicare was first introduced in Congress. Each of these senators became a major Medicare supporter. Eugene McCarthy (D-MN) in 1959, Vance Hartke (D-IN) in 1961, and Abraham Ribicoff (D-CT) in 1963 joined the Finance Committee and formed what had now become a sizable liberal block. Byrd, aging and near the end of his Senate career, could not control this block. Even his legendary grip over Virginia politics was waning. In 1964 the Democratic Party in Virginia backed Lyndon Johnson, and he carried the state, a sharp contrast with the four previous presidential elections. Byrd could no longer effectively separate the Democratic Party in Virginia from the national Democratic Party, either in Richmond or in Washington.[7]

The situation in the House Ways and Means Committee was quite different. In 1956 Jere Cooper (D-TN) had chaired the committee, but his death at the end of 1957 allowed Wilbur Mills to take over as chair. Mills played a very active role in the committee's affairs and achieved success in bringing the committee to consensus on important matters. His success followed from his willingness to do the necessary homework on tax and Social Security legislation that made him the near equal of the bureaucratic experts and lobbyists when it came to the fine points of the law. Mills did not have a very large staff working on Medicare and relied on outside help from the Congressional Research Service. He also came to depend on people like Ball and Cohen and actuary Robert Myers on Social Security legislation. The 1958 promotion of Wilbur Mills to Chairman of Ways and Means made a great difference in the 1965 passage of Medicare.[8]

Medicare in the Kennedy Administration

The team of Cohen, Ball, and Cruikshank put together the administration's Medicare proposal of 1961, drawing upon a bill already considered and rejected by the Senate during the 1960 presidential campaign. The basic idea was relatively simple: use the Social Security program, already in the business of dispersing money from payroll taxes, to administer a program that provided an elderly beneficiary with up to 90 days in the hospital and up to 180 days in a skilled nursing facility per year.[9] Doctors' bills were not covered, perhaps out of deference to the political power of the AMA and the precedent of previous bills but perhaps because hospital care was considered the more serious risk. People regarded doctors as familiar figures who worked in their hometowns, and they admired them in much the same way as they did their local congressman. A doctor might offer an elderly patient, who might be his neighbor, a substantial discount or some other special treatment. Hospitals, like Congress, were more alien and forbidding places. To reach them many rural and suburban residents had to travel to urban centers, and hospitals stays could be lengthy, even for relatively routine things like the birth of a baby, a spell of pneumonia, or a tonsillectomy. Hospital visits were often costly endeavors, and the federal government volunteered to step up and pay much of the cost for elderly people who were at risk for such diseases as cancer, heart disease, and the many other maladies of old age.

As one might expect of a high-profile issue, alternatives to the administration proposal abounded. Some conservatives, such as Congressman Thomas Curtis (R-MO), argued that aid should be limited to people in poverty—many Social Security beneficiaries were in fact quite wealthy and could afford to buy their own health insurance or simply pay their medical bills out of pocket—and any government program should be administered by the states, not the federal government. One notion was to work with the Kerr-Mills program, created in 1960 in the heat of that year's battle over Medicare. It provided federal grants to state programs that helped to finance health care to the indigent elderly. Wilbur Cohen, eager to establish the idea of national health insurance, even in a very elementary form, had created the program, and Senator Robert Kerr and Representative Wilbur Mills had seized upon it as a convenient alternative to Medicare.[10]

Liberal Republicans, such as Governor Nelson Rockefeller and Senator Jacob Javits of New York, thought something more was required. They had a different idea than Congressman Curtis. Rockefeller proposed that people should have a choice between a higher cash Social Security benefit and Medicare. To be eligible for the cash, a person needed to prove that he already had health insurance that was as least as good as Medicare. Rockefeller and others seeking a middle ground received some pushback from Social Security bureaucrats who preferred that all Social Security taxes and benefits be mandatory. Social Security Commissioner Robert Ball believed, for example, that Rockefeller's option plan would be difficult to administer and it would leave the Medicare program with the sickest people to insure.[11]

Opening bids in the Medicare debate began in 1961. Few people expected Medicare to pass in that year. As an example of this cautious and tentative attitude, Ways and Means hearings did not even begin until late July, and they were lengthy and inconclusive. The next year, which culminated in a Senate vote on Medicare, featured the sort of veiled politics that was common to social welfare policy at the time. In particular, Wilbur Mills favored the administration's welfare reform proposal and was confident it would get through his committee. At the time Ways and Means handled all legislation related to both Social Security and public assistance. He therefore acquiesced in a plan to pass an omnibus Social Security bill that included welfare reform but omitted Medicare. Perhaps Medicare might be added as an amendment when the Senate received the welfare reform bill from the House. Mills, whose predilections were extremely difficult to read, might accept some health insurance provisions in conference.

Even though Medicare had little chance of passing the Ways and Means Committee, a major task of the Kennedy administration in 1962 was to produce modifications of the Medicare bill, perhaps acceptable to Mills in conference and maybe acceptable to one or more of the four undecided Democratic votes within his committee. Representative Burr Harrison (D-VA), one of the wavering congressmen on the Ways and Means Committee, wanted to limit Medicare to those people who had in some sense paid for it. That meant that people who were already retired, a sizable percentage of the elderly, would not be covered. Harrison favored a plan in which eventual recipients would need to pay into a special trust fund for five years, with special discounts for people nearing retirement age. Although this idea never gained much traction in the Medicare debate, another of Harrison's proposals did. He wanted to allow hospitals to designate private, voluntary Blue Cross plans as their agents. In Harrison's scheme (or the one Social Security staffers created for him) money would go from the federal government to Blue Cross rather than directly to the hospital. Starting in the summer of 1962, therefore, the administration's Medicare bills came to contain what policy insiders would call "intermediaries," illustrating how the 1965 Medicare bill acquired pieces that had been developed over the course of the long congressional debate between 1961 and 1965.[12]

The tactical problem in 1962 and beyond for Medicare proponents was how much to bend their proposal into a shape that liberal Republicans or wavering Democrats would find acceptable without destroying its structural integrity. One idea current at the time allowed the federal government to make direct payments to private insurance carriers for those already covered by private plans. This proposal went so far in the direction of mollifying Medicare's critics that it divided the normally united group of Medicare supporters. The influential Nelson Cruikshank thought this notion very ill-advised because private companies wasted too much money administering and advertising their plans.

The government could use the broad base of Social Security beneficiaries to reduce those costs substantially. Others in the Medicare coalition thought that any compromise that might bring Wilbur Mills to the cause was worthy of serious consideration.[13]

A channel of political communication opened in 1962 between Senator Clinton Anderson and Senator Jacob Javits. By June 28, 1962, they had come up with a variation on the administration plan that preserved a role for private health insurers. In addition to the administration's Medicare plan, known at the time as the King-Anderson bill, the new measure included an option for the reimbursement of private plans. If a person was covered by an approved private health insurance plan, one that contained equal or better benefits than specified in Medicare, then the person could continue the coverage at retirement but at the government's expense. The federal government would pay all or part of the person's premiums by reimbursing the private health insurance company.[14]

The Javits-Anderson amendment figured in the July 1962 Senate debate on Medicare, after organized labor and others in the Medicare debate reluctantly agreed to go along with it. Even this watered-down version of Medicare met determined opposition from key Finance Committee senators, particularly Robert Kerr of Oklahoma. Similar to the situation in 1956 with disability and again in 1960 with Medicare, it failed to pass the Finance Committee, requiring Medicare proponents to offer it as an amendment to the Finance Committee's welfare reform bill on the Senate floor. The climactic vote came on July 17, and it appeared that it would be close, just as the 1956 Senate vote on disability insurance had been. This time the liberals lost by a vote of 52–48 after Senator Kerr put pressure on the normally reliable Jennings Randolph (D-WV) and forced him to vote against the measure.[15]

The battle for Medicare rolled into 1963, and this time the measure did not even come to a vote. The proponents' strategy, which shifted with the political whims of the moment, now called for the Ways and Means Committee to pass Medicare before sending it to the Senate. Wilbur Mills kept stalling; he did not announce hearings on Medicare until October 29 and set November 18 as the date for them to begin. The hearings ended abruptly on November 22, the date of Kennedy's assassination, and never resumed.[16]

Throughout this desultory process, the proponents kept rejiggering the bill in the hope that one version would satisfy Mills. The trouble with this strategy was that Mills and a majority of his committee might never accept Medicare, and if they did not, liberals thought they might proceed with their own vision of Medicare that would offer health insurance to the elderly on more generous terms. Senator Pat McNamara (D-MI), who held a seat on the Labor and Public Welfare Committee, which had been a traditional home of health insurance advocates such as Senator Robert Wagner (D-NY), objected to deductibles and preferred what the insurance industry called "first dollar" coverage. The Social Security technocrats, who doubted that liberal senators like McNamara would ever get their way with Mills, nevertheless drafted a plan that included a uniform benefit with no deductible but also allowed individuals to elect, once a year, a longer duration of benefits with a deductible. Such proposals strained the Social Security coalition. Even the accommodating Robert Ball found this plan to be administratively unworkable. In an often repeated piece of Medicare lore, Ball requested an appointment to register his complaints with President Kennedy. When he got to the Oval Office, he found Wilbur Cohen and Kennedy waiting for him. Ball said that the proposed plan would produce administrative chaos. "Well, then, let's have a little chaos," the President supposedly replied.[17]

Lack of success led to a loss of discipline in the legislative process. Some, including White House staffer and Kennedy crony Kenny O'Donnell and HEW Undersecretary and former Madison, Wisconsin, Mayor Ivan Nestingen, thought Mills could be worked around or forced by the weight of popular opinion to back Medicare. The proponents just needed to rally the people behind the presumably popular cause. The policy insiders, such as Cohen, Ball, and Cruikshank, who worked in the Social Security issue network rather than in the broader realm of conventional partisan politics, disagreed with this approach. So amenable to compromise in their basic posture toward Congress, they nonetheless believed that the administration had nothing to trade with Mills, who held a secure seat in a conservative region where President Kennedy was not very popular. They could not purge him from Congress if he failed to support Medicare. Instead they needed to keep working with him patiently, despite all of his false starts and hesitancies. Both sides in this dispute saw the other as naïve—one too willing to compromise on the contents of the Medicare legislation and the other too eager to apply political muscle where it would not gain any ground. The Kenny O'Donnells of the world wanted to pass Medicare at any price; they needed the win. The Social Security insiders wanted to maintain a good working relationship with the program's chief congressional proprietor.[18]

1964: LBJ Tries His Hand at Medicare

Kennedy's death changed things and altered the tone of the discussion. Things that looked deadlocked in 1963 appeared more hopeful in 1964. Still, the Johnson administration could not reach agreement with Wilbur Mills in 1964, and the matter carried over into 1965 before it finally came to rest.

In 1964, as in previous years, the Republicans felt obligated to come up with alternatives. The idea associated with Governor Nelson Rockefeller, a potential Republican presidential candidate, of offering a choice between increased Social Security or Medicare benefits remained in play. In the meantime, Senator Javits and the liberal Republican senators moved closer to the administration. The new Javits plan, which had been developed by a group called the National Committee on Health Care of the Aged, offered forty-five days of hospital care and up to two hundred days of home health treatment to be financed with a one-half percent increase in the Social Security tax. At HEW Wilbur Cohen explained to his boss, "It is significant that a bipartisan committee representing a cross-section of various interests, including persons connected with Blue Cross plans, the American Hospital Association, private insurance, business, law, and medicine, should have endorsed the principle of providing basic hospital insurance protection for the aged through the social security mechanism."[19]

The Javits bill also contained something new, one of a number of innovative proposals to cover the costs of doctors' bills. He called it "Complementary Private Health Insurance for Individuals Aged 65 or Over." The idea was for private insurance companies, acting through a nonprofit association chartered by Congress, to offer a standard medical-surgical policy at a relatively low price to people over sixty-five. "I do not think," said Cohen, that "the inclusion of the new title raises any difficult policy problems for us in relation to the hospital insurance proposal as we are advocating it."[20] Cohen asserted that the issues had now "worked themselves out." Medicare would cover hospitalization, and something along the lines of Javits's proposal would cover other medical bills.[21]

Throughout the year the President and his staffers like Cohen and

Ball and virtual staff member Cruikshank chased Wilbur Mills. Cohen, an indefatigable optimist, and Ball, who believed in "running out every hit that didn't have a chance in hell," as one of his staffers put it, kept meeting with Mills and asking him for suggestions for them to develop. In April during the executive sessions of the Ways and Means Committee Cohen wrote to a former colleague that "I am still optimistic that I can work something constructive out with Mr. Mills—but only time will tell."[22]

On May 5 Wilbur Cohen told Kennedy's former speech writer Ted Sorensen, now ensconced at Harvard writing his memoirs of the Kennedy administration, "I have been deeply involved these past few weeks in working out with Wilbur Mills a 'solution' on the hospital insurance bill. I'm still hopeful. . . . Mills has been reasonably cooperative." Cohen hoped that Mills would accept one of the solutions, "but I won't be sure until the last minute." The current solution on the table included a 5 percent increase in Social Security benefits but with an option for an additional increase in cash benefits for those who did not want hospital insurance and a provision to use Blue Cross to administer the hospital plan. The hospital insurance would include forty-five days of hospital care.[23]

In May Wilbur Mills remained deeply engaged with the details of the Medicare legislation. He reached out to Walter McNerney, the National Director of the Blue Cross Association that represented the interest of Blue Cross hospital plans across the nation, and tried to convince him that his association should administer Medicare. He favored Blue Cross over private insurance companies because the Blue Cross plans were quasi-public agencies chartered by the states in a different manner than the for-profit insurance companies. The depth at which he probed the details suggested that he was giving Medicare very serious consideration.[24]

On May 22, 1964, President Johnson flew to the University of Michigan to deliver the commencement address in the massive football stadium that locals called the Big House. On this occasion he unveiled the theme of the Great Society as the banner for his domestic program. On the flight between Washington and Ann Arbor, Assistant Secretary Cohen traveled with the President on Air Force One. Johnson invited him to the presidential cabin for a discussion of Medicare. Cohen said he was "very hopeful" of Mills reporting out a bill that would please Johnson.[25]

In June things fell apart with Mills, whose support for Medicare had always been tenuous. He postponed a committee vote on Medicare on

June 23. One version of what happened was that he had been ready to capitulate to the President but had become convinced that Barry Goldwater would be the Republican candidate for president and, in the wake of the 1964 Civil Rights Act, he would carry Arkansas (as indeed he did). One journalist reported that Mills thought his political future would be safer if he continued to follow a conservative line and oppose Medicare. Internal committee dynamics also influenced his decision. Even with all of the White House pressure and persistent efforts to produce an acceptable plan for wavering members such as John C Watts (D-KY) and Sydney Herlong (D-FL), Mills did not think he had a majority in favor of Medicare.[26]

By July it was all over, and the politics of Medicare reverted to its familiar form. On the first day of the month, the Ways and Means Committee reported out a bill that contained many provisions related to Social Security and welfare but failed to include either Medicare or some extension of Kerr-Mills.[27] For Medicare to be successful, the Senate, as it had in 1956 deliberations over disability, would have to wait for the Finance Committee to report a bill, offer a Medicare amendment during the ensuing floor debate, hope that the Senate passed it, and pray that the wavering Mills would accept some part of the Senate bill in conference.

Final passage in the House did not come until July 29. Behind the scenes, the Medicare proponents worked feverishly to come up with a Medicare bill that would pass the Senate. They fiddled with the number of days of hospital care that Medicare would fund. They also continued to refine the notion of a choice between higher cash benefits and Medicare.[28]

The Finance Committee still needed to hold hearings and report out a bill, even though close observers realized that its bill would not contain Medicare. Everyone conceded that Harry Byrd was an unrepentant opponent of Medicare, and he could bring enough Democrats and nearly all the Republicans with him. Finance Committee member Abraham Ribicoff tried to lay the groundwork for a compromise plan, perhaps acceptable to Wilbur Mills, that offered beneficiaries a choice between Medicare and increased Social Security benefits. Ribicoff persisted in his belief that the option plan might be a way out of the morass, and he gained administration approval to introduce it in the Senate.[29] Considerable skepticism remained. Even the liberal Finance Committee members, such as Vance Hartke, were wary of Mills and thought it might be inadvisable to pass Medicare in any form so late in the session. It was a presidential election year, and the members of Congress were eager to leave Washington, have their conventions, and get on with the campaign.[30]

The Finance Committee completed its work on August 17 and followed the lead of the House in offering a 5 percent benefit increase and rejecting Medicare. Southern Democrats including Russell Long, George Smathers (FL), William Fulbright (AR), and Herman Talmadge (GA) voted with the majority. Their votes caused them to go against the advice of the administration and the congressional leadership, even though people like Smathers were nominally a part of that leadership. Ribicoff did not even bother to attend the meeting, leaving Paul Douglas to carry the liberal load. The consensus at this point was that the administration had the votes to add Medicare to the bill on the Senate floor but Mills's persistent opposition made the chances of getting such a package through a conference committee "dim."[31]

The full Senate took up the measure at the end of August. The President had sweetened the pot at the Democratic convention by announcing that the country wanted Medicare "and so do I." The President's advocacy failed to sway Senator Long, a key member of the Finance Committee and someone almost certain to be a member of the Senate's conference committee. Long offered an amendment that would raise the Social Security benefit increase in the House and Senate Finance Committee bills. Instead of a 5 percent increase, he proposed a 7 percent increase. His move created disarray. Senator Douglas accused Long of "legislative legerdemain" to block Medicare. Senator Gore, who stood out as a liberal member of the southern congressional delegation, said that Long's amendment would kill Medicare. "Well, that's the idea," agreed Senator Smathers.[32]

The proponents had to cook up an alternative on short notice. They already had the Ribicoff option proposal, but they also reworked Senator Gore's basic Medicare amendment. It now included a seven-dollar across-the-board increase in Social Security benefits to accompany the costs of 45 days of hospital care, 60 days in a nursing home, and 240 home visits by a nurse.[33]

The climactic debate occurred on September 2. In a roll call vote, the Senate accepted Gore's Medicare amendment by a margin of 49 to 44. Sixteen Democrats, all but one from the South, voted against the amendment, and five Republicans voted in favor. The price for the support of Jacob Javits and the four other liberal Republicans was acceptance of the Javits plan to encourage private insurance companies to write low-cost policies that would fill in the gaps that Medicare left behind.[34]

The formal Medicare part of the final legislation showed the erosion that had occurred in the course of the long debate. Medicare beneficiaries would have to choose between ninety days of hospitalization with a deductible or forty-five days with no deductible. What had once been 180 days in a skilled nursing facility had changed to 60 days. Although the Ribicoff option proposal did not come up in the Senate debate, it waited in the wings. The proponents now considered using it as a compromise they could offer in the conference committee.

The Medicare debate in the Senate also featured a play within a play. President Johnson was on record in favor of Medicare and expected to make it an issue in the campaign. Barry Goldwater, his Republican opponent, came out squarely against Medicare. Minority leader Everett Dirksen (R-IL) convinced the Arizona Senator that his vote was needed on Medicare. Piloting his own plane, Goldwater made a special trip from Phoenix to Washington and arrived in time for the vote. Before the vote, he offered a statement of his views. It featured typically forthright language that, although out of sync with Great Society politics, anticipated the language of Ronald Reagan's, George W. Bush's, and Donald Trump's later campaigns. Goldwater said that the proponents believed that the elderly were "incapable of deciding how to spend their own money." They showed "contempt for the intelligence and judgment of our people." The elderly wanted their benefits in money and not in kind. Medicare marked a step along the path to the destruction of the Social Security in favor of a "public relief or charity program." Goldwater faced a world with Medicare "with deep foreboding."[35]

As Goldwater knew, the measure still required the approval of a House-Senate conference committee, which in practical terms meant the approval of Wilbur Mills. It went without saying that Mills would be the chair of the House conferees, and it was expected that he would prevail among them by a vote of three to two. The Senate conferees were pledged to Medicare as a result of the Senate vote, but people like Long and Smathers who were personally opposed to Medicare might drop their support at the earliest opportunity.

Even at this late stage, the Medicare advocates continued to search for the Medicare plan that Mills would accept. Among the features they explored were making Medicare a separate social insurance program from the rest of Social Security, with its own trust fund and with separate contributions (rather than a single contribution as, for example, applied to old-age insurance and disability). Presumably that protected the finances of the Social Security program and kept a financial crisis in Medicare from bleeding into the rest of Social Security. Mills also wanted to be sure that everyone who received Medicare benefits paid into the trust fund supporting them. Even Social Security recipients who were already retired would have to pay seven dollars a month, which would be deducted from their Social Security benefits. People would therefore have the option of getting the seven dollars a month or taking health insurance. Officials in the Social Security Administration, although anxious to pass Medicare in almost any form, thought that seven dollars a month might be more than many elderly individuals could afford. They might decide not to take the insurance. As always in voluntary insurance, the problem of adverse selection arose. The government might end up insuring the poorer health risks and the older members of the aged group. No one thought the plan ideal.[36]

For a time there appeared the real possibility that Mills might agree to this sort of plan, perhaps limited to working-age people who would build up Medicare coverage over their working lifetimes, leaving those already retired to their own devices. When the conferees met on September 25, reports circulated that the impasse had been broken. Mills, it seemed, had accepted a plan, with all of the many provisos that had been developed for him but with forty-five days of hospitalization. The morning session of the conference committee appeared to go well, and afterward Mills sought out the House parliamentarian to confer on the proper procedures to follow. The afternoon session of the conference committee went less well and hope faded. Senator Long said that he had seen "some daylight at the end of the tunnel," but "as of now, I can't make that statement."[37]

On September 30, 1964, Mills joined Republicans John Byrnes (WI) and Thomas B. Curtis (NE) in voting against Medicare. The Senate conferees refused to back down from their support of the bill that had been passed in their chamber. In a showdown vote among the Senate conferees on October 1, the decision to stand firm passed by a four to two margin. With the exception of Harry Byrd, who was present but did not cast a vote, all of the Democrats—Senators Long, Smathers, Gore, and Anderson—voted *not* to recede from the Senate position. Still, the conference ended in deadlock, with the passage neither of Medicare nor of increased Social Security benefits.[38]

After the Election of 1964

When Lyndon Johnson returned from Texas after his smashing electoral victory, he went to a party for the departing economist Walter Heller in the State Department building. Spying Wilbur Cohen in the crowd, he approached him and told him that Medicare would be the top priority for 1965. He urged Cohen to touch base with the AFL-CIO and with everyone in the cabinet. Using the telephone as an instrument to keep in touch with his staff at all hours of the day and night, LBJ hectored Cohen over the course of the next few days, telling him to work faster on a draft of the new bill and again urging him to "touch all the bases," not only with the AFL-CIO but with congressional leaders as well. Cohen, Robert Ball, and Nelson Cruikshank turned their full effort toward writing the new bill.[39]

The 1964 election did appear to be, at least in part, a mandate for Medicare. Lyndon Johnson carried all ten of the states with the highest percentage of the nation's aged citizens. The list included Vermont, which had never before supported a Democratic candidate for president. The election also shed some of Medicare's strongest opponents in the Ways and Means Committee, including three Republican members from Texas, Michigan, and New York. These results pointed to the fact that, as the *Washington Post* journalist who had covered the Medicare story most closely put it, "the Administration is now in a better position to bargain with Mills than it ever has been before." As if to confirm that fact, Wilbur Mills announced that his committee would get to the Medicare legislation at the very beginning of the session.[40]

Mills appeared to be softening. Early in December he spoke before the Lions Club in Little Rock. Ordinarily such an event would have little news value; congressmen gave speeches to local audiences all the time. On this occasion Mills's remarks made national headlines because they appeared to indicate, for the first time in a public forum, that he would accept a payroll tax to finance health benefits for the elderly. He did insist that the Medicare tax be separate from the Social Security tax and, as always, he proposed a number of alternatives. One was to raise the eligibility age for Medicare from sixty-five, as proponents had simply assumed it would be, to sixty-eight. Another would be to vary the medical benefits according to the income of the recipients, with well-off beneficiaries receiving less government help with their medical bills than those closer to the poverty line but all within a social insurance format.[41]

At almost exactly the same time, Donovan Ward, the President of the AMA, said that his organization would not bow to the political realities and abandon the campaign against Medicare. "The battle must go on," he said. The medical profession could not compromise on "matters of life and death." Every doctor had the duty to make every effort to block the Medicare legislation. To be sure, the politics were now more difficult, but Ward found no evidence that the 1964 election provided a mandate for Medicare. People, he said, voted against Barry Goldwater, not in favor of Medicare. Still, he conceded that "the outlook is neither pleasant nor easy."[42]

The proponents used the bill that the Senate had passed as a basic text on which to base the new bill. In that sense the Medicare bill was an incremental endeavor: the 1965 Medicare proposals and the Medicare law itself bore the imprint of the previous discussions. The first drafts of what was called the "Hospital Insurance and Social Security Amendments of 1965" read like a compendium of previous Medicare bills. None of the proponents took the position that, with the results of the 1964 election in hand, they could simply dictate their preferences to Wilbur Mills, Harry Byrd, and the other congressional proprietors of social legislation. If nothing else, they had to be ready for the AMA's opposition.

The November 24 draft of the Medicare bill showed how ungainly it had become. It gave beneficiaries a choice of three different hospital plans. These included 45 days in the hospital with no deductible, 90 days in the hospital but with a variable deductible of ten dollars a day, or 180 days in the hospital with a flat deductible of one hundred dollars until 1970 and thereafter two and a half times the average daily hospital rate. The plan would be financed through a completely separate hospital insurance trust fund and administered by the HEW Secretary through the Social Security Administration. The Social Security tax rate would not include Medicare. Rather, Medicare tax payments would be levied as a separate payroll tax, and pay stubs would reflect that payment. Hospitals would have their own options. They could elect to be represented by a private organization, such as Blue Cross, to negotiate their contracts with the government to pay their Medicare claims. The beneficiaries could also, if they wished, buy insurance from "an association of private insurance carriers," operating on a nonprofit basis, to cover their remaining health care costs, such as doctors' bills. Carriers who participated in this association would receive an exemption from antitrust laws.

As always, the 1965 legislation would come bundled with improvements in regular Social Security benefits. All Social Security recipients would receive a 7 percent increase in their benefits, and these would be paid retroactively to January 1, 1965. Widows would now be able to receive benefits at sixty rather than sixty-two, and dependents of beneficiaries could continue to receive benefits until the age of twenty-one rather than eighteen as in the previous law. Improvements, or better put, liberalizations of welfare programs and disability also received mention.[43]

The Medicare proponents did everything they could to grease the skids for their bill. They pushed to have the Medicare bill introduced as HR 1 because that would have "a great psychological impact." It would indicate that the bill had priority and should be passed early in the session. They met with as many sympathetic groups as possible. All of the groups offered advice, but the proponents thought it less important to heed the advice of groups already committed to Medicare and more important to satisfy the congressional leaders and the members of the proprietary committees.[44]

Everyone knew that the first of the year constituted a deadline to get a bill to Mills and his committee. One issue that remained unsettled in December concerned the duration of hospital benefits—how many consecutive days in the hospital Medicare would insure. Some wanted to give people only one choice of hospital plan rather than the three that were in the draft bill. It made for a simpler proposal that would be easier to explain to Congress and the public.[45] Another issue concerned Wilbur Mills's desire for a separate tax for hospital care. Congressional leaders would have preferred that the Medicare tax be buried in the Social Security tax that people were already paying rather than singled out on people's pay stubs.[46] A third issue involved how to package all of the many Social Security, Medicare, and welfare proposals. Should there be one large omnibus bill in the manner of the 1935 Social Security Act or a series of smaller bills? Perhaps Medicare should stand alone to give it the attention that it demanded. Congressional leaders appeared to prefer that the Social Security benefit increase, the proposed changes in the welfare program, and Medicare all be included in one bill. The Social Security benefit increase would make it easier to vote for Medicare.

Because of the many delays in the consideration of Medicare, this benefit increase, intended in part to cover the rising cost of living, was overdue.[47]

As these discussions took place, the Department of Health, Education, and Welfare culled the legislative proposals from its various bureaus. One in particular related to Medicare. It came under the heading of a new child health services program and included increased funds for infant and maternal health services but also funds "for the children from needy poverty families." If enacted, this proposal would provide medical assistance for needy children in a manner similar to the way the Kerr-Mills program already provided care for the elderly. The Child Health Act would operate on a welfare format, which meant that there would be a means test to determine who would be eligible for its services and that the individual states would administer the program.

Although the Department of Health, Education, and Welfare did not rank the child health proposal high among its health care priorities, Congressman Mills regarded this measure as an appropriate way to broaden the Kerr-Mills program, and his opinion always mattered. The Child Health Act came from the welfare bureaucracy rather than the Social Security Administration, and that meant that the Medicare proponents did not consider it as important as the rest of their legislative proposals. Because of a departmental reorganization in 1963, the federal employees who worked on welfare had left the Social Security Administration and become part of a new office known as the Welfare Administration. The fact that the proposal for a Child Health Act came from the Welfare Administration meant that the Social Security officials struggling to create Medicare ignored it or saw it as a needless complication.[48] White House officials shared similar concerns. Larry O'Brien, a key congressional liaison, worried, for example, that the Child Health Act would simply add to the Ways and Means Committee's heavy legislative load and distract it from Medicare. Perhaps the Child Health Act might be introduced in 1965 for consideration in 1966 with all welfare categories included in the bill, rather than just dependent children.[49]

The AMA, by way of contrast to the Medicare proponents, thought that the Child Health Act was just the sort of health insurance program that the federal government should propose. It believed that coverage restricted to the needy and administered by the states would interfere least with the expansion of private insurance and lessen the threat that the federal government would come to dominate the practice of medicine. They agreed with the head of the Welfare Administration, who argued there was "sound justification for the child health act."[50] The Medicare proponents, who saw social insurance as a superior form of social policy to welfare, regarded the AMA as their main enemy. Unlike many incidental policy discussions, this one mattered because it contained the seeds of what became Medicaid, which would grow into America's largest federal health insurance program.

On New Year's Eve, Wilbur Cohen, on behalf of his associates Ball and Cruikshank, sent the legislative leaders the latest version of the Medicare bill. It was comprehensive in nature, covering Medicare, Social Security, and welfare. On the advice of the majority of people with whom the Medicare proponents had consulted, it would have only one option for hospital care, and that option would be compulsory. The basic package included sixty days of hospital care with what was described as a "one day" deductible, as well as sixty days of post-hospital care in an approved nursing facility, sixty days of home health visits, and various diagnostic services. Elderly people not covered by Social Security, a dwindling number destined to grow even smaller as the effects of expanded coverage took hold, would nonetheless receive the hospital benefits funded from the general revenues. The bill did not contain the separate payroll tax that Mills wanted, apparently because Senator Anderson thought it a bad idea. It did, however, include the Javits notion of authorizing the formation of an association of private insurance carriers to sell an inexpensive plan to cover medical costs beyond hospital costs.[51]

1965: "This Is the Year"

The bill met with an initially favorable reaction. Even Republican Ogden Reid (NY) conceded it would have "strong bipartisan support in the House." "This is the year," said Senator Anderson. "We're not drafting a bill. We're writing a law." The President told Congress that hospital care for people sixty-five or older was of the "utmost urgency." "This year is the year when with the sure knowledge of public support," Medicare should be enacted, he said.[52]

In aid of passing that law, the House of Representatives made changes to the way it filled its committees to reflect the outcome of the election. For more than two decades, the ratio of majority to minority members of the Ways and Means Committee had been fifteen to ten. Under the new arrangement, the ratio would be seventeen to eight. As a practical matter, it meant there would be three vacancies for the Democrats to fill and one for the Republicans. Before Philip Landrum (D-GA), Charles A. Vanik (D-OH), and Richard Fulton (D-TN) were asked to join the Ways and Means Committee, they gave their assurances that they would support Medicare. Two of the three new members came from the South, but they did not have the same allegiance to Wilbur Mills as the members they replaced. Dan Rostenkowski (D-IL), another dependable vote for Medicare, had joined the committee during the preceding summer as a replacement for an Illinois Democratic congressman who had died. Rostenkowski, who held a safe seat as a member of Mayor Richard J. Daley's Chicago machine, stayed with the committee long enough to become its chairman.[53]

In the Senate not everyone rushed to endorse the proposal. Some members of the southern delegation continued to resist what seemed inevitable. Louisiana's Democratic Senator Allen Ellender announced his opposition to Medicare because "it would do violence to the Social Security program and not accomplish the purposes for which it is intended. It would cost the taxpayer more than is anticipated." His words were similar to those of his fellow senators who had opposed disability insurance in 1956. Liberal Republican senators, such as Javits and Senator Clifford Case (NJ), who were content with the efforts the administration had made to work with them, disagreed. They announced their support for Medicare.[54]

As always, the Medicare opponents sought alternatives. The American Medical Association made the first move by offering a plan in which the government subsidized the premium costs of private health plans for the elderly. In keeping with past AMA proposals, states rather than the federal government would run the programs. Under its terms, an elderly individual would purchase a policy from Blue Cross Blue Shield or a commercial insurance carrier. The states, using state and federal money, would pay part or all of the cost but only for people whose incomes fell below a certain level. The AMA touted its plan as superior to Medicare in that the people who received its benefits would get "comprehensive health care benefits" rather than just hospital and nursing home benefits. It also had the purported advantage of operating within the established insurance system rather than creating an entirely new one. The proposal for what came to be called Eldercare went beyond the terms of previous AMA plans. It nonetheless involved state administration and a means test, which meant that its contents would vary by state, and not all of the elderly would be eligible to participate.[55]

Not all Republicans were satisfied with the AMA plan, and Republican members of the Ways and Means Committee sought still another plan to introduce in the committee. They worked with the tacit approval of Gerald Ford (R-MI), who had just become the House Minority Leader. Ford wanted the Republicans to go beyond simply opposing Great Society legislation and instead offer constructive alternatives. Ranking member John Byrnes took the lead on this project.[56] Byrnes unveiled his plan at a crowded news conference on January 28, the same day that the Ways and Means Committee began its deliberations over Medicare. In contrast to the administration's Medicare bill, Byrnes's plan was both voluntary and more comprehensive. Those who elected to join the plan would have money deducted, on a sliding scale that ranged from $4.00 to $11.50, from their Social Security benefits. The federal government would also use general revenues to meet some of the costs of the plan. Beneficiaries would receive a package that included the payment of the first $1,000 dollars of hospital bills, plus 80 percent of the balance. The package would also contain 80 percent of all other hospital, surgical, and medical expenses after a fifty-dollar deductible.

The Byrnes plan, which came to be called Bettercare, differed from most of the Republican alternatives to Medicare in that it paid uniform benefits and was administered by the federal government and not by state governments. Byrnes argued that his plan was more adequate than the administration's, which only paid hospital bills. Furthermore, its voluntary nature and financing scheme would not, as Byrnes put it, "push the regressive payroll tax to the limits of acceptability." It was, at one and the same time, a form of comprehensive health insurance for the nation's elderly and a means of easing some of the financial pressure on Social Security. Byrnes insisted that it was a better bill than the one offered by the administration. Although the Republican congressional delegation remained split among several alternatives, support for the Byrnes plan developed among six of the eight Republicans on the Ways and Means Committee, and floor leader Ford endorsed it as well.[57]

The Byrnes bill gave the administration something to consider. It provided the first hint of serious competition in a political atmosphere still infused with postelection euphoria. The Medicare proponents still found many things to criticize in the Byrnes bill. The voluntary nature of the bill and the Social Security benefit deductions it entailed meant that "many aged persons with low incomes or who were very old and senile and who need the protection would not take it." Unlike the administration's bill there was no cost sharing by the employer (who paid half of the Social Security payroll tax), and the Byrnes alternative had the potential to become a big charge on the general revenues when there were many other demands on those revenues. The administration asked people to contribute during their working lives for the health insurance they would receive at retirement; the Byrnes plan required people to pay at a period of their lives when they could afford it least. The administration reimbursed hospitals for their costs; the Byrnes plan reimbursed them for their charges, which might be considerably higher. The administration bill left room for private insurance to supplement Medicare, as in the Javits component of the administration bill, which might ultimately provide the elderly with more benefits.[58]

As the Republicans considered their various alternatives, Wilbur Mills got down to business. At an organizational meeting, the Ways and Means Committee decided not to hold public hearings on Medicare, of which there had been many in the past, such as the ones that had taken three weeks in 1964. This was something of a partisan move. The Democrats wanted a bill on the House floor by March. The Republicans preferred a more leisurely process that would allow them to put testimony in favor of the Byrnes bill on the public record. Medicare proponents dismissed the bills offered by Representative Byrnes and the AMA as "last-minute, last ditch, last gasp" efforts.[59]

Mills, who felt the strong administration push to get Medicare through Congress, assembled his committee for executive sessions on Medicare on January 27.[60] The Medicare legislative process now moved behind closed doors, where it had been at the end of 1964. The private sessions served some useful purposes. Republicans coalesced around the Byrnes bill as their Medicare alternative. The AMA endorsed the bill it had proposed, yet also used its testimony to recommend that the services of radiologists, pathologists, anesthesiologists, and psychologists—doctors whom patients were likely to encounter in the hospital—be dropped from the definition of "hospital services." With this recommendation the AMA sought to get doctors completely out of Medicare, which also had the effect of narrowing the range of benefits offered by the bill. When the Vice President of the Equitable Life Assurance Society testified, he recommended that the Javits proposal be dropped from the bill. His testimony, as a representative of the health insurance industry, cut the legs out from under Javits's proposal. It was easier to make this sort of suggestion in private than in public.[61]

As the Ways and Means Committee did its work, President Johnson urged on its members. "We are in sight of the promised land," the President told the members of the President's Council on Aging in a public ceremony in the Cabinet Room on February 16. The President believed that the people were ahead of the politicians on the issue: "They want this program. They are going to have this program. The question now is just timing."[62]

The Transforming Event

In fact, though, the most crucial part of the legislative process lay just ahead. On March 2, 1965, Chairman Mills completed his review of all the major alternatives to Medicare, including the AMA bill and the Byrnes bill. As always, even though the sessions were closed to the public, government officials like Wilbur Cohen, Robert Ball, and Robert Myers were in the room in a staff capacity to help the committee with its deliberations (and Nelson Cruikshank could not have been too far away). Mills turned to Cohen and asked him to develop the details for a new bill that combined the features of all three of the major bills. It was a transforming and apparently spontaneous moment in the debate. Each of the three bills had been offered as an alternative to the other two. Now Mills wanted somehow to put them together.[63]

Mills suggested as the basic architecture of the new bill that it include the hospital insurance of the administration's bill, the administration's Child Health and Medical Assistance Act (as it was now called), and an adaptation of the Byrnes plan to cover doctors' bills. Although the details remained to be worked out by Mills and the government officials in the room, this third part of the bill was something new. As Byrnes had suggested, it would be financed in part by general revenues and in part with voluntary deductions from an individual's Social Security benefits. The new element was that it would be limited to supplemental health care costs like doctors' bills that were not covered in the hospital insurance part of the bill.

Mills's suggestion reflected his objective of creating a comprehensive bill that would gain the overwhelming approval first of his committee and then of the House of Representatives. He had become worried, as had many of the Medicare proponents, that the Byrnes bill was so much broader in scope than the administration bill. People might criticize the administration bill for omitting any number of things, such as physicians' services. Republicans who supported the Byrnes bill could tout it, as Wilbur Cohen put it, as "more liberal and a more comprehensive and better total package than the Administration's program." The new "super" bill that Mills wanted to create would protect him and the administration from the Republicans' attacks.[64]

Journalists Rowland Evans and Robert Novak commented that at a time when Congress was losing the ability to legislative independently, Mills "has written his own bill." Yet he was not veering too far from what had already been proposed. All of the elements of the new bill had been discussed in the Ways and Means Committee between 1961 and 1965. The hospital insurance provision went back to the very first Kennedy and Johnson proposals. Mills had objected to this provision and obstructed its passage, but he had remained open to considering various versions of it that the Medicare proponents had presented to him, such as during the protracted negotiations in the spring and summer of 1964. The 1964 elections convinced him that Medicare was inevitable, and he should get out ahead of the process. He could then write the bill in a way that reflected his priorities, such as safeguards against Medicare dragging Social Security into insolvency. If the Medicare proponents wanted to expand medical services in the future, for example, they would have to do so through a program financed by general revenues and the elderly themselves rather than by Social Security payroll taxes.[65]

Although the Medicare proponents continued to believe that Social Security represented a form of social protection superior to welfare, the "super" bill nonetheless expanded the nation's welfare programs in a very significant way, by calling on the states to fund medical care for dependent children, disabled individuals, and the elderly. Medicaid, as this program would be known, would soon become the most expensive part of the nation's welfare system. Mills endorsed it with a sense of pride that it expanded on the Kerr-Mills legislation that he had helped to create in 1960. It was also on the administration's list of approved bills and indeed had been developed by the administration. It had the further political appeal of following the approach to health insurance that the AMA had recommended in its bill. And the Medicare proponents entertained the notion that someday Medicare might be expanded to reach people under sixty-five and would, in turn, diminish the need for Medicaid. No one in 1965 could have known that this would never happen.

As always, the invention of new social policy institutions went unremarked, and instead people concentrated on how the super bill solved the political problems of the moment. Supplemental medical insurance, which became known as Medicare Part B, would become a permanent part of America's welfare state, just as the system of state disability determinations did in 1954 and 1956. In both of these cases, considerations related to public administration took second place to partisan political considerations that were embedded in the history of the moment. With the passage of time, these inventions came to be historical curiosities that few people understood but few people questioned.

The President endorsed the new bill as soon as its contents were presented to him. He dismissed the unanticipated increase in general revenues that Part B would entail as well within the government's financial capabilities. His reaction became part of the Johnson lore. Told that the Mills bill would cost an extra half a billion dollars, the President reportedly replied, "Five hundred million. Is that all? Do it. Move the damn bill out now, before we lose it." Mills might have had a few more qualms about half a billion dollars, but he also embraced the bill, which was, of course, his bill. Much of the work on the bill had been done in private, although the press soon got word about Mills's legislative maneuvers. When the story broke, Mills endorsed the bill in public, although he lacked the President's flamboyance. He characterized it as "a satisfactory, proper, and correct way of dealing with this particular problem." It was the final blessing from a legislative leader who had been reluctant to endorse the measure. Johnson, who could be cruel in the way he characterized people, regarded Mills as a "prissy, prim and proper man" who worried more about "saving his face . . . than saving the country." Johnson was nonetheless more than happy to share credit for Medicare with Mills.[66]

The Inner Politics of Medicare

It was not as if all the political problems associated with Medicare evaporated after the Mills moment on March 2. For one thing, the new bill was more objectionable to doctors and the insurance industry than the old one had been, because Part B covered doctors' services. The proponents worried that the President would be "besieged by demands by the private insurance companies for dropping the new feature which Mills is adding." Although the new legislation gave the Republicans more political cover than the old one and HEW officials believed that most of them would vote for the measure on the House floor, Representative Byrnes continued to press his opposition. Byrnes said he was pleased that the Democrats on the Ways and Means Committee had agreed to the principle of financing medical benefits through general revenues. He remained opposed to splitting off hospital benefits and financing them through what he regarded as a regressive payroll tax.[67]

The details of the bill also harbored more subtle political conflicts. The Medicare proponents wanted to make the premium for the supplementary benefits as low as possible so that more people would sign up for them. Congress, never eager to impose visible taxes on constituents, settled for three dollars a month and buried the charge within an increase in the level of Social Security benefits. Mills wanted to be sure that the premiums were set at a level that, along with the required general revenues, would adequately fund the program without imposing too large a burden on the federal budget.[68]

Part B also carried another danger for both Mills and the Medicare proponents. Neither wanted the federal government to be in the position of setting doctors' fees, since the hands-off attitude had been crucial in selling Medicare to the Congress. All parties wanted to avoid the charge of socialized medicine. One way around this problem was to allow the private intermediaries to perform sensitive operations. The private intermediaries, such as Blue Cross and Blue Shield rather than the federal government, would be the ones to decide whether a particular claim from a hospital or doctor should be paid.

Although Mills wanted to keep the federal government out of the doctors' way, he worried that some doctors might use Medicare to raise their fees in what the elderly might regard as an unfair way. The fact was that some doctors charged different fees for the same services, depending on the customs of the area in which they practiced and their perception of a patient's ability to pay. With Medicare this element of charity would no longer be necessary, since all of the elderly would be covered by Medicare. Working with the government staffers who remained by his side, Mills agreed to put language in his committee's report to the effect that doctors' charges must be "reasonable." He assigned the intermediaries the responsibility of making sure that physicians' charges were "not higher than the charge applicable, for a comparable service and under comparable circumstances, to the policyholders and subscribers of the carrier."[69]

Another sensitive issue that required political negotiations concerned the boundary line between the hospital insurance program, now known as Part A, and the doctors' services program, now called Part B. Mills took the position that no doctors' services should be included in Part A. Instead they all should be concentrated in Part B. He wanted to be able to say on the House floor that physicians were not covered under the Social Security part of the bill. The proponents hoped to make such things as radiology and pathology—services routinely received in the hospital—a component of Part A, just as they had been in the previous drafts of the Medicare legislation. In general the Medicare proponents wanted to put as many things as possible in Part A, which would be compulsory and run on social insurance principles. They did not want to put patients in the position of having to pay out of pocket for things like reading X-rays to determine if a bone were broken or reading slides to determine if a tumor were malignant.[70]

The Speaker of the House of Representatives, the House Majority Leader, and the President all tried to get Mills to change his mind on this matter. Mills resisted the pressure. None of the other committee members understood the legislation well enough to argue with Mills on this point or any other. "Their total tendency is . . . to support Mills in all committee matters," Larry O'Brien told the President. Since Wilbur Cohen, the administration's expert on Mills, believed Mills was "completely opposed," O'Brien advised that the matter could not be resolved in the administration's favor in the Ways and Means Committee.[71]

Still another potential problem with the super bill, with its vast array of benefits and financing schemes, was its effect on the economy. Before the administration could fully support the bill, it needed to engage in what might be called Keynesian accounting. There were two steps in this accounting. One was to determine whether the bill put more money into the economy through its benefits or took money out of the economy through its tax features. Preliminary estimates showed an excess of collections over disbursements of $1.3 billion. The second step was to make changes in the bill so as to lower this amount and reduce what the economists called the fiscal drag on the economy in 1966. This change fell into the realm of the government staffers, particularly actuary Robert Myers, who needed to make adjustments to the various implementation dates and tax schedules so as to pass muster with the economists.

The contention that Medicare created a fiscal drag on the economy was a political as well as an economic argument. By identifying a defect in the bill, its opponents could try to use it to derail the bill. Every time a new version of the bill appeared—whether a product of the Ways and Means Committee, the Finance Committee, or a house of Congress—the score of disbursements and collections changed, requiring more consultation among the Social Security experts, the members of the President's Council of Economic Advisors, and Treasury Department officials. If the press got word of these consultations, it could publicize the fact that Medicare was a fiscal drag on the economy and produce more harm than good. HEW Secretary Anthony Celebrezze saw such negative reports as more than benign matters. He regarded the attacks as the final push of Medicare's proponents to derail it. Celebrezze talked to Jack Valenti in the White House about this matter, urging him to tell the President to do all he could to keep the stories from appearing.[72] President Johnson knew that the primary thing was to pass a law. He therefore told his economists "to pipe down" until the bill was passed.[73]

Another issue that arose in the final drafting of Medicare related to civil rights. During the 1950s and early 1960s, one of the strategies that both conservatives and liberals used in debates over such questions as federal aid to education was to insert a civil rights rider—banning racial discrimination in school districts that received federal funds, for example, into the bill. With the civil rights rider, the legislation became much less desirable to the southerners, who controlled many of the major committees. In 1964 the Civil Rights Act included in its Title VI a provision that stated that recipients of federal funds could not discriminate on the basis of race. Title VI appeared to take the civil rights matter off the table in the Medicare deliberations. Hospitals and medical practices that received Medicare funds would not be allowed to discriminate. When the measure got to the Senate Finance Committee, Senator Byrd nonetheless inquired of the Department of HEW whether Title VI would apply to the Medicare program. Surprisingly, the matter had not come up before, despite the long Medicare deliberations.

Senator Byrd was no friend of either Medicare or civil rights, but liberal groups, such as the AFL-CIO and the Civil Rights Leadership Conference, also wanted the matter clarified. The liberals were solid Medicare supporters, not likely to jeopardize the Medicare bill by adding a civil rights rider. White House staffer Lee White told the President that the "opponents of Medicare have no such inhibitions." If Byrd were told that the federal government could not prevent discrimination, however, then liberals would insist on an amendment to the bill. The proposed solution was to finesse the matter and to "make every effort to find authority to prevent discrimination without a specific amendment to the Medicare bill."[74]

The administration tried to resolve most issues of this sort behind closed doors, away from the prying eyes of the press. By March 17 most of the House Ways and Means Committee bill had been drafted. The more the committee got into the details of the bill, the more complex it became, until the final version read something like a document prepared by a Wall Street lawyer. The basic architecture of the bill, with Medicare Parts A and B and Medicaid, was relatively simple. The original benefits in the bill, such as 60 days of hospitalization and 60 days of nursing home care and up to 240 home health visits a year, were also clear. The committee's bill adjusted the nursing home benefit so that it varied from twenty to one hundred days, depending on the length of the hospital stay. The shorter the hospital stay, the more days of nursing home care a person could receive. The benefits applied to each "benefit period," defined as the span between when a person entered the hospital and up to ninety days after he or she had left the hospital or nursing home. In accordance with Mills's instructions, Medicare Part A failed to cover radiology, anesthesiology, and pathology. Those activities fell into the realm of Part B, which had its own complicated rules.[75]

The Ways and Means Committee approved the new Medicare bill on March 23 by a straight party vote. Some of the Republicans who voted against the bill indicated they might support it on the House floor, and House passage of the bill appeared to be assured. The President issued a statement calling the committee's action "an historic one" that marked "a tremendous step forward for all of our senior citizens." He praised the work of Wilbur Mills.[76]

Four days later the President pulled off one of his patented maneuvers during a meeting with House and Senate leaders in the White House. He realized that the problem for Medicare now was the Senate Finance Committee, and he wanted to bend Harry Byrd to his will and prevent him from obstructing the legislation. After the meeting he took the leaders into the Cabinet Room, where he asked them to express their support for Medicare in front of the television cameras. All of the members, none of whom had expected to be on television, said it was a great bill, until finally the President got to Senator Byrd, who was seated on his left. He asked the senator to make an observation. Byrd demurred, "All I can say is . . . that I will see that adequate and thorough hearings are held on the bill." The President, who delighted in violating the senator's sense of decorum, pressed further. He asked whether there was anything ahead of Medicare in the committee, and Byrd said there was nothing. "So when the House acts and it's referred to the Senate Finance Committee you will arrange for prompt and thorough hearings," the President asked. The thoroughly cowed Byrd could only answer yes. Carl Albert commented that it "was the best example of 'The Treatment' in public that anyone ever got."[77]

The President also used the telephone to speed up the legislative process. He urged Wilbur Mills to get a rule from the Rules Committee just as quickly as he could, so that nothing stalled Medicare's momentum. "Tell the Speaker and Wilbur [Mills] to get a rule just the moment they can," he told House congressional leaders. "That damn near killed my education bill, letting it lay around. It's just like a dead cat on the door. When a Committee reports it you better either bury that cat or give it some life." The fastidious Mills tried to reassure the earthy President that the matter was in hand and there would be no dead cats. One cannot conceivably imagine John F. Kennedy using the same language when he addressed Mills, who had held up so much of his legislation, including Medicare, for his entire term.[78]

Enactment

The House debate on Medicare, the first ever to take place on the floor of that body, began on April 7, and the House of Representatives passed the legislation the very next day. Mills gave a bravura performance in presenting the bill that was loaded with so many health insurance, Social Security, welfare, mental retardation, and child and maternal health features to his colleagues. He pointed out the administrative complexity of implementing Medicare but expressed confidence in the Social Security Administration's "outstanding record for service and efficiency." He tasked the Social Security Administration with completing agreements with "fiscal intermediaries, insurance carriers, State agencies and others." He urged the SSA to engage in "broad-scale consultation" with "professional organizations representing the Nation's hospitals and others who furnish reimbursable health services." He realized that "operational policies and recordkeeping procedures will have to be worked out on a scope never before undertaken in the health field." Among many other tasks, the SSA would have to get information about the two health insurance programs in the hands of nineteen million aged people, not to mention setting up records about who had elected to receive Part B and delivering "identification cards" to all who were eligible. Mills's statement belied the claim that the federal government would not be very involved in the American health care system.[79]

Despite laying out an ambitious work plan for the Social Security Administration, Mills contended that the giant Medicare program needed to be separate from the rest of the Social Security program. Against the wishes of the Social Security proprietors, he had insisted on this point and gotten his way. "For years I have contended," he told his House colleagues, "the basic difference between the two types of benefits makes it essential that we have two separate systems." Toward that end the hospital program would be financed through its own tax. The schedule of tax rates for hospital insurance would be in a separate subsection of the Internal Revenue Code, and hospital insurance would have its own trust fund. Even the W-2 forms that workers received from their employers would show separate deductions for Medicare and Social Security.[80]

One of Mills's concerns had always been that payroll deductions for Medicare would strain the Social Security system and block future improvements. For that reason he welcomed Medicare Part B because he did not think the medical costs of the elderly "could be financed only through a payroll tax." Too high a payroll tax would "interfere with our capacity to compete in the world." At the same time, if the costs were left to general revenues, the nation ran the risk of "bankrupting the Federal Treasury once and for all." The situation required a combination of payroll taxes and general revenues, and Medicare Part B met that objective.[81]

Mills realized that the bill put a great deal of responsibility on the federal government, and he was sensitive to the charge that the program would "in time regulate the relationship between the physician and the patient by saying this physician you can go to and this physician is not on our list" and ultimately "control and regulate physicians' fees." To avoid that situation, Mills insisted that no doctors' payments be made under

Medicare Part A and pointed out that the plans for Part B were identical to the ones in Representative Byrnes's substitute for the committee bill. He emphasized the prominent role that Blue Cross, Blue Shield and private insurance carriers would play in the program. "They are the ones who are going to pay the bills," he said. Neither the physicians nor the hospitals need ever come into contact with the federal government.[82]

It left little room for Byrnes to defend his substitute bill. His plan would be voluntary, but so would Part B. It would put less of a strain on the payroll tax. Even with all of the separations between Social Security and Medicare in the Mills bill, Byrnes believed that the practical effect, as the *New York Times* reported, would be "to jeopardize future improvements in the cash benefit system." Byrnes warned that Mills would come to regret his decision to preempt "the payroll tax as a source of cash benefits by tying hospitalization to it."[83]

In the end both the Byrnes and the Mills bills endorsed the concept of national health insurance for the elderly. The similarities made it difficult for Byrnes to preempt Mills, who enjoyed the advantages of a considerable Democratic majority in the House and the strong support of President Johnson, the labor unions, and senior citizen groups. First the House turned down the Byrnes substitute by a vote of 236 to 191, with 63 Democrats and 128 Republicans voting in its favor. Then it passed the Mills bill by a vote of 313–115, with 65 Republicans and 248 Democrats voting in favor.

The President, who understood better than most how his ability to get legislation through Congress would wax and wane, wasted no time in lauding the Medicare bill as a "landmark day in the historic evolution of our social security system." Secretary Celebrezze praised the bill as the greatest step forward "in the advancement of security and dignity" since the 1935 passage of the Social Security Act. Neither politician referred to the fact that the bill was also a tremendous extension of the power of the federal government.[84]

As the bill headed toward the Senate, the administration faced problems from the American Medical Association or at least from some of its members. In May Dr. Jack Schreiber, an Ohio doctor, proposed that doctors boycott Medicare and predicted that the boycott movement would spread to at least six states. The Ohio State Medical Association had already passed a resolution that urged doctors to refuse any fees from Medicare. Schreiber hoped that the national AMA would take up the matter when it met in June. He had already told his patients that he would not accept federal fees, directly or indirectly, under Medicare and had gotten a "fine response."[85]

The boycott of Medicare became a big issue at the AMA convention held in the middle of June, at the same time that Medicare remained under active consideration by the Senate Finance Committee. Groups like the conservative American Association of Physicians and Surgeons pushed the boycott, sending every doctor in the country a letter telling them they should "voluntarily pledge non-participation" in Medicare, described by the association as "the socialized hospitalization and medical care program for the aged." Physicians in Texas, South Carolina, Louisiana, Ohio, Florida, and Oklahoma appeared to be sympathetic to the appeal.[86]

Some in the AMA leadership began to have second thoughts. Writing in an AMA trade journal that he edited, Morris Fishbein, the longtime editorial voice of the AMA, thought that the organization would have more influence if it participated in the development of Medicare rather than opposing it at every turn. Fishbein believed that recent events made it clear that "the AMA's crusade has failed." Because of the AMA's intransigent attitude, it was losing ground in medical policy circles to the American Hospital Association, which the AMA accused of trying to seize "ever-widening control over the provision of medical care in this country."[87]

When the AMA convention convened in New York, Dr. James Z Appel, its new president, warned the delegates that a Medicare boycott would be unethical. Instead, the medical profession should "actively participate" in Medicare's development. Boycotting Medicare would "discourage respect for the law." "It is the only way we can and should travel," he added. Appel assured the delegates of his credentials in the Medicare fight. He opposed the law but thought the organization should accept its passage and prevent its expansion.[88]

Appel carried the day, but feelings against Medicare ran high among the nation's practicing physicians. "I do not propose to be chicken in my resistance to a program that will destroy the high quality of medical care in the country," a New Jersey physician said. According to the President of the Chicago Medical Society, a boycott would tell Congress that Medicare was "seriously wrong."[89]

This sentiment reflected the accurate sense that Medicare demarcated a point of change for the practice of medicine in America. Dr. Schreiber, the proponent of a boycott, believed in the sliding-scale method of health care finance. He treated some people for free and sent others only small bills. Those with deeper pockets paid more for his services. The doctor sensed that Medicare would help to put an end to this practice and change the way he practiced medicine. The Medicare proponents thought that Dr. Schreiber and his allies were reactionaries intent on blocking progress. "I do not look upon the United States Government as a foreign institution that is out to regiment the physicians of the country," Wilbur Cohen told Dr. Schrieber. Instead he viewed the government "as a cooperative enterprise which is under the control of democratic procedures and processes."[90]

These democratic procedures and processes were painfully visible to the Medicare proponents in their dealings with the Senate Finance Committee. The Senate moved at a more deliberate pace than the House. Senator Byrd, the head of the Finance Committee who lacked Wilbur Mills's desire to expedite the passage of Medicare, insisted on new public hearings, something he knew would slow down the process. Byrd remained a Medicare opponent and cast the sole dissenting vote on the final bill among the Democrats on the committee. Senator Russell Long, second in seniority on the committee and the Senate Majority Whip, was a very cautious supporter. Senator Byrd was passive, but Senator Long insisted that government staff members explore alternatives to the Mills bill.

The liberals, acting in concert with the administration, did their best to remove some of the objectionable features that Wilbur Mills had inserted into the bill in the House, in the hope that they could prevail in conference. Senator Douglas removed the services of radiologists, anesthesiologists, pathologists, and rehabilitation doctors from Part B and put them back in Part A. He defended his proposal on the grounds that, in most cases, the services of these specialists were included in hospital bills and that practice should continue in Medicare. Douglas's motions occasioned no arguments in the committee and were approved by a voice vote.[91]

By way of contrast, Long's actions fit a long pattern in which Democratic leaders, not coincidentally from the South, failed to support the party's position on a key piece of domestic legislation. In 1956 Senator Byrd felt it was his duty not only to oppose disability insurance in committee, against the wishes of Majority Leader Johnson, but also to lead the fight against it on the Senate floor. Now it was Senator Long who was causing trouble for President Johnson over the Medicare legislation, although his actions were difficult to categorize as either liberal or conservative. One of Long's ideas, for example, was to provide longer durations of hospital stays, beyond the sixty days of hospital care for each spell of illness in Part A, for those who were catastrophically ill. To finance the added cost, he suggested that there be a variable deductible, based on a person's income, instead of the uniform forty-dollar deductible in the administration bill. The Medicare proponents tried to dissuade him from this idea. Robert Ball suggested that there were "very, very few cases" that required hospitalization for more than sixty days. People who needed more care should be moved to nursing homes and not allowed to linger in the hospital. The last thing the proponents wanted was to have the hospitals be the providers of long-term custodial care.[92]

"I begged, cajoled, argued to get the Senator not to touch the King Anderson portion of the bill but, if he insists on any amendments, to make them only to the voluntary, supplementary plan," Wilbur Cohen reported to Larry O'Brien. Neither Cohen nor O'Brien relished the prospect of the Majority Whip sponsoring major changes in the bill. Their reaction was to send Nelson Cruikshank and Andy Biemiller to see Long and dissuade him from doing anything rash. Long stuck to his course and offered a measure to cover catastrophic costs with $1,000 as the upper end of the deductible. At the same time, the senator made it clear that he was not a fiscal conservative in the manner of Senator Byrd. Long said that he would support any Medicare bill that came out of the committee and back the Senate position in conference. He also promised not to push his ideas on the Senate floor if the Senate Finance Committee rejected them.[93]

Instead of supporting the administration, the Finance Committee obliged Senator Long. It accepted his amendments on June 17. One eliminated all durational limitations on inpatient services, post-hospital extended health services, and home health services. Another provided for a variable deductible that depended on the income an individual had in the year preceding his spell of illness. Observers regarded the changes in the bill as altering its fundamental character. "Medicare Revised to Help the Poor," headlined the *New York Times* on its front page.[94]

The Medicare proponents fought back. They mobilized President Johnson, Nelson Cruikshank, Andrew Biemiller, the American Hospital Association, and the American Public Welfare Association to persuade the committee to reverse its actions. Senator Anderson underscored the importance of this maneuver when he said that Long's amendments, with their use of a means test to determine the deductible, violated "the whole principle of Social Security."[95]

The pressure worked. Less than a week after supporting Long, the Finance Committee removed his amendments from the bill by votes of ten to seven. On the first vote, all of the Democrats, with the exception only of Long himself, voted to remove the variable deductible from the vote. The second vote concerned unlimited hospital benefits, and liberals Vance Hartke and Abraham Ribicoff sided with Long on this matter, but Republican conservatives Frank Carlson (KS) and Wallace Bennett (UT) turned against him. These votes did not end the bidding. Instead, the committee accepted Hartke's measure, which he billed as a compromise, retaining the sixty days of hospitalization in the administration bill but adding another thirty days of hospital benefits at a daily patient cost of ten dollars.[96]

The next day the Senate Finance Committee reported out its version of the bill but not before adding another thirty days of hospital insurance, with the ten-dollar-a-day copay, at the instigation of Russell Long. The final vote was twelve to five, with all of the Democrats, with the exception only of Harry Byrd, and two of the Republicans including Senate Minority Leader Dirksen, in favor. The outcome meant that Long's efforts to extend the reach of the legislation had paid off, and the Senate version of the bill came loaded with more benefits than the administration, mindful of the upcoming conference with Wilbur Mills, would have preferred.[97]

Somewhat to the chagrin of Senator Anderson, Senator Long served as the floor manager for the bill in the Senate. Senator Byrd, who recognized the futility of continuing to take a public role in opposing the measure, stepped aside for Long, who assured his colleagues that despite his earlier misgivings he would move the debate along expeditiously. Long praised the measure "as the largest and most significant legislation ever to pass the Congress," which "would do more immediate good for more people . . . than any bill the Congress has ever enacted." The bill offered senior citizens a very comfortable deal. Social Security benefit increases would more than cover the three-dollar monthly premium for Part B, and even those elderly individuals not covered by Social Security would be able to receive the Part A hospital benefits without having to pay anything beyond the proscribed deductibles and other cost-sharing features. Senator Anderson believed that Medicare showed off the American government to best advantage, demonstrating that it had the "vitality and the will to provide a good way of life for the people when private measures are of no avail."[98]

Unlike in the House, senators felt free to offer as many amendments as they wished to the committee bill on the Senate floor. Senator Robert Byrd (D-WV), for example, argued in favor of allowing workers to retire at age sixty with reduced benefits. Although it was a major change that the Senate Finance Committee had not had a chance to consider, the Senate approved it by a voice vote. Wilbur Cohen, in the thick of monitoring the debate, advised the President not to support the Byrd amendment, which died in conference.[99]

The bill still faced challenges from the left and the right. On the left, Senator Ribicoff, who had voted to remove all of the time limitations on hospital and nursing home care benefits in committee, offered the same amendment on the Senate floor. In this case, the senators demanded a roll call vote, and the measure failed by the close vote of 43 to 39. More Republicans voted yes than no. It took a five-vote margin on the part of the Democrats to defeat the amendment.[100] Senator Carl Curtis, a longtime opponent of Social Security expansion, challenged the bill from the right. Curtis wanted to alter the financing provisions of both Parts A and B. Wealthier people would be asked to pay more for their Medicare benefits, a form of what might be called reverse means testing. His amendment failed by a vote of 51 to 41.[101] After adopting eighty amendments, most of a minor nature, the Senate passed its version of the Medicare bill on July 9 by a vote of 68 to 21.[102]

A conference committee now needed to reconcile the differences between the House and Senate Medicare bills, including the changes in the duration of benefits that the Senate Finance Committee had made at the behest of Russell Long and Vance Hartke. These changes reflected important philosophical differences between Long's desire for the bill to cover catastrophic illnesses and the Ways and Means Committee's desire for definite limits on government expenditures. They nonetheless succumbed to the sort of hard bargaining common to conference committees. The conference committee decided, for example, on sixty days of hospitalization, as in the Ways and Means bill, but with an extra thirty days at a copay of ten dollars a day.[103]

The issue over the duration of benefits differed from the major difference between the House and Senate bills on whether specialist services like radiology should be covered by Part A or Part B. This question mattered so much to Wilbur Mills that it was difficult to find common ground. Senator Douglas just wanted to split the difference, with radiology and pathology under Part A and anesthesiologists and other medical specialties under Part B. Such an accommodation could not pass muster with Representative Mills because he regarded the matter as one of fundamental principle: all doctors' services should fall under Medicare Part B. Senate conferees yielded only after what the *New York Times* described as "much resistance and attempts to compromise." Congressman Hale Boggs (D-LA) and Senators Long and Smathers accepted Mills's position.[104]

The conferees issued their report on July 21 and launched a race to get the measure passed by the end of the month. Congress, having settled all of the major issues over the course of a protracted four-year period, passed the final measure with alacrity. The House acted on July 27 and the Senate on July 28. The bill passed by substantial margins in both houses, although seventeen Republicans voted against it in the Senate and a bare majority of Republicans, 70–68, supported it in the House.[105]

Celebrating Medicare

Only symbolic and ceremonial occasions remained. On July 29 the President received a delegation from the AMA at the White House. The President, who was briefed on all the many ways that the Medicare proponents had tried to accommodate the doctors, hoped, as one White House staffer put it, "to smooth the way for implementation of Medicare and convince the doctors that the Government was not planning to straitjacket the medical profession." Somehow the President got the AMA officials to greet the press and make conciliatory statements in public about Medicare. The Chicago doctor who headed the AMA Board of Trustees said, "We realize we are part of the citizenry and we were grateful for a chance to discuss problems of mutual interest." AMA President Appel made the point that LBJ most wanted to hear. "We are after all law abiding citizens, and we have every intention of obeying the new law," he said. The doctors' boycott of Medicare never occurred, at least in any organized way, and soon the doctors were too dependent on Medicare revenues even to suggest that the measure be repealed.[106]

The ceremony occurred on July 30 when President Johnson signed the Medicare bill into law in the presence of President Harry Truman in Independence, Missouri.[107] The White House did its best to make it a special occasion. A large delegation of congressmen and senators flew out to Kansas City on Air Force One to witness the ceremony at the Truman Library and take home one of the signing pens. Former President Truman greeted President Johnson and his party at the Truman Library. They moved to the library's auditorium, where both spoke to the assembled crowd. After the remarks, the President moved to the signing table, which Truman had once used to sign the peace treaty with West Germany, and gave the first pens to Mrs. Truman, President Truman, Vice President Humphrey, and Wilbur Mills. As a reward for the services they had performed, Wilbur Cohen and Andrew Biemiller of the AFL-CIO received two pens. The President then flew to his Texas ranch for a weekend of rest and relaxation. In what might have been a portent of his future, he had spent, as the *Chicago Tribune* reported, "an arduous week dealing with the Viet Nam crisis."[108]

The ceremony highlighted the achievements of President Truman, who was the first American president to endorse the idea of national health insurance as part of his postwar Fair Deal program. The notion of signing the Medicare law in Independence had worried some White House staffers. As some of the government veterans, such as Wilbur Cohen and Robert Ball, remembered, Truman had proposed health insurance for people of all ages, and Medicare covered only the elderly. The careful staffers wanted to continue the process of conciliation that had begun with the President's meeting with the AMA delegation. They wanted to do nothing to suggest that Medicare would be the prelude for a national health insurance program for all Americans.[109]

At the ceremony, the President said that the people had voted for Harry Truman "not because he gave them hell but because he gave them hope." By signing the Medicare law, President Johnson transformed "the hope he offered" into a "reality for millions of our fellow citizens."[110]

Conclusion

The effort to implement the law started almost immediately. The Social Security Administration made plans to add 6,000 workers to its 34,500 employees. Julius Gross, the president of a company that designed and furnished nursing home interiors, said, "We're getting ready for a rush of orders that should dwarf anything that has gone before." In November new HEW Secretary John Gardner announced the appointment of a sixteen-member Health Insurance Benefits Advisory Council, composed of representatives of many of the interests that had contended over the bill, from the AMA and the Health Insurance Association of America to the ubiquitous Nelson Cruikshank. As the year reached an end, the Director of Retirement Planning for the Continental Casualty Company predicted that Medicare would be an opportunity rather than a catastrophe for companies in the private insurance market who targeted senior citizens. Insurance salesmen should expect a "positive climate" for the senior citizen market, "not in spite of Medicare but because of it."[111]

The ceremony in the Truman Library marked the high-water point of the Great Society. Over the course of two weeks, the House had passed both Medicare and federal aid to education—the very measures that President Kennedy had tried so hard to get through Congress without success. Both the education and the Medicare bills differed in form and content from what President Kennedy had originally proposed. As Congress considered the measures over four years, it put its own imprint on the legislation. Although both reflected the short-run optimism of the era that the government could undertake difficult tasks, both went to great lengths to keep the federal government out of the classroom and the examining room, respectively. And both benefited from the prior passage of the civil rights legislation, which took this divisive subject off the table in the congressional debates. Furthermore, the robust shape of the economy facilitated the passage of both of the very expensive bills. The conditions of a relatively benign attitude toward civil rights and an expanding economy—as well as a labor movement that enjoyed considerable influence over legislation—would last for only a few years longer. No one knew it at the time, but the window for expansive social legislation would close relatively quickly. The year 1965 joined 1935 as a year of tremendous expansion of the American welfare state, although as the 1956 passage of disability insurance made clear, laws could be liberalized in other years as well.[112]

The long effort to pass President Kennedy's health insurance legislation had left a permanent mark on American social policy. In place of his original proposal for a program of hospital benefits, the nation acquired a much more comprehensive measure. To be sure, the new law followed the principles that had been in place since the early 1950s to limit national health insurance to the elderly and to use the Social Security program as an administrative delivery mechanism. Instead of being pared down, as disability insurance was in the legislative process, Medicare bulked up to include a major expansion of health services for welfare beneficiaries of all ages, a new program of supplementary health insurance to cover medical expenses that was offered to Social Security beneficiaries on very attractive terms, and more days of hospital and nursing home visits than anyone could have predicted in 1961. Government officials did most of the conceptual and leg work to create Medicare, but they did so with the close collaboration of their counterparts in the labor movement. Congress also played a very active role, taking the Medicare proponents along paths that government officials and labor leaders did not wish to travel, such as a voluntary health insurance plan.

The entire process was filled with the usual political horse-trading that made the final result rather ungainly. Allowing private intermediaries to administer the program was probably not what Medicare proponents had in mind. They nonetheless made many compromises in search of a health insurance plan that would satisfy all of the interests involved, and even then they failed to take the American Medical Association along with them until after the legislation had been passed. As always, short-term political bargains laid the foundation for enduring social institutions.

The fight for Medicare was an uphill battle as the continuing resistance of the House Ways and Means Committee indicated. It took the 1964 elections and the large Democratic (and liberal) majorities they brought with them to spring Medicare from the clutches of Congress. After the Senate passed but the House rejected Medicare in 1964, Lyndon Johnson made it into a campaign issue, sensing that it highlighted the differences between him and Senator Goldwater in a way that worked to his advantage.

If the 1964 presidential election paved the way for Medicare, it still gave Congress a great deal of freedom to work its will. The Ways and Means Committee played a vital role in shaping the final bill and in letting it veer from the administration's recommendations. The fact that there were more liberal members on the Senate Finance Committee than before helped to get the measure through the Senate, without needing to stage a dramatic floor fight such as occurred in 1956 and again in 1964. Indeed, the Senate felt free to add its own features to the bill, making its own mark on the final legislation.

Even more than with most laws, the implementation process mattered with Medicare. The results of the new law differed from any that either Wilbur Cohen or Harry Byrd would have predicted. In this case, origins were important but so were the dramatic changes in health care costs and other factors in health care finance that followed. These matters take up the next two chapters and attempt to provide a history of the way Medicare was both expanded to provide more benefits to more people but also altered to reflect new policy regimes and new policy ideas.

CHAPTER FOUR

The Consequences of Medicare from Accommodation to Regulation

Between 1965 and 1972 Medicare followed a pattern of incremental growth, not unlike the early expansions of disability insurance. The program added significant new groups to those entitled to federally funded health insurance, including people with disabilities. The addition of disability insurance beneficiaries to the Medicare program allowed the program to cover all Social Security recipients, not just those receiving old-age retirement benefits. In a sense, it eliminated what could be portrayed as an arbitrary program boundary, just like the age fifty limit for disability beneficiaries in the 1956 legislation. Legislators also made ad hoc additions to Medicare, such as extending the program to people with end stage renal disease. That change reflected the predilections of influential congressmen, such as Wilbur Mills, and effective interest-group lobbying.

After 1972 the pattern of incremental growth slowed, despite real gaps in the program, such as its lack of prescription drug coverage. Financial pressures on the program made it harder to expand Medicare. Between 1972 and 1983, policy makers sought ways to reduce the rate of growth in the program's expenditures. This process culminated in 1983 legislation that changed the way that the Medicare program reimbursed hospitals for their services. Significantly, the 1983 law did not change the benefits that the program offered so much as it tried to create incentives for hospitals and other health care providers to act in a cost-efficient manner. Overt benefit cuts were a much harder sell.

This chapter chronicles the early incremental expansions of Medicare and then looks at President Nixon's and President Carter's failed efforts to regulate and contain hospital costs. It concludes with an account of the 1983 legislation. The chapter argues that between 1965 and 1983 Medicare moved from accommodating doctors and hospitals to regulating them.

Some General Considerations

Although Medicare may not have developed in the way that its creators intended, it succeeded in its basic objective of providing health insurance for America's elderly population. The program never served, as some of its proponents intended, as a model for national health insurance in which the entire population was brought under its protection.[1] The strength of the private health insurance system prevented that, and the high costs of the program, which exceeded expectations, made health care reform—as national health insurance came to be called—an increasingly difficult proposition. Instead of the model for national health insurance, Medicare became the nation's single most important health insurance program in a very heterogeneous system. In the years between 1965 and the present, it exerted substantial influence over the development of health care in America. Few Americans escaped its consequences.

The history of Medicare, like the history of most social programs, contained many unintended consequences. For one thing, historical fashions changed, and the program that started as what health insiders called a single-payer program evolved into a program that offered the elderly choices in the sort of health insurance or prescription drug coverage they received (the subject of the next chapter). In this sense the public Medicare program mimicked the private health insurance market, and the policy goal for many conservatives became to make one system look much like the other. Managed care, which came to imply cheaper but somehow more efficient and more complete care, became a feature of both types of programs.

Any historical consideration of Medicare must begin with its size and its cost. In fiscal year 2016, according to preliminary estimates, some 56.5 million people received Medicare protection, either from Parts A or B but usually from both, each month (see figure 4.1). That included 8.9 million people with disabilities. As for Medicaid, the program reached a staggering 71.1 million people in a given month in 2016.[2] As the numbers implied, health expenditures played a large role in the nation's economy. They accounted for 17.5 percent of the nation's gross domestic product in 2014. In that year the nation spent more on Medicare and Medicaid than it did on private health insurance.[3] The situation presented a sharp contrast to the pre-Medicare era. In 1960 the government estimated that personal health care expenditures amounted to some 4.3 percent of the nation's GDP, and the federal government paid for a very small part of them.[4]

Medicare, unlike the basic Social Security program, became a large and expensive program early in its history. On July 1, 1966, when the program began formal operations, some nineteen million people enrolled (see figure 4.2). The large number reflected the fact that the program covered not those who had contributed to the program through payroll deductions throughout their working lives (as Social Security did) but people already receiving Social Security old-age benefits. There was, in effect, a large pent-up demand for the program.[5] In the program's

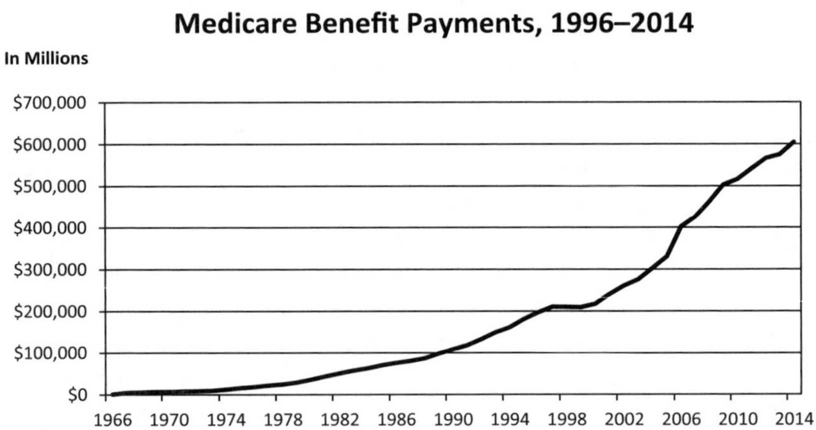

FIGURE 4.1. Medicare Benefit Payments, 1966–2014.

Note: Chart includes Part A, Hospital Benefits, and Supplemental Benefits under Parts B, D, and Medicare Advantage plans. Figures are benefit payments only and do not include administrative expenditures.

Source: *Social Security Bulletin, Annual Statistical Supplement, 2015*, Tables 8A1 and 8A2. US Social Security Administration.

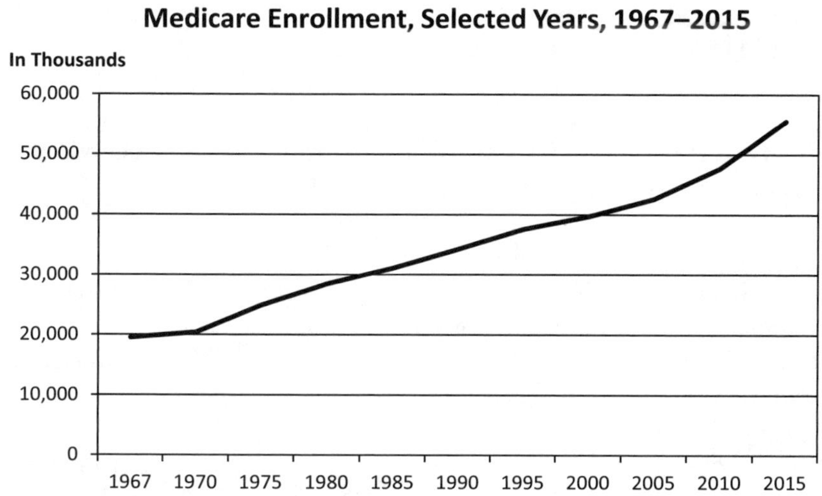

FIGURE 4.2. Medicare Enrollment, Selected Years, 1967–2015.
Note: Includes enrollees in hospital insurance and supplemental insurance.
Sources: *Social Security Bulletin, Annual Statistical Supplement*, 1986, Table 145. *Annual Report of the Board of Trustees of the Federal Hospital Insurance and Federal Supplementary Medical Insurance Trust Funds*, 2012 Report, Table VB3, and 2017 Report, Table VB4.

start-up years between 1966 and 1969, the average annual increase in Medicare expenditures was 32.3 percent, caused among other things by a rapid increase in hospital costs (which the program agreed to pay as part of the legislative bargaining in 1965) and the high usage rate for skilled nursing facilities (which owed much of their prominence to the 1965 Medicare legislation). This initial growth, far beyond the actuarial estimates, put a damper on plans for the program's expansion. Nor was the start-up period an anomaly. In the years between 1974 and 1982, for example, the average annual increase was 20 percent. Analysts explained the increase by an expansion of the program to include people with disabilities (legislated in 1972) but also by what one actuary described as "rapid general and medical inflation."[6]

As the program matured, it cost more and more money. In calendar year 2014 the nation spent $618.7 billion on Medicare. That was a significant percentage of the nation's 3.3 trillion in medical costs (or more than $9,523 per capita).[7] Although the large numbers meant nothing in and of themselves, the high cost of Medicare became a target for criticism. It became harder to argue that the program should be expanded to take on new populations, and it became fashionable to portray it as an out-of-control funding source that could not be sustained into the future.

Getting Started and Extending Medicare to People Receiving Disability Insurance and People with Kidney Disease

Even before Medicare went into effect, it changed the American health care system by serving as a force for the racial integration of southern hospitals, an early indication of the program's potential clout. Most of the early work in Medicare was not nearly so dramatic. It consisted of putting a system of intermediaries and carriers in place to handle the billing operations of the program, signing people up for the voluntary Part B of the program, and writing the many rules and regulations that would govern the administration of the program. The federal government devoted a substantial amount of manpower to accomplishing these tasks and adopted a conciliatory approach toward the doctors and hospitals who would have the real responsibility for implementing the program. There were people, particularly a group of influential staffers who worked for Russell Long and Herman Talmadge on the Senate Finance Committee, who criticized the program for paying hospitals more than they typically received from Blue Cross and thus aggravating medical cost inflation. For the most part, the accomplishments of the program—launching a major new health insurance program with only a few glitches—overshadowed the criticisms.[8]

From the beginning people had suggestions for the expansion of the Medicare program. One critical dimension was age, leading to the notion that newborns and children, whose future well-being was vital to the nation, might have their medical expenses subsidized by the federal government. Another critical dimension was health status. Perhaps sicker people needed Medicare more than others in the general population. Still another dimension was the scope of care. Maybe the government could do something about the critical cost of drugs that were cost effective in terms of prolonging life and reducing morbidity but were increasingly expensive for the elderly to pay for out of pocket. The need for prescription drugs extended well beyond hospital stays, when many drugs were covered by Medicare, to reach the daily lives of many elderly Americans. A final dimension concerned the fact that some Social Security beneficiaries but not others were eligible for Medicare. People receiving Social Security Disability Insurance benefits, although retired, could not qualify for Medicare until they reached the age of sixty-five.

Of all these potential areas of expansion, Medicare for disability insurance recipients appeared to enjoy the most political support. President Johnson proposed this measure in 1967, but at the time the program was still trying to sort out its start-up problems. In the Nixon years, a new controversy over the Family Assistance Plan and welfare reform distracted the Ways and Means and Finance Committees, with the result that only ad hoc Social Security benefit increases, rather than substantive new reforms, cleared Congress in the President's first term. Nonetheless, Medicare benefits for disability beneficiaries passed the Senate in 1970 but stalled in the House. Their eventual passage appeared to be, in one policy insider's term, "a foregone conclusion."[9]

When Congress finally passed omnibus Social Security legislation in 1972 and President Nixon signed it at the end of October, it contained, among its many features, Medicare benefits for people on Social Security Disability Insurance. Congress required a substantial waiting period of twenty-four months between the receipt of SSDI and the start of Medicare benefits, making Medicare for people with disabilities more stringent than Medicare for the elderly. In a manner that was typical of American social policy, Congress made no other significant distinctions between the health insurance program for the elderly and the health insurance program for people with disabilities, even though some might argue that the two groups had different medical needs. Rehabilitation medicine, for example, had more potential benefit for people with disabilities than for the elderly. Such matters received no consideration at all.[10]

Medicare's extension to people with disabilities was the most important but not the only Medicare feature of the 1972 amendments. Instead, public policy took an unexpected turn, and Congress added people with end stage renal disease to the Medicare program.[11] Patients with kidney disease were a deserving group, but they were just one of many. Just as Congress in 1935 decided to make the blind but not other handicapped groups eligible for public assistance, so Congress made a similar decision to promote kidney disease over other worthy impairments in the 1972 legislation. As a result, the Social Security Amendments of 1972 authorized Medicare entitlement for individuals with a diagnosis of chronic renal failure who were "fully or currently insured under social security." The provision also applied to the spouses and dependent children of such individuals.

The key feature of the new provision declared that anyone with a diagnosis of chronic renal failure was "deemed to be disabled," without having to prove, as did most other disability applicants, that they were unable to engage in substantial gainful activity. Similarly, Medicare benefits were available immediately upon eligibility rather than requiring the twenty-four-month waiting period. People with end stage renal disease passed the disability requirement by virtue of their impairment alone.

For a Congress that had labored so hard and long over the creation of disability insurance and Medicare, one might wonder how the same body could enact the kidney disease program almost as an afterthought in 1972. The matter came up only at the end of a very long process and was the product of an amendment offered by Senator Vance Hartke on the Senate floor that was ultimately adopted in conference.

Part of the reason was that influential legislators like Hartke and Wilbur Mills had been looking for a suitable legislative vehicle for the kidney disease program. The interest followed from years of technological developments that resulted in the creation of an effective dialysis program for treating people with kidney disease. Such treatment prolonged lives but was too expensive for most patients to afford—the classic conundrum of modern medicine and one that seemed to imply a role for the federal government. Parts of the federal bureaucracy with an interest in the problem, such as the Veterans Administration and the Public Health Service, pursued some sort of remedy. These agencies mobilized a network of public and private practitioners who continued to improve the process of dialysis and to increase the efficacy of kidney transplantation. These procedures went from experimental to established therapies for kidney disease.

By 1972 a substantial legislative record had been worked up in favor of government aid for people with end stage renal disease. In November 1971, for example, the Ways and Means Committee heard testimony from representatives of the National Association of Patients on Hemodialysis in which a patient was dialyzed in front of the committee. The hearings focused on national health insurance rather than on Medicare per se. They prompted Wilbur Mills to introduce a personal, as opposed to a committee, bill at the end of 1971 that would have authorized appropriations to assist needy individuals with the cost of dialysis. The bill would have created a budgeted program and not an entitlement like Medicare. In the Senate, Hartke and Senator Alan Cranston (D-CA) proposed to use the Public Health Service Act as a vehicle to establish and operate "cooperative community programs for patients with kidney disease" and provide "financial assistance to individuals suffering from chronic kidney disease." Neither of these measures passed, but Hartke continued to pursue the matter in the Senate Finance Committee as an amendment to the Medicare bill that ultimately succeeded and became part of the 1972 omnibus legislation. Like all programs, once in place the program stayed in place, but the rising costs of Medicare and medical care more generally made it difficult to extend the disease-specific approach to new groups.

National Health Insurance and Its Demise

If nothing else, the End Stage Renal Disease Program reinforced the concept, also promoted by the extension of Medicare to people with disabilities, that Medicare had the potential to serve the nonelderly population. In an indirect manner, it served as a preview for a more general national health insurance program. In the early 1970s, as Congress was considering the various components of the 1972 Social Security Amendments, the discussion over national health insurance took a serious turn. It seemed at times that some form of national health insurance would pass Congress and at a minimum change the place of Medicare in the American health policy system.

The period of intense discussion of national health insurance lasted until 1974, when inflation and other economic difficulties ushered in a new era of social welfare policy. During the Nixon administration's first term, it paid close attention to the debate over national health insurance and felt obligated to offer its own proposal. It was typical of the rhetoric of the time that HEW Secretary Elliot Richardson told a congressional committee in 1971 that he was certain that the hearings would culminate in national health insurance. Richardson proposed a scheme that became known as mandating: requiring employers to provide a basic health insurance package for their employees. More liberal Democrats favored a scheme closer to Medicare, in which payroll taxes would create a more complete and more universal system of health insurance.

Neither of these approaches became law. In the end, liberals, particularly the labor unions that remained front and center in national health insurance politics, gambled that the 1974 elections would bring a more receptive Congress to Washington and put off making a deal. Because

Watergate so discredited the Republicans, the Democrats made substantial gains in 1974, but the economic conditions in 1975 changed the political picture.[12]

Even when national health insurance was under serious discussion, the rising cost of Medicare and health costs in general caused policy makers to examine the system with an eye to reducing health care cost inflation. The precipitous increase in expenditures during the first five years of Medicare helped to focus the discussion. The rise in hospital charges, aided by the decision to pay hospitals on a "reasonable cost basis" under Medicare Part A and allow them to recover their direct and indirect costs (such as the depreciation of equipment and the cost of capital indebtedness), brought particular attention to hospitals and medical care more generally as a source of inflation. The Nixon administration went after this problem aggressively in its price and wage control program announced in August 1971. With the exception of oil prices, hospital costs were at the very center of the effort. The hospital cost controls lasted until May 1974. Their removal led to a precipitous increase of 30 percent in health care costs in the second half of that year. In a typical move, the George Washington University Hospital, an important health provider in the capital area, announced a 23 percent rate increase in 1975; that meant that many consumers faced a 60 percent rise in hospital costs between 1972 and 1975.[13]

The precipitous rise in costs indicated that there might be a flaw in Medicare and other health insurance systems. One notion was that insurance payments, such as Medicare and private health insurance, shielded doctors and their patients from cost concerns. The more tests they ordered, the more operations they performed, the more the doctors received in reimbursement, often with no increase in the patient's insurance costs, at least in the short run. The situation caused policy makers to become more interested in what came to be called health maintenance organizations (HMOs). These organizations set a limit on what HMOs received for the care of patients, reducing the incentive to order extra tests or provide extended periods of hospital care. The hope was that preventive medicine and better access to primary care doctors might reduce expensive hospital stays. HMOs were not new—prominent health maintenance organizations already existed in the District of Columbia, Minneapolis, and Seattle—but they gained much more prominence in the early 1970s. A new object of federal health policy became the promotion of HMOs.[14] In 1973, even as it delayed or discarded many other things, Congress passed the Health Maintenance Organization Act. It mandated, in the manner of the era, that employers of twenty-five persons or more offer a choice of a prepaid group practice plan to their employees, provided such a plan existed in their area.[15]

Although this legislation did not revolutionize American health care or have an immediate effect on Medicare, it did indicate the direction of future change. Increasingly policy would center on cost controls and not on the expansion of public programs such as Medicare. Particularly after 1983 the idea of choice figured into health policy discussions, with the ultimate result of allowing Medicare beneficiaries to elect an HMO-style plan rather than the traditional "single-payer" Medicare program.[16]

Jimmy Carter and Hospital Cost Containment, 1977–1978

In 1977 the emphasis on cost control moved to the very center of health care policy discussions. For nearly all of the Jimmy Carter years, containing hospital costs through regulation remained a hot political issue. Medicare, once relatively removed from the public eye after its 1965 passage, emerged as a politically charged area of public policy. The once orderly policy apparatus that administered the program became increasingly unruly, with scores of committees and subcommittees entering the fray. Considerations related to the economic power of health care providers and the desires of congressmen to preserve their political turf became part of the process. And the lengthy discussion largely went nowhere, at least in the short run, maybe because so many parties with an interest in the matter participated and maybe because almost any solution to the problem of health care cost inflation was politically unattractive. The fact that Congress refused to pass Carter's legislation meant the perpetuation of health care cost inflation as a policy problem and an item on the Medicare agenda.

Jimmy Carter, a Democrat, was expected to carry the usual Democratic policy baggage, such as plans for welfare reform and national health insurance. Both of these items, particularly national health insurance, continued to be high priority items of the party's liberal wing as personified by Senators Edward Kennedy and Gaylord Nelson (D-WI). Carter, with a much wider array of issues to consider, regarded inflation as a more immediate and therefore important policy problem. He believed he needed to perform a two-step. First, he would slow down the inflation rate and only then pursue expensive new programs like national health insurance. Medicare policy thus became health care cost containment policy rather than a means of expanding the program to reach new people and provide new services. The era of big government was, if not entirely over, at least becalmed. As Carter put it in a 1979 speech delivered at the dedication of the John F. Kennedy Library in Boston, America was struggling with a "profound transition" from JFK's New Frontier to a new, still undefined era. As part of this transition, America had acquired "a keener appreciation of the limits" in domestic and foreign policy.[17]

As Carter prepared to take over the government, his emerging health care policy team turned its attention to writing a hospital cost containment bill. Health economist Karen Davis, who was to play an important role in health policy from her position in the HEW Secretary's office concerned with policy planning and research, explained that "you needed to control health care costs in order to convince people to pay for coverage of the uninsured." The public simply would not support expanding a public health care system that was "running out of control." If consumers were concerned about such things as increases in the price of food and fuel, "health care inflation was a bigger problem."[18]

As someone versed in economics, Davis and her colleagues in the administration, such as Brookings economist Henry Aaron who was detailed to the Department of Health, Education, and Welfare as an Assistant Secretary, recognized the inherent problems of any hospital cost containment proposal. First, there were the general regulatory problems that arose when the government tried to control something in the private sector whose inner workings were largely beyond its control. The specter of more paperwork, intrusive bureaucracy, and smaller revenues stirred up the opposition of the organizations representing the interests of hospitals. Furthermore, the interests of hospitals were themselves fragmented, since all hospitals were not the same in their basic mission and financial schemes. Instead, as Davis put it, the heterogeneous hospital industry took "care of all sorts of patients" and their costs were "at all kinds of levels." From a health policy point of view, that created a tradeoff between a measure that was "simple and unfair" and one that was "fair and complicated." It appeared likely that adjustments would need to be made for hospitals with special missions, such as rural hospitals, teaching hospitals, and hospitals that treated many very sick patients, such as the Mayo Clinic. The Carter administration ended up putting in "lots of adjustments," making hospital cost containment legislation, according to Davis, "difficult politically for the Congress to swallow."[19]

Whatever hesitations the members of the Carter administration might have had, they recognized inflation—and hospital cost inflation—as a problem that required their immediate attention. The fact that work on a hospital cost containment bill began in the transition period rather than the early months of the administration was significant. So was the decision, apparently made very early, that hospital cost containment measures should apply to all payers, not just the health insurance programs under the federal and state governments' immediate control, such as Medicare and Medicaid. Hospital cost containment would not only affect private and community hospitals; it also would intervene in the private health insurance market.[20]

By April 1977 the Carter administration decided that the hospital cost containment measure was ready for its close-up. The President issued a statement on inflation that noted that "the cost of hospital care is increasing at more than twice the overall rate of inflation." He promised the introduction of a "hard-hitting hospital cost containment measure" within a few weeks. The measure was touted as a means of saving health insurance plans and the federal government $2 billion a year by putting a cap or ceiling on increases in hospital charges. The operating principle was to tie permissible hospital cost increases to rises in consumer prices. If, for example, the inflation rate for 1978 was 6 percent, then hospitals would be allowed to increase their charges (and hence the Medicare Part A payments they received) by only 9 percent regardless of the financial pressures associated with medical cost inflation they faced. The legislation promised to save $695 million in Medicare and $134 million in Medicaid in 1978.[21]

Opposition to the legislation developed even before it was formally introduced. Both George Meany, the indefatigable head of the AFL-CIO, and Sidney M. Wolfe, the Director of the Public Citizen's Health Research Group associated with consumer advocate Ralph Nader, praised the legislation as a step in the right direction but thought that it was not strict enough with the hospitals. Other liberal health policy advocates believed that the administration's endorsement of hospital cost containment signaled that it was stepping away from a national health insurance program. Groups that protected the interest of hospitals wasted no time in attacking the measure. John Alexander McMahon, the President of the American Hospital Association, said that he was "certain that any across-the-board ceiling will bring the total opposition of the hospital field" and put the sick and the injured at risk.[22]

The President responded that, contrary to the desires of special interest groups, the legislation was in the public interest. The President stressed the precipitous rise in health care expenditures—some 1,000 percent since 1950. The average American worker was devoting one month of his annual salary to pay for health care costs. The President singled out hospital costs as an important component of these rising medical costs. He noted that hospitals absorbed some forty cents of each health care dollar and "the cost of hospital services is growing faster than the cost of other health services."[23]

The President saw hospital cost containment as transitional, a first step along the path toward a new reimbursement system that would not accept a hospital's base price as given. For example, instead of hospitals receiving reimbursement for any service they performed, they might receive a fixed amount of money from Medicare and presumably private insurers as well that would create incentives to lower their costs. Hospital cost containment was also transitional in the sense that it might mark a step toward national health insurance or some other health care financing scheme. Unconstrained health care costs "restrict our ability to plan necessary improvements in our health care system," the President said, implying that national health insurance advocates should get behind hospital cost containment as legislation that advanced their policy goals. Carter's Secretary of HEW Joseph Califano, a Washington lawyer who had made a name for himself as a domestic policy aide in the Johnson White House and who considered himself very knowledgeable in the ways of Washington, made a similar point at a White House briefing. Hospital cost containment would supply the "financial underpinning" for national health insurance or whatever other improvements came along.[24]

Everyone realized that the hospital cost containment proposal was key to the future of Medicare and Medicaid. These programs made more payments to hospitals than did any private insurer. One sign of rising program costs was that the deductible that Medicare required beneficiaries to pay out of pocket before its benefits kicked in had recently risen from $124 to $144 dollars. Administrators worried that the program, and indeed medical practice more generally, had become bloated through such practices as performing unnecessary operations. In keeping with the new conventional medical wisdom that showed the slow creep toward managed care, Medicare officials announced they would reimburse patients for a second opinion on the necessity of an operation.[25] Medicare and Medicaid were also keys to the operation of a hospital cost containment program. Data from these programs were essential to establishing the level of hospital costs that would form the basis for permissible increases in hospital cost.

By the end of 1977 it had become evident that hospital cost containment would not clear Congress in that legislative session. Congressional and administration leaders believed that further staff discussions were necessary in order to fashion an acceptable bill for 1978. The hospital industry continued its unrelenting opposition, and subcommittee chairmen, who held near veto power over the bill, continued to express their reservations. The disciplined committee structure that had produced Medicare in 1965 no longer existed. Now at least four committees and their attendant subcommittees had stakes in the hospital cost containment legislation.[26]

In the House, Dan Rostenkowski, who represented a district in northwest Chicago and maintained close relations with Mayor Richard Daley, headed the Ways and Means Subcommittee on Health. He favored the hospital cost containment legislation less vigorously than did the liberal members of the Health Subcommittee of the Commerce Committee. Committee Chair John Dingell, who had presided over the House during the final Medicare debate and whose father was an early leader in the fight for national insurance, helped to steer that committee in a liberal direction.

Like all congressmen, Rostenkowski received considerable pressure from the many hospitals in his district, which had become important sources of employment in Chicago and many other cities. Rostenkowski's Chicago district was also close to the national headquarters of many medical organizations, and by virtue of his membership on the Ways and Means Committee he benefited from their financial contributions. Rostenkowski, in keeping with the more conservative approach of his committee, challenged the hospital industry to engage in a voluntary campaign to reduce costs. As a legislative tactician, he realized that the threat imposed by the Carter proposal might compel action in the private sector. He hinted that such an effort might forestall the need for hospital cost containment legislation.[27]

In the Senate the measure fared better. It passed the relatively liberal and prolabor Human Resources Committee. Edward Kennedy became a major supporter, presumably because he wanted to pass the measure quickly and move on to national health insurance, which was slipping from the administration's list of priorities. The Senate Finance Committee took a more cautious approach. Georgia Senator Herman Talmadge, who had taken Walter George's seat in 1956, regarded his chief specialty as agriculture, but he also chaired the Finance Committee's Subcommittee on Health. His staffer Jay Constantine, although liberal in his political leanings, had been an acerbic critic of Medicare and its expenditures since 1965. Constantine regarded the hospital cost containment measure as imperfect. He urged Senator Talmadge to produce his own plan, in which hospitals would be split up into groups with different cost increases for each group.[28]

Rumors that the monthly premiums for Part B of Medicare would rise from $7.70 to $8.20 began in 1978.[29] Meanwhile the hospital industry hastened to create a network of committees that would spearhead the effort to reduce hospital costs on a voluntary basis. The President of the American Hospital Association said that the trend was already favorable. Hospital costs rose by 19 percent in 1977, down from a rise of 19.1 percent in 1976. Michael Bromberg, Executive Director of the Federation of American Hospitals, added that it was the "first time in history that the whole health industry is working toward the exact same goals."[30]

These actions mollified Dan Rostenkowski, who appeared to be more favorably disposed to the hospital industry than he was to the Carter administration. Speaking before the House of Delegates of the American Hospital Association early in February, he announced his intention to set aside the administration's hospital cost containment bill in favor of the voluntary actions that the hospitals were undertaking.[31]

Senator Kennedy and Representative Paul Rogers (D-FL), a genial congressman with increasing influence over health policy from his post as chair of the Commerce Committee's Health and Environment Subcommittee, continued to make the case for hospital cost containment. Kennedy, whose actions were being watched closely by journalists who wondered if he might challenge Carter for the Democratic nomination in 1980, said the voluntary effort was doomed to failure. Secretary Califano, who found himself increasingly in the role of intermediary between Carter and Kennedy, characterized the voluntary effort as offering "false hope" to the American people.[32]

Relations between the Democratic Congress and the Carter administration were becoming more strained over hospital cost containment and other issues. Congressmen accused the Carter administration as being lackadaisical and ineffective in its lobbying efforts. The congressmen complained of lack of access to the White House and a lack of leadership from HEW. "We don't even know who is making the policy on cost containment in HEW," one Senate staffer said.[33] Members of Congress felt that they had taken considerable risks in supporting the legislation and received no rewards. Rostenkowski had his own feud with Califano. He wanted Califano to appoint Kenneth Sain, a former Chicago assistant mayor and a confirmed member of the Daley machine, to the post of regional director of the department. Califano felt Sain was nothing more than a political hack and made only a grudging offer that Sain turned down. Chicago alderman Chris Cohen, the eldest son of former HEW Secretary Wilbur Cohen and something of an independent in Mayor Daley's Chicago, became the regional commissioner. Rostenkowski said he was not "the only one having trouble with Califano." He suggested that the President would enjoy more legislative success if he paid more attention to congressional patronage.[34]

Kennedy and Herman Talmadge continued to negotiate over hospital cost containment in the hope of getting it to the Senate floor in 1978. One stumbling block to passage was the attitude of organized labor, a group ardently courted by Kennedy. Labor leaders supported the general concept of containing the costs of health care—they were after all major health care consumers—but worried that the Carter bill would adversely affect the wages of hospital workers: they were also health care producers. This ambivalence meant that organized labor did not lobby vigorously for hospital cost containment. Like Kennedy, the labor leaders reserved their enthusiasm for national health insurance. Kennedy, Meany, and United Auto Workers President Doug Fraser met with Carter in the White House and got him to agree on what journalists described as "a broad approach to health insurance."[35]

In the spring of 1978, the Democrats in the Senate, including Majority Leader Robert Byrd, agreed to make hospital cost containment a priority for the legislative session. The House continued to struggle with the bill. The climactic moment came in the Commerce Committee in a July vote that substituted voluntary cost controls for mandatory controls in the legislation. It passed by a close vote of 22–21.[36] Within the House Commerce Committee, Martin Russo (D-IL), another member of the Chicago delegation who previously had supported the administration bill, decided to oppose it and go with the voluntary approach.

His failure to inform the White House of his decision infuriated President Carter. In a meeting with Democratic congressional leaders, Carter said he would like to hear "why Rostenkowski's colleague from Chicago stabbed me in the back." Russo, for his part, said that he had decided that the measure had become "an administrative nightmare." Better, he thought, to take the voluntary approach.[37]

President Carter had proclaimed ownership of the hospital cost containment bill, calling it the "most important anti-inflation decision of this congressional session." If Congress killed the measure, it would be a very visible defeat. Secretary Califano slammed the Commerce Committee bill as "a sham." Robert Hunter, the Chairman of the Board of the American Medical Association, expressed pleasure in the committee's action. He claimed that physicians needed protection from the tightening grasp of the federal government over their activities, just as they had ever since the passage of Medicare, and that the voluntary approach was working. The first four months of 1978 saw a rise of 12.7 percent in hospital costs, down from 15.6 percent in the previous year. That enabled Congressman James Broyhill (R-NC) to argue that the Commerce Committee's measure would encourage hospitals in their efforts to cut costs.[38]

With all of its committees and subcommittees, Congress contained many avenues for passing legislation. Attention shifted to the Senate Finance Committee, where Senator Talmadge continued to tinker with the bill. He suggested that the cost controls be applied to Medicare and Medicaid patients and not to private insurance. He focused on routine services, such as room fees and meals. Although the Carter administration complained about the limited focus and the exclusion of such things as surgery, X-rays, and drugs from cost controls, Senator Talmadge's bill won the approval of the Senate Finance Committee and headed for the Senate floor.[39]

There remained the tradition of amending legislation on the Senate floor. The Carter administration backed Senator Kennedy's and Senator Nelson's efforts to change the bill so that it was closer to Carter's original bill rather than what might be called the Talmadge-Rostenkowski substitute. The Carter team was not unwilling to compromise. Nelson's amendment, for example, would impose mandatory cost controls only if hospitals failed to achieve cost reductions of 2 percent a year. In a concession to organized labor, Nelson's plan would exempt the wages of nonsupervisory hospital employees in computing hospital costs. Watching from the House, Paul Rogers said that the cost containment bill was "still breathing." President Carter remained all in. Secretary Califano said the President wanted to make "an all out effort to get hospital cost containment this year." Responding to Carter's and Kennedy's efforts, the Senate passed a hospital cost containment bill that was acceptable to the administration.[40]

The Senate actions brought the measure back to the House and the Committee on Ways and Means (which had not yet considered this specific bill, with its version of hospital cost containment). There the measure died by a margin of four votes, despite the intense lobbying of Joseph Califano. For this Congress at least the measure was dead, part of Carter's unsuccessful effort to discipline the health care system in the face of persistent inflationary pressures. The episode further soured the Kennedy-Carter relationship and added to the impression that the administration was somehow not up to dealing with the complex problems of the era. Medicare and Medicaid would remain largely in place and cost more and more money.[41]

Hospital Cost Containment, 1978–1980

Rather than cut its losses, the administration decided to pursue hospital cost containment as a priority matter in the Congress that convened in 1979. Although the congressional elections failed to provide a mandate for the measure, some changes in Congress altered the political environment at least a little. Dan Rostenkowski decided he had had his fill of the Ways and Means Health Subcommittee and stepped down as its chairman. Paul Rogers, an effective legislator who had left behind many health care laws that made him a hero at the National Institutes of Health, retired. Henry Waxman (D-CA), small in stature but energetic in his pursuit of liberal legislation, took over from Rogers as chair of the Commerce Committee's Health Subcommittee. For the rest of the century, Waxman, a Watergate baby who came to Congress in 1975, would make his mark on health policy through such things as the expansion of Medicaid.[42]

Edward Kennedy, another key legislative player, decided not to be front and center in the renewed campaign for hospital cost containment. Instead he concentrated on presenting his national health insurance proposal, apparently unwilling to wait for the Carter administration to make the first move. His advocacy of national health insurance would be one of the things that impelled him to challenge Carter for the 1980 Democratic presidential nomination.

The administration decided that the White House rather than the Department of Health, Education, and Welfare would take the lead on hospital cost containment. Carter stressed the link between the legislation and the more general fight against inflation, a problem that showed no sign of abating and would only get worse before the end of his term. The cost of hospital care continued to skyrocket. Over the course of the past twenty-seven years, the nation's hospital care bill had jumped from $3.8 billion to $55.4 billion, more than twice the rate of growth in the nation's gross national product. With hospital costs doubling every five years, one could imagine the nation spending $220 billion on hospital care in 1985.[43]

President Carter doubled down on hospital cost containment. "One of the highest legislative priorities for this year is hospital containment. It will be one of the clearest tests of the seriousness of the Congress in dealing with the problem of inflation," he declared in his State of the Union address at the beginning of the session.[44] Carter cast the legislation in moral terms. "It is time for the public interest to prevail. It is time for Congress to demonstrate its commitment to end inflation," the President said.[45] Carter used the rhetoric of the progressive era to conjure up a battle between the public and the special interests, with the President on the side of the people and the hospital industry putting profits above the nation's true needs. Hospitals needed to be less selfish and more altruistic. Congress needed to do what was right rather than what was politically rewarding or expedient.

The White House geared up for a major battle. It wanted to build on its Senate success in the previous year, pass the measure in the Senate, and concentrate on the Commerce Committee in the House, with Henry Waxman now directing traffic there. The idea was to move quickly before the hospital industry had a chance to mobilize its formidable opposition. During a February 1979 meeting of congressional leaders, the President pulled Dan Rostenkowski aside. "We really need your help on this one," the President said. He hoped that Rostenkowski would pressure his Chicago colleague and Commerce Committee member Martin Russo to go along with the measure. Rostenkowski, who described hospital cost containment as a "no-win proposition," remained openly skeptical. Henry Waxman agreed that it would be "very tough" to get the measure out of his committee. Although Waxman was more liberal than his predecessor, his subcommittee had become more conservative after the 1978 elections.[46]

Under the terms of the legislation introduced in March, hospitals had until the end of the year to cut costs voluntarily before the mandatory controls took effect. The measure also exempted many hospitals from cost controls, including those in states such as Maryland that already had all-payer cost controls in place, small rural hospitals, hospitals less than three years old, and hospitals in states that succeeded, on average, in meeting the voluntary targets. Officials estimated that more than half of the nation's hospitals would be exempt. The hospital industry remained wary. Carter's legislation, according to Alex McMahon of the American Hospital Association, would create a "huge federal bureaucracy," with people like the implacable Joseph Califano in charge. The hospital industry could solve the problem on its own and in a way that did not put patients at risk.[47]

The measure proceeded to run the congressional gauntlet. The Ways and Means Health Subcommittee approved the measure on April 25. Members of the subcommittee amended the administration's measure to exempt more hospitals in their districts from the cost controls. Representative Charles Vanik, who represented the Cleveland area, put clinics that specialized in the treatment of cancer, such as the Cleveland Clinic, on the exemption list. Representative Harold Ford (D-TN) made sure that children's hospitals that drew patients from across the nation and engaged in research were exempt. One of these hospitals happened to be the St. Jude's Children's Hospital in Ford's hometown of Memphis.[48]

Senator Edward Kennedy put forward his own pet project, a national health insurance bill "to make quality health care a right for all our people" on May 14. Other prominent liberals in the health insurance coalition, such as Douglas Fraser of the United Auto Workers, stood beside Kennedy as he made the announcement. The Senator spoke in the Senate Caucus Room, the very location in which his brothers had announced their presidential candidacies. The press was not slow to pick up on the symbolism. In response to the reporters' questions, Kennedy criticized Carter's "piecemeal" approach to health care but said he still expected to support the President in the 1980 election. Representative Waxman vowed to introduce Kennedy's legislation in the House. A prominent part of the Health Care for All Americans Act was an expansion of Medicare to reach more of the uninsured.

The administration, concerned about its hospital cost containment bill and the need to cut down on federal spending, tried to be as conciliatory as it could. Secretary Califano had the unpleasant task of answering press queries. He said that the President shared the goals of Kennedy and Waxman for a "universal comprehensive national program" but wanted to start with what Califano called a "first phase" bill. Stuart Eizenstat, who played the same role for Carter that Califano did for Johnson, added, "You can't have all these additional demands on the system without some sort of controls."[49]

The hospital cost containment bill lumbered through Congress. In July the Ways and Means Committee gave its approval to the measure. Discussion of the bill within the Commerce Committee dragged on through the summer. The Health Subcommittee included at least six members who remained firm opponents and a handful of liberals such as Waxman who wanted to advance the measure. Three wavering members of the committee appeared to hold the key to the measure's success. They included Richard Shelby, a freshman Democrat from Alabama, who first gave his support to the measure but retreated in the face of hospital industry pressure, as well as two Republicans, including the ranking GOP member of the subcommittee. In early September, the health subcommittee defeated the bill by a substantial eight-to-four margin.[50] The full Commerce Committee then considered the measure without a positive recommendation from its health subcommittee. In an unlikely victory for the Carter administration, the Commerce Committee passed its version of the bill. With the approval of both the Ways and Means and Commerce Committees, the bill could now proceed to the House floor.[51]

The final vote, which came on November 15, resulted in a decisive defeat for the administration. The hospital industry pressed the point that its voluntary controls were working and the Carter controls were unnecessary. Its spokesmen argued that there had been a steady decline in the rate of hospital cost increases over the past four years. Democrat Richard Gephardt, a rising member of Congress from the St. Louis area who had first been elected in 1976, agreed to offer an amendment to the bill on the House floor that would eliminate all mandatory price ceilings and hence gut the bill. The Gephardt amendment carried.[52]

Following the vote, the President did not face the press directly, but his press secretary Jody Powell said that the President was "quite upset." Powell characterized the House's action as "a defeat in the fight against inflation and a victory for a well-financed interest lobby group." In other words the special interests had succeeded in putting their interests above those of the people. Henry Waxman conceded that the measure's chances were now "very slim."[53]

In the uneasy period leading up to the 1980 election, in which Carter would defeat Kennedy in the primaries but lose in the general election to Ronald Reagan, health care and Medicare politics returned to their familiar forms. Secretary Califano was gone, a victim of Carter's summer 1979 purge of his cabinet. Patricia Roberts Harris, the new Secretary, turned her attention to eliminating waste and fraud in Medicare as a means of reducing costs. Congress obliged her by holding hearings that exposed wide variations in the costs of medical supplies that Medicare reimbursed and that called attention to the use of drugs in the Medicare program that the National Academy of Sciences considered ineffective.[54] The Carter administration came away with little or nothing to show for its efforts to lay the foundation for national health insurance by controlling the growth of hospital costs.

Reagan and the Creation of TEFRA

Ronald Reagan arrived with his own agenda for Medicare and health care politics. Much of what followed, including the passage of key legislation in 1982, was motivated by concerns about rising health care costs. In 1981 Americans spent $287 billion on health care, or 9.8 percent of the gross national product. Although the GNP increased by 11.4 percent between 1980 and 1981, total health expenditures rose by 15.1 percent in the same period. Nearly 43 percent of those health expenditures occurred in government programs. Increasing Medicare and other health care expenditures put pressure on the entire federal budget. Administration officials estimated that health care programs such as Medicare and Medicaid would take up a tenth of the federal budget for 1983. "The message of these statistics," said the new Department of Health and Human Services (HHS) Secretary Richard Schweiker (who became the first head of that successor department to HEW), "is that the policies of the past are bringing us health cost increases well above the rate of inflation."[55]

Beginning in 1982 the Reagan administration could offer its own proposals, free from the shadow of Jimmy Carter's budget. In January of that year journalists speculated that the administration would reduce reimbursements to hospitals for their Medicare patients by 2 percent. This proposal followed the spirit of Jimmy Carter's hospital cost containment but applied, unlike Carter's most ambitious proposals, only to Medicare patients. The Reagan administration, unlike the Carter administration, hesitated to tell private health insurers and the quasi-public Blue Cross plans what to do.[56]

The Reagan administration also pushed proposals that reflected what might be called the neoconservative beliefs of Ronald Reagan and his advisors. A good example was the encouragement of vouchers, set just below Medicare per capita cost, which would allow elderly people to opt out of the traditional Medicare system and instead use their voucher to purchase private medical care.[57] These sorts of proposals, unlike the administration's hospital cost cutting measures, faced a difficult reception in Congress that made their passage unlikely.

Robert Rubin, a former chief of nephrology at Tufts and now the Assistant Secretary for Planning and Evaluation in HHS, directed much of the staff work that went into the Reagan health proposals. He had met Schweiker while detailed to the Senate's Human Resources Committee in 1977 and 1978 as a Robert Wood Johnson health policy fellow. He returned to Tufts after that year but continued to consult with the committee, and he remained in touch with Schweiker. He was not political in the conventional sense—he had been a registered Democrat in Massachusetts—but he had the sort of decisive personality, deference to his superiors, and practical skills at meeting deadlines that worked well in Washington. His relationship with Schweiker, who had a deep interest in Medicare, boosted his influence within the department.

Looking back on his experience in government, Rubin noted that "we couldn't stand the growth of Medicare and we needed to do something about Social Security." Rubin also understood the ideological direction in which the Reagan administration wanted to drive policy. He said the administration favored "pro competitive things that fostered the free market." Looked at another way, the Reagan administration wanted to make health providers "conscious of the economic consequences of their decisions," something that Medicare, with its accommodating attitude toward doctors and hospitals, emphatically failed to do. Hospital stays, for example, might be shorter without creating adverse effects. Not all of the procedures and tests that patients received were cost effective or even necessary.[58]

Hospitals reacted most sharply to the things in Reagan's proposals that were most like Carter's proposals and in particular to the idea of a

2 percent across-the-board cut in Medicare payments to hospitals. They argued that this sort of regulatory measure would not reduce health care expenditures but rather shift them from the public to the private sector. "When the government refuses to pay its full share, everyone else must pay more," said Philip Briggs, a Metropolitan Life Insurance executive speaking on behalf of the Health Insurance Association of America, which represented the interests of large health insurers. His well-heeled organization launched a $2 million advertising campaign designed to publicize the problem of cost shifting, and that was only the opening salvo in what promised to be a difficult legislative session.[59]

As in the Carter years, health care providers were under pressure to control costs or, as Secretary Schweiker put it, face "cost containment by government fiat." Representative Dan Rostenkowski, the Chicago congressman who now chaired the Ways and Means Committee, added, "I don't like mandatory cost controls. But unless you can find a way yourselves, you will suffer arbitrary regulations from Washington." The facts of medical cost inflation remained obvious. Federal health care expenditures were growing even faster than defense expenditures, rising at a rate of 19 percent in 1982. They threatened to swallow all available funds and crowd out other domestic expenditures.[60]

The need for a constructive alternative led to a change in attitude on the part of hospitals and other health care providers. Some people in the industry began to argue that, if regulation were inevitable even in an administration with a professed love of the free market, then it should be done the right way. Rather than the federal government paying the bills it received from hospitals and doctors, it might be better to convert to what people were calling "prospective reimbursement." The details of such an arrangement remained vague, but the essence of the idea was that the government should set reimbursement rates in advance. One way to think of the notion was to compare two methods of reimbursing employees for travel expenses. One way was to pay all of the traveler's bills; that meant the traveler might stay in a fancy hotel, eat deluxe meals, and use the minibar (or in the pre–cell phone days the telephone). Another way was to give travelers a per diem and allow them to pocket the difference between their expenditures and their allowance. Under such a system, the frugal traveler might come out a little ahead and still save the company money. In the language of the times, the new idea might change the incentives in the health care system.[61]

In March 1982 word leaked to the press that work proceeded within

HHS on a prospective payment plan. The *New York Times* said that the system would apply to Medicare patients and "end . . . the practice of paying hospitals for whatever services they rendered and would require them to accept a single overall payment for Medicare expenses, payable in advance."[62] It was one of those policy proposals that was simple in concept but that might prove difficult to implement in a health care system with so many different types of hospitals in so many different areas of the country. Was Medicare a one-size-fits-all program, or should different payments be made for different illnesses or health conditions? Should hospitals receive the same amount for treating someone with hemorrhoids as it did for open heart surgery? Should short hospital stays receive the same reimbursement as longer hospital stays for the same diagnosis? What if a person came to the hospital with one problem but developed another one during his hospital stay? Willis Goldbeck of the Washington Business Group on Health, which represented two hundred major corporations that provided health insurance for some fifty-five million people, said that health services could simply not be treated like other commodities.[63]

Robert Rubin was in a feisty mood. He said that the health care industry was betting "that if we cannot get competition, we're going to do nothing. They are making an error. If we have to choose between regulating or deficit financing, we are going to go to regulation." The American Hospital Association appeared to get the message. Its support of a prospective payment system represented a sharp break with the association's previous position on Medicare reimbursement. "It has never happened before," said Michael Bromberg, Director of the Federation of American hospitals. Indeed, the federation had been a major opponent of President Carter's hospital cost control legislation.[64]

It took little imagination to see that both Medicare and Social Security posed huge political problems for the Reagan administration. The President had gotten nowhere with his earlier Social Security proposals, such as lowering the benefits that early retirees received and tightening the disability insurance program. His Medicare proposals, particularly those that increased the out-of-pocket cost of the program for its elderly beneficiaries, were similarly vulnerable. The Democrats, with no management responsibilities of their own, felt free to attack the administration on both programs. Still in control of the House if not the Senate, Democrats reflexively defended the Medicare program and resisted efforts to raise out-of-pocket costs. They highlighted the fact that the administration wanted to change popular programs in substantive ways. Henry Waxman, who had retained his chairmanship of the Commerce and Energy Committee's Health Subcommittee, said he did not "believe members of Congress who are facing elections this year will be willing to turn their backs on Medicare patients and further burden state governments for the cost of the Medicaid program." House Speaker Thomas P. O'Neill (D-MA), who held Jack Kennedy's old congressional seat in the Boston area, referred to the "cruel and unwarranted Republican attack on the Medicare program." "I am determined," he said, "that America's senior citizens be protected" from such disasters as having to pay $534 for a two week hospital stay."[65]

With this background of partisan conflict, Congress set about making changes in Medicare that would meet predetermined budget targets as defined by the budget reconciliation procedure that Congress now used to conduct much of its business.[66] It did so knowing that any cuts in Medicare would be unpopular. Nonetheless, In June 1982 the Republican-controlled Senate Committee on Finance voted to cut some $15.2 billion from Medicare over the next three years. The proposed changes included increases in the Part B premium that beneficiaries paid for doctor's visits and an increase in the Part B deductible from sixty to eighty dollars. Senator Moynihan, the acerbic Democratic Senator from New York, said that "we are being very casual with the lives of very sick people." Senator Robert Dole (R-KS) replied, "We are not being casual. We are being very sensitive." The American Association of Retired Persons (AARP) felt that more sensitivity was required and lobbied against cuts that would increase the out-of-pocket costs of beneficiaries.[67]

If Senator Moynihan and the AARP worried about Medicare beneficiaries, other politicians grew concerned over the reactions of the hospital and other medical interest groups. Cuts in hospital reimbursement rates elicited strong reactions from the Federation of American Hospitals, and the American Hospital Association vowed to fight the cuts in the House Ways and Means Committee. Interest increased in a prospective payment system that the federation offered as an alternative that might solve the problem of painful budget cuts in the future.[68]

The Democrats on the Ways and Means Committee decided not to offer a plan of their own, putting the burden on the Republicans. In July 1982 Willis Gradison, an Ohio Republican who would later head the Health Insurance Association of America, took the lead in the committee's efforts to make $11.5 billion in cuts. The committee came up with a rule that required hospitals whose costs rose faster than the national average to receive less than the "full" compensation for their services. The committee hoped to save some $5 billion over three years and reward the hospitals that kept their costs below the average.[69]

By the middle of August 1982, conferees from the House and the Senate were close to agreeing on a measure that would make some $12.5 billion in cuts over three years in Medicare, Medicaid, and welfare programs. More than half of the money came from Medicare, such as what the *Washington Post*'s Spencer Rich described as a "limit of 9 to 10 percent on how much average payments to a hospital per Medicare patient could rise from year to year."[70]

The Tax Equity and Fiscal Responsibility Act of 1982 (TEFRA), signed by the President in September 1982, contained a provision that limited the per-case rate of increase in hospital revenue for three years beginning September 30, 1982. And the change related to hospital reimbursement rates was just one of at least twenty-eight major changes in the Medicare program contained in the legislation and the accompanying Omnibus Budget Reconciliation Act of 1982.[71]

Diagnosis-Related Groups and the Rise of Regulation

The hospital industry could not have viewed the legislation as anything other than stringent, but it contained an implicit escape clause. Congress directed the HHS Secretary, in consultation with the Ways and Means and Finance Committees, to develop proposals for new prospective payment plans. It set a tight deadline of December 31, 1982, for the department to report to the committees, which suggested that much of the work had already been done. It signaled a readiness on the part of Congress, and presumably many of the key interest groups that looked over its shoulder, to make major changes in the 1965 Medicare legislation. The problem of the inflation of hospital costs that had been a perpetual feature of the program and had so preoccupied President Carter and Secretary Schweiker appeared to be heading toward a legislative solution.

Reading the signals from Congress, the HHS Department wasted no time in getting down to work. Only a few days after the President signed TEFRA, Secretary Schweiker announced that he had made the first basic decisions on the prospective payment system. Schweiker's key decision was to compute different cost rates for different illnesses in place of a single blended rate. The fear that motivated the decision was that hospitals might respond to the single rate by taking as many easy cases as possible and avoiding more costly and possibly more urgent cases.[72] Schweiker then asked Carolyne Davis, who headed the Health Care Financing Administration (HCFA), to refine the proposal and come up with appropriate legislative language.[73]

Carolyne Davis, like Robert Rubin, played a key role in health policy during the Reagan administration.[74] From an early age and early experiences caring for an ailing grandfather, Davis felt drawn to the field of nursing. That led her to follow her undergraduate education at Dickinson College with training at Johns Hopkins to become a registered nurse. She eventually became interested in medical and educational administration and became the Dean of the School of Nursing at the University of Michigan. Her work there drew her into lobbying the federal government on behalf of the university and its medical school. She established a connection with Congressman David Stockman (R-MI), who would later head President Reagan's Office of Management and Budget. Stockman persuaded her to testify against the Carter hospital cost containment bill, which she agreed to do because, as she put it, "I was dreadfully against heavy-handed regulation." As a partial reward for her efforts and in recognition of her administrative competence, Richard Schweiker decided to make Davis his HCFA Administrator. He advised Davis to sit down with the congressmen and brief them on the prospective payment plan.

As the process of creating federal prospective payment legislation intensified, Schweiker signed new regulations, an easier way for him to make policy than going through the legislative process. They provided guidelines for states that sought waivers from the traditional Medicare system in favor of some sort of prospective payment system. States had the option of including Medicaid in their plans, and in some states "all payer" systems operated that also covered hospital payments from private insurers. By the fall of 1982, prospective payment experiments were running in more than a dozen states. Among the states with recently approved plans were New York and Massachusetts, with half a dozen states expected to follow.

In encouraging states to assume their traditional roles as laboratories of reform, Schweiker continued to stress that the Medicare program was badly out of fiscal control. He predicted that hospital costs if unchecked would rise at three times the inflation rate in 1982. Schweiker suspected, as did many Medicare critics, that the system encouraged unnecessary tests in part because health insurance shielded both doctors and patients from the costs of those tests. Advance payment would discourage such excesses in which hospitals were paid "whatever they spent" and encourage thrift. Schweiker touted the "positive incentive to control costs" because the prospective payment system would create "a reward for efficient delivery of care."[75]

Disagreements continued over the question of method. Here was an area of policy in which the design of legislation really mattered. Schweiker based his plan for state waivers on 467 standard diagnoses in 23 major disease categories. He claimed that the system was the product of previous research paid for by the federal government and carried out in such places as the Yale University medical school. There remained the vexing matters of putting a price tag on each of the 467 diagnoses and of incorporating capital costs, such as hospital construction to serve Medicare patients, into the formula. Neither the American Hospital Association nor the Federation of American Hospitals was entirely sold on using the 467 standard diagnoses. Alex McMahon of the American Hospital Association said that basing payments on diagnostic groups is "exactly the wrong way to go." Michael Bromberg of the Federation of American Hospitals wondered if the federal government had the "correct data" on hospital costs.[76]

Democrats in Congress also had their reservations about Schweiker's emerging proposal. Henry Waxman's Health Subcommittee considered the matter in November 1982 hearings. Alice Rivlin, the Director of the Congressional Budget Office, raised the matter of hospitals shifting costs from Medicare to Blue Cross or commercial insurance. Waxman feared that a stringent system of hospital cost reimbursement under Medicare would lead to a "two track system of health care, one for the elderly and poor; one for the rest of the nation." Such an outcome was contrary to Medicare's original purpose of providing access to "mainstream" health care. Representative Ronald Wyden (D-OR) worried that the new system would encourage hospitals to turn away sicker and poorer patients.[77]

Schweiker filled in many of the details of his plan at the end of 1982. In pushing the notion of prospective payment, Schweiker used examples of wide variances in the cost of the same procedure. Treatment of a heart attack could cost $1,500 in one hospital and $9,000 in another with, Schweiker claimed, no difference in quality. One major advantage of the Schweiker approach was that it preserved all of Medicare's benefits, so that beneficiaries would receive the same services. All of the adjustments would have to be made by the hospitals.[78]

Schweiker admitted that he still did not have a detailed bill, and Robert Rubin added that the White House had not agreed to all the details. Nonetheless, they hoped that a bill would be ready in time for the new session of Congress that would begin in January 1983. Despite the partisan reservations expressed in the November hearings, the politics still looked favorable. Democrats could point to the preservation of Medicare benefits, and groups like the Federation of American Hospitals indicated that their support was "very likely" for the simple reason that, in Michael Bromberg's words, "We think the present system is terrible." The administration could also argue that limiting the measure to Medicare patients was preferable to previous proposals because, as Robert Rubin put it, "It does not interfere with the private sector," such as the private health insurance plans that companies offered to their workers. That lucrative market would remain the private domain of private insurance companies.[79]

The administration's cost-cutting proposal for a prospective payment system made key concessions to the complexity and wide scope of the American health care system. These concessions made it harder for even health policy veterans, let alone average American citizens, to follow the details of the proposal. Among the types of costs that the new system would not cover, for example, were capital costs for construction and equipment, the direct costs of medical education such as the salaries of interns and residents, and the costs of outpatient care. The program would continue to pay such costs in the traditional way. Certain specialized hospitals would also not be subject to the new system, including pediatric hospitals, on the theory that treating a child with a particular diagnosis was a different matter than treating an elderly adult, and psychiatric hospitals, which typically had long rates of stay.[80]

By congressional standards, Congress took up the prospective payment system quickly and did not subject it to the long delays that often characterized health care legislation. Serendipity intervened, as it often did in free-floating legislative discussions. The fact that policy makers discussed time-sensitive changes in the Social Security program at the same time that they considered the Medicare prospective payment system opened an unexpected window in the legislative process. The Social Security legislation addressed an immediate problem. Without some sort of intervention, Social Security would not be able to meet its obligations by July. That situation ensured the passage of a Social Security law developed in early 1983 that enjoyed bipartisan support.[81] The Social Security bill fell into the same category as increases in the debt ceiling (not yet a catalyst for government shutdowns) and other must-pass legislation and invited the same sort of legislative response. Congressmen tried to add features to it as a means of sweeping otherwise controversial proposals through Congress.

In a stroke of good fortune, the administration managed to put the provisions for prospective payment in Medicare into the Social Security "rescue" bill. That almost guaranteed its successful passage through Congress. "At first," said Robert Rubin, "we thought we'd have a much more leisurely pace" to introduce the prospective payment legislation. Then, after the two sides struck a Social Security deal, it became clear that the rescue legislation would become the legislative vehicle for the prospective payment system. Since the Social Security bill was bipartisan and tamper proof, it provided a means of protecting the prospective payment proposal and speeding its legislative passage. Rubin explained that the measure was veto proof and had the blessings of the Speaker and the President. "The skids were really greased on this baby," he said.[82]

The Ways and Means Subcommittee on Health, now chaired by Representative Andy Jacobs (D-IN), considered the Medicare parts of the Social Security rescue legislation. On February 24, the subcommittee gave unanimous approval to the measure by a voice vote. It nonetheless continued to make adjustments to the legislation as it heard from the various interest groups. For the most part, the Reagan administration proved agreeable to these changes because it very much wanted the passage of legislation that would solve some of Medicare's problems and take it off the table as an issue that the Democrats could use against the Republicans. It helped that the proposal came from the administration and could be presented as a bipartisan achievement in a difficult area of social policy.

Unlike the Social Security parts of the legislation, Congress felt free to alter the Medicare provisions (although not enough to jeopardize the whole bill). The Ways and Means Committee diluted the concept of one grand Medicare hospital reimbursement scheme for the entire nation. The committee set one rate for urban hospitals and another for rural hospitals. It added a phase-in period with only 50 percent of a hospital's reimbursement rate being based on the new system during the first year.

It also required that state waivers for hospital cost reimbursement be continued. The committee's bill also directed the Department of Health and Human Services to "make appropriate adjustments for hospitals that serve a disproportionately large number of low-income and Medicare beneficiaries." Presumably such hospitals could count less on payments from private insurance companies to make up any deficits in their operating costs. All in all, Michael Bromberg of the Federation of American Hospitals believed that the legislation marked "a historic change in the way hospitals are reimbursed."[83]

The implicit strategy involved taking sensitive political issues off the table and leaving them to be settled by means of automatic formulas, without the need for Congress to get its hands dirty in the matter. This strategy followed from one adopted in the Social Security program in 1972 that created an automatic formula for the cost of living increases that beneficiaries received each year. To be sure, arguments persisted over such things as how to measure increases in the cost of living for elderly citizens. Occasionally, too, something fell off the table that required congressional attention. The Social Security rescue legislation under consideration in 1983, for example, included a provision that delayed the annual cost of living adjustment for six months, in an effort to cope with the system's financial problems. For the most part, however, the annual cost of living arrangements happened every year without any action required of Congress. Policy makers hoped that the new prospective payment system would function in a similar manner and adjust payments to hospitals without creating the sort of political uproar that accompanied President Carter's efforts at hospital cost containment.

The administration's hospital cost provisions moved smoothly through Congress, even though Richard Schweiker, who was the main champion of prospective payment in the administration, announced in late January that he would leave his post. Schweiker made an appearance before the full Ways and Means Committee in early February in which he gave the new system his blessing and explained how it would work. He stressed that that the committee had before it a measure that would deal with rising hospital costs and maintain quality. The main mechanism was to relate payment to output, putting payment on a per-discharge basis using what policy makers were now calling diagnosis-related groups (or DRGs, as nearly everyone referred to them). Schweiker hoped that there would be similar payments for similar services in a particular geographic area and that there would be provisions to provide extra compensation for medically justified "extraordinary lengths of hospital stays." In other words, so-called tertiary care hospitals, such as Johns Hopkins in Baltimore, saw Medicare patients whose cases were more complicated than those with the same diagnosis in, say, a county general hospital. Perhaps there needed to be special provisions for such "outliers." In this respect and others Schweiker tried to keep the heterogeneous nature of the hospital system in mind. The system would apply mainly to the short-term general hospitals rather than, say, psychiatric hospitals. Hospitals that were the only providers in their communities also received special consideration.[84]

The legislative process continued to move quickly. The Ways and Means Committee's Social Security Subcommittee marked up its portion of the rescue bill on February 22 and sent it along to the full committee. The full committee marked up the provisions submitted by its subcommittees on March 1 and 2. It further refined the Medicare recommendations so that, for example, separate DRG rates would be established for nine census divisions and the phase-in period would be extended to four years. The committee also determined that at least 4 percent of the Medicare cases would be treated as atypical outliers. The House managed to pass its version of the bill by March 9.[85]

That same day the Senate Finance Committee began marking up the bill. It tackled the prospective payment provisions on March 10.[86] Although it tinkered with some of the provisions, it did not change them substantially. In place of the nine census divisions that the House preferred, the Senate suggested four regions. It mandated that the secretary would be required to adjust the DRG payment rate at least every five years. By March 16 the latest version of the Social Security rescue bill, complete with the Medicare provisions, reached the Senate floor and that body passed the legislation a week later. The differences between the House and Senate versions were relatively minor, such as whether the prospective payment system should be phased in over three or four years.

A conference committee convened promptly, and the measure cleared both houses of Congress on March 25. In the House the bill passed by a two-to-one majority, and in the Senate the margin was five to one. On April 20, 1983, President Reagan signed the measure into law in a grand ceremony outside the White House on an unseasonably cold day.

The Medicare provisions of the law that President Reagan signed made careful distinctions among the many hospitals that did business with the program. Some hospitals, because of their isolated location or the severity of their climates, received special treatment as sole community providers. Public hospitals, hospitals serving a disproportionate number of Medicaid patients, hospitals that were national or regional referral centers, hospitals in Alaska and Hawaii, and, in an odd bow to other public health measures, hospitals extensively involved in cancer research all became exceptions to the general rule. The law also recognized as "outliers" the cases that exceeded the mean length of stay and made provisions for them. The law also called for a host of studies, demonstrations, and reports that indicated there were still many unresolved problems in the Medicare program. The Congress asked the Secretary of HHS to report on how capital-related costs could be incorporated into the prospective payment system and how the program should deal with skilled nursing facilities that received Medicare patients discharged from the hospital. The law also contained provisions intended to establish the prospective payment system on a permanent basis. For example, the law created the Prospective Payment Assessment Commission, composed of independent experts, to make recommendations to the Secretary on the proper hospital reimbursement rates for 1986 and beyond.[87]

Many things got set aside, but the urgency of the problem and the bipartisan consensus on legislation that had been approved by the Speaker of the House and the President accounted for the quick congressional action on a major piece of social legislation. The bill marked the resolution of policy disputes in Social Security and Medicare that had been brewing since the Ford administration. Both the Social Security and the Medicare provisions acted as cost-saving reform measures without at the same time disturbing the basic structure of either Social Security or Medicare benefits.[88]

Conclusion

Although the legislation's phase-in provisions absorbed some of the shock, the prospective payment system represented a new way of doing business in the Medicare program, one that, if it were rigorously applied, might reduce the rate of growth in hospital cost reimbursements. The 1983 legislation differed in content and tone from the original 1965 legislation. Medicare shifted its identity from an accommodating partner of doctors, hospitals, and nursing homes in serving the elderly to a vigilant purchaser of health services that looked to make the best deal with health care providers. In other words, the program took a decisive regulatory turn and realized some of the worst fears of national health insurance opponents such as the American Medical Association. As in 1965, the hospital industry accepted the necessity of making some accommodation to the government in order to forestall more draconian legislation. Many believed that the DRGs were the best deal the hospitals could get.[89]

The entire exercise depended on the way Congress dealt with health legislation. The Finance Committee and the Ways and Means Committee handled both Social Security and Part A of Medicare. That followed from the 1935 decision to label Social Security as tax legislation and put it under the jurisdiction of the congressional tax committees. It also was a direct result of creating two separate Medicare programs: one for hospitals and the other doctors, each with its own trust fund. The arrangement led to jurisdictional battles between the Commerce Committee, with its historical interest in health legislation, and the Ways and Means Committee. The Commerce Committee eventually obtained substantial control over Medicaid, which did not depend on payroll taxes, and Part B of Medicare, which relied on user fees and a trust fund that could be replenished from general revenues. As a result the Social Security rescue legislation of 1983, which put a premium on quick passage and dispensed with many congressional formalities, such as lengthy hearings, applied to Part A of Medicare rather than to Medicaid and Part B.

The 1983 legislation began a regulatory regime for Medicare that could easily, or at least conceivably, be extended to other parts of Medicare, such as payments to doctors or nursing homes or home health providers. In this era when Congress no longer had the luxury of adding costly programs to America's social welfare arsenal, Congress turned instead to automatic formulas, often reliant on statistical projections of the economy's future growth, to predict and control the future growth of entitlement programs. In 1983 one could have envisioned a Medicare program that operated on automatic pilot with only an occasional glance from Congress.

At the same time, the 1983 legislation established a system that eventually enabled Congress to extract large savings from the Medicare program. According to a senior congressional analyst, congressional leaders came to regard the Prospective Payment System (PPS) as a means of reducing fiscal deficits that would be so troubling for the rest of the century and also increasing spending for other programs such as Medicaid. "Oh God," said congressional staffer Lisa Potetz, "we had those huge deficits. . . . And conveniently we now had a system in place, the PPS, that had a lot of levers you could pull in order to generate a tremendous amount of savings." One such lever was the update factor, which changed hospital reimbursement from Medicare for DRGs from year to year and could be "tweaked" according to the fiscal needs of any given year. In this regard and others, the 1983 legislation initiated a new era in Medicare policy.[90]

After 1983 Medicare policy took a different turn that facilitated a new round of expansion. This expansion followed a different policy format than had the 1965 law or the 1972 additions to Medicare. The next chapter considers these developments.

CHAPTER FIVE

The Continuing Consequences of Medicare

Choice and Prescription Drugs

Although the 1983 legislation was important to Medicare, it marked only the beginning of a tide of Medicare reform that crested around the turn of the century. The period after 1995 became very significant in the program's history, with Republicans gaining control of the House of Representatives for the first time since 1953. The Republicans sought to recast social policy in their image. In place of the Great Society's push for equity and inclusion and its emphasis on the federal government as a prime investor in the nation's health and welfare, the Republicans, who ran under the banner of the Contract with America, wanted something different. They proposed that social welfare programs be modernized so as to reflect important developments in the private sector and to support their major policy goals: a balanced federal budget and a tax cut.[1] Medicare legislation in 1997 and 2003 illustrated the new Republican influence on social welfare policy.

As a general proposition, Republicans of the Newt Gingrich era offered a critique of social welfare programs that highlighted their anachronistic practices. Social Security, for example, remained an entitlement that in the policy jargon promised to pay a "defined benefit" to the nation's elders and people with disabilities. Many private employers no longer offered such a benefit to their retirees. Instead, they made "defined contributions" to retirement funds that workers could manage themselves, thus reducing the employer's future liability and promoting job mobility in a newly fluid economy. The implication was that public Social Security should look more like private pensions and offer people more freedom to build their nest eggs and keep the federal budget free of catastrophic future commitments.[2] The Republicans felt even more strongly about welfare programs such as Aid to Families with Dependent Children (considered in chapter 7). With the mass entrance of young mothers into the labor force, it seemed hypocritical to have most mothers working outside the home while offering welfare recipients money that allowed them to stay home with their young children.[3]

This chapter provides a narrative history of the 1997 legislation, which offered consumers choices among Medicare plans, and the 2003 legislation, which created a prescription drug program for Medicare beneficiaries. It argues that these changes, created in the shadow of Newt Gingrich's victory in the 1994 congressional elections, represented a conservative approach to the program's expansion and hence a decisive break with Medicare policies between 1965 and 1972. The previous chapter emphasized the importance of the 1983 reforms as a turn away from accommodation toward regulation. This chapter shows that Republicans became more ambitious in the 1990s and the early twenty-first century and promulgated reforms that went beyond regulating the program in the interest of cost containment to embrace proposals such as prescription drug coverage once thought to be the domain of liberals. Where the early Medicare reforms simply inserted new groups—people with disabilities, people with end stage renal disease—into the existing program, the Republican initiatives required that new parts be added to the 1965 policy apparatus.

Newt Gingrich and Bill Clinton Debate Medicare's Future, 1995

On the one hand, the late twentieth-century debate over social welfare policy involved philosophical principles. On the other hand, it became a contest of political will played by two consummate masters. The competition highlighted Medicare because of the program's prominence in the federal budget and because historical contingencies just happened to move Medicare to the center of the political stage at the time of the contest.

Led by Newt Gingrich (R-GA), the author of the Contract with America who became Speaker of the House in 1995, the Republicans knew that their legislative agenda needed to include the Medicare program if for no other reason than its prominence in the federal budget. Speaker Gingrich believed that Medicare required "systemic" changes if the federal debt were to stop growing and a balanced budget to be achieved. He called Medicare "a large, clunky inefficient government system." "Clunky, centrally designed bureaucratic systems don't work very well; market driven systems work better," he said. Gingrich took pains to point out that he did not want to abolish Medicare. Instead, he wanted to bring it up to date and give every senior citizen "greater choice of better health care at lower cost."[4] If nothing else, Gingrich's pronouncements made it clear that President Clinton's national health insurance plan, which he had pushed in the period preceding the 1994 elections, was off the table, and people could expect something different.[5]

It was, however, a tricky proposition. Medicare was a large program with many followers who were wary of program changes. Democrats who had little to lose could argue that Gingrich wanted to end Medicare as we know it and, in the process, "get rid of Medicare," as Democratic House leader Richard Gephardt of Missouri put it. No, insisted Representative John Kasich (R-OH), the Republicans simply wanted systemic changes that would improve the program. Speaker Gingrich promised "to rethink Medicare from the ground up." He vowed to work with senior citizens to produce a better Medicare system that "actually works more effectively, that gives them greater choices."[6]

In the background of the Medicare discussion was the fact that Medicare Part A's hospital trust fund was, in the words of Spencer Rich, the *Washington Post*'s veteran social welfare reporter, "hemorrhaging even faster than expected." The trust fund ended fiscal year 1995 with $4.7 billion less in its coffers than experts had predicted. It did not bode well for a program preparing to meet the ballooning costs of the retirement of the baby boom generation in fifteen years. No one wanted to go into this precarious period with the program already in a shaky financial position.[7]

The Medicare program's precarious condition contrasted with the apparently robust shape of private health insurance and suggested that the public program might incorporate mechanisms such as "managed care" that increasingly characterized the private sector.[8] At the same time that the public sector was announcing it "will be able to pay [Part A Medicare benefits, financed with a trust fund] benefits for only about seven years and is severely out of balance in the long-range," word came that the medical costs paid by employers fell for the first time in a decade: increases in the price of health insurance were lower than the rate of inflation.[9] Perhaps Medicare recipients should also be able to benefit from "managed care" and be offered a wider choice of health care plans rather than the rigid "single payer" system that prevailed.[10]

Choice sounded like something positive. It stood in contrast to other suggestions for reducing Medicare costs. One could, for example, increase the age of eligibility from the current sixty-five to sixty-seven, the new official Social Security retirement age for younger workers by virtue of changes made in the 1983 amendments. That was a crude benefit cut that would be felt by the beneficiaries. One could also increase the out-of-pocket charges for Medicare, such as the monthly premium that beneficiaries paid for Part B. Representative Bill Thomas (R-CA), the new Chairman of the Ways and Means Health Subcommittee, believed that the premium, which covered less than 30 percent of the actual costs of the program (with the rest funded from general revenues), raised fundamental questions of equity. He asked whether taxpayers "who now fund more than three-quarters of the costs of Medicare Part B benefits [should] subsidize other Americans who can well afford to pay more of the tab for their own care." Thomas conceded, however, that "there's going to be some political expense of making this change."[11]

President Bill Clinton charged that the government had a moral responsibility to protect Medicare.[12] He suggested that the real Republican motivation for Medicare changes such as those proposed by Representative Thomas was to generate savings to finance tax cuts for the rich. Not so, countered Newt Gingrich. Less expensive health cost options and increased attention to fraud and waste would make it possible to cut Medicare spending significantly for the next seven years.[13]

The Republican balanced budget plan passed by the Senate on May 25 proposed $288 billion in Medicare savings and $187 billion in Medicaid savings. The exact ways to realize these savings were not fully spelled out in either the House or the Senate budget bills, but one proposal was to eliminate the Medicaid program in its present form by offering a federal block grant and turning over responsibility for running the program to the states. If that plan were followed, it would mean that Medicaid would no longer be an entitlement program with many of the benefits specified by the federal government and become instead a state program with limited federal assistance. For both Medicare and Medicaid, it appeared that the Contract with America, particularly as interpreted by the Democrats, meant major changes, not just the beneficial cost saving measures that Gingrich had suggested.[14]

The interest groups watched the sparring between Clinton and Gingrich with more than casual interest. As always, the groups representing the interests of hospitals and elderly health beneficiaries were quick to notice that the Gingrich plan could induce major changes. The American Hospital Association took the line that Medicare and Medicaid cuts could mean that community hospitals would have to reduce their services or even close their doors. The hospitals made no effort to disguise the fact that federal reimbursements drove the financial health of hospitals—a good example of the prominence of the public sector in the private medical system. Tom Scully, the President of the Federation of American Hospitals who had worked closely with President George H. W. Bush on his health care proposals and would be instrumental in shaping health policy for Bush's son, said, "It was almost impossible to find a serious health care or budget analyst who thinks this level of cuts is justified by rational health policy."[15]

The Republicans in the House tried to shift the terms of the discussion. The hospital groups wanted "to defeat the balanced budget" and opposed the effort to save Medicare from bankruptcy. In the summer of 1995 Republicans on the Senate Finance Committee chastised the President for walking away from Medicare's financial problems. They argued that the program's costs needed to be controlled or the program would go bust and leave the beneficiaries stranded. This rhetoric might be called the Republican doomsday scenario. Democrats responded with their own doomsday scenario. They charged that the Contract with America sacrificed the interests of Medicare beneficiaries in favor of the political goals of a balanced budget and tax cuts. Both sides realized that the stakes were high. "If we solve Medicare, I think we will govern for a generation," boasted Speaker Gingrich.[16]

The Republicans insisted that anyone who wanted to remain in the traditional Medicare program could do so, implying that Parts A and B would remain in place. They hoped, though, to create attractive and cheaper alternatives. They suggested, for example, providing beneficiaries with a voucher with which they could purchase their own medical care. If they chose a PPO (preferred provider organization) or some other form of managed care, the government's financial liability would be limited to the amount of money in the voucher. In other words, Medicare would become a defined contribution rather than a defined benefit program, in the same way that conservatives hoped to change Social Security so that it looked more like a private pension. Meanwhile, health care providers would strive to deliver care at a cheaper price, forcing them to be more efficient. Medicare beneficiaries would reap the benefits of marketplace competition, just as airplane passengers did.[17]

As this discussion took place on Capitol Hill, the White House, and the K Street offices of private lobbyists, Medicare celebrated its thirtieth anniversary in the summer of 1995. The celebration had a muted tone in contrast to Social Security's thirty-year anniversary in 1965, and it had a hard political edge. In 1965 the triumphant passage of Medicare had taken place. The summer of 1995 brought concerns that Medicare would go bankrupt and leave the baby boomers, who had faithfully been paying into the program throughout their working lives, high and dry. In 1965 a Democrat sat in the White House and a large Democratic majority ruled in Congress. In 1995, the Democrats held on to the White House but had lost their congressional majority. President Clinton had proposed a bold health insurance plan. Now, only a few months later, he and the Democrats were playing defense, defending the status quo and protecting Medicare from change. Senior citizens, said James McCrery (R-LA), deserved the same health care choices as other Americans. "Vouchers," countered HHS Secretary Donna Shalala, "are a cruel birthday present on the 30th anniversary of Medicare."[18]

Both sides took their case to the public. In radio advertisements the Democrats charged that the Republicans wanted to cut Medicare. Preserving the benefits, as the Democrats wished to do, was "moral, good and right by our elderly." Republicans countered with advertisements in strategic congressional districts, such as Richard Gephardt's St. Louis district, that accused politicians like Gephardt of "ignoring Medicare's looming bankruptcy." Haley Barbour, the Republican National Committee Chairman, said that people understood that Medicare was in trouble and in need of a major overhaul. The Democratic National Committee responded that people realized that the Republicans wanted to make "extreme cuts in Medicare."[19]

The era of Newt Gingrich had begun like a juggernaut, and the Democrats tried to slow the process down.[20] They hoped to build up their case that the Republican proposals represented a fatal assault on the popular Medicare program. "We are going to do everything we can to slow the process down," said Minority Leader Gephardt, "so that the American people have a chance to know what's happening." His colleague John Dingell (D-MI), the veteran Chairman of the Commerce and Energy Committee, introduced a resolution demanding that there be at least four weeks of hearings on the Republican Medicare proposals. He hoped to return to the deliberate and resolute policy-making style that had characterized Medicare in its early years.[21] Delay nearly always favored the status quo.

Shutting Down the Federal Government in Part Over Medicare

So that there was no mistake about the Democrats' intentions, President Clinton said he would veto legislation that contained the Republicans' Medicare and Medicaid proposals. If enacted, they would have what the President called "Draconian consequences" and would completely "dismantle" Medicare. The congressional Democrats applauded the President's rhetoric and hoped that the veto threat would energize their natural allies, such as organized labor and the AARP. Dick Armey (R-TX), the House Majority Leader, responded in kind. He called the Democrats' approach to Medicare "craven," because they preferred to let the program go bankrupt in return for "short-term political gain." Armey said that the tactics would not succeed because "public tolerance for demagoguery is at an all time low."[22] "We want a solution to preserve and protect Medicare," the Speaker proclaimed. He called the vote to reform Medicare "the most decisive vote on the direction of government since 1933."[23]

On October 19 the House passed legislation, along largely partisan lines, that contained the Republican Medicare proposals. First, the measure emphasized choice with the creation of something called MedicarePlus. Recipients would have the choice of remaining in the traditional Medicare program or joining MedicarePlus, which meant choosing an HMO, PPO, or some other private health plan (with the proviso that the benefits in the private health plan equaled or bettered the benefits in Medicare). MedicarePlus plans combined Medicare Part A and Part B in one. Second, the Republican measure introduced the concept of Medical Savings Accounts into Medicare.[24] Third, the Republican legislation called for increases in the Medicare Part B monthly premium from $53.50 in 1996 to $87.60 in 2001, with higher premiums for the wealthy—a new form of means testing in Medicare. Combined with various provisions to limit reimbursements for health care providers, the Republican measure promised $270 billion in Medicare savings over seven years.[25]

The Medicare legislation became part of the budget reconciliation process and therefore part of a massive budget bill. The Senate passed its version of this bill on October 28, with Majority Leader and presumptive presidential candidate Robert Dole touting it as "a vote for America's future." The Senate made some changes to the House bill but left most of the Medicare provisions intact. Perhaps the most important Senate changes came in Medicaid. The Senate preserved the state-run program as a federal entitlement.[26]

President Clinton wasted no time in reaffirming his intention to veto the bill. "There is nothing for us to talk about," he said. "I am not prepared to discuss the destruction of Medicare and Medicaid." Refusing to back down, Gingrich warned the President "to think twice about vetoing the balanced budget and jeopardizing long-overdue revolutionary change." The apocalyptic rhetoric suggested it would be the Washington equivalent of a fight to the death. Clinton vowed not to let the Republicans put pressure on him by refusing to extend the federal debt limit unless he signed the bill. "I am not about to give in to that kind of blackmail," he said.[27]

Democrats sensed an opening. According to a *New York Times* / CBS poll, people, particularly the elderly, disapproved of the Republican Medicare plan by a sizable margin. That caused Gephardt to comment that the real debate was "about whether we will have Medicare at all." White House Press Secretary Michael McCurry added that the reason that the Republicans wanted to slow down the program's rate of growth was because "eventually they'd like to see the program just die and go away."[28]

The situation escalated over the course of the next month. On Monday, November 13, Congress considered a short-term spending bill. Failure to pass the bill would mean that the federal government could shut down the next day. Senator Dole lamented that Clinton was "going to shut down the entire federal government because he thinks it will be a little political gain for him and the senior citizens." It was a highly stylized version of the larger dispute, with Gingrich continuing to insist that Medicare was going bankrupt and a decrease in the Medicare Part B premium would only make it worse and Clinton continuing to defend the integrity of the program. He wanted to hold the line on Part B premiums, and the Republicans wanted to increase them so as to maintain the share of Medicare's costs for which the premium paid. That would mean an increase of about seven dollars a month beginning in January 1996 and larger increases in future years.[29]

The two sides met into the night on November 13 but came to no agreement. Clinton held firm and vetoed first a two-week extension of spending authority for the federal government and then, the next morning, a four-week extension of the spending authority. The timing of Clinton's vetoes meant that some 800,000 federal employees would be furloughed after reporting for work in the morning. Each side blamed the other for the federal government's imminent shutdown. Senator Tom Daschle (D-SD) said that "as long as Medicare is on the table, there is no deal." Representative Gingrich said that the President's objections centered on the fact that "we are committed to a balanced budget that controls spending instead of raising taxes, that we are committed to shrink the size of the Washington bureaucracy."[30]

Both sides appeared to think that they held the winning hand. The freshmen Republicans elected in 1994 believed that they had been sent to Washington to balance the federal budget in seven years no matter what obstacles the Democrats threw in their way. "Forget popularity," said Zach Wamp (R-TN). "This is a gut check for what we're doing here." Before Speaker Gingrich set off for the White House negotiating sessions on Monday evening, he received a vote of confidence from his Republican caucus. "Do what you think is right," said representative and future cabinet member Raymond LaHood (R-IL). "We're with you." Even LaHood conceded, however, "We're getting killed on Medicare."[31]

The dispute dragged on, with Clinton refusing to sign a temporary spending bill without resolving the budget issue and the Republicans holding out for what they believed were necessary spending cuts in the federal budget. The cuts affected more than Medicare. They also involved an array of environmental and education measures that the President wanted to preserve. There had been similar work stoppages before, but the federal government had never shut down for more than a day. This closure lasted for almost a week before Congress cobbled together legislation that allowed the government to reopen but still left open the possibility of another closure on December 15.

The shutdown became the main story. Federal employees who were designated essential continued to do things like deliver the mail, process Social Security checks, and maintain the military readiness of the

United States. That left another 800,000 employees and meant that federal parks and attractions like the Statue of Liberty and the Smithsonian Institution were closed and travelers had to do without passport services. These things were important because they put a human face on the activities of the federal government. Both President Clinton and Senator Dole made changes to their schedules to respond to the growing emergency. The President canceled a trip to Japan, and the Senator skipped a Republican presidential debate. Meanwhile the Speaker felt slighted by Clinton on a presidential trip to Israel for the funeral of Prime Minister Yitzhak Rabin. He claimed that Clinton refused to talk with him on the long flight when they should have been discussing the budget and that he suffered the indignity of having to exit the aircraft from the rear.[32] There were also more subtle clashes between Gingrich, the Republican hero of the hour, and Dole, the man who would have to carry the Republican banner in 1996. One passenger on the plane to Israel noted, for example, that Gingrich and Dole barely spoke to one another.[33]

The Government Closes Again

With the government back in business on November 19 but with the threat of another government shutdown on December 15, Clinton and Gingrich girded for another round of budget negotiations. Chief of staff Leon Panetta, a former Democratic congressman from California and Budget Committee head, led Clinton's team of negotiators, and the chairmen of the Budget Committees in the House and Senate—Representative John Kasich and Senator Pete Domenici (R-NM)—headed the Republican delegation. Speaker Gingrich and Majority Leader Dole kept a close eye on the proceedings.

Both sides tried to spin things their way. The Republicans thought it significant that the President had agreed to enact legislation that would balance the budget in seven years. The Democrats found reassurance in a CBS news poll that showed that more people blamed the shutdown of the government on the Republicans than on the President and that the public trusted the President more than the Congress on budget matters. Everyone realized that the matter was not settled. Representative Bill Richardson (D-NM) called the interim agreement that had reopened the government "a temporary cease-fire."[34]

The negotiations moved at a glacial pace that cast doubt on meeting the December 15 deadline. On Tuesday, December 5, President Clinton said that by the end of the week he would produce his proposal to erase the federal deficit in seven years. It would include detailed plans on how he proposed to cut $124 billion from Medicare over a seven-year period. The President appeared to accept many of the elements of the Republican plan, such as giving Medicare recipients more choices among the types of plans they could choose. That meant that Clinton stressed choice, just like the Republicans did. He objected only to the medical savings plans, which he said would undermine traditional Medicare. He also held firm on his desire to preserve the Medicaid program in its present form. Clinton claimed that his plan would keep the hospital trust fund solvent to 2011 and achieve $124 billion in savings "without undermining the structural integrity of program or imposing new costs on beneficiaries." The plan even included some expansions in the Medicare program, such as respite care for families taking care of Alzheimer's patients.[35]

On December 6 President Clinton vetoed the latest version of the Republican comprehensive budget plan. In a piece of political theater, Clinton ordered the Social Security Administration to find one of the pens that Johnson had used to sign Medicare in 1965, and Clinton then used the pen to sign his veto message. The Republicans were not impressed. They noticed that the pen had run out of ink during the signing ceremony and as Newt Gingrich's noted, "The President has to realize that Lyndon Johnson's Great Society has failed." The President countered that the Republican program was an attack on fundamental American values.[36]

On December 15 budget negotiations again collapsed, and another partial shutdown of the federal government began.[37] Medicare remained central to the dispute, both because of its large size and hence great importance in balancing the budget, which attracted the attention of Republicans, and because of its popularity, which made it an attractive program for Democrats to defend. The Republicans as the party proposing fundamental changes faced the more difficult task. They had somehow to convince people that cutting $270 billion from Medicare was compatible with their pledge to "preserve, protect and improve" the program. Clinton had the comparative luxury of endorsing the Republican ideas with political appeal, such as choice, and still arguing that he did not intend to change the program in any fundamental way. The poll numbers continued to lend encouragement to President Clinton. Fifty-four percent of the people polled by the *New York Times* and CBS said that they disapproved of the Republican plan to overhaul Medicare, and only 33 percent approved of it. More than half of the people in the poll believed that the real Republican motivation was not to save Medicare but rather to balance the budget and finance a tax cut.[38]

The debate underscored the fact that, whatever people felt about the health care system and however much they criticized its rising cost, they were reluctant to endorse change. They wanted to keep their doctor and to maintain their treatment regime. They wanted less managed care, not more, in their lives. Opponents of President Clinton's health care plan were able to exploit these feelings in 1993 and 1994. In 1995 President Clinton used those same feelings to gain a political advantage over the Republicans. The situation differed from previous disputes about Medicare. In 1983 the parties managed to hide fundamental change in the program's arcana and complexity. All people had to know was that the benefits would remain the same in a prospective payment system. In 1995 the politicians made the debate very visible to the public, triggering the public's protective feelings toward Medicare.[39]

The Election Year

The second federal stoppage lasted until January 6, 1996, and even then there was no resolution of the Medicare dispute. Much of the potential disruption was muted by the fact that the shutdown occurred over the Christmas holidays. The new agreement on January 6 permitted a three-week hiatus during which the federal government would remain open.[40] As it turned out, however, neither side wanted another federal shutdown and in effect agreed to a truce that would carry Medicare and the government itself through the 1996 election. The remarkable thing was that the stalemate did not continue indefinitely. Instead the two sides reached an agreement that led to important Medicare legislation in 1997.

Over the course of the dispute, the differences between the congressional Republicans and Clinton had narrowed. As matters stood at the beginning of 1996, both sides had a plan that they believed would balance the budget by 2002. The Republicans emphasized tax cuts and Medicare savings in their seven-year plan. The Democratic plan also had tax cuts and cuts in Medicare, but they were substantially lower than the Republicans wanted. Clinton insisted, "You can balance the budget and still provide adequate protection for Medicare, Medicaid, education and the environment and provide tax relief for working families." Both sides realized that they were entering an election year in which Republicans hoped to consolidate the gains they had made in 1994 and recapture the White House.[41]

The tendency in election years was to postpone controversial legislation, and 1996 was no exception. In this becalmed atmosphere, Medicare nonetheless remained in the news because of the problems with the Part A Hospital Insurance Trust Fund. As early as February 1996 it became clear that the trust fund had lost money in the previous fiscal year for the first time since 1972. The actuaries had expected the fund to increase by $4.7 billion in the 1995 fiscal year. Instead it fell by $35.7 million. The actuaries had expected that 1997, not 1995, would be the first year in which the trust fund would experience a shortfall, although it still had more than enough money to cover its current expenditures. The problem seemed to be arising two years early. "Things turned out a little worse than we expected," said Medicare actuary Richard Foster. Everyone realized that the gap between income and outlays would only grow in future years and eventually deplete the trust fund. Foster explained that "you can't continue very long with a situation in which the expenditures of the program are significantly greater than the income. We have enough assets to cover the shortfall in each of the next few years. But once the assets of the trust fund are depleted, there is no way to pay all the benefits." People now thought that the date of the total depletion of the fund might be the middle of 2001 rather than the end of 2002 as previously expected.[42]

The situation suggested that Congress and the administration needed to resume their negotiations and come to an agreement on Medicare and the budget. It also showed how the institutional structure of Medicare that had been developed in 1965 continued to influence Medicare politics. As usual, no one talked about the Medicare Part B trust fund. Instead, discussion centered on the hospital trust fund because of the way it was funded from payroll taxes rather than general revenues. If this fund went bankrupt, one either had to cut benefits or increase taxes or change the way Medicare Part A was administered to permit general revenues. Because this fund attracted so much attention, it became shorthand for the entire Medicare program rather than just its hospital components. If the Part A trust fund went bankrupt, that meant, as the Republicans stressed, that Medicare went bankrupt.[43]

The formal report of the trustees of the Medicare Part A trust fund did not appear until June, and as expected it predicted that the program would run out of money in 2001 and that the problems would cascade after that. By 2005 the trust fund deficit would exceed $400 billion dollars. As usual, the politicians in Washington cared more about the election of 1996 than they did about the hypothetical problems of 2005 and beyond. Republicans planned to blame Clinton for the impending problem because he had not agreed to their cost-saving Medicare proposals. The Democrats stressed that their opposition to the Republican cuts had preserved the Medicare program. Both sides continued to believe that they held the winning hand. Republicans could appeal to the young and tout their efforts to keep Medicare solvent for the baby boomers and their children. Democrats could count on the strong support of senior citizens and the hope that younger voters would recognize these seniors as their parents and grandparents.[44]

Although both sides tried to make the dispute as crisp and clear as possible, the discussion often went into the weeds. Because the bankruptcy of Medicare was an artificial problem created by the structure of the trust funds that supported the program, the problem could be "solved" by changing the structure. In particular, the Clinton administration proposed to save the Part A trust fund by shifting some of the fast-growing costs of home health care from the Part A to the Part B trust fund. Republicans attacked this proposal as an accounting trick or sheer gimmickry. Washington insiders realized, however, that home health care costs had little to do with hospitals and hence it was, as AARP Legislative Director John Rother said, "arbitrary where you put home health care." Health policy expert Stuart Altman described the situation in subtle terms. There was the Medicare trust fund crisis and the long-term health care financing problem. The Clinton maneuver handled the trust fund crisis by making the long-term problem a little worse. In an election year, patchwork rather than major renovation was the order of the day.[45]

As in the Reagan era, when Social Security was the issue, it seemed best to postpone serious discussion of Medicare until after the election and even then leave it to a presidential commission or some other external body to solve. In other words, Clinton wanted, as Reagan had with Social Security, to dance around the issue. As Gail Wilensky, a highly respected health policy expert who had advised President George H. W. Bush, put it, "The rhetoric of this political season will make it much more difficult to make the difficult reforms needed to save a very important program." If anything, Clinton's strong attacks on the Republicans would only make the issue more difficult to face after the election.[46]

Toward the Balanced Budget Act of 1997 and the Creation of Medicare Part C

The window for the consideration of Medicare's future reopened in 1997 and resulted in the passage of the Balanced Budget Act that the President signed into law in August. This legislation resolved many of the issues that had developed in the contentious period of the preceding two years. It also made major changes in the program that reflected the policy predilections of the era.

As before, Medicare politics was contained within budget politics. In January President Clinton prepared to introduce his budget for fiscal year 1998. He approached the task with a greater desire to be conciliatory to the Republicans than he had shown in previous years. People within the administration, including the Secretary of the Treasury and the Director of the National Economic Council, lobbied to subject Medicare premiums to a means test. Under this arrangement richer beneficiaries would pay higher premiums than poorer beneficiaries, and the flat system in which everyone paid the same amount for Medicare Part B would end. The people in the administration who supported the measure thought it was good public policy and also something the Republicans might welcome. The feature survived until it was deleted by the conference committee considering the Balanced Budget Act. It would take until 2003 for this provision to be included in Medicare.[47]

Another issue that remained alive in the discussions was President Clinton's notion of transferring home health services from Part A to Part B in Medicare. Republicans continued to oppose this measure. Trent Lott (R-MS), who had taken over from defeated Republican presidential candidate Robert Dole as Majority Leader, called it a "shell game." Clinton's new proposal contained the added twist that a beneficiary's first one hundred home health care visits would be paid from the Part A trust fund and the remainder in a given year from the Part B trust fund. The final law adopted Clinton's proposal but modified it so that the transition to the new system would be gradual. In order to reduce the future costs of the home health care program, it called upon the

Secretary to implement a prospective payment system for home health visits by October 1, 1999. The transfer from one trust fund to the other would take place over six years. Home health care visits used to be free to the beneficiary, but now the Medicare Part B premium would be adjusted to pay for this care, with the added fees phased in over a seven-year period.[48]

As discussions on these complicated matters took place, the policy environment continued to change. In January, for example, the Prospective Payment Assessment Commission, which was in the business of advising Congress on Medicare payments to hospitals, voted to recommend no increase in Medicare payments to hospitals for the next year. Both the President and the Republicans in Congress reacted sympathetically to this proposal because it would make it easier to reduce the federal budget deficit and to improve the position of the Part A trust fund. The hospitals reacted with less enthusiasm, charging that they were being penalized for their successful efforts to hold down costs.[49]

The trustees of the Part A trust fund continued to call attention to its deteriorating position. In April 1997 they reiterated that, in the absence of new legislation, the trust fund would run out of money in just four years. Although there was nothing new about this warning, it came one year after the previous ones. Reducing the time available to restore funds made the problem more difficult to solve. "It's time for action," said HHS Secretary Shalala.[50]

In a slow dance that consumed most of the winter and spring, the President moved closer to the Republican position on Medicare. On January 21, for example, he announced that his proposals would reduce the rate of Medicare spending by $138 billion over six years. In the beginning of 1996, the President and the Republicans had been some $42 billion apart in their suggested Medicare savings. Now the President said, "I'm going to do my best to reach out to the Republicans" and "meet them half way of this and many other issues."[51]

On May 2, 1997, the two sides came to an agreement on the broad outline of a budget plan. They pledged to balance the budget by 2002 and to cut taxes. Although the details on how to handle Medicare were not yet final, they included the pledge to realize $115 billion in savings so as to assure the program's future solvency. It helped in the negotiations that the Congressional Budget Office announced that it believed the federal government would get $225 billion more in revenues over the next five years than it had previously expected. This "found" money lubricated the process and eased the concerns of congressional Democrats that the agreement gave away too much to the Republicans. It allowed the creation of an expanded program for the health care of low-income children to remain in the legislation, and it protected Medicare beneficiaries from steep rises in Medicare premiums.[52]

There remained difficult details to be worked out. By this time some Democrats had adopted the Republican line that the program was out of date and needed to be modernized. Senator Ron Wyden (D-OR) described Medicare as "a bureaucratic Tin Lizzie." He added that the Democrats could still win on the issue by "guaranteeing well-defined secure benefits for seniors" while acknowledging that the Republicans were "absolutely right about the need to increase competition and choice in the program." Such philosophical statements did little to assuage the concerns of the hospital industry, which worried about the freeze in Medicare payment rates, or reduce the displeasure of the National Association for Medical Equipment services, which complained about a possible 40 percent cut in Medicare payments for home oxygen therapy. Medicare, in other words, remained thickly populated with interest groups whose private businesses depended on the largesse of the public program.[53]

Clinton and his congressional adversaries continued to work on a legislation package that they could both accept. The President had, for example, opposed the Republican proposal to create Medical Savings Accounts as alternatives to Medicare. Medical Savings Accounts, the President and other health policy experts believed, would lead to an "adverse selection problem." Younger and healthier individuals, who anticipated having few health problems, would sign up for the accounts, leaving older and sicker people in the traditional Medicare program. In the process, the costs of running the traditional Medicare program would rise, adding to its long-term problems. Republicans hoped that the entire Medicare program would eventually go the way of Medical Savings Accounts—that was the sort of minimum government and maximum private responsibility they wished to see in the American welfare state. In 1997, knowing President Clinton's feelings but wanting to get a foot in the door, they proposed setting a limit on the number of people who could choose such accounts. Instead of a radical change in the Medicare program, Medical Savings Accounts would be part of a demonstration project that policy makers could evaluate. The President and the Republicans agreed to this approach.[54]

Both sides also realized that Medicare faced long-term problems that would coincide with the entrance of the baby boom generation into the program. In the interest of making short-term progress, they decided to put this problem aside, even though it probably offered more political advantages to the Republicans than the Democrats. As a substitute for serious congressional debate, the two sides agreed to leave it to a bipartisan commission similar to the one that had considered Social Security in 1982.[55]

In this manner, both sides worked hard to accommodate the concerns of the other. Representative Bill Thomas, a senior member of the Ways and Means Committee, explained that in the past the Republicans had sought out confrontation with the White House. They now put a premium on producing legislation that the President would sign. Clinton's acceptance of the notion that Medicare beneficiaries should have a wider range of choices in their health care plans helped the two sides come together.

Even in the newly accommodating political climate, some issues remained difficult to resolve. An important one concerned the age for Medicare eligibility. Republicans wanted to increase the age for eligibility from sixty-five to sixty-seven, under the rationale of making the age for receiving Social Security and Medicare benefits the same. Although such a change would save substantial sums of money, its transparent nature invited criticism, particularly from citizens younger than sixty-seven, who did not relish the prospect of waiting longer for their Medicare benefits to begin. Senator Kennedy called the proposal "hogwash." He believed it would "throw millions of seniors into the ranks of the uninsured." Despite Kennedy's fiery warnings, the Senate agreed to raise the eligibility age to sixty-seven in a series of gradual steps in the bill it sent to conference. The House showed little inclination to follow the Senate's lead. Representative Bill Archer (R-TX), the head of the Ways and Means Committee, suggested that the matter be left to the commission that would consider Medicare's future. The conferees soon announced their intention of keeping age sixty-five as the age to receive Medicare. "I don't think the system can accommodate that yet," said Representative Kasich.[56]

On July 28, 1997, the White House and the Republican congressional leaders announced that they had come to a final agreement on an omnibus budget bill. Both houses of Congress had passed the bill by the end of July. The long standoff that had twice shut down the federal government and motivated many of the political battles between Representative Gingrich's victory in 1994, and the fruits of President Clinton's victory in 1996 appeared to be over.[57]

The Balanced Budget Act of 1997 stood as a testament to Speaker Gingrich's Contract with America. It made substantial changes in the Medicare program. As passed in 1965, Medicare contained Part A for hospital services and Part B for doctor's services. The new legislation introduced Part C and the Medicare+Choice program. For many years, members of the health policy community had assumed that Part C, when and if it arrived, would extend the Medicare program to working Americans and be the legislative vehicle for national health insurance. The Part C that materialized in 1997 was something completely different. Under the new arrangement, individuals qualified to receive Parts A and B of Medicare could sign up for the existing program, identified as a fee-for-service program, or opt for Part C or Medicare+Choice. Part C would cover both doctors' and hospital expenses through such arrangements as a health maintenance organization, a private fee-for-service plan,[58] a preferred provider plan, or, for some 390,000 individuals, a Medical Savings Account. The change would take time to implement, and it would require regulations to govern the relationship between Medicare and the private health plans. It nonetheless made the Medicare program look more like the plans that private employers offered their employees, an important convergence of the private and public sectors in America's welfare state.[59]

At the same time, the windfall produced by economic growth made it easier to fund new initiatives, just as in the Great Society days. One of the most important initiatives concerned uninsured children. The Balanced Budget Act established a child health block grant to fund state programs that reduced the number of uninsured children in the state. States could use the money to expand their Medicaid programs to cover low-income children or, if they preferred, to establish a separate state program for this purpose. It was a significant exception to the rest of the law in that it expanded rather than contracted the welfare state.[60]

Prescription Drugs: Preliminary Battles

Adding Part C to the program took more than thirty years. Because of the partisan battles that appeared to be a distinguishing feature of late twentieth- and early twenty-first-century politics, one might have expected a similarly long wait for Part D. As it happened, Medicare Part D arrived in 2003, only six years behind Part C. Products of the same era in Medicare policy, the two new parts of Medicare resembled one another in their reliance on the private sector to deliver benefits (although with federal money) and on market competition to control costs (although with federal regulation). One could regard Part D as another legacy of the Gingrich revolution, even though it was passed after Gingrich had left Congress.

Part D concerned prescription drugs, which had been a preoccupation of Medicare administrators since the program's creation. In 1965, during the passage of Medicare, participants in the political debate recognized the importance of prescription drugs but regarded insurance against the cost of hospital stays as a higher priority. Almost as soon as Medicare was passed, however, calls rose to expand the program to include prescription drugs. The first things that influential Social Security Commissioner Robert Ball put on the incremental expansion list in 1969 were health care benefits for people on the Social Security disability program, which was soon achieved, and prescription drug coverage, not achieved until the next century.[61]

From the program's very beginnings, Part A covered the cost of prescription drugs that Medicare patients received in the hospital. During a hospital stay, it was almost routine for a patient to be taking a prescription drug after surgery or some other event. If a patient was already taking prescription drugs at home, the hospital, as directed by the treating doctor, supplied those he or she still needed to take in the hospital. When the person got home from a hospital or rehabilitation facility, however, he was largely on his own—dependent on his own funds or his private insurance coverage to pay for drugs. Even then there were exceptions to this general rule. Patients being treated for end stage renal disease often became anemic, and the drug to treat that condition was reimbursable by Medicare. During the AIDS epidemic, immunosuppressive drugs were added to the list. If a drug needed to be administered in a doctor's office or if its cost or efficacy came to the attention of an interested congressman, it had a chance of being added to the list of physician-dispensed drugs. By 2001 the program reimbursed 454 of these drugs.

These incremental and stop-gap methods failed to solve the general problem of making sure that Medicare beneficiaries could afford prescription drugs. As early as 1967, President Johnson asked HEW Secretary John Gardner to convene a task force on prescription drugs, headed by Assistant Secretary for Health Philip Lee, an important advocate of increased government financing for health care. Johnson might have proposed the task force as something of a delaying tactic, as the many parts of Medicare still needed to be implemented and the initial costs of the program exceeded expectations. The task force did not issue its final report until after Richard Nixon assumed office, and its recommendations tended to be cautious, such as limiting the drug benefit to people seventy or older. The Nixon administration gave some consideration to a prescription drug plan but soon got caught up in the debate over national health insurance and the federal role in the promotion of health maintenance organizations. Then the drive to create a prescription drug benefit hit the wall of escalating health care costs and a deteriorating economy during the 1970s.[62]

Congress revived the matter in the late 1980s in a series of events that led to the passage of the Medicare Catastrophic Coverage Act of 1988. Most accounts highlight the role of Otis Bowen, a physician, former Governor of Indiana, and Secretary of Health and Human Services in Reagan's second term. He pushed the idea that Medicare ought to cover catastrophic costs that a beneficiary who ran out of permitted hospital days faced. He raised the matter in a 1984 Social Security Advisory Council meeting and became its advocate in the Reagan administration. Reagan mentioned the proposal in his 1986 State of the Union address and requested that Secretary Bowen develop legislation. Bowen presented his plan to the White House Domestic Policy Council in November 1986. According to Richard Himmelfarb, an academic who has made a close study of the matter, Bowen wanted to extend "Medicare protection to acute hospital and physician costs in excess of $2000 yearly." Ignoring the significant opposition of many of Reagan's advisors, he then announced his plan at a news conference. He said nothing about prescription drugs.[63]

In November 1986 the Democrats strengthened their position by winning the Senate for the first time since 1980. At the time, the matter of long-term care, championed by Representative Claude Pepper among others, stood high on the Democrat's agenda. Pepper and other liberals wanted to "establish a long-term care benefit for anyone who needed assistance in two or more of the recognized activities of daily living." Medicare handled acute care medical expenses, not the expenses of someone bedridden with a chronic condition and living at home or in a nursing home. Democrats hoped that the need for long-term care would become an issue in the 1988 campaign. The Democrats also had their eye on a prescription drug benefit and saw Bowen's legislation as a means of promoting both of the items on their agenda. House Speaker Jim Wright (D-TN) got the heads of his health committees and subcommittees, primarily Ways and Means and Energy and Commerce, to support a prescription drug benefit so that, in effect, the Democrats could share credit with the Republicans for the bill. Representative Henry Waxman, already a major player in the field, added the drug benefit to the House bill. In the Senate, Finance Committee members John Heinz (R-PA) and William Mitchell (D-ME) pushed a prescription drug benefit. The only difficulty was that the White House and Secretary Bowen both opposed the idea for fear it would upset Medicare's delicate financial balance.[64]

The Iran-Contra scandal and the new Democratic majority in both houses of Congress sapped some of the administration's bargaining power. The key issues centered on how the new drug benefit would be financed. Senator Lloyd Bentsen (D-TN), who as the head of the Finance Committee played a key role in the negotiations, agreed to a supplemental premium for the drug benefit based on a person's wealth as measured by the income tax he paid—a means test, in other words. In the final legislation, passed in July 1987, two-thirds of the program was to be financed by these supplemental premiums and the final third by a premium paid by all Medicare beneficiaries (similar to the Part B premium). Medicare beneficiaries would have no choice about accepting the new benefit. To keep the system solvent, premiums (which could be as much as $1,600 for married couples, plus a $600 deductible when the plan started, plus an increase in the Part B premium) for the new benefits in the bill would begin in January 1989. The drug benefits themselves would not be fully phased in until 1993. Unlike the usual largesse in Medicare, authorities estimated that a third of the Medicare beneficiaries would actually be worse off under the legislation, and all beneficiaries would have to wait to receive their new benefits.[65]

Although the new law enjoyed the support of the AARP, new organizations on the scene, such as the National Committee to Preserve Social Security and Medicare, began actively to oppose the legislation and urge its repeal. In an amazing reversal, Congress repealed the measure outright in November 1989. It became a newly accepted part of Medicare lore that, at minimum, programs should offer something positive before the costs kicked in. Imposing new costs on program beneficiaries was always a difficult exercise, even with the promise of future benefits.[66]

When Bill Clinton made his proposals for national health insurance, he revived the idea of a prescription drug benefit. The idea faded again with the demise of his health care reform plans. After the long battles over Medicare that culminated in the Balanced Budget Act of 1997, policy makers cleared some space for a reconsideration of prescription drugs. The strong economy worked wonders on the program. In 1999 the cost of Medicare actually declined for the first time in the program's history. Good economic predictions and the Balanced Budget Act helped to extend the life of the Medicare Part A trust fund from 2001 to 2029. Budget surpluses attracted the interest of policy makers anxious to expand Medicare. Many people who had signed up for managed care plans already enjoyed coverage of their prescription drug costs; perhaps the government could bring such coverage to all beneficiaries.[67]

Prescription Drugs and George W. Bush

In the history of Medicare expansion, the 1972 addition of people with disabilities was rather simple; it expanded the existing Medicare program without changing its benefits or structure. By way of contrast, the 2003 prescription drug program marked an effort to reorient the Medicare program—reform it in a fundamental way—so that it utilized private companies, stimulated competition, and facilitated the use of managed care. In this new version of Medicare, recipients could choose a privately managed drug plan, and the George W. Bush administration hoped to direct Medicare recipients away from single-payer "traditional Medicare" into managed care plans—now known as Medicare Advantage—that would drive down the cost of care.

Different political eras produced different types of reforms. In 1972 these reforms still followed an expansionary Great Society model, although the federal government relied on nongovernmental organizations to run the program and permitted both hospitals and doctors a great deal of autonomy. In 2003 the reforms bore the marks not only of the Reagan era, with its emphasis on trying to cut down on costs and federal responsibilities, but also of the Republican revolution of 1995, with its emphasis on balancing the budget and making private and public social welfare benefits conform to one another. Before 1999 reform proposals for prescription drugs involved what Philip Lee and his collaborators described as a "straightforward expansion of Part B." In the new century, policy makers envisioned "a separate drug benefit administered by private organizations."[68]

Prescription drugs became a major issue in the 2000 presidential election. George W. Bush, the victor by a narrow margin, expressed an interest in Social Security and Medicare. In a familiar Republican maneuver, he wanted to preserve Social Security by privatizing a major part of it—a proposal that went nowhere—and he showed an interest in creating a prescription drug plan. Unlike a plan that might have come from Bill Clinton or Al Gore, Bush thought in terms of creating what his Centers for Medicare and Medicaid Services (CMS) administrator described as "a market oriented, fairly conservative, fairly cheap drug benefit that will cover poor people."

The Bush era initiative began in earnest in 2002, after 9/11 but before the Iraq War and at a time when there were "still surpluses as far as the eye could see" and when a Republican victory in the 2002 congressional elections was just around the corner. Bush had already enacted a tax cut, leading some administrative figures to argue that the right thing to do with the remaining surpluses was to create a prescription drug benefit. The President, who took an active interest in the discussion in a way that belied his reputation as a passive figure in the policy process, agreed. As always, though, the Republicans, who hoped to make inroads among elderly voters, faced competition from Democrats, who had been seeking a prescription drug benefit from the beginning of the program. One key difference was that the Democrats favored a relatively expensive plan that covered all Medicare beneficiaries. The Republicans tended to think of prescription drug benefits as an adjunct of managed care. If one joined a prepaid Medicare plan, one of the benefits would be prescription drug coverage. The President decided that he wanted to spend $400 billion over ten years "and not a penny more."[69]

The prescription drug plan became embroiled in the usual partisan politics that delayed final passage of the measure until the end of November 2003. The conference report that preceded the bill ran some 678 pages, a good illustration of the technical complexity and detail that attended Medicare. Even with the conference report in hand, the measure still faced rough treatment in the House when it came up for a vote at three in the morning on Saturday, November 22. At the end of the normal time for voting, the bill was behind by fifteen votes. After the Speaker of the House applied pressure on his members, the margin stood at two. At that point the Secretary of Health and Human Services took the floor, and the Republican leaders woke up President Bush. Only after the roll call remained open for nearly three hours did the House finally pass the bill by a vote of 220 to 215. Three days later the measure prevailed in the Senate by a vote of 55 to 44. The *Washington Post* editorialized that the "controversial" bill cleared Congress "by the tiniest of margins" after the House leadership "cajoled, berated and twisted arms, barely containing a conservative revolt" and the Senate Democrats "used a bag of parliamentary tricks" in an unsuccessful effort to defeat the bill.[70]

The press dwelled on the horse race aspects of the measure when the contents of the legislation itself were what mattered most. The chief difference between President Bush's original proposal and the final legislation concerned the availability of prescription drug benefits to people enrolled in the traditional Medicare program. President Bush initially wanted to exclude them; the Democrats and such organizations as the AARP made sure that the final version included them. The main feature offered beneficiaries a choice between maintaining the prescription drug coverage that they already had or, beginning in January 2006, enrolling in stand-alone drug plans that would be a feature of the new Medicare Part D.[71]

If a person enrolled in the new Part D, he or she faced a premium that began at $35 a month and received 75 percent of approved prescription expenses between $250 and $2,250, nothing for expenses between $2,250 and $5,100—the so-called doughnut hole—and then 95 percent of expenses above $5,100. The law prohibited beneficiaries from supplementing their Part D coverage to insure against the drug prescription expenses that were not covered by the program and required that all Part D beneficiaries have at least two options of plans they could join. But the law failed to include a national "fallback plan." Instead, private Prescription D drug plans, run by large companies like Humana, secured approval from the government and then negotiated independently with drug manufacturers to secure the best price for their clients. The law did not allow the federal government to negotiate directly with the manufacturers.[72]

In the end, the new prescription drug plans looked a great deal like private medical insurance. A person signed up with a particular plan, not a federal program. The plans subsidized prescription drugs that a senior citizen might be taking. The proprietors of these plans expected their clients to be familiar with concepts such as out-of-pocket costs. According to the boilerplate that the participating insurance companies sent to beneficiaries, out-of-pocket costs did not include a plan's premiums, drugs not covered by the plan, non–Part D drugs a person might receive during a hospital stay, or drugs obtained at a "non-network pharmacy." Furthermore, the company reserved the right to make coverage decisions "when we decide whether a drug is covered and how much you pay for it."[73] Private employers were required by CMS to send Form 10182-CC to their employees. It explained that the employees were eligible to join a Medicare drug plan when they first became eligible for Medicare and each year after that from October 15 to December 7. Employees who were sixty-five or older and still working continued to receive their prescription drug benefits from their private plan.[74]

Aftermath of the Medicare Modernization Act

The final measure passed with few votes to spare and soon ran into a controversy that was related to the design of the policy apparatus for Medicare. In particular, the way policy makers estimated the program's future costs incited partisan conflict. The Office of the Actuary in the Social Security Administration played a major role in the 1965 Medicare legislation and in its 1972 expansion. The actuary made estimates of the costs of legislative proposals on which the Office of Management and Budget in the executive branch and the Ways and Means and Finance Committees in the legislative branch relied.[75] The actuary operated at some remove from political considerations in order to serve as an impartial umpire and produce the best estimates possible. That always mattered because each side in the political conflict wanted the estimates to come out their way. Those who favored expansions sought evidence that they were within the nation's means. Those who opposed the expansions wanted data to show that the new initiatives would break the bank.

By the time of the Medicare Modernization Act, the arrangement of making cost estimates for Medicare proposals had changed. For one thing, Medicare now resided in a different agency than Social Security.

Creation of the Health Care Financing Agency in 1977 put both Medicare and Medicaid in a new bureaucratic entity that concentrated on health care finance. A Medicare Actuary worked at the Health Care Financing Agency.[76]

For another thing, in the years between putting people with disabilities on the Medicare rolls and creating a new prescription drug benefit, Congress had acquired a greater capacity to act independently of the executive branch. The Medicare actuary might estimate the cost of a particular proposal from HCFA (and later CMS), but Congress relied on a new agency (established in 1974) called the Congressional Budget Office (CBO) for its estimates. This office owed its existence to budget battles between the Democratic Congress and the Nixon administration at a time of particular ill will between the two branches of government. Once in place, it became the official scorekeeper for Congress. As the search for budget-neutral programs intensified in the late 1970s and as the Budget reconciliation process took hold throughout the 1980s, the scorekeeper function emerged as a vital part of the legislative process.[77]

Estimating the cost of a new benefit over a ten-year period was not a straightforward exercise for any actuary. The annals of social policy contained many programs that greatly exceeded their initial cost estimates, including disability insurance and Medicare itself. As one insider described the new prescription drug benefit, "Nobody had any idea that it was going to work. It was all guess work." Not surprisingly, then, the Congressional Budget Office and the Medicare actuary did not come up with the same scores for Bush's bill. Bush administration officials even anticipated this contingency, predicting that the CBO would score the proposal lower than the Medicare actuary. Congress would then take Bush's bill and fill it up until the cost reached $400 billion, the President's limit, according to the CBO scores. The Bush administration, in other words, decided to work around its own actuary in the executive branch under the rationale that the CBO score, the one that favored the administration, was the only one that mattered.[78]

The bill as passed had a CBO score of $399 billion. But the administration's budget that came out at the beginning of 2004 used CMS rather than CBO numbers. The media accused the administration of lying to Congress about the cost of the prescription drug benefit and trying to sell a $500 billion program for $400 billion. When CMS officials (CMS was the bureaucratic successor to HCFA as a result of a name change in the Clinton era) refused to let the Democrats on the Ways and Means

Committee see the Medicare actuary's scores, the Democrats charged that the Republicans were trying to muzzle the presumably independent Medicare actuary. Pete Stark (D-CA), a particularly partisan Democrat, put out a press release that said the CMS Administrator was threatening to fire the actuary.[79]

These sorts of partisan fights related to the policy-making structure obscured even more fundamental changes over time that affected the government's and the private sector's ability to deliver benefits. The fight over drug benefits lasted a long time, and as a result the measure that was finally passed in 2003 took advantage of advances in technology that had not been so readily available in 1988, the year of the ill-fated Medicare Catastrophic Coverage Act. Although hidden from public view, the HCFA employees who would have had to implement the 1988 prescription drug benefit had serious doubts about their ability to administer it. The man in charge of the agency envisioned what he called the "shoebox approach." Under this arrangement, people would keep the receipts of their prescription drug expenditures and when those expenditures reached a certain level, "somehow they would make their claim to be reimbursed, which would obviously be horribly complicated and inefficient." By 2003 the available technology had improved.[80]

Hence the new prescription drug program benefited from the latest technology but still began with considerably more acrimony than did the extension of Medicare to people with disabilities. The fact that 2004 was an election year added to the political jockeying. Still, partisan bickering that impeded the policy process appeared to be a permanent fixture of health care policy, in stark contrast to the period before the battle over hospital cost containment.

The Unanticipated Rise of Medicaid

Few of the changes in health care policy between 1972 and 2003 could have been anticipated in 1972. Perhaps the most surprising of the changes and the one with the greatest effect on the nation's health policy concerned Medicaid. Rather than Medicare, Medicaid became the key vehicle for the expansion of health care coverage beginning in the 1980s. One of the most notable features of President Obama's 2010 Affordable Care Act centered on the widening of Medicaid eligibility to include adults without children (who were the least likely to fall into the traditional welfare categories and hence already be receiving Medicaid) and to raise the eligibility across the nation to 133 percent of the federal poverty line. Income level, rather than the receipt of welfare benefits, now determined Medicaid eligibility.[81]

That development would have surprised policy observers in 1965. Both Medicaid and Medicare began with the notion that social insurance represented a better form of social protection than welfare or public assistance. The mantra at the Social Security Administration was that programs for poor people made poor programs. Medicare was tied to the Social Security program and the respected Social Security Administration and Medicaid to the welfare system and the much less well-respected welfare and rehabilitation bureaucracy. When President Carter put Medicare and Medicaid together in a new agency, Medicare quickly established itself as the "dominant partner."[82]

Federal administrators favored Medicare in part because they had more control over it. One set of Medicare rules, at least in theory, applied to the entire nation (although these rules were interpreted by widely dispersed "fiscal intermediaries" and "carriers" and after 2003 by Medicare Administrative Contractors). Hence Congress could create something like the diagnosis-related groups and expect them to govern Medicare expenditures across the nation. The same fiscal controls did not operate in Medicaid. The common wisdom was that, in the words of CMS Administrator Michael McMullen, "Medicaid was a different program for every state." Another former CMS administrator noted, "There is not just one Medicaid program; all of them are different in the states and territories."[83]

Based on that sort of evidence, one would have expected Medicare to expand at a greater rate than Medicaid and eventually subsume Medicaid. There was historical precedent for that. The old-age insurance program largely replaced the old-age assistance welfare programs in the states during the 1950s. However, nothing similar happened with Medicaid. By the time the Affordable Care Act came along, Medicaid had 20 percent more people than Medicare on its rolls. More people received Medicaid than received Social Security.[84] Medicaid cost less than $1 billion in 1966 and more than $200 billion in 2000. At the beginning the program had something like four million people on its rolls and spent about $200 per year on each of the people enrolled. By the end of the century, the rolls had swelled to thirty-three million and the program spent $750 per year on each of them.[85]

Medicaid owed its survival and eventually its inclusion in the Affordable Care Act in part to the way that Congress protected the program at critical junctures. In 1989 Congress repealed all of the social insurance aspects of the Medicare Catastrophic Coverage law but left the Medicaid provisions intact.[86] In 1996 the largest welfare program—Aid to Families with Dependent Children—became incorporated into a federal block grant. The states received considerably more leeway to deal with dependent children on welfare, and welfare as an entitlement, in which everyone who qualified received benefits, ended (as we will see in chapter 7). Instead of allowing the states a similar leeway to end the Medicaid entitlement of dependent children and their parents, Congress created the State Children's Health Insurance Program in 1997, which broadened health insurance protection for children.[87]

If Medicaid lacked uniformity from state to state, it also enjoyed more freedom to experiment and even became known as a center of health innovation. For example, state Medicaid programs began to experiment with health maintenance organizations and other health care delivery systems that were touted as more efficient and inclusive than traditional health insurance. Earlier than Medicare, Medicaid, to the extent that one could talk about a national program, changed "from merely paying claims to managing services and the costs of care as well." By the year 2000 more than half of all Medicaid clients were in some sort of managed care plan.[88]

Medicaid also profited from the fact that it filled a key niche in the nation's safety net. Medicaid became the major vehicle for financing long-term care, paying nearly half of the nation's total costs. When the program began, the bias among policy makers was that the federal government should not support custodial care, such as the large insane asylums that could still be found in many states. No one wanted hospitals, widely hailed as places where people went to be cured, to become, in health policy expert Judy Feder's words, "warehouses for frail elderly people."[89]

Here Medicaid's loose structure facilitated its growth. Congress, reflecting the fashions of the day, explicitly prohibited Medicare from covering custodial care. Instead the program limited its long-term care benefits to post-acute care that followed a hospital stay and would lead to the recovery of the patient. Medicaid, from the beginning, had fewer constraints and quickly became a major supporter of nursing homes. (It was also an early leader in prescription drug care.) Nursing home care for individuals over twenty-one was one of five basic benefits that the federal government required the states to have in their Medicaid programs. As early as 1971, Medicaid was disbursing more money on nursing homes "than had been spent in the entire industry five years earlier."[90]

Long-term care brought a new clientele to Medicaid. The residents of nursing homes were not traditional welfare recipients. Instead they might be elderly women who had outlived their husbands and spent down their assets. The nursing homes themselves became a powerful political force—supposedly the most influential force in twenty-one states according to Medicaid authority Laura Olson. That changed the configuration of health care politics. Republicans interested in ending federal matching grants in Medicaid and replacing them with block grants needed to counter the argument that most of the money in the block grants would go to nursing homes.[91]

Beyond these important structural factors, Medicaid benefited from congressional champions who knew how to use the budget reconciliation process to expand the program. The most prominent in the period from 1975 to the Obama era was Congressman Henry Waxman. He used his seat on the Energy and Commerce Committee to become a major player in both Medicaid and Medicare.[92] Waxman, who headed the committee's important Health Subcommittee, led the way in the incremental expansion of Medicaid in the 1980s. Each year after 1984, Congress passed laws that expanded Medicaid coverage in the states and affected infants, children, pregnant women, low-income Medicare beneficiaries, and other disabled and aged enrollees.[93] Washington insiders, like Michael Hash who worked on the Affordable Care Act for the Obama White House, called it "the Waxman wedge," which over a period of eight or nine years changed Medicaid from a program that served welfare beneficiaries to one that brought care to low-income individuals. A former head of CMS called Henry Waxman and Commerce Committee chair John Dingell "raging incrementalists" who fundamentally changed the Medicaid program in the 1980s.[94]

Conclusion

In 1965, in the heady days of the Great Society, legislators had hoped to give the elderly the same generous health insurance coverage that Americans of working age and their families received through their employers. At the same time, Congress rejected the idea of giving people a choice of the Medicare plan they would receive. Instead of allowing beneficiaries to choose their own health insurance to cover doctor's visits, Congress decided instead to create Part B. It was voluntary but, as in the rest of Medicare, there was the implication that one size fit all. The premiums and the benefits of Part B would be the same for everyone.

In the thirty-five years that followed Medicare's passage, Medicare and private insurance fell out of synch with one another. The economic changes of the 1970s, with their soaring inflation and lagging productivity, appeared to mark the point of discontinuity. Medicare remained what the health policy experts called a single-payer plan, and private health insurers, responding to the needs of private employers, emphasized the concepts of managed care and consumer choice. The Social Security rescue legislation of 1983 and the Balanced Budget Act of 1997 recalibrated Medicare so that it once again reflected developments in the private sector. Gone were the incremental expansions such as extending coverage to people on disability insurance or people with end stage renal disease. Instead, policy makers intended diagnosis-related groups and Medicare+Choice as instruments to contain the growth of Medicare's costs. The era ended with Bill Clinton preserving most of Medicare's original benefits but with first Ronald Reagan and then Newt Gingrich inducing major changes in the Medicare program that President George W. Bush brought to fruition in 2003. President Obama completed the modern medical system by passing a liberal variation on ideas such as the expansion of Medicaid that were already in wide circulation.

The result was the preservation of the 1965 law, although with internal improvements, such as diagnosis groups, designed to reduce costs. Subsequent reformers needed to build on to this basic structure and create new layers of programs in Part C and Part D. This result differed from what happened to disability insurance which, once in place, remained in place with initial incremental expansions but no major changes. It also differed from what happened in the field of welfare, which is the third of this book's three case studies. Chapters foregrounding the 1996 welfare reform law and narrating its passage follow.

CHAPTER SIX

The Welfare Reform Debate from JFK to Reagan

If the Gingrich revolution had a profound effect on Medicare, it left a more permanent impression on the nation's welfare program that supported mothers with young children who were in need of financial aid. It transformed the Aid to Families with Dependent Children program from an entitlement, available to anyone who met its terms, to a much more discretionary program that granted a great deal of freedom to the states. The 1996 welfare reforms represented a real change in direction in the nation's social policy, and unlike the Medicare reforms of the same era that added Parts C and D without disturbing Parts A and B, the welfare reforms jettisoned the existing program in favor of something new. At the same time, policy makers did not write the 1996 reforms on a blank slate. A long line of incremental reforms and policy discussions that were well under way by 1967 led to the 1996 law. By virtue of these discussions, welfare (or at least the Aid to Families with Dependent Children component of it) became a transitional benefit that prepared welfare mothers for the world of work rather than a regular payment to mothers so that they could make ends meet and raise their children at home.

In the book's third and final case study, this chapter chronicles what might be called the prehistory of the 1996 reforms, and the next chapter narrates the passage of the reforms. Welfare reform has similarities to the other case studies. As with disability insurance, policy makers tried without much success to introduce the element of rehabilitation into AFDC and to find ways to stem the growth of the program. As with Medicare, policy makers fiddled with the economic incentives contained within the program in an effort to change the behavior of welfare recipients. Medicare and AFDC, both expensive and in some people's view also underperforming, led the social welfare agenda of the Gingrich era and beyond. It was inevitable that one policy discussion affected the other. In particular, both programs received criticism that they were anachronistic and unable to meet modern needs.

This chapter argues that the Social Security Act of 1935 set the institutional terms of AFDC, just as it did for disability insurance and Medicare. Complicated institutional and economic factors pushed AFDC to prominence by the end of the 1950s. During the 1960s and early 1970s, both liberal and conservative reformers tried to change AFDC from a check-cashing operation to a workfare program. Like that of disability insurance, the program's structure made it hard for policy makers to realize their goals. It was difficult to transform a program designed to allow women to raise their children at home into a manpower program. When the 1996 reforms arrived, therefore, they required policy makers to make fundamental alterations in the program's structure.

Welfare programs proved to be more pliable than social insurance programs such as disability insurance and Medicare because they were less popular. The receipt of welfare, particularly for single mothers, carried a stigma that motivated the passage of the 1996 welfare reforms. The stigma was not endemic to American social welfare programs, and the Social Security program worked around it. Even for welfare, the stigma arose over time and did not take firm hold of welfare policy until perhaps 1967. That was because until the late 1950s most welfare recipients were elderly, and hence members of the deserving poor or widows who were also considered worthy of government aid. People regarded the periodic scandals that arose in welfare—a welfare mother who could somehow afford a fur coat of a fancy car, for example—as anomalies. As a general proposition, though, people valued welfare as an institution that protected vulnerable populations from hunger and poverty. During much of the postwar era, people also believed that welfare could also be a force for positive change, an institutional mechanism for making families function more effectively. Only by the end of the 1960s was the stigma of single mothers strong enough to motivate policy makers to take punitive action.

The Origins of the Aid to Families with Dependent Children Program

The pre-1967 view of the world has largely faded from historical memory. Social critics have set up a dichotomy between Social Security, often viewed as a successful program that has kept many elderly and disabled people out of poverty, and welfare, often regarded as a policy failure that encourages immoral behavior and prevents its recipients from working their way into the middle class. This view suffers from historical amnesia. Welfare's bad image in contemporary America makes it easy to forget the fact that Social Security and welfare have a common history and, for many years, coexisted in a common bureaucracy and were governed by the same congressional committees. Even more importantly, welfare was a more popular program than Social Security between 1935 and 1950.

Both the old-age insurance or Social Security program and the modern welfare program originated as parts of the 1935 Social Security Act. That year marked President Roosevelt's ambitious effort to reshape the nation's social welfare programs by giving the federal government more of a role to play in them. Social welfare had traditionally been a profoundly local concern. Different areas of the country treated those who they believed to be in genuine financial need differently. At base welfare was a community responsibility, with the communities given wide latitude to deal with the problem as they saw fit. In this regard, Americans inherited their social welfare system from the English poor laws that dated back to the seventeenth century.

The 1935 Social Security Act changed that arrangement. This legislation made a distinction between social insurance and welfare. Social insurance covered the relatively new industrial hazards of unemployment and retirement in old age. The idea was that workers or their employers paid into a fund that yielded benefits when the contingency arose. Welfare or public assistance covered the more immediate problems of people in need. The Social Security Act left much of the existing locally oriented welfare system unchanged but singled out certain groups as worthy of special support from state governments. The federal government made matching grants to the states to aid people who fell into these special categories. The Social Security Act, therefore, did not start a program of federal assistance to the poor. Rather, it designated specific categories of people as worthy of state benefits that were partially financed by federal funds. The choice of these original categories made a great deal of difference in the development of America's welfare state. The 1935 legislators chose the elderly, dependent children, and the blind, not so much because these groups were the most needy as because they were the most worthy, and many states had already established statewide (as opposed to local) programs for people in these three groups. The Social Security Act gave these state programs a financial boost at a time of economic depression and encouraged lagging states to start their own programs.[1]

The key thing about these welfare programs was that they involved a means test. A person needed to prove he or she was poor—lacking in income and assets—in order to qualify for benefits. By way of contrast, Social Security benefits went to anyone who had paid into the relevant fund. One purchased Social Security retirement benefits in advance during one's working lifetime. Welfare relied on government funds, general revenues in the policy jargon, to cover special cases.

In another serendipitous but fateful step, Congress put both welfare and Social Security under the control of the Social Security Board, later (in 1946) converted into the Social Security Administration. That bureaucratic placement of the programs meant that they developed in tandem. Some employees of this agency worked with welfare programs in its Bureau of Public Assistance, and others worked in the branches of the agency concerned with establishing wage records and computing old-age benefits for Social Security. Those on the Social Security side needed to cajole employers to establish Social Security accounts for their employees and, in a larger sense, to sell the somewhat alien concept of social insurance to the general public. Those who worked on public assistance needed to offer advice and guidance to the state agencies that ran the programs and to make sure that the states received the right amount of money, as defined by requirements in the legislation for the federal government to match state contributions to the program.[2]

The welfare arrangement permitted a great deal of discretion to the states. The benefit levels for an indigent blind person in Mississippi came nowhere near those levels in Massachusetts. Some states had a larger income base and a greater inclination to come to the aid of the poor than others. The federal overseers of the program could do little about that, but they could make sure that states followed the rules and procedures established by the Social Security Act. An important one was that a state's welfare laws needed to cover the entire state. No counties or other government units were excused from the obligation to pay welfare to those who passed a means test and fell into one of the designated categories. States also needed to follow certain procedural rules in paying welfare. It could not, for example, be used as a mechanism to reward one's political friends and punish one's political enemies. The right to welfare also included procedural guarantees so that welfare benefits would not be awarded or rescinded capriciously. States that disobeyed the federal government faced the very real threat of losing their federal contributions to their welfare programs. In a celebrated case, the federal government refused to make payments to the state of Ohio in October 1938 because the Governor of that state had used welfare payments to boost his reelection efforts.[3]

The federal bureaucrats in charge of welfare wanted to establish a working welfare program that paid benefits to all elderly and the blind and dependent children who needed them. Others, such as able-bodied males in families with no children, depended on the more uncertain generosity of state and often county governments in general assistance programs. The federal government had nothing to do with those. Its clients fell into categories of people who had long since made their case to the community that they needed special attention. A blind person required welfare to survive in a sighted world and was an obvious candidate for a community's charity. The elderly had often put in long working lives before running out of resources in their old age. Dependent children shared no blame for the economic misfortunes of their parents.[4]

Although the employees of the Social Security Administration did their jobs in relative harmony, the top levels of the agency regarded old-age insurance (Social Security) as superior to old-age assistance (welfare) and wanted to promote one above the other. It did not seem much of a stretch. The one program paid benefits as a matter of right without the need for intrusive needs tests. The other, despite the best efforts of the Bureau of Public Assistance, was more discretionary. One program drew on payroll taxes for most of its revenue and did not need to rely on the more uncertain stream of general revenues. The other represented a potential drain on general revenues that, because of a growing elderly population, would only increase in future years.

But this argument only went so far, because Social Security had obvious limitations. Restricted by act of Congress to industrial and commercial workers, it excluded other large employee groups, such as the self-employed or agricultural workers, who had to rely on welfare, not

Social Security, should they meet financial misfortune. Nor were its benefits available immediately after the passage of the Social Security Act in 1935. Only those who paid into the program on a regular basis could receive its benefits, and these payments did not even begin until January 1937. Changing that situation required an act of Congress, and Congress initially regarded Social Security as a tax and hence more of a political liability than a benefit. Little support for the expansion of Social Security developed in the years between 1935 and 1950. It paid relatively low benefits to relatively few people and in its initial years between 1937 and 1940 collected payroll taxes from employers without paying regular benefits. In the face of this program that represented the federal government's preferred way of doing business, the Bureau of Public Assistance had to establish its programs as a right of poor citizens in the designated categories but only as a residual and secondary right.[5]

Even in the midst of the campaign to promote Social Security, welfare to the elderly, rather than Social Security, dominated the social policy scene between 1935 and 1950. There were more people receiving old-age assistance than received old-age insurance. Among the welfare categories, old age was by far the largest in terms of both recipients and expenditures. Little evidence suggested that welfare was somehow a stigmatized social benefit. After all, most of those on old-age assistance had worked their entire lives and somehow managed to survive.[6]

Even after 1950, welfare still had political advantages over social insurance. It could expand without making the federal bureaucracy larger. It brought the administration of social welfare benefits closer to the local level where, at least in theory, officials could better supervise the caseload. In both of these regards, it raised fewer political issues than did the expansion of Social Security to cover a new field like disability. When Congress finally passed legislation in 1950 that extended Social Security coverage and raised benefit levels for the elderly, it did not hesitate, in the very same legislation, to expand the welfare system. The 1950 Social Security Amendments created a new welfare category for the permanently and totally disabled. At the time, Congress preferred that to the creation of a Social Security Disability Insurance program, which would require the political machinations of 1956 (described in chapter 1) to become law.

The bureaucratic marriage of welfare and Social Security continued uninterrupted until 1963. In that year the Welfare Administration came into being as a constituent agency of the Department of Health, Education, and Welfare. Its emergence coincided with the first major change in the welfare law since 1935 and signaled that the Social Security Administration no longer considered welfare as central to its mission. As it turned out, however, the separation was temporary. In 1972 the Social Security Administration once again received permission to run the welfare programs for the aged, blind, and disabled under the banner of the Supplemental Security Income program. In 1977 responsibility for the administration of Aid to Families of Dependent Children, which had become the most important of the welfare programs, reverted to the Social Security Administration, only to be set loose again in the 1990s. This bureaucratic history showed how interwoven the two programs were between their origins in the New Deal and the policy upheavals of the 1990s.[7]

Rehabilitating Welfare Recipients in 1962

The 1950s marked an important era of change for welfare programs. In 1957, for the first time, more people received AFDC than received any other category of welfare. (By 1970, AFDC would cost more than all of the other welfare categories combined.) This development reflected the expansion of the Social Security program in every Congress that met between 1950 and 1958, combined with the nature of the welfare categories created in 1935. Because of the Social Security expansion, more of the elderly could now depend on Social Security rather than welfare in their old age. People covered by Social Security also benefited from survivors' benefits (1939) and disability insurance (1956). Old-age insurance (social insurance), therefore, came close to replacing old-age assistance (welfare) and left AFDC as the largest welfare category. Because the only other recipients were the blind and the permanently and totally disabled, AFDC became the most flexible welfare program, the closest thing the nation had to a federally supported general assistance category.

The AFDC program swept up people in need, even as the nature of those people changed. In the 1950s, a different group of people became the clients of the AFDC program than had been the case in 1935. At first the AFDC program mainly served widows whose husbands had died and left behind dependent children, but they were exactly the sort of people who entered the Social Security survivors program. By mid-1959, fewer than 15 percent of the children on AFDC owed their benefits to the death of their father; most received welfare because their fathers had left home or never lived with the family in the first place. Welfare beneficiaries were no longer the children of widows who deserved the nation's sympathy. They now became more closely associated with such perceived problems as illegitimacy.

Welfare was no longer so tightly woven into the fabric of American society. It was increasingly perceived as something that applied to the cities more than to suburban or rural communities. More tellingly, it acquired a racial connotation as a program that paid benefits to blacks rather than to whites. That was a consequence of the state administration of welfare programs. As black families moved from the South to the North, they arrived in states that made fewer racial distinctions in awarding welfare benefits. It was easier for a black person to get welfare in Philadelphia, Pennsylvania, than in Philadelphia, Mississippi. But as that happened AFDC recipients lost their identities as members of the deserving poor, and the welfare rolls became blacker. Welfare, therefore, changed its character as the program that came to the aid of worthy people in need and became something else. In other words, it was now something alien and somewhat menacing to many Americans. That change, visible by the end of the 1950s, motivated welfare politics from the late 1950s to the end of the century.[8]

The presence of even a few blacks on the welfare rolls stirred up community fears, much like the sale of a house to a black family raised fears that the entire neighborhood was turning black. By the beginning of the twenty-first century, it became commonplace among academic researchers to demonstrate that opposition to welfare among white voters reflected their attitudes toward race. Just as many people overestimated the percentage of black people in the nation's cities, so they tended to regard the welfare rolls as being blacker than they actually were. In a 2001 review of the literature, social scientists Robert Moffitt and Peter Gottschalk reported that "the general popular perception that minority racial and ethnic groups dominate the welfare rolls has been historically incorrect." If one were to examine the welfare caseload as late as 1998, one would discover that blacks made up only a slightly larger percentage of the caseload than whites (37.1 percent compared to 35.6 percent), and that trend would be reversed by 2009. One could say, however, that blacks were overrepresented on the welfare rolls compared to their percentage of the general population, a trend reinforced by the relatively low black participation rate in AFDC in 1935 and higher participation rates in the 1950s, 1960s, and 1970s. Hispanics also became a prominent feature of the modern welfare rolls; 20 percent of welfare recipients in 1998 fell into that demographic category.[9]

The turn against welfare took hold gradually. In a sense, welfare, as a proven social program, had money in the bank. In the 1950s, most policy makers continued to regard welfare as a necessary obligation of government, and little political capital could be made by attacking welfare recipients as indolent, irresponsible, or dysfunctional. Instead, new situations required new responses. In 1955, for example, President Eisenhower spoke of the need for new grants to the states to finance programs that combated juvenile delinquency. According to the President, more money should be spent on welfare because the present arrangements for the aged, blind, and disabled and dependent children were "far from adequate." The precipitous rise in the welfare caseload that would take place between 1965 and 1975 was not yet in sight.[10]

Congressmen like Wilbur Mills saw welfare as one of their important responsibilities. At the beginning of 1962, for example, Mills, in a confidential conversation with Kennedy administration officials (discussed in chapter 3), articulated his opposition to health insurance but affirmed his desire to secure more public assistance for the state of Arkansas. Liberals had their own agenda for welfare expansion that they pushed on the obliging Mills. Wilbur Cohen, the HEW official as involved in welfare policy as anyone, explained to a correspondent that "the whole tenor of my study and of my present views is that we need to be more vigorous and creative in using Federal, State, and local funds and personnel for rehabilitation of welfare recipients." Legislation to that effect was submitted to Congress early in 1962, and it followed upon temporary welfare legislation that had already been approved in 1961. The 1962 legislation, passed without much opposition, would "reinforce and extend the rehabilitation objective and spell out how Federal funds may be used for work and training projects," according to Cohen.[11]

In other words, families with dependent children needed more than money or a pension that would allow mothers to stay home with their infants, toddlers, and young children. The Social Security Act of 1935 encouraged the view of welfare as a pension. Women, often widows with children in their care, formed one of the protected classes in social policy. Beginning in the late 1950s, dependent children and their mothers became candidates for a different sort of treatment. "My idea was to develop a plan for each child," Cohen explained. The plan would vary with the specific needs of the child, but it would be more than a simple cash grant. "It might be counseling, it might be referral to a job, it might be the mother going back to high school or a job," said Cohen. The new approach put an emphasis on the casework skills and methods of trained social workers who were experts at diagnosing the social problems that arose in a family context. It also emphasized the extension of welfare programs to embrace job training, something that by its very definition undermined the 1935 objective of keeping mothers at home so that they could raise their children.[12]

Policy makers therefore wanted the program to continue its legitimate function as a source of aid for needy dependent children but also to assume a new identity as a force that cured dysfunctional families and transformed people from welfare consumers to independent members of the labor force. It was similar to the situation of disability insurance. Although some of the people on the disability rolls were truly disabled and belonged there, policy makers believed that others could be rehabilitated and returned to the labor force. Similar problems of public administration applied to both cases. Once beyond the procedures that got someone onto the rolls, both disability insurance and AFDC were essentially mass check-writing operations, even though local authorities kept a closer eye on AFDC beneficiaries than on the disability rolls. Rehabilitation, by way of contrast, proceeded on an individual basis and required a great deal of discretion on the part of policy makers to motivate people and create a plan for them that took their individual circumstances and natural abilities into account. One style of administration devoted to issuing checks did not match the other devoted to individual case work, making it doubtful that either the AFDC program or the disability insurance program could meet its rehabilitation objectives.

The lure of rehabilitation nonetheless remained strong. "From the day of my confirmation hearing I have been convinced that the demand for changes in the welfare laws would become a hot issue," noted Abraham Ribicoff, a former Governor and future Senator of the state of Connecticut who served as Kennedy's first HEW Secretary. Ribicoff believed that there was still room for political consensus on welfare between conservatives who were beginning to worry about welfare abuses and liberals who wanted to reorient the "whole approach to welfare from a straight cash-hand-out operation to one in which the emphasis is on rehabilitation of those on relief and prevention ahead of time." Lurid tales were circulating, as Ribicoff put it, about the "AFDC mother with a dozen illegitimate kids, the relief checks that buy liquor instead of food and rent, the able-bodied man who spurns a decent job to stay on relief." Something needed to be done before a welfare backlash set in and changed the entire tone of social welfare policy.[13]

Ribicoff and his colleagues thought that the rehabilitation of welfare beneficiaries would handle the problem and showcase the ability of the federal government to promote the social good. In rhetoric that would soon become outdated, they spoke of a "tremendous improvement in our welfare programs which will greatly help to strengthen family life and prevent continued dependency of many families." Kennedy-era welfare reform meant spending more money to bring services to dysfunctional families so that the recipients could function better as parents and take their place among the nation's citizens in prosperous postwar America. A new feature in the law also made it possible for children in "intact" families to receive benefits, if the family were poor enough and if the father were unemployed. In the style of welfare legislation, the new rehabilitation features would be optional in the sense that the states did not have to adopt them. If they did, however, they would be reimbursed on liberal terms.[14]

All of the political elements fell into place for passage of the 1962 Public Welfare Amendments, which among other things increased from 50 to 75 percent the federal portion of the cost of rehabilitation services for welfare clients and allowed federal funds to be used for community work and training programs. The President sent a special message to Congress about public assistance. Wilbur Mills started hearings promptly, perhaps eager to have a distraction from Medicare. The President signed the bill into law on July 25 and repeated the hope that the new law would provide "rehabilitation instead of relief."[15]

For all of the enthusiasm and hype that accompanied their passage, the 1962 Public Welfare Amendments produced disappointing results discrediting the rehabilitation approach to welfare reform. In fiscal year 1960, there were already 2,982,083 AFDC recipients, a figure higher than the populations of Philadelphia or Los Angeles (see figure 6.1). The state of California alone had nearly 262,000 AFDC recipients. By 1967 when Congress had an opportunity to reauthorize the 1962 amendments, the number of welfare recipients in the fiscal year reached 4,854,972, including some 740,000 who lived in California. In New York City, the city's cash spending on categorical public assistance programs (which included more than AFDC) more than doubled between 1961 and 1966 and more than doubled again by the end of the decade (see figure 6.2). And that was only the beginning of welfare's rapid rise. By fiscal year 1975 the

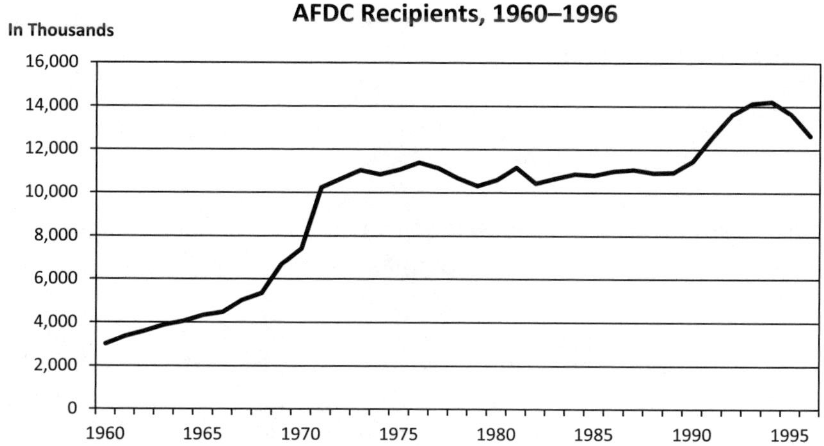

FIGURE 6.1. AFDC Recipients, 1960–1996.
Sources: Office of the Assistant Secretary for Planning & Evaluation, US Dept. of Health and Human Services, "Welfare Indicators and Risk Factors: Thirteenth Report to Congress." AFDC/TANF Program Data, 3/1/2014, Table TANF 1. Available online at https://aspe.hhs.gov/report/welfare-indicators-and-risk-factors-thirteenth-report-congress/afdctanf-program-data.
Additional data points from *Social Security Bulletin, Annual Statistical Supplement*, 1986, Table 204, p. 282.

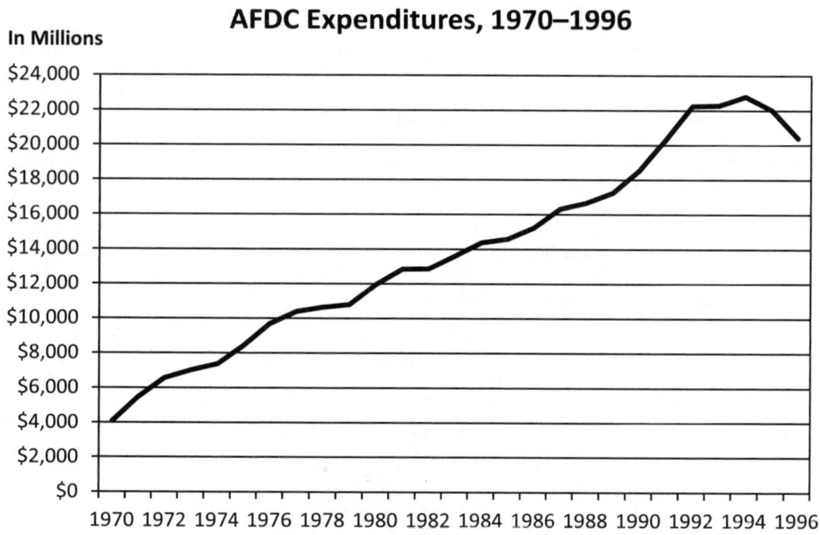

FIGURE 6.2. AFDC Expenditures, 1970–1996.
Note: Includes both federal and state benefit payments. Does not include administrative costs.
Sources: Office of the Assistant Secretary for Planning & Evaluation, US Dept. of Health and Human Services, "Welfare Indicators and Risk Factors: Thirteenth Report to Congress." AFDC/TANF Program Data, 3/1/2014, Table TANF 4. Available online at https://aspe.hhs.gov/report/welfare-indicators-and-risk-factors-thirteenth-report-congress/afdctanf-program-data.

national AFDC caseload stood at 11,203,027, and there were 1.4 million AFDC recipients in California.[16]

1967 and the Turn against Welfare

The rising caseloads drew unwelcome attention to welfare and made policy makers less receptive to calls for its expansion. The liberal idea of investing in people no longer had the same resonance, and people began to turn to a more punitive version of welfare reform that sought to discourage people from entering the rolls. What happened to welfare in 1967 resembled what happed to the disability insurance program in 1981. In both cases, policy makers tried to trim the program rolls without making substantive changes in the basic structure of the programs.

The 1967 Welfare Amendments indicated the turn in policy. Liberals, who remained firmly in control of the federal executive branch, believed in such things as expanding the state AFDC unemployed parents programs so that mothers and fathers would no longer need to separate in order to be eligible for welfare. They called for more work training, as a way of not so much of disciplining welfare recipients as improving them and adding to their stock of human capital. Day care for the children of working mothers, provided at government expense, would ease the mother's transition from home to the labor force. Liberals also wanted to create work incentives for welfare recipients. People on welfare should be allowed to keep the wages they earned without reductions in their welfare grants. In a policy idiom that became fashionable a generation later, policy makers would "make work pay" rather than taxing a welfare mother's wages to the point where she was actually better off not working. In addition to all that, liberal policy makers wanted to bring more uniformity to welfare practice so that, for example, the rules for how to calculate benefits and to define a person's assets were not so different from state to state. Liberals criticized the wide disparity in benefit levels from state to state. The Johnson administration brought these ideas and more to Wilbur Mills and the Ways and Means Committee in 1967 as part of what the administration envisioned as an omnibus Social Security law that, among other things, would contain large Social Security benefit increases.[17]

Wilbur Mills did not balk, at least not initially. He proceeded to mark up a comprehensive bill that, among other things, contained a provision that an AFDC recipient could keep the first thirty dollars she earned and one-third of the remainder (not unlike the provisions in the Carter-era disability insurance law). Then the situation changed. The riots that occurred in cities such as Detroit and Newark, New Jersey, in the summer of 1967 were an important catalyst. They seemed to indicate a breakdown in law and order in the very places where the funds from the Great Society and its War on Poverty had been directed. The political logic of the riots was for Congress to take a different tack toward welfare, away from generosity and toward discipline. The senior staff member of the Ways and Means Committee tried to explain the situation to staffers in Lyndon Johnson's White House. He said that members of Congress worried about the growth of the AFDC rolls and were particularly upset by stories of three generations of a family going on welfare. Some of these congressmen believed that welfare was self-perpetuating and therefore self-defeating or, as future generation of welfare reformers would put it, that welfare bred dependence and imprisoned people in its grasp.[18]

The Ways and Means Committee came up with a new set of welfare ideas or at least temporary provisions that would send a signal that it did not approve of the welfare expansion and expected the states to get serious about work and training programs. One was to initiate a freeze on the number of welfare grants to families with absent parents. If the population of such families increased, states would no longer receive automatic funds to make up the difference from one year to the next. The committee also decided that a welfare mother's participation in a work and training program should not be by choice. Instead the government could compel her to enter such a program. Representative Mills told his colleagues that welfare should not become "a way of life." Instead, as historian Molly Michelmore reminds us, Mills believed they should "submit themselves to a test of their ability to learn a job." The Senate backed away from some of the House provisions. It removed the freeze or cutoff from its version of the bill and permitted, in an amendment offered on the Senate floor, mothers of young children more of a choice about participating in a work and training program. The House dominated the conference committee and moved it toward the House position. The Ways and Means rebuke of the welfare program would stand.[19]

Mayors, such as New York's John Lindsay, reacted with alarm to the welfare provisions in the 1967 amendments. John Gardner, Lyndon Johnson's Secretary of Health, Education, and Welfare, warned the President that "these are going to be celebrated issues in the liberal community," ones that Bobby Kennedy, the Senator from New York who was moving closer to entering the 1968 presidential race, would surely exploit to his advantage. Joseph Califano advised the President, who was receiving strong pressure to veto the bill, that many people perceived the bill as anti-Negro and feared it would become the pretext for urban riots in the campaign summer of 1968. The controversy delayed final passage of the bill until December 18, and President Johnson allowed it to become law at the beginning of 1968. He called upon Secretary Gardner to establish "compassionate safeguards to protect deserving mothers and children." The President suggested that maybe the time had arrived for a fundamental reexamination of the nation's welfare laws. "The welfare system in America," he said, "is outmoded and in need of major change." Wilbur Cohen, who had done as much as anyone to create the 1962 amendments, believed that "there is an urgent need for new blood, new and imaginative thinking, and competent administrative experience in the Federal welfare program."[20]

As Cohen suggested, the top-level officials of the Department of Health, Education, and Welfare no longer held much confidence in the Welfare Administration that had been created to administer the 1962 law. Ellen Winston, the former head of the welfare program in North Carolina and the first head of the Welfare Administration, found the job of supervising the welfare programs at the federal level too daunting and resigned in 1967. The new idea was to create something called the Social and Rehabilitation Service, headed by Mary Switzer, who had developed a tight relationship with Lister Hill (D-AL), John Fogarty (D-RI), and other powerful members of Congress in her role running the vocational rehabilitation program. Switzer would emphasize work and not merely cash payments. Even Wilbur Cohen suggested that "welfare departments have not always been in the forefront of providing training or work for welfare recipients." He and his colleagues hoped that the new arrangement, which would administer the 1967 laws, would satisfy welfare's critics while at the same time assure liberals that the program would keep vulnerable children out of poverty.[21]

The presence of new participants in the welfare debate made it particularly hard to find the appropriate balance. On the left the National Welfare Rights Organization (NWRO) emerged as a powerful voice articulating the demands of welfare recipients. This organization reflected the influence of the 1960s on American social policy. An offshoot of the increasingly confrontational civil rights movement, it built upon the new rights consciousness that characterized the American legal system in the years after *Brown v. Board of Education*. Lawyers working for public interest groups, themselves largely the product of the legal aid programs established by the War on Poverty, sought to make welfare easier to get and a more secure right for those on the rolls. In sharp contrast to congressional leaders who governed the program from the top down, the lawyers, working from the bottom up, fought to expand the rolls to include more of the people who were eligible and to limit the state's power to remove people from the rolls.[22]

Representatives of the NWRO became a staple feature of hearings on welfare in Congress and in state legislatures. Their testimony lacked the deferential tone of most of the others who testified. They believed that welfare benefits were too low, not too high, and they failed to embrace the new idea that welfare recipients should work in return for their benefits. Beulah Sanders confronted the formidable Martha Griffiths (D-MI) by saying, "One of the things we are concerned about is being forced into these nonexisting positions that might be going out and cleaning Mrs. A's kitchen. . . . I feel I am more valuable and can do something else." George Wiley, the leader of the group, found the administration's welfare proposals "too timid, token, tardy and toothless."[23]

The NWRO received prime exposure during the Senate Finance Committee hearings to consider the 1967 amendments. Its testimony contained a threat in the form of a warning. If welfare benefits were not raised, more riots would occur in the cities. The organization compared workfare to slavery. Mrs. Margaret McCarty of Baltimore explained, "It's another form of slavery, baby. But I'm black and I'm beautiful. They're not gonna take me back." In its September 19, 1967, testimony before the Senate Finance Committee, one NWRO representative characterized the House-passed bill as a form of "dictatorship" that imposed new demands on welfare recipients without giving them any say in the matter. The September 19 testimony featured a sit-in at the hearing room that triggered a confrontation with the Capitol Police. Committee Chairman Russell Long remained unimpressed. He had no particular complaint against welfare and became a leader in the fight to raise the welfare benefits of the elderly and disabled. He felt differently about AFDC and about welfare mothers and sought to turn the NWRO's behavior to his rhetorical advantage. "If they can find time to march in the streets, picket and sit in all day in the committee hearing rooms, they can find time to do some useful work," he famously said.[24]

A different critique of the welfare program emerged from the right.

Almost as soon as Ronald Reagan became Governor of California in 1967, he became an important figure in the nation's politics. Already famous because of his Hollywood career and blessed with both personal charm and a gift for oratory, he held one of the nation's most visible political posts and unlike many national political leaders, articulated a conservative point of view. He made welfare one of his issues. "Here in California," he said, "nearly a million children are growing up in the stultifying atmosphere of programs that reward people for *not* working, programs that separate families and doom these children to repeat the cycle in their own adulthood." AFDC should not be treated as an "inalienable right" but rather as "something of a gift" from working Americans to those in need. The community had every right to put work requirements on those welfare recipients capable of joining the labor force.[25]

The Family Assistance Plan and the Promise of a Guaranteed Annual Income

By the 1970s the consensus that had made the 1962 amendments possible had largely disappeared, in part because it was difficult to find a welfare reform plan that would satisfy both the NWRO and Ronald Reagan. A new political divide developed between supporters of guaranteed annual income on one side and advocates of the traditional welfare system, with benefits limited to people deemed to be truly deserving and with no effort made to create work incentives, on the other. As the conscious efforts of the NWRO and the poverty lawyers and more impersonal political and demographic factors fueled the expansion of the AFDC rolls, that very expansion strengthened Ronald Reagan's position in the national debate. Particularly in the years before the economic crises of the 1970s made social reform much more difficult, politicians and the experts who advised them conducted a frenzied search for an acceptable welfare policy. Contrary to the conventional wisdom, the policy makers of the early 1970s did not come up empty. Instead the period ended with a major addition to America's welfare state but not one that applied to the AFDC program.

One idea that emerged at the time held that policy makers should set aside the existing welfare programs and instead institute a guaranteed annual income that would take care of all poor people's financial needs. Such an action would require substantial changes to the existing welfare structure, such as abolishing the 1935 welfare categories, substituting federal for state administration of welfare programs, and trimming some of the other programs that supported welfare recipients such as public housing. It was, therefore, a difficult "ask" but one that seemed plausible during the urban riots and social disruptions of the late 1960s and early 1970s. One source of this idea was the President's Commission on Income Maintenance Programs. Started in 1968 in part to quiet some of the furor created by the 1967 amendments, it issued its report in 1969, when President Johnson had already left town, and Richard Nixon, the beneficiary of the backlash against Johnson's war and Johnson's Great Society, was President of the United States. Neither Johnson nor Nixon showed much interest in the report. Nixon's staff nonetheless absorbed some of its ideas and in an unlikely turn of events proposed its own version of a guaranteed annual income.[26]

Nixon unveiled his Family Assistance Plan (FAP) in a televised address to the nation on August 8, 1969. He proposed scrapping AFDC (but not the other welfare categories) and replacing it with a federal program that would pay a family of four with no other source of income $1,600 a year. Families of four with one of the parents in the labor force could still receive money from the federal government because the first $720 of the parent's wages would be disregarded and the remaining income taxed at the rate of 50 percent. In addition, all poor families would benefit from an expansion of the Food Stamp Program that would cover the costs of some of that family's food budget. The complicated arithmetic of the plan permitted a family earning $3,000 a year to receive an additional $460 from the government plus assistance in the form of food stamps.[27]

It was an audacious proposal, and many, even within the Nixon administration, opposed it. The opponents argued that the federal government should not be in the business of supplementing the wages of working Americans. Instead it should subsidize state welfare payments for people excused from the labor force because of their age, physical condition, or family circumstances. Proponents of the plan argued that, unlike the AFDC program, it encouraged work, paid its benefits in always welcome cash rather than in sometimes unwanted advice or training, and gave a mother and father no reason to separate just to receive welfare benefits. From a more political point of view, the measure was, if not race neutral, then at least color-blind, removing the Nixon administration from some of the contentious clashes that had occurred in 1967. It diminished the influence of social workers, who often acted as advocates to build up a client's welfare grant and who protected Democratic rather than Republican interests in the inner cities, on social welfare policy. It marked a step toward ending a system that many people believed encouraged the birth of "illegitimate" babies. The proposal also allowed the President to preempt his political opponents who were more inclined than many of the President's political allies to back a guaranteed annual income. There was a bold, Nixon-goes-to-China quality about it.[28]

FAP failed in Congress. Conservatives thought its benefits too generous and liberals regarded its benefits as too low. The National Welfare Rights Organization, for example, became a dedicated opponent of FAP. The measure could not get past both houses of Congress, despite the fact that Wilbur Mills, desperate for a solution to the welfare problem, endorsed it and got the House to pass it three times. Russell Long and the Senate Committee on Finance blocked its passage in the Senate. Long regarded FAP as something like a liberalization of the AFDC program, an expensive undertaking that, whatever the economists' theories, would encourage indolence rather than work. It would also have the undesired effect of increasing the size and influence of the federal bureaucracy.[29]

Although these sorts of arguments mattered, FAP stumbled over a structural impediment that would have doomed it even in a more accommodating political system. Simply put, a guaranteed income was a difficult measure to introduce into a mature social welfare system. People might agree to abolish AFDC. States might welcome the fiscal relief such a move might bring, and many people would agree that AFDC was an anachronistic program that was not suited to modern conditions. Instead of a program that paid pensions to deserving widows, as originally intended in 1935, it had become an inefficient and self-defeating income maintenance program for many of the nation's most poor. The revolution in labor force expectations that made it common practice for mothers to work outside of the home undermined the original rationale for AFDC. Even if getting rid of AFDC enjoyed wide political support, outside of groups like the NWRO whose political identity depended on it, other social welfare programs that interacted with AFDC benefited from bipartisan support and could not be abolished so easily. Nixon, for example, felt obligated to accompany his welfare reform proposal with a liberalization of the Food Stamp Program, which had the strong backing of Senator Robert Dole and other politicians who promoted agricultural interests. Other members of Congress strongly supported Medicaid and still others backed public housing. If enacted, FAP would be added to these existing programs.

These political facts of life increased the difficulty for FAP or any guaranteed annual income plan to create work incentives. Senator John Williams (R-DE) made this point with devastating effect at an April 1970 Senate Finance Committee hearing. He used charts that the Department of Health, Education, and Welfare had prepared for him to show that under the President's plan a welfare mother in Chicago who made $720 a year ended up with $6,128 year in the form of cash benefits, public housing, food stamps, and medical care. A mother in similar circumstances who earned substantially more—$5,560—received a total of only $6,109. The working mother ended up nineteen dollars poorer for her time on the job. It would take a great deal of money and considerable political effort to correct this problem. In general, the stronger the work incentives, the more expensive a plan like FAP would be. Policy makers never figured out a way to solve this problem because abolishing AFDC did not give them a clean slate on which to work.[30]

The introduction of FAP did little to quell the growing public discontent over welfare. Congress sent another message to welfare recipients in 1971 legislation sponsored by Herman Talmadge of Georgia. The law now required all AFDC mothers who were not caring for children under six to register for the Work Incentive Program (WIN). Like many manpower programs aimed at welfare recipients, WIN failed to make much of an impression on the caseload. In December 1974, for example, 3.3 million heads of household received AFDC. Approximately 1.3 million of them registered for WIN. Authorities selected fewer than 250,000 to participate in the program. Including people chosen in previous years, the total number of participants was 500,000. Half of these people required subsidized childcare, which represented an additional cost to the government. About a third of the participants took jobs in what authorities termed "unsubsidized employment." For the most part, these were low-level jobs with few entry requirements, the very sorts of jobs that the National Welfare Rights Organization found demeaning. Of the group that started jobs, about a third quit within ninety days. Only fifty-two thousand people left the welfare rolls, with no guarantees that they would not be back. Such results brought little honor to the beleaguered welfare program.[31]

Contrary to the conventional wisdom and the low expectations generated by WIN and other welfare initiatives of the time, Nixon's campaign on behalf of FAP resulted in a major expansion of the American welfare state. The dynamic behind this expansion was that one could not raise benefits for families with children, as FAP proposed to do, without also raising the benefits of the people in the other welfare categories. If anything, increasing the benefits to the elderly, blind, and disabled was easier than raising them for dependent children. The biggest difference was that Russell Long opposed one and supported the other. He saw himself as a legislative champion of the needy elderly and disabled, just as his father Huey had been. As Congress toyed with various iterations of FAP between 1969 and 1972, Long kept the focus on the "adult" welfare groups. In October 1972, President Nixon signed a law—the same one that extended Medicare coverage to people with disabilities and end stage renal disease (described in chapter 4)—that initiated the Supplemental Security Income program.

The new program, destined to become a major part of America's welfare state, combined aid to the blind, disabled, and elderly into one program that was administered by the federal government. The new national standard for indigent people in these categories, who still needed to pass a means test in order to receive benefits, was $130 a month for an individual and $195 for a couple. But the program never worked quite as smoothly as its creators intended. Supplemental state benefits assured that the program would be different from state to state. Many mistakes attended the January 1974 launch of the program, and SSI recipients did not entirely escape the welfare stigma. The creation of the program nevertheless demonstrated that even in 1972 policy makers were still not hesitant to expand welfare programs under the right circumstances. The period that coincided with the defeat of the FAP, despite the continuing conflict over AFDC, marked the height of the Great Society era of welfare state expansion. Increases in Social Security benefits accompanied by indexing benefits to the rate of inflation, the broadening of Medicare to include new groups, and the creation of SSI testified to that.[32]

Workfare and the Reagan Approach to Welfare

The broad issue of welfare reform remained a challenge for all of the presidents of the 1970s, although a leveling off of the AFDC caseload at the end of the decade eased some of the pressure. Each administration came up with a welfare reform plan that Congress balked at passing. In the AFDC program, the actions of individual states eventually overshadowed the activities of the federal government. California, with its ambitious and charismatic governor, attracted much attention. Ronald Reagan touted his state plan as superior to the Family Assistance Plan. In 1971 the California rolls were growing at the rate of forty thousand a month. In March of that year, at the same time that federal legislators were struggling with the FAP, Reagan announced his new welfare plan for California, which the state legislature adopted. In broad outline, the plan had three main objectives: to "purify" the rolls so that only those who met the eligibility criteria stayed on them, to force fathers and other responsible relatives to accept financial responsibility for their children, and to make the able-bodied poor work for their grants. The California Community Work Experience Program (CWEP) required welfare recipients, or at least those who did not have to care for young children or those who were not too sick or disabled to work, to "pay off" their welfare grants by taking minimum-wage jobs. By February 1, 1972, with the Family Assistance Plan still under consideration, Governor Reagan felt sanguine enough about the California results to tout them to the Senate Finance Committee. Russell Long welcomed such testimony, since it suggested that the states might handle the welfare problem better than the federal government.[33]

In fact, the results were modest. The number of welfare recipients in California began to drop in April 1971 and continued to drop for eight straight months. At the same time, the benefit levels of those remaining on the rolls increased, and at least some former welfare recipients got jobs. In May 1971 the rolls of the basic AFDC program (not the related AFDC–Unemployed Parent program) contained 1,285,742 mothers and children. In June 1972, three months after Governor Reagan's testimony before the Senate Finance Committee, 1,270,972 remained on the rolls.[34]

Even the California Community Work Experience Program failed to produce a miracle and to reverse the indifferent record of state manpower programs for welfare recipients. During 1974, for example, 182,735 Californians were eligible for CWEP, 5,712 were assigned to work sites, and 4,760 actually worked. The low numbers occurred partly because less than half of the state's counties participated and many of the caseworkers in the counties that did participate lacked enthusiasm for the plan. In touch with their caseload and aware of its many needs, they refused to regard the program as mandatory or even helpful for that matter.[35]

The numbers could be arrayed in all sorts of ways, depending on the point that an advocate wanted to prove. Evangelistic governors such as Reagan became increasingly important in social welfare policy because they were able to cast the most favorable light on their experiences. And in a sense things were moving in their direction. The era of presidents who had served in Congress or spent their career in the military (another twentieth-century federal institution) lasted from 1945 to 1977. Governors took over for the rest of the century and well into the next. As a result state policy became more relevant to federal policy. In 1972 Congress had authorized the federal government to assume the administration of the adult welfare categories. After that things tended to move in the opposite direction.

Reagan's relevance became undisputable after he became president in 1981. He helped to initiate a significant round of welfare reforms that had a different tone from those of his immediate predecessors. The liberal welfare regime that lasted into the Carter years appeared to be over, and a new, more conservative regime began. One indication of this trend was that the guaranteed annual income—or variations such as Nixon's Family Assistance Plan—received little serious consideration from Reagan or from Congress during the 1980s. The first Republican Senate since 1955 and Reagan's own popularity, particularly after the assassination attempt on his life on March 30, 1981, made it easier for him to sell his version of welfare reform.

Reagan benefited from having staff workers in the Department of Health, Education, and Welfare and the White House who had previously worked in California and knew the California system. John Svahn, for example, served as California's Acting Director of Social Welfare and helped with Governor Reagan's welfare reform plan before he came to Washington during the Nixon-Ford era to become, among other things, the Administrator of the Social and Rehabilitation Service, the federal agency in charge of the AFDC programs. During Reagan's first administration, Svahn headed the Social Security Administration and worked in the White House as an advisor. Caspar Weinberger, a key Reagan advisor whom the President appointed to be Secretary of Defense, had worked in the Nixon-Ford administration as the Director of the Office of Management and Budget and the Secretary of Health, Education, and Welfare in 1972 and 1973. As HEW Secretary, Weinberger brought Robert Carleson into the department to be the US Commissioner of Welfare. Another veteran of California's welfare reform, Carleson worked on the domestic policy staff in the White House and helped to formulate and implement the welfare reforms that the Reagan administration made in 1981.[36]

According to a story that Carleson liked to tell, he met with the President-elect in January 1981 while Reagan was staying in Blair House. The two men talked about welfare reform for two hours. Reagan, in Carleson's telling, reacted positively to his ideas. Later Carleson approached former Michigan congressman and current Office of Management and Budget Director David Stockman and told him, "Here is something that has been approved. All you have to do is plug it in. It's like a cassette."[37]

In the Reagan era, welfare reform, like Medicare and Medicaid, became part of the budget reconciliation process that had become standard practice in American policy formulation. Congress set budget targets, often budget cuts or reductions, and asked the various authorizing committees to meet them. The measures devised by these committees, covering a wide range of government programs, were then consolidated into one large bill, known in 1981 as the Omnibus Budget Reconciliation Act (OBRA). Although not as dramatic as stand-alone legislation such as the 1935 Social Security Act or the 1965 Medicare law, OBRA took its place among the nation's most important social policy measures.[38]

OBRA put the lid on the drive to create work incentives within welfare programs, such as the 1967 rules the allowed welfare recipients to keep some of the money they earned. As befit Reagan's desire to restrict welfare to the truly needy, it limited eligibility for AFDC to families with gross incomes less than 150 percent of a state's standard of need. Reagan strongly opposed the features of the law that were intended to encourage work effort among welfare recipients. No longer would various exemptions and work disregards allow relatively advantaged families to receive welfare. According to the new 1981 rules, a welfare recipient lost her work bonus after only four months of working and could not reclaim that bonus for a year. The new law also limited the work expenses, such as the cost of the bus ride to work or childcare, that a welfare recipient could claim. The changes meant that a welfare recipient now had a brief trial work period. After this trial she either lost her welfare because her earnings took her beyond the 150 percent of the state standard of need or found her grant greatly reduced—a reduction of one dollar for every dollar she earned.[39]

The 1981 changes in the law sent a strong signal to potential welfare recipients that the benefits might not be worth the effort they put into obtaining them. Almost as soon as OBRA went into effect, the AFDC rolls began to dip. Federal expenditures for AFDC declined from fiscal year 1981 to fiscal year 1982 by half a billion dollars. These "gains" could not be sustained, in part because of a rise in the unemployment rate that people took to calling the "Reagan recession." Nonetheless the changes showed that the administration was serious about reducing the growth of the rolls in the same way that Wilbur Mills had been in 1967. Neither Representative Mills nor President Reagan wanted welfare to become a way of life for young mothers with children. Liberals reacted with alarm that the nation's leaders were putting the nation's children at risk for harm.[40]

Reagan remained a believer in his version of workfare, the Community Work Experience Program, and thought it should be instituted in all the states. Congress refused to mandate CWEP as standard welfare practice and instead crafted a measure that permitted (but did not require) various forms of workfare in the states.[41]

Workfare gave welfare reform a new meaning. Liberals believed in training programs as agents of benevolent change for welfare recipients because they provided the recipients with valuable human capital. They also respected, to a far greater degree than many of the conservatives who professed a belief in family values, the right of a mother to stay home and raise her children and not be forced to join the labor force against her will. CWEP implied something different. It was a form of coercion or discipline and not intended in any way to be voluntary. If liberals thought the state had a vital mission to protect the welfare of children that entailed giving indigent mothers a right to receive welfare, conservatives regarded welfare as a grant from the state that carried certain obligations on the part of the recipient. "We have to use welfare," wrote Lawrence Mead, an academic who became one of the new conservative welfare theorists, "to set some standards for the recipients." Welfare grants carried "social obligations."[42]

The Family Support Act of 1988: Enter the Governors

OBRA came in the Reagan administration's first year, and Congress passed the Family Support Act, a second major piece of welfare legislation, in the administration's last year. Over the eight-year course of Reagan's presidency, his political situation, like that of most presidents, had changed. A lame duck, he faced a Congress with Democratic majorities in both houses. His popularity, tarnished by the Iran-Contra scandal and the simple passage of time, no longer stood at the high levels he had enjoyed in 1981 or during his landslide reelection in 1984. More than before, he needed to cooperate with the Democrats to achieve legislative success. On both Medicare and welfare Reagan managed to strike a deal with the Democrats. The Catastrophic Health Coverage Act of 1988 expanded the Medicare program, at least until it was repealed a year later, to include prescription drugs (as discussed in chapter 5). The prescription drug proposal came from the Democrats, not the Reagan administration, but found its way into a bipartisan bill. In a similar manner, the Family Support Act of 1988 followed the suggestions of the Democrats to provide welfare recipients with social services that they believed were necessary to facilitate the transition from welfare to work. It also emphasized Republican ideas that welfare grants carried obligations that the recipients needed to meet if they wanted to retain their benefits. Both sides agreed to put the emphasis on work. Just as in health care policy, the private sector would lead the way.

Over the course of the Reagan administration, the nation's governors had emerged as an important influence over welfare politics. In the field of welfare, with its matching grants from the federal government to the states, the opinions of governors who had the ultimate responsibility for administering the law always mattered. At the same time, the federal government enjoyed an advantage over the states because it had more money at its disposal as a result of its larger tax base. Within the Social Security Administration, the federal agency with administrative responsibilities for welfare from 1935 until 1963, an unspoken assumption prevailed that there was less corruption and a higher level of professionalism and expertise in Washington than in Albany, Trenton, or Springfield. That feeling began to erode in the 1970s, when fiscal stringency was the order of the day at all levels of government and when the Social Security Administration's reputation for competence suffered a serious decline. The welfare agencies that had taken over from the SSA, such as the Welfare Administration and the Social and Rehabilitation Service, had never enjoyed a reputation for competence in the first place. By 1972 the Senate Finance Committee actively solicited the opinions of Governor Reagan and of the less well-known Governor of Georgia when it considered the Family Assistance Plan and created the Supplemental Security Income program.[43]

By the Reagan era, the National Governors Association met regularly in Washington and offered suggestions to Congress that were taken seriously. It was a bipartisan organization whose recommendations reflected a consensus among Republican and Democratic governors. That dynamic gave it more of a good government aura than other organizations that lobbied Congress. As with all organizations, however, self-interest prevailed. The governors sought to prevent what they called unfunded mandates that imposed responsibilities on them without supplying what the governors deemed to be adequate compensation. The governors also favored a smooth interface, to use a term just coming into vogue in the early personal computer era, between the state and federal governments. They sought discretion rather than what they regarded as intrusive oversight and like any citizen or organization hoped not to be ensnared in mountains of paperwork.

In February 1987, at the beginning of the congressional term in which the Democrats regained their majority in the Senate, the governors, led by Arkansas Governor Bill Clinton, issued a welfare reform plan. They saw themselves as ideally suited to this task because, as they or their press agent put it, "The leading innovations in this area have come from the states." Leading lights in Congress, such as New York Senator Daniel Moynihan—perhaps the best-known and most respected welfare expert in the Senate—hastened to agree. "It is now the states—not the federal government," said the creator of the Family Assistance Plan and the former Harvard academic, "that seem to have the energy and creativity necessary to develop new, more productive approaches to public assistance." According to the *Congressional Quarterly*, the governors "jump-started" welfare reform.[44]

The governors synthesized the conventional wisdom of the era. They called for a "binding, contractual agreement" that spelled out the responsibilities of both sides. The contract specified that mothers with children older than three had an obligation to work toward self-sufficiency by acquiring training and looking for work. If they failed to meet their obligations, they could lose their welfare benefits, although the governors were very squeamish about taking away their children's benefits. The government also had its obligations, such as to supply the necessary education and training, childcare, medical care, and job placement for the welfare caseload. In the governors' view of the world, these initiatives, such as

Medicaid, would benefit from federal dollars but would also allow them the freedom to devise programs best suited to their states.[45]

Ronald Reagan signed the Family Support Act of 1988 into law in October, just a month before his Vice President defeated Massachusetts Governor Michael Dukakis in the general election. The law, billed as emphasizing work, child support, and family benefits in an effort to avoid long-term welfare dependency, led with its most popular feature. Nearly everyone supported increased efforts to determine the paternity of a welfare baby in order to collect payments from the father or other responsible relative.[46]

This feature provided the government with found money that would otherwise be used to pay welfare benefits, and it prodded fathers to assume responsibility for the lives they had created. It also marked a congressional response to lurid television news stories such as Bill Moyers's shocking *The Vanishing Family: Crisis in Black America* (1986). The documentary featured a young black male who lived in Newark, New Jersey, the site of the debilitating 1967 riots. "Timothy," although still a young man, was the father of six children to whom he felt no responsibility. "That's on them" (meaning the children's mothers), he said. "I ain't gonna let no woman stand in the way of my pleasures." The new law reinforced a child support enforcement program that dated from 1975 and required, beginning in November 1990, all states to withhold the wages of people who owed child support payments in cases handled by the federal Office of Child Support Enforcement. The legislation benefited from the improving technology that allowed authorities to locate missing fathers, to garnish state and federal income tax refunds, and to use federal and state unemployment records in the effort to find deadbeat dads.[47]

Establishing paternity mattered because child support could not be enforced without it. The Family Support Act instituted penalties for states that lagged in this effort but provided federal funds for any laboratory costs that might be involved. States also had the responsibility of getting the Social Security numbers of both parents when birth certificates were issued and to make those numbers available to state welfare authorities if necessary.

The new law also tackled the more difficult and contentious problem of preparing welfare recipients for jobs. It created a new job training program, the latest in the long line of such programs that included the 1967 Work Incentive Program and the community work experience and other such programs authorized by OBRA in 1981. Now came the Job Opportunities and Basic Skills Training program (JOBS); its acronym emphasized its purpose. The law required all states to establish a JOBS program intended to allow needy families with children to get the necessary education, training, and employment to avoid long-term welfare dependence. JOBS required caseworkers to assess the skills and needs of a welfare recipient and then to develop an "employability plan" uniquely tailored to the needs and skills of the recipient. Recipients would receive assistance in obtaining childcare so that they could pursue the education, job skills training, job readiness preparation, and job search activities contained in their particular plan. Clients might also receive postsecondary education or some form of vocational training, all in an effort to make them more employable.

Although participation in JOBS was mandatory for all welfare clients, the law permitted many exceptions to the rule of the sort that had hindered participation in previous welfare-to-work programs. A JOBS program or suitable childcare might not be available in a particular locale. Individuals who were ill, incapacitated, of advanced age, under the age of sixteen, needed at home to care for a relative, already working thirty hours a week, a full time student, or in the second trimester of pregnancy received exemptions from the program. At the same time, participants in the JOBS program who failed to follow through on the activities in their employment plan faced real penalties of a sort that would have created a furor in earlier welfare discussions. On the one hand, the states needed to provide childcare and Medicaid in the transitional period between welfare and regular work. The state also had the obligation of making sure that all parents under the age of twenty and on welfare attended school. Those without high school diplomas were required to be working toward one and could substitute their classes for formal participation in JOBS. On the other hand, a welfare recipient who did not show up for a prescribed activity or who turned down a legitimate employment offer could have her welfare grant reduced by the amount that was considered to cover her needs, rather than the needs of her children. For families with two parents who violated the JOBS rules, both parents faced the loss of their benefit. Successive violations led to progressively longer sanctions.

Although the Family Support Act established a flexible format for state welfare administrators to create pathways toward employment, it was not successful enough to forestall efforts to move AFDC further in a conservative direction. One temptation was to take only the easy cases with the most possibility of success: a woman with a college degree taking care of her child who met the state's standard of need, for example. Finding a job for her would be easier than dealing with a twenty-one-year-old school dropout with more than one child and a record of encounters with the juvenile justice system. The law provided financial incentives for the states to focus on the hard cases.[48] These regulatory measures were, however, difficult for the federal government to enforce, and conservatives could still argue that the Family Support Act left much of the basic AFDC program structure intact and impeded the ability of individual states to create their own program.

Conclusion

The Family Support Act, like other welfare measures before it, relied on the federal power of the purse to discipline the states that failed to meet its standards. At the same time, the law reinforced the trend to make states rather than the federal government the locus of social policy. In this regard it showed the influence of the National Governors Association in its creation. State power appeared to be a new feature of welfare politics. Earlier laws, such as the 1962 Public Welfare Amendments, had assumed that the states needed advice and guidance from Washington if they were to rehabilitate people on welfare. In that sense welfare reform was a top-down exercise. Many influential people in the executive branch believed that programs that increased federal control over welfare policy marked improvements over their predecessors. The Supplemental Security Income program of 1972 followed that design principle, and so did the presidentially launched Family Assistance Plan. Passage of the Family Support Act in 1988 showed that things were now heading in the opposite direction—toward the states and away from Washington, toward welfare programs that varied from state to state and away from programs that fit a rigid federal mold. At the same time, welfare programs acquired a new modesty. The Family Support Act had a fairly narrow reach and modest goals. If successful, it would create marginal improvements in the welfare program that could be sustained over time.

The day of the big play in welfare reform that would transform the welfare system in a single stroke, such as the Family Assistance Plan, appeared to be over. Instead, states assumed their traditional role as laboratories of reform. The use of the states as laboratories implied a willingness to experiment without knowing the outcome in advance. The belief that experts, whether they were social workers dispensing therapeutic services in 1962 or economists designing a guaranteed annual income in 1969, could "solve" the welfare problem was waning.

If the revival of state power and the willingness to experiment were features of modern welfare reform, so was the notion of a contract between the state and the welfare recipient. It mimicked the legal transactions that took place in the private sector and reinforced the notion that welfare grants carried obligations. In the past these obligations involved a mother's duty toward her children. In the 1960s, they widened to include the notion that mothers with dependent children, like other heads of households, had an obligation to join the labor force or at least take positive steps, such as getting a high school diploma, that prepared them for the world of work. Liberals could assuage some of their guilt over the coercive aspects of these contracts by insisting that the state provide the necessary social services, such as day care and health care, that were necessary for welfare mothers to work.

All of that set the stage for the fundamental welfare reform that occurred in 1996 that will be the focus of the next chapter. A resurgent Republican Party and the state governors had earned their place at the table and pushed the welfare reform discussion in a conservative direction. In 1935, at the start of the process, the Democrats exerted their power both in Congress and the White House, although as the majority party they covered a wide ideological spectrum. The Social Security Act set up the basic structure that included categories of people eligible to receive welfare benefits that were supported by federal grants. The interplay of the welfare categories and the drive to expand Social Security and make it the nation's retirement benefit, combined with the demographic and political forces of the postwar era, centered welfare reform initiatives on families with dependent children. Through the course of significant legislation in 1962, 1967, 1972, and 1988, the nation never found a stable solution to the growth of the welfare rolls. This social policy failure paved the way for the 1996 welfare reform legislation.

CHAPTER SEVEN

Clinton, Gingrich, and Welfare Reform in 1996

In the early 1990s, as a new round of welfare reform got under way, it became increasingly common to refer to the AFDC program as an anachronistic failure. In his testimony before Congress in 1994, Sam Griswold, the Director of the South Carolina Department of Social Services, observed, "Our assessment suggests that the AFDC program was designed back in the thirties for women and orphans. The number of widows and orphans in our AFDC caseload is infinitesimal." Few people thought that AFDC handled the problems of poverty among dependent children well. Donna Shalala, Clinton's Secretary of Health and Human Services, described welfare as a "national tragedy." Congressman Kweisi Mfume (D-MD), the head of the black caucus, characterized welfare as "terrible."[1]

A rational response to something anachronistic is to trade it in for something new and modern. Essentially that is what happened in 1996. Both President Bill Clinton and House Speaker Newt Gingrich supported welfare reform, and over the course of a nearly two-year period they eventually found common ground. The AFDC program proved to be much more malleable than did either Social Security Disability Insurance or Medicare. Unlike those programs, both of which survived into the twenty-first century, it could safely be jettisoned. This chapter details the circuitous route that led to the 1996 jettisoning.

In the 1990s, welfare had far more critics than defenders. Those who wished to preserve the program tended to be politicians in districts that included many welfare recipients, and even these politicians admitted that the welfare program contained many flaws. Representative Harold Ford from Memphis, who was very solicitous of welfare recipients, many of whom were his constituents, objected to the fact that "we are talking about welfare recipients like they are somebody else." In a bow to current fashion, he admitted that "abuse, fraud and waste must go" and that the system should emphasize work, but he emphasized that the children on welfare were "innocent." "I hope," added his colleague Charlie Rangel, a congressman from Harlem, "in the future we can get rid of this mean-spirited language that makes it appear that every program designed to give assistance to the poor . . . is going to become a federal target." Talk of limiting the amount of time a person could receive welfare struck Representative Cardiss Collins of Chicago as racist. She observed that "two years and out is like three strikes and you are out in the crime bill. It sounds more like a discussion about criminals than about Americans who happen to be poor and unemployed." Although conservatives emphasized welfare's destructive features, Cardiss reminded her colleagues that welfare was also a force for good. As one welfare recipient put it in very plain language, "If it had not been for the system being there, even in the condition that it is, how would I have fed my kids?"[2]

These words tended to go unheeded. A consensus developed that the AFDC program needed to be abandoned and replaced by a new program that was more effective in bringing welfare mothers into the labor force. The proximate causes of the 1996 law included a sharp spike in the monthly AFDC caseload between the end of the 1980s and 1994—exactly the sort of enrollment spike that motivated policy makers to make changes in the disability insurance program in 1980. After the steep rise in cases in the 1960s and early 1970s, the number of AFDC recipients remained relatively constant from 1971 to 1989. Then the AFDC caseload grew by over one million families between July 1989 and January 1993, a 29 percent increase. Analysts attributed as much as half of this growth to an increased number of mother-only families in which the mother had never married. These mothers and their babies born out of wedlock became a particular target of politicians invested in welfare reform. The statistical trends were difficult to ignore. Speaking before a Senate Finance subcommittee early in 1994, welfare expert David Ellwood, on leave from Harvard to serve as Assistant Secretary for Planning and Evaluation at the Department of Health and Human Services, noted that in 1960 some 9 percent of all children were in one-parent families but in 1991 nearly 30 percent of children lived in such families. Ellwood added that the poverty rate for single-parent families was 46 percent, compared with 8 percent in two-parent families.[3]

Candidate Clinton and Welfare Reform

President Bill Clinton had his eyes on the growing welfare caseload. He had played a prominent role in the Family Support Act (1988) due to his leadership in the National Governors Association. Clinton had served as Governor of Arkansas between 1979 and 1981 and again between 1983 until his resignation to become president in 1992. George H. W. Bush, his 1992 opponent, faced the consequences of the rise in the welfare rolls. According to the *New York Times*, the rolls "exploded to record highs" and reached 4.8 million families or 13.7 million people during the Bush presidency. Clinton, as a governor who had been active in welfare reform, ran as someone who had an answer to the problem.[4]

Clinton made a TV ad that aired on September 9, 1992. It featured a neatly appointed Clinton leaning on the desk from which he governed the state of Arkansas. His often hoarse voice sounded soothing and confident as he looked into the camera and faced the viewers. One of government's "worst failures," he said, was welfare. Luckily, though, Governor Clinton had "a plan to end welfare as we know it—to break the cycle of welfare dependency." The government would supply "education, job training and childcare," but those who were able would have to join the labor force. Clinton assured his audience, "I know it can work. In my state we've moved 17,000 people from welfare rolls to payrolls." Echoing rhetoric that went back at least as far as 1967 and Wilbur Mills, Clinton said it was time to make welfare work as it was intended to work—as "a second chance, not a way of life." The advertisement positioned Clinton as proactive, tough on welfare recipients yet protective of their rights to vital social services. He was a new-style Democrat not afraid to abandon the orthodoxies of the past.[5]

Having identified welfare as a priority, Clinton set his administration to work on a viable piece of legislation. A decision to move health insurance ahead of welfare reform delayed the process, but by June 1993 he had created the President's Working Group on Welfare Reform, Family Support and Independence. There would be a formal welfare reform bill in the summer of 1994. David Ellwood, Bruce Reed of the White House domestic policy staff, and Mary Jo Bane, the Assistant Secretary for Children and Families at HHS, led the group. Bane, a former Commissioner of the New York State Department of Social Services, promised to repair the deficiencies in what she described as the "organizational culture of the welfare system." She and her colleagues sought ways to strengthen that culture so that welfare became "a transitional period of preparation" with a greater "emphasis on self-sufficiency." Bane said very little about welfare as a secure entitlement that kept children out of poverty.[6]

These Clinton administration activities did not occur in a vacuum. Republicans also seized on welfare reform as a popular cause with which they wanted to be associated. The Republicans had their own working groups on the issue that went back at least as far as October 1991. With the help of influential minority staffer Ron Haskins, who was a valuable staff resource on the subject of welfare, the Republicans on the Ways and Means Committee produced a policy paper that they called *Moving Ahead: Initiatives for Expanding Opportunity in America.* It led to several bills that emphasized the need for welfare recipients to work but that failed to get much attention from the Democratic majority. Despite this frustration that came from their minority status, the Republicans persisted, operating through a House Republican task force to produce a bill filed on November 10, 1993, with the support of 164 of the 178 House Republicans. In line with the Clinton administration's thinking, the bill had a strong work component. Clay Shaw (R-FL), a member of Congress since 1981 and hence a senior member of an increasingly southern Republican congressional caucus and a former mayor of Fort Lauderdale, told his colleagues, "We have got to stop the welfare trap that has been produced in this country and it has just been lying dormant with the Congress doing absolutely about it."[7]

Newt Gingrich Enters the Battle

Even before the election of 1994, therefore, a consensus had developed in favor of some sort of welfare reform. The Republican victory and the accompanying ascendance of Newt Gingrich to the post of Speaker sped up the process. Gingrich and the Republicans came to power with legislative proposals that included a welfare reform bill. Both sides knew that

1996 marked an important election year for both Clinton and Gingrich. Clinton wanted to win a second term and become the first Democratic president since Franklin Roosevelt to serve two full terms. A welfare reform law would be a solid domestic achievement that he could add to his résumé. Gingrich wanted to maintain and possibly even strengthen the Republican majority in the House. As a historian and a student of social policy, he knew that the Republican majorities achieved in 1946 and 1952 lasted for only two years each time. Welfare reform had a prominent place in his plans to make the revolution permanent.

The battle over welfare reform in the Clinton-Gingrich era had a different political configuration than either disability insurance or Medicare. In strictly institutional terms, the circumstances most closely resembled 1947, when the Democrats held the White House but Republicans gained control of Congress. The Republicans of that era wanted to put their stamp on the nation's social policy and chose the Taft-Hartley bill, which put new constraints on what they perceived to be powerful and Democratic-oriented labor unions, as their means of doing so. They passed the bill but lost the next election. In 1952 the Republicans again won control of the Congress, and this time they secured the White House as well. Dwight D. Eisenhower presided over an expansion of the Social Security program, a consensus item in 1953. He held the line on disability insurance, however, and the Democrats pressed for that measure in 1955 after reestablishing control over both houses of Congress. Disability insurance became part of a social welfare agenda that the Democrats used to win the White House in 1960 and pass Medicare in 1965.

In 1995 the situation had reverted to that of 1947, except that the Republicans had a much firmer legislative agenda than they did in 1947 and there was a great deal of bipartisan agreement on welfare reform, the lead item on that agenda. Republican leaders faced pressures from the newly elected members of their caucus to move the discussion further to the right, and many Democratic liberals, such as the members of the Black Caucus, steered Clinton to his left.

Straw Men in the Welfare Reform Debate

In the ensuing debate, congressmen used straw men, stylized portrayals of welfare recipients resembling stereotypes, to simplify the issues and strengthen their cases. The most important of the straw men were the children born out of wedlock to welfare recipients. Neither Republicans nor Democrats could condone out-of-wedlock births. "Out of wedlock births are a national tragedy," said Mary Jo Bane.[8] Republicans, who had fewer minority and inner city constituents than did the Democrats, tried to top the Democrats in their condemnation of babies born out of wedlock. Clay Shaw believed that illegitimacy was "really tearing up society" and that welfare recipients were also cunning. "These people that are on welfare aren't stupid," he said. They knew that more children meant more welfare, which "makes the choice about having a baby out of wedlock a lot more desirable than if there were no payments to be made." Jane Meyers (R-KS) did not believe that people "have babies to get the money. . . . It is because they are in poverty, under peer pressure, they are under friend pressure, they are unhappy at home. . . . But then along comes the federal government and says 'I will give you $18,000 a year if you have two children with no man in the house.'"[9]

Illegitimate children undermined the legitimacy of the welfare program. Children in single-parent families dropped out of school, committed suicide, took drugs, and got arrested at greater rates than other children. In welfare communities, reported welfare authority and journalist Mickey Kaus, young people channeled their "entrepreneurial drive" into "gangs and crime." Inner city families, argued Glenn Loury, an academic economist with a conservative bent, "cower because of the fearsome behavior of young men who have not been civilized within a family context." Welfare, it seemed, contributed to the wilding of America. Congressman Tim Hutchinson (R-AR) believed that it might be better to place the children in orphanages rather than to allow them to grow up in dysfunctional single-parent families in violent settings. Representative Dave Camp (R-MI) summarized the situation by saying, "Republicans have succeeded in drawing the nation's attention to the magnitude of the illegitimacy crisis. Millions of Americans now understand that out of wedlock births are at the center of social pathology."[10]

This sort of lurid testimony tended to drown out the views of people who disagreed. "I believe," said Mike Kopetski (D-OR) of the Ways and Means Committee, "that every child is legitimate in the eyes of God and there is no such thing as an illegitimate child." Some social scientists questioned the notion that more welfare produced more illegitimacy. They posited that something more complicated was going on, such as the increased ability of women to get jobs and men's decreased ability to support families. "Unfortunately," said the noted economist Rebecca

Blank, "the world we live in is far from simple." Such academic advice was not particularly helpful to politicians who faced a firestorm of outrage over illegitimate births.[11]

Children who pretended to be disabled joined illegitimate children as a stigmatized group in the welfare reform debate.[12] The Supplemental Security Income program, which had been legislated in 1972 to deal with the problems of adults on welfare, also contained provisions for disabled children, who became another of the straw men in the debate. This anomalous category reflected developments in the legislative process during the creation of SSI. It became part of the legislation but did not attract much attention since Congress had seemingly more important things on its plate. An SSA staffer described the addition of benefits for disabled children as "one of those annoying details." By federal standards, the number of disabled children on the SSI rolls remained relatively low, with about fifty thousand children added to the rolls each year between 1974 and 1990. Then a 1990 Supreme Court decision changed the procedures used to determine if a child was disabled and led to a surge in the rolls, which never returned to their earlier levels. The surge attracted the attention of first the media and then Congress.

On February 4, 1994, the *Washington Post* ran a story on disabled children under the byline of venerated journalist Bob Woodward. The story highlighted the ways in which less-than-honest parents coached their children on how to get SSI benefits. They encouraged their children to act out in ways that would make state disability determination officers certify the children as disabled. Because of the 1990 Supreme Court decision, the determination process placed great emphasis on age-appropriate behavior rather than an organic impairment as the criterion for disability. A Pennsylvania employee of the State Disability Determination Services told Woodward that "children who curse teachers, fight with classmates, perform poorly in school or display characteristics of routine rebellion are often diagnosed with behavioral disorders and therefore qualify for the program's cash benefits." As was the case with illegitimate children, irresponsible parents appeared to be driving an increase in the welfare rolls.[13]

Television producers and congressional staffers read the *Washington Post* in search of material for their news shows, such as ABC's *Prime Time*, and hearings. In October 1994, the ABC prime time news magazine ran a piece on what veteran White House reporter Sam Donaldson referred to as "how easy it is to get on the receiving end of what some are calling 'crazy checks.'" The ABC producers interviewed the Pennsylvania official quoted in the Bob Woodward story, who told them in comments that aired with the piece that only 30 percent of the children on SSI actually deserved their benefits. In the manner of media stories from a different era that featured women who lived in the lap of luxury as "welfare queens," the state official said that a family of disabled children could buy a Mercedes with its benefits. A congressional subcommittee showed the *Prime Time* segment at one of its welfare hearings. It produced a sense of outrage similar to the 1986 Bill Moyers documentary on welfare fathers and mothers in Newark that had so alarmed policy makers in 1986 and influenced the tone of the 1988 Family Support Act.[14]

The Subcommittee on Human Resources of the Ways and Means Committee also invited Wayne Parker, the manager of the Shreveport, Louisiana, office of that state's Disability Determination Service, to testify. He told the subcommittee about how SSI caused average students to become behavior problems who performed badly in school. He said that the students discussed the best ways of getting "crazy checks." Parker quoted one as saying, "My mother said I had to be crazy to get a check."[15]

Jim McCrery, the congressman who represented Shreveport from 1988 to 2009, drew lessons from the testimony. "Frankly," he said, "the SSI Children's Program has grown out of control" because of "generous cash benefits, loose eligibility criteria and lack of proper Congressional oversight." He favored eliminating the cash benefit for disabled children except in extreme cases where children would otherwise require institutional care. Representative Rick Santorum, a Republican from Pennsylvania who made himself something of an expert on SSI, described the program as "the most fraudulent welfare program of all the programs out there."[16]

Although this sharp critique received some pushback from liberals who fought for the rights of disabled children, the defenders faced an uphill battle in the blizzard of so much adverse publicity. One key interest group consisted of the parents of what were still called retarded or developmentally disabled children. The Arc, a group devoted to the interests of people with developmental and intellectual disabilities, maintained a strong lobbying presence in Washington. Leaders of this group testified that mental retardation, the reason that 44 percent of the children were on the rolls, could not be faked and that 62 percent of the applicants who applied for child disability benefits in Louisiana ended up being rejected. Cutting off the cash benefit would lead to a regime of inappropriate and costly institutionalization.[17]

Immigrants who came to this country to take advantage of its welfare benefits became another straw man or stereotype in the welfare reform debate, and they had fewer defenders than disabled children.[18] From the very beginning of the SSI program in 1972, aliens admitted to the United States for permanent residence qualified for SSI on the same basis as American citizens. At first this provision in the SSI program attracted little attention in the same manner as child disability benefits. But by 1994, as the welfare reform discussion heated up, nearly a third of the aged people who received SSI were noncitizens, and their numbers on the SSI rolls had increased from 3 to 10 percent. What appeared to be happening was that immigrants arrived in the United States, became citizens, and then sent for their parents. They supported their parents for a minimum legal interval and then, in the words of the *Washington Post*, "slough[ed] them onto the rolls."

The presence of noncitizens on the rolls outraged many in Congress. Rick Santorum noted with disapproval, "We now spend $7 billion a year on welfare for noncitizens." He charged that they arrived in the country "with fairly in depth knowledge of our welfare programs and go on and qualify for those benefits, particularly SSI." "We have a responsibility to the taxpayer," Santorum argued, "which doesn't encourage this country to be the beacon of SSI payments as opposed to the beacon of economic opportunity." Although like almost all Americans he came from immigrant roots, he preferred immigrants who "will take responsibility for themselves and not rely on the federal government." Clay Shaw spoke for his party when he said that "noncitizens should not qualify for welfare." Cutting benefits for noncitizens became a convenient way of funding welfare reform and a consensus item in the welfare reform discussion.[19]

That did not exhaust the list of straw men or stereotypes used to raise the emotional temperature of the debate. Senator William Cohen, the moderate Republican senator from Maine, released a report with the lurid title "Tax Dollars Aiding and Abetting Addiction" through the Senate Special Committee on Aging, although the report was not really about aged people. The word on the street, Cohen reported, was "that SSI benefits are an easy source of cash benefits for drugs and alcohol." Like the mothers of children born out of wedlock, the mothers of children receiving "crazy checks," and the parents of immigrants, addicts and alcoholics manipulated the system. Their manipulations served to "subsidize and perpetuate drug and alcohol abuse." Government money went for self-defeating purposes because the disabled welfare category had been extended to drug addicts and alcoholics with no other major impairment. The situation led to perverse policy outcomes. Cohen's report chronicled what happened on the first day of the month in a Denver homeless shelter. With money in their pockets, addicts binged on drugs and alcohol and only returned to the shelter and any modicum of supervision when the money ran out.[20]

Each of the straw men and stereotypes became the subject of discussion in the welfare reform debate that produced the Personal Responsibility and Work Opportunity Act—the seminal welfare bill—in 1996. The alcoholics and addicts provided such an inviting avenue for politicians that two laws to deal with them preceded the main welfare reform bill. On August 15, 1994, President Clinton signed a bill that imposed a three-year limit on SSI benefits for alcoholics and drug addicts. The law required alcoholics or drug addicts to receive their benefits through a representative payee who would guard against spending the money on drink or drugs. Someone entitled to retroactive benefits would not receive a lump-sum check but rather would be paid in safer installments.[21] The Contract with America Advancement Act of 1996, the second of the new laws, went on the books in March of that year. It prohibited SSI benefits "to individuals whose drug addiction and/or alcoholism is a contributing factor to their disability." As one congressman put it, "This should put an end to having disability being misused by drug and alcohol addicts to support their habits."[22]

Welfare Reform in Wisconsin

Throughout the debate on welfare reform, the examples set by state governments remained central to the discussion, continuing a trend that had begun with the Family Support Act of 1988. State governors became one of the key interest groups in welfare politics. Although many states promoted their success stories in improving welfare program administration and saving taxpayer money, Wisconsin, under the leadership of Governor Tommy Thompson, attracted the most attention. A state that set itself up as a model for the nation needed a governor like Thompson to call attention to the state's achievements, much as Ronald Reagan and Bill Clinton, eager for national audiences, did in California and Arkansas.

The political environments of Wisconsin, California, and Arkansas differed from one another. In Wisconsin, unlike in California and Arkansas, whites made up 93 percent of the population in 1990, and most of the black population lived in Milwaukee. Wisconsin also had a fabled progressive tradition that made it a pioneer in workers' compensation during the progressive era and unemployment compensation during the New Deal. For many years, the state also had a high percentage of foreign-born citizens; in 1930 it ranked only behind New York in this category. Immigrants became an important force in the state's politics because the state had an agency to attract European immigrants, and after a year's residence these immigrants gained the right to vote. Despite the presence of heavy industry in such locations as Milwaukee and Kenosha, the state remained more agricultural than did its midwestern neighbors. How these historical trends affected the state's approach to welfare at the end of the twentieth century remained unclear, but the state's social welfare practices had always attracted outside interest.[23]

Governor Thompson, who won reelection in 1990, 1994, and 1998 and served from 1987 to 2001, sold welfare reform in the same optimistic way that President Trump would later tout a border wall. Like Trump, he was not a particularly polished speaker, in his case dropping the letter *g* from his gerunds, but he was an effective communicator. In the manner of Trump, he conducted pep rallies in which he claimed credit for any and all improvements in the Wisconsin welfare rolls. Born in 1941, Thompson differed from Trump in that he came from middle-class roots and grew up in a small Wisconsin town. His father of German and English ancestry worked as a grocer. Thompson took advantage of Wisconsin's public education resources by attending the University of Wisconsin, which had been the home base for many of the people who created and implemented Social Security, and the University of Wisconsin's law school. During the 1960s, he fell under the influence of Barry Goldwater's conservatism that the Republicans had featured in the 1964 election. Overcoming any natural shyness, he was elected to the state assembly and enjoyed a long career there, rising to the rank of minority leader.

Thompson made a successful run for governor in 1986, at a time when welfare reform ranked high among the state's political issues. That year the state created a Work Experience and Training Program, which became a precursor of the 1988 Family Support Act. During his first year in office, Thompson proposed several welfare demonstrations for which the state sought waivers (permission to deviate from standard state practice) from the federal government. For example, the state gained approval to impose more stringent requirements for participation in the Job Opportunities and Basic Skills Training program (the JOBS program created in the Family Support Act) than those in federal regulations. In Wisconsin, beginning in the spring of 1988, mothers with preschool children could participate in JOBS activities for more than the federal maximum of twenty hours a week. Thompson packaged another demonstration as "Learnfare." This program required teenage AFDC recipients, including teen mothers, to attend school regularly. If they failed to do so and, for example, accumulated more than ten unexcused absences during a school semester, then the state penalized them by not counting them in the determination of the family's welfare benefit (which reduced the benefit).[24]

Learnfare, launched in Milwaukee in spring 1988, eventually went into operation statewide, but it was not without problems. The Milwaukee schools could not locate the enrollment records for over half of the students who faced Learnfare sanctions. Legal Action of Wisconsin, a public interest organization of the sort that had worked with the National Welfare Rights Organization, filed a federal lawsuit on behalf of families it believed had been improperly sanctioned by Learnfare, prompting a judge to put an injunction on the program. Welfare recipients, even in Tommy Thompson's Wisconsin, still had their defenders.[25]

Another round of Wisconsin welfare reform demonstrations began in 1992. These demonstrations dealt with problems of national interest, such as how to reduce illegitimacy and promote marriage and how to collect child support from recalcitrant fathers. The Personal and Family Responsibility Initiative, according to historian Rebecca Barrett, "removed the financial penalty or cap if families chose to marry." It offered a carrot for welfare recipients who behaved in what the state regarded as a socially responsible manner. The Child First initiative used the stick to attack the problem of collecting child support payments by threatening nonpaying parents with jail time.[26]

The culmination of the Wisconsin experiments came in the Clinton era when both Democrats and Republicans were fixated on the problem of welfare reform. In the spring of 1995, the state announced the completion of an initiative it called "Wisconsin Works." Its importance lay in the fact that it presented one version of what might happen if, as Congress was contemplating, welfare became a block grant to the states, with the states free to design their own welfare programs. The plan represented a more complete, statewide version of a 1992 demonstration project called "Work Not Welfare" that had been tried in two relatively rural counties. Among other things, Work Not Welfare put a two-year limit on welfare receipt, with a one-year extension of transitional benefits, and made AFDC clients work for their cash benefits and food stamps. It eliminated an increase in the AFDC benefit if the family had an additional child.[27] Wisconsin Works took ideas from Work Not Welfare and other waiver-based demonstrations and, in the words of one authority, generalized "them to the caseload as a whole." The new plan linked cash assistance to some form of employment. It reduced the automatic linkages between welfare receipt and other assistance, such as childcare. "Many individuals," state authorities argued, "will do better with just a light touch." Finally, the plan put welfare administration under the control of the state's employment service agency rather than its Department of Health and Human Services.[28]

The change emphasized that welfare would be primarily an employment operation, not a form of therapy or other social work–oriented intervention to treat dysfunctional families. It represented the death knell, at least in Wisconsin, for the vision of welfare reform that President Kennedy had promoted in 1962. It also gave a sense of legitimacy to conservative plans to "end welfare as we know it." Proponents argued that measures that looked repressive and even dangerous had been tried before in states like Wisconsin and found to be effective.

Wisconsin officials were not bashful about touting their achievements beyond the state boundaries. When Gene R. Kussart of the Wisconsin Department of Health and Human Services appeared before the Senate Finance Committee in 1994, he noted that Wisconsin, under Governor Thompson, had received more federal waivers than any other state in order to experiment with welfare reform. He said that the state had made "remarkable progress" and produced an enviable "track record." When Governor Thompson took over in January of 1987, the caseload stood at 98,300, but at the beginning of 1994 it was down to 78,000. At the beginning of the Thompson era, Wisconsin had the nation's tenth largest percentage of households on welfare, but in 1994 it ranked thirty-first.[29]

As always advocates such as Gene Kussart used statistics to prove their case, yet the statistics could also be arrayed in ways that made the

Wisconsin experience look like less of a total triumph. Between 1990 and 1994, for example, the state caseload had declined at an annual rate of 6.3 percent, but in Milwaukee, where most of the state's welfare residents lived, the rate had actually increased by 0.4 percent during those years.[30] Such things were like the fine print in a financial contract—widely ignored. The basic message was that the Wisconsin experiments had worked and that Governor Thompson would be pleased to run his welfare program by himself without Washington's help. "Two years and you're out" and "work not welfare" became mantras in the national welfare debate.

The National Governors Association as Interest Group

Thompson and his fellow Republican governors had the full attention of Speaker Gingrich and Senate Majority Leader Bob Dole in 1995. The governors pushed the idea of flexible block grants that they could use as they saw fit in return for a freeze on federal spending at 1994 levels for the next five years. "Every city and state is different," said Governor John Engler of Michigan, who rivaled Governor Thompson in his efforts to "own" the welfare issue. Engler wanted "the flexibility to be different and to be creative in our strategy to reform welfare and restore hope." In keeping with the rhetoric of the Gingrich revolution, Engler believed that cutting welfare, far from endangering the nation's vulnerable children, would actually restore hope. "One size does not fit all," Governor Thompson added.[31]

The bipartisan National Governors Association suggested that the states be offered a choice: they could elect to take a block grant to assist poor families and children "with no federal restrictions," or they could continue to run the welfare program as an entitlement program but with considerably more freedom than they presently enjoyed and without even a need to match the federal dollars they received.[32]

This choice exposed the question of whether welfare should remain an entitlement in which the government had an obligation to aid any needy family that qualified or should be more discretionary, with the states allowed to turn people away or cut people from the rolls. Liberals in the Clinton administration believed strongly that welfare should remain an entitlement. Secretary Shalala argued, for example, that President Clinton would make a mistake if he left "welfare reform to the states in a grand bargain with the governors." Chief of Staff Leon Panetta insisted that Clinton should protect "the entitlement side" of welfare. Nonetheless the White House still had a considerable amount of give on the welfare issue, agreeing with the Republican governors on the need to emphasize work, to impose time limits on welfare recipients, and to give states more flexibility in setting eligibility levels and work requirements in their welfare programs.[33]

Governors Engler, Thompson, and William R. Weld of Massachusetts, with the approval of Speaker Gingrich, pushed the idea of consolidating some three hundred federal programs into eight block grants. Their colleagues failed to give them the necessary three-quarters of the votes, and the Governors Association decided to put the entitlement/block grant issue aside. It was clear, though, that the notion of block grants in place of entitlements for a wide variety of purposes had strong congressional support, particularly in the House. Representative Clay Shaw, the new head of the House Ways and Means Subcommittee on Human Resources, told the governors that the Republicans in the House were determined to create a block grant for welfare and had similar plans for other programs.[34]

Despite the setback in the National Governors Association on the issue of entitlements, Governor Thompson felt confident that time was on his side. "The train is leaving the station. It behooves the Democrats to get on board," he said. President Clinton, a former governor, continued to insist that he wanted the states to have maximum flexibility, but he asserted that there was a "national interest in protecting the welfare and the possibilities of our children."[35]

The Welfare Contest in 1995

January 1995 and the arrival of the Republican Congress marked the start of the political competition that culminated in the passage of a major welfare reform law that President Clinton signed into law in August 1996. The Republicans, fresh off their stunning 1994 victories, appeared to hold an initial edge because of the public dissatisfaction with welfare programs. Feeling the disorienting effects of losing control of the House of Representatives for the first time in more than forty years, the Democrats found themselves reacting to the Republican moves rather than initiating their own actions.

Child welfare advocates sensed that the situation had changed with the 1994 election and knew they would have to ratchet up their rhetoric. They fell back on their traditional defense of children rather than of the welfare system itself. "When the American people voted for change, and for less government, I don't believe they voted to hurt millions of children, or to make them hungrier and homeless, or to take them away from their families," said Marian Wright Edelman of the Children's Defense Fund. In the words of welfare reform veteran Daniel Patrick Moynihan, "You can't abandon children. You just cannot do it."[36]

The Republicans had what they hoped was a winning counter to this argument. Congressman Clay Shaw, the Republican congressman now in charge of the key Ways and Means Subcommittee on Welfare Reform, said that "nothing is crueler to our children today than the present welfare status quo. It's not working and it has to be changed." Since welfare did more harm than good, children on welfare needed tough love. It all fell in with Speaker Gingrich's desire to fulfill the Contract with America and create what he described as "the conservative opportunity society."[37]

Things moved swiftly in the House, with hearings on welfare reform beginning on January 5 and passage of the Personal Responsibility Act on March 24. The House measure amounted to a catalog of Republican approaches to welfare reform: deny aid to legal immigrants, deny cash assistance to families headed by unmarried women under eighteen, replace the federal school lunch program with lump-sum payments that the states could spend as they wished to aid the poor, and replace the old welfare entitlement with a new block grant. Representative Jim Talent (R-MO) proclaimed the House vote "a big victory for Republicans in Congress and for the children who will grow up in the next century."[38]

The Republicans realized that welfare reform would be a heavier lift in the Senate. Old hands like Senator Moynihan described the House bill as "a Draconian measure," and Senator John Chafee (R-RI), who was apparently willing to end welfare as an entitlement, was nonetheless reluctant to part with federal programs such as the Special Supplemental Nutrition Program for Women, Infants, and Children more commonly known as food stamps. Chafee promised that the Senate Finance Committee, unlike its counterpart in the House, would make every effort to come up with a bipartisan bill. All of the participants conceded, however, that Senate passage of a welfare reform bill was, in the words of Senator Don Nickles (R-OK) "not going to be easy."[39]

In April President Clinton promised that, unless the Senate made substantial changes to the House bill, he would veto the Republican welfare reform bill. Clinton argued that the Republicans only wanted to reduce welfare costs and made no realistic plans to help welfare recipients get jobs. The resulting bill would harm innocent children, particularly such provisions as denying aid to children born out of wedlock in a family already receiving welfare. Whether or not children were born out of wedlock, they would grow up someday, according to the President, and the Republican plan doomed these children to failure and the very real possibility that they would spend time in jail. The President and his fellow Democrats claimed they wanted to give these children the same opportunities as other Americans, so that they might attend Berkeley or Stanford rather than serve time in San Quentin.[40]

The governors joined the President in seeking to influence the welfare legislation that had been passed by the House. The Republican governors believed that the House bill was overly prescriptive and might interrupt the "progress" that Wisconsin and other states were already making toward reducing their welfare loads. They objected in particular to the federal mandates concerning illegitimacy that were in the bill to appease conservatives. For example, in an effort to punish women who bore babies out of wedlock, the bill would deny benefits to unmarried teenage mothers or to children born into families already receiving welfare. The governors wanted to make those calls themselves. Governors were also wary of cutting off welfare to families of noncitizens for fear that the responsibility for supporting legal immigrants would fall to them.[41]

The Senate Finance Committee plowed ahead on welfare reform, reporting out a bill on May 26 that modified the House bill but preserved its basic approach. As the governors had suggested, the senators removed some of the more hortatory features of the House bill and allowed the states to handle such matters as denying welfare to unmarried teenage mothers, additional children born to families already receiving welfare, and legal aliens on their own. In general the bill treated the states well: they could, for example, receive block grants from the federal government for welfare without having to spend any of their own money. Senator Carol Mosely Braun (D-IL) believed that the bill did not uphold the federal government's duty to make sure children "will not go homeless or hungry, [or] die from deprivation." But Senator Chafee, who was among the most liberal members of the Republican delegation, believed that governors "are going to be extremely conscious of taking care of children."[42]

President Clinton stopped short of saying that he would veto the Senate Finance Committee bill. Throughout the long welfare reform debate, he always kept the window for compromise open even as he deployed the threat of a veto. He criticized the bill in much the same way that he attacked Republican proposals on Medicare and other social welfare programs. The Republicans, according to the President, just wanted to save money, balance the budget, and offer tax cuts to the rich. Clinton portrayed himself as someone who wanted to end welfare as we know it and replace it with work. Unlike Senators Moynihan and Mosely Braun, for example, the President could live with time limits on welfare as both the House and the Senate favored. Yet he objected to Republican cutbacks to vital social services such as childcare and job training that he believed were necessary to turn welfare recipients into working Americans who paid taxes. He also presented himself as someone concerned about the living conditions of the poor children on welfare and their parents. Reduced welfare benefits would work to the extreme disadvantage of the children in welfare families, particularly during economic downturns. With the end of welfare as an entitlement and the initiation of federal block grants for welfare, child welfare advocates would have to compete against other strong interest groups such as nursing homes for funds in the state capitols.[43]

The Republicans, as much as the Democrats, faced ideological disagreements over the welfare reform bill that delayed party leaders from bringing the Senate Finance Committee bill to the floor. Some conservatives, such as Senator Lauch Faircloth (R-NC), believed that welfare reform should change the behavior of people seeking and living on welfare. They wanted to end the scourge of illegitimate births by, for example, cutting payments to unmarried teenage mothers and rewarding states that succeeded in reducing out-of-wedlock births. Conservatives believed it was a matter of fundamental principle, a moral matter in which the federal government needed to encourage responsible behavior that conformed to Christian family values. Although states should have maximum flexibility, the federal government needed to use its power to set moral standards at a national level. Hence conservative senators were willing to undercut the governors by not leaving all of the details of welfare policy to them, just as liberals had once tried to move welfare in their direction by making the rehabilitation of welfare beneficiaries a federally supported goal. The conservative focus on illegitimacy made more moderate Republicans, who believed that the federal government should neither impose its policy preferences on the states nor dictate the behavior of welfare recipients, uneasy (particularly since there was no guarantee that cutting benefits to unmarried teenagers would reduce illegitimate births). When Governors Thompson and Engler attended a Republican caucus, they urged the senators to create a block grant with no strings attached. But Senator Faircloth objected to the governors lecturing to him and his colleagues in a forum designed to allow senators to talk among themselves.[44]

The issue spilled over into the Republican battle for the 1996 presidential nomination. Front runner Senator Robert Dole put a premium on getting a welfare reform bill passed, even if that meant some compromise with the Democrats. Senator Phil Gramm (R-TX) placed more emphasis on getting the details right, including the provisions related to illegitimate children. He wanted to maintain the bright line between the Democrats and the Republicans on welfare reform. "We cannot let the commitment we made in the [1994] election perish on the ramparts of compromise and status quo and a deal-cutting in Washington," Senator Gramm told the Republican National Committee. The Senator insisted, in the manner of Senator Faircloth, that the welfare reform bill should cut off welfare payments for unmarried teenage mothers and not increase benefits for women who had additional children while on welfare.[45]

Where Gramm believed that the Senate Finance Committee bill was "not worthy of the name Republican welfare bill," Dole continued his efforts to broker a compromise between the Finance Committee and the bloc of twenty-four conservative Republicans, including Gramm, who did not think the Finance Committee bill was tough enough on illegitimacy or work requirements. At the same time, he attempted to allay the concerns of Governor Thompson that the bill would be loaded up with "conservative prescriptions" that, according to the Governor, were like the liberal mandates of the past because they limited "our flexibility, our ability to get the job done."[46]

Dole remained committed to the idea, favored by Newt Gingrich and the Senate Finance Committee, that welfare should be funded by a lump sum in the form of a block grant that would put a cap on federal welfare spending and end the status of welfare as an entitlement. He realized, however, that any grant formula produced winners and losers and created grounds for political if not ideological disagreements. States with growing populations, for example, did not want to lock themselves into formulas that kept their grants at a flat level over a number of years. Senator Kay Bailey Hutchison (R-TX) predicted that the proposed formula, which would freeze the level of federal spending for five years, "would produce devastating results." She wanted a formula that would distribute money according to the number of poor children in each state and make allowances for inflation and population growth. Although some Republicans believed that they "should not be fighting with one another over how to divide up the spoils of the welfare state," Senator Dole, his eyes on the prize of a Republican welfare reform bill, assured Senator Hutchinson that no state would get less than it already received and that there would be an allowance for population growth.[47]

Still another disagreement to which Dole needed to attend arose over whether it was good public policy for states to receive federal grants for welfare without having to spend at least some of their own money. Senator Pete Domenici wanted to amend the Senate Finance Committee bill to include a "maintenance of effort" provision. Under this provision, which was also supported to Senator James Jeffords (R-VT), states that reduced their welfare spending below the 1994 level would lose some of the money they would receive from the federal block grant.[48]

The Democrats encouraged these interparty squabbles. They hoped that Congress would fail to pass a welfare reform bill and that they could blame inaction on welfare reform on, in the President's words, "some people on the far right." "If the Republicans can't get their act together," said Senator John Breaux (D-LA), "it may mean we can't do welfare." That outcome did not upset Senator Moynihan, who said, "Maybe the best thing would be no thing. It may turn out that it can't be done in this Congress."[49]

On August 4 Dole unveiled his compromise plan that he hoped would settle the matter. Although President Clinton reacted relatively sympathetically, conservatives immediately attacked it. Dole's rivals for the Republican nomination, such as Senator Gramm and California Governor Pete Wilson, took to the Sunday television news shows with their criticisms. The Christian Coalition denounced the bill because it would do little "to change the alarming rate of illegitimacy." Senator John Ashcroft (R-MO) demonstrated the fervor of those who, like the Christian Coalition, saw welfare reform as a means of protecting morality, arguing that "illegitimacy is a threat to the survival of our nation and our culture." In the manner of disputes over abortion, such a matter did not yield itself easily to political compromise. The views of the libertarians clashed with those of the Christian right, even though both groups identified themselves as conservative. Despite Senator Dole's considerable skills as a negotiator, he could not repair the breach that had developed in the conservative ranks.[50]

The President tried to preserve his position in the welfare reform debate by offering a critique of the Dole bill that took the views of some liberals into consideration. The President continued to believe that a bipartisan agreement—by which he meant one that would leave his imprint on the final bill—was possible. He had four fixes for Dole's bill. One was a maintenance-of-effort provision. Another was the need to earmark federal money for childcare. A third was a financial incentive in the form of a bonus for states that succeeded in moving people from welfare to work, and a fourth was a guarantee of more money for states that experienced population growth or increased unemployment. Dole's bill set aside some money for this purpose, but, in Clinton's view, it did not provide enough. Clinton's suggestions put the Democrats in a reactive mode with Republicans controlling the action.[51]

Senate debate on Dole's compromise bill began on August 7. Dole believed that the welfare issue was important enough and the need to settle the issue urgent enough that the Senate should suspend its regular routines and work on the nation's business in the August heat. The debate featured the universal view shared by Democrats and Republicans that welfare was an anachronistic failure in urgent need of repair. Senator Robert Packwood (R-OR), the head of the Finance Committee, reminded his colleagues that "welfare started as a substitute for a deceased breadwinner. But it became a lifetime support system for someone who never had a breadwinner." The trouble was that welfare was such an inadequate support, not only because it paid low benefits but also because it failed to cure poverty and instead increased dependency.[52]

After only a few days of debate, Majority Leader Dole sent the members home without an agreement. Although Dole tried to blame the situation on the Democrats, who wanted to offer a series of amendments that would delay the legislative process, the split in the Republican Party motivated his decision. To Dole's regret, his failure to end the debate and reach consensus gave the President license to resume his political posturing: "It is time to put partisanship and politics aside and get the job done. I hope the Senate will place welfare at the top of its agenda in September and take swift action." The President clearly hoped that he, rather than Dole or Gingrich, would gain the credit for ending welfare as we know it without at the same time alienating his liberal base. Senator Moynihan, for example, loomed over the debate like an Old Testament prophet. He regarded the welfare reform bill as a disaster that grew worse the more he studied the measure.[53] "If, in 10 years, we find children sleeping on grates, picked up in the morning frozen," lectured the professor, "it will have begun on the House floor this spring and the Senate chamber this autumn."[54]

Dole, an indefatigable worker who had little use for leisure, courted conservatives during the recess in an effort to pick up enough votes to get the welfare reform bill through the Senate. Much like the President had to heed Moynihan's jeremiad, Dole had to listen to the voices of evangelical Christians buzzing in his ear. The Majority Leader came to appreciate what Ralph Reed, the head of the Christian Coalition, described as "the significance and centrality of the religious conservative constituency" in the welfare reform debate.[55]

By September 8, the recess over, Dole thought he might be ready to move the welfare bill to the floor. Differences between the moderate and conservative senators remained, and Dole moved to the right. His major concession was to include a family cap in the bill, which served to prevent increases in benefits for welfare families that had another child. Some Democrats reacted by becoming more vocal in their criticisms of the bill.[56]

A coalition of Democrats and moderate Republicans succeeded in making changes to the Dole bill on the Senate floor. Using the rationale that childcare was crucial to moving people from welfare to work, Christopher Dodd (D-CT) managed to earmark $8 billion for childcare over five years. The moderate Republican-Democratic coalition also won votes that eliminated the family cap and the provision prohibiting the payment of benefits to women who had more babies while on welfare. Conservatives such as Robert Rector of the Heritage Foundation believed that these votes stripped away the very essence of the bill and preserved a system that promoted illegitimacy and destroyed marriage. Even before the final vote on the Dole bill, Rector and his allies such as Senator Gramm turned their attention to the conference committee.[57]

President Clinton gave a radio address in which he praised Dole and his associates for bringing the nation "within striking distance of transforming the welfare system." His words sent a favorable signal to Democrats who were conflicted about voting for the bill. They created a final break between New Democrat Clinton and New Deal / Great Society /

neoconservative social critic Daniel Moynihan who refused to be associated with the latest iteration of welfare reform.[58]

On September 19, the Senate approved the Dole bill by an overwhelming margin of 87–12. Even Senator Gramm, if not Senator Faircloth, and liberal Senator Barbara Mikulski (D-MD), if not her Maryland Democratic colleague Paul Sarbanes, voted in favor of the measure. Senator Daschle expressed the opinion of many of his Democratic colleagues that it was the "best bill we're going to get." Senator Dole was euphoric that his efforts had succeeded, and Speaker Gingrich came over to the Senate chamber to congratulate the senators on their work. Sounding very much like someone running for president, Dole said he was proud that the Republicans had kept their promise to end business as usual and resisted "tinkering around the edges." Bill Clinton, who was also running for president, predicted that if welfare reform remained a bipartisan effort, promoted work, and protected children, "we will have welfare reform this year and it will be a very great thing."[59]

Welfare Reform Stalls in 1995

Despite the optimism of Clinton, Dole, and even Gingrich, the year came to a close without a new welfare reform law. The differences in the House and Senate versions of the bill reflected the unresolved issues. Both houses of Congress had adopted measures that would end welfare as an entitlement. Yet the House bill projected greater savings over seven years—$102 billion in the House compared to $65 billion in the Senate. The difference reflected the desire of House members to remove any vestige of the old welfare system that they could in an effort to save money and ultimately balance the federal budget. The Senate thought much more explicitly about protecting groups such as dependent and disabled children from the subway grates or some similar misfortune. The House bill included prescriptive measures to end illegitimacy, and the Senate bill eliminated them, even though such measures were becoming increasingly important to conservatives in both houses.

As the welfare conference committee began to meet, the President sent lawmakers a letter warning them not to "walk away from the bipartisan common ground" or he would veto the bill. Meanwhile, he emphasized the work his administration had done by granting waivers to thirty-five states and permitting them to experiment with time-limited welfare grants and other innovations. If Congress got welfare reform wrong, then, the President said, "I will be forced to continue to end welfare through the waiver process, one state at a time, until Congress gets it right."[60]

For the Republicans getting it right involved deciding how tough to be on illegitimacy. For many congressmen, illegitimacy constituted the heart of the welfare problem. Charles Murray, whose 1984 book on the failures of the Great Society had brought him to national attention, expressed the view that welfare grants were bad for children, and policy makers should consider such drastic remedies as putting children into orphanages. In 1993 he wrote a widely noticed *Wall Street Journal* op-ed in which he argued that welfare grants increased the rate of illegitimacy, and illegitimacy was nothing less than the "single most important social problem of our times." But not everyone on the Republican side shared that view, and the forty-four-member welfare conference committee searched for a compromise. One such compromise, supported by Jim Talent, a leading proponent of the Republican illegitimacy measures, was to leave the federal mandates in the law but to allow the states to opt out through legislative action. As Talent pointed out, that would at least raise the issue in the state capitols.[61]

The politics of the already complicated issue took a new turn in October when, in the words of former Republican staffer and welfare authority Ron Haskins, the welfare reform bill "got swallowed by the whalelike budget reconciliation bill." The move to incorporate welfare reform into the budget reconciliation process made sense when one considered that the welfare reform bill offered substantial savings of some $80 billion over a seven-year period. Unlike earlier efforts at welfare reform, the 1995 version had been about reducing federal government expenditures from its very beginnings.[62]

The budget reconciliation process, already well along, needed to acquire a welfare reform component. During the preceding June, the House and the Senate had passed budget resolutions that called for a reduction of a trillion dollars in government spending in order to balance the budget by 2002. The budget committees had incorporated the suggestions from the committees with jurisdiction over the various programs into huge reconciliation bills of some two thousand pages. The final bills came to a vote at the end of October. Meanwhile, the welfare reform conference committee worked independently of the budget reconciliation process but, as staffer Haskins put it, "It was a foregone conclusion that if the welfare bill had not passed by the time the reconciliation bill was ready for the floor, a version of the welfare bill would be included in reconciliation." Hence the final budget reconciliation bills contained the welfare provisions. If the President vetoed the budget reconciliation bill that contained the welfare bill, as seemed likely, then the welfare bill would be pulled out of the reconciliation bill and sent to the President as a separate measure.[63]

On Saturday, October 28, the Senate passed its version of the budget reconciliation bill by a vote of 52 to 47. In a move that added another level of complexity to an already very complicated process, the Senate used the "Byrd" rule, named after the West Virginia Senator, to strip forty-six provisions from the bill because they were considered "extraneous matter" that did not produce a change in outlays or revenues. Those included the illegitimacy measures in the welfare section of the large bill. Such differences between the House and Senate versions of the budget reconciliation bill created the need for a conference committee, which meant that two conference committees were considering welfare reform. As Congress worked through these bureaucratic details, the President stood by with his threat to veto the final reconciliation bill when it reached his desk.[64]

In the midst of these political maneuvers, a flap developed in November that energized liberals and encouraged their efforts to get the President to veto the welfare bill whether it appeared as part of the large budget reconciliation or as a stand-alone measure. The liberal apparatus shadowing the welfare reform process uncovered an HHS study that predicted that the welfare bill would push 1.1 million children into poverty. That was ground zero for the liberals, like Senator Moynihan, who worried that welfare reform would put children in danger (in some ways the flip side of the conservative concerns about illegitimacy). Clinton's press secretary confirmed that the President had received the poverty study from Secretary Shalala, and a White House official told the *New York Times* that the study created "a ruckus" among the White House staff.[65]

There followed another report, prepared by the Office of Management and Budget in the Clinton White House, that was written at the request of congressional Democrats on the welfare conference committee and released to the press on November 9. It confirmed the results of the earlier study, predicting that the Senate version of the welfare bill could push 1.2 million children into poverty. "I don't think it took a genius to tell us the Senate bill would make more children poor," said Marian

Wright Edelman, a go-to figure among advocates for children and someone who had close connections to Hillary Clinton and whose husband worked as a Clinton appointee in the Department of Health and Human Services. "But now that you document it, how in the world could you support it? It's just unconscionable and it's a failure of moral leadership on the part of the President," she added. Conservatives countered that the reports just prepared the way for another of Clinton's flip-flops.[66]

As the Democrats attended to their internecine conflicts, Republicans continued to work on their differences. Top Republican leaders met with Gingrich and Dole to determine if they could reach an acceptable compromise that they could include in both the budget reconciliation bill and the stand-alone welfare bill. On November 14, the first day of formal meetings of the budget reconciliation conference committee, the Republicans announced that they had reached an agreement, at least among themselves, on welfare. In the words of Finance Committee chair William Roth (R-DE), the agreement would "test whether President Clinton is indeed a New Democrat or whether he is the final defender of the failed welfare state."[67]

The items in this latest iteration of a welfare reform bill reflected the Republican effort to satisfy the many conservatives in the party without alienating the few liberals. For example, states would have to spend some of their own money on welfare—at least 75 percent of their 1994 expenditures for at least five years. On the critically important illegitimacy provisions, the new draft of the bill allowed states to override them on the vote of their legislatures. On a related matter, the bill narrowed the definition of a disabled child, as the Republicans wanted, but retained SSI as a federal entitlement program rather than folding it into a block grant, as the Democrats preferred.[68]

Some Republicans continued to grouse. The compromise did not satisfy Senator Faircloth on illegitimacy. He insisted that "I do not intend to support any bill that continues to support illegitimacy, which is the root cause of the welfare disaster we are seeing in this country." Other issues involved the welfare programs run by the Department of Agriculture, such as food stamps. Senator Richard Lugar (R-IN), who chaired the Agriculture Committee, wanted to limit the number of states that could opt out of the Food Stamp Program. He also defended the idea of the school lunch program as a federal entitlement. But Representative Bill Goodling (R-PA), the House's chief negotiator on school lunches, insisted on giving the states "substantially greater flexibility" in their approach to child nutrition.[69] This dispute delayed the filing of a conference report to accompany the stand-alone welfare bill since Senator Lugar refused to sign it. These disagreements reflected both the depth of the conservative feeling on illegitimacy and the way committee chairmen defended their turf and protected the interests of groups that their committees served.[70]

The President decided that the latest Republican compromise on welfare veered far enough from the Senate version of the bill to warrant his veto should it reach his desk. The President's decision reflected the careful polling that his administration did on public issues and continuing discussions with his advisors on how best to position himself for the 1996 election. Social welfare politics was no longer an arcane matter debated by experts and handled by a faceless bureaucracy. Welfare reform was now a highly visible issue on which both sides jockeyed for advantage, with the media reporting on every move. Among the things on which the administration focused were cuts in the school lunch program, one of the more popular in the array of social welfare programs, and cuts to disabled children and immigrants. Other notions such as devolution of power from the federal government to the states, work requirements after two years of welfare, and five years of lifetime welfare benefits passed by without notice. Despite the intensity of the political conflicts, a consensus on the broad aims of welfare reform still existed.[71]

1995: Endgame

The Republicans finished up their work on the budget reconciliation bill—the one with the first version of the welfare bill tucked within it—on November 20. On November 29 administration officials such as Donna Shalala and Leon Panetta sent a signal to Democrats that the President would veto it. Shalala cited concerns over childcare that she called "the foundation of any real approach to welfare reform." The President met with Democratic senators and tried to reassure them of his intentions. Since he had supported the earlier Senate version of welfare reform, the senators were reluctant to get too far out in front of the agile Clinton, who was continuing with his efforts to get a balanced budget on his own terms. Senator Bob Kerrey (D-NE) left the meeting convinced that the President "doesn't like the welfare bill. He will veto that by itself."[72]

On December 6, the President delivered his promised veto on the reconciliation bill, dooming its chances of passage. "With this veto the extreme Republican effort to balance the budget through wrongheaded cuts and misplaced priorities is over," the President said.[73] Meanwhile Congress wrestled with the stand-alone welfare bill, which the House adopted on December 21 by a vote of 245 to 178.[74] Fewer Democrats voted for the bill than had voted in favor of the earlier welfare bill passed by the House. As would become standard procedure on big-ticket items such as welfare reform, the Republicans, the party in power, wrote the bill with little or no Democratic input. Moynihan, continuing his role as the weary veteran of previous battles, warned, "This is not the way that great social political efforts are addressed successfully."[75] "This welfare bill," said the President, "includes deep cuts that are hard on children and at odds with my central goal of moving people from welfare to work."[76]

The Senate passed the bill the next day, only three days before Christmas. The timing allowed Democrats to characterize the bill as uncharitable and not in the spirit of the season. The Senate vote indicated the parties had become more polarized in the course of the welfare reform debate. September's tally had been 87 to 12, indicating bipartisan support. In the Christmas season vote, only one Democrat, who faced a tough reelection fight in conservative Montana, voted in favor. Clinton's veto threat helped many wavering Democrats to make up their minds, as did the party's improving position since the early onslaught of the Gingrich revolution.[77]

When Clinton vetoed the welfare bill on January 9, it made little news because it was so expected. The President reiterated his by now familiar argument that the cuts in the welfare bill "would fall hardest on children and undermine states' ability to move people from welfare to work." Representative Bill Archer said that the veto demonstrated that the Clinton pledge to end welfare as we know it was "just another campaign slogan, not a meaningful policy objective." Not so, said Senator Breaux, who noted that the welfare reform process would continue in 1996. "This is a time to take a deep pause," said Speaker Gingrich.[78]

First Moves in 1996

All sides needed to consider their next moves in what was now an election year. The Republicans thought of passing the September version of the welfare reform bill (the one that had done well in the Senate) and sending it to President Clinton. They knew that the President would face great pressure to sign the bill, thus alienating the liberal wing of his party. The Republicans thought they could win either way, either forcing the President to capitulate to their welfare bill or, if he vetoed the bill, calling into question his previous endorsement of the Senate bill and his commitment to welfare reform. Of course, obstacles remained in the path of passing the bill. Representative Talent still thought that the Senate bill was weak on illegitimacy, and no one knew if senators like Barbara Mikulski and John D. Rockefeller (D-WV), who had voted for the measure in September, would support the measure this time around.[79]

The governors remained another interested party in the welfare reform debate. The thirty Republican governors had already contributed to the bill that the President had vetoed twice. At the beginning of February, the bipartisan National Governors Association offered a new welfare proposal that continued its efforts to reduce federal oversight and increase the amount of federal funds going to the states. The governors reiterated their endorsement of federal block grants for state welfare programs but with states allowed to reduce their welfare spending by 25 percent without losing money, the continuation of food stamps (a program financed entirely by the federal government), and a change in the Medicaid program to increase the federal share of the costs in wealthier states like New York and New Jersey. Speaking with the blithe optimism of Franklin Roosevelt, President Clinton told the governors, as he had previously told Congress in his State of the Union address, "I believe we're going to pass welfare legislation." As always, the administration wanted it both ways: endorsing the governors' general objectives but reserving the right to criticize their proposals.[80]

Liberals were less eager to entrust the welfare of children to the states than the President appeared to be. Some Democratic congressmen preferred no action in 1996 to some version of the governors' bill. Sander Levin (D-MI) worried about what would happen during a recession when the demand for welfare benefits but not necessarily the federal block grants would increase. Robert Matsui (D-CA) called it a "great deal for our governors. We raise taxes. They spend the money and are not accountable." Sharon M. Daly of the Catholic Charities attacked the governors' plans because "they would repeal the Federal guarantee of protection for poor children" and "allow states to turn their backs on their obligations to poor families." One of the more articulate of the advocates who followed the welfare debate, Daly said that the welfare discussion had focused on individual responsibility, ignoring the government's responsibility to assure that people had suitable employment and adequate welfare benefits when no jobs were available.[81]

The states continued to enjoy an advantage in the welfare discussion because of the federally approved waivers that allowed them to make changes in their welfare programs. Some believed that the national level was not the right level of government to address the welfare problem because, for example, the culture of welfare offices could not be changed by federal edict. Efforts to put welfare recipients in jobs required the energy and creativity of dedicated employees who knew the ins and outs of their local labor markets. There was no one-size-fits-all approach that could be mandated in Washington.[82] Wisconsin and its ambitious governor, who was interested in running for vice president on the 1996 Republican ticket, passed legislation that would abolish cash welfare payments in the state by the fall of 1997 and replace them with work programs. These were things that Congress had not been able to enact at the national level.[83]

Both sides pushed whatever advantages they had in the welfare reform debate. For Clinton that meant executive actions that demonstrated his bona fides in the debate and kept the spotlight on him. In May the President used his weekly radio address, one of his regular media opportunities, to broadcast a new initiative dedicated to keeping welfare mothers in school. In June the President announced new federal actions, based on things already being undertaken in Florida, New York, and Washington State, to track down fathers behind in their child support payments. In July came word that the President would require through executive action that welfare recipients go to work after two years. Throughout he continued to stress the state waiver process as one of his accomplishments, noting that his administration was reforming the welfare system "state-by-state." He demonstrated his commitment to the process by giving permission for Wisconsin to undertake its effort to end the cash welfare system. Clinton continued to portray himself as a willing partner in the effort to pass a welfare reform bill in Congress. Republicans in Congress complained that the President wanted to take credit for the achievements of Republican governors and that he was playing politics with welfare reform.[84]

The Republicans had the great advantage of controlling Congress, even if they did not have enough votes to pass legislation over the President's veto. They used this advantage to produce another welfare bill, introduced in April 1996, which demonstrated their dedication to the cause and renewed the Republican stamp on welfare reform. The new bill ended welfare as an entitlement and included term and lifetime limits on welfare receipt, but it also required the states to put at least half of their adult welfare recipients to work by 2002.

Even though presidential candidate Dole resigned as a member of Congress in June, he played a key role in how the Republicans shaped and presented their welfare reform bill, such as separating their controversial Medicaid proposals from the welfare bill but including the more popular provisions that banned noncitizens from getting welfare benefits. The Clinton administration, as usual, offered its own critique of the bill, arguing, for example, that the work requirement needed to be accompanied by adequate provisions for childcare and that the cuts in the Food Stamp Program were too deep. At the same time, his press secretary said that the situation presented a "historic opportunity, and the President believes we can get this done."[85]

The House of Representatives passed the new welfare reform bill on July 18 by a vote of 256 to 170. The Senate passed its version of the bill on July 23 by a vote of 74 to 24 with all but one of the Republicans voting in favor and half of the Democrats voting against. The issues that arose at this stage of the debate did not involve the time limits on welfare or the end of welfare as an entitlement—the two things that represented the sharpest breaks from the past. Instead, debate centered on important but peripheral details. As the debate proceeded, most advocates realized that the legislation would pass and therefore concentrated their attention on publicizing features in the bill that might cause the President to veto it.[86]

One hot issue concerned immigrants who had not become citizens. Despite pleas from senators from states with large immigrant populations, such as California and Florida, the Senate voted to follow the lead of the House and exclude noncitizens, even the ones already legally living in the country, from receiving federal benefits. The Senate rejected Bob Graham's (D-FL) amendment to make legal immigrants eligible for welfare, food stamps, and Medicaid by a vote of 62 to 34. Graham argued that, if the benefits were cut off, his state and others like New York and Illinois would be faced with high extra costs. The other senators thought the general principle that welfare benefits came only with citizenship was more important than the specific needs of relatively affluent states like New York. Rick Santorum, who had started the welfare reform debate in the House but had graduated to the Senate in the 1994 Republican landslide, pointed to the high percentage of immigrants on the SSI rolls as part of a "real pattern of abuse." Denying benefits to immigrants saved money at little political cost. It was not a likely reason for a Clinton veto.[87]

A second issue that occasioned debate concerned the future of the federal Food Stamp Program. The rather convoluted provision in the Senate bill stated that prime-aged able-bodied adults with no dependents could receive food stamps for no more than four months a year unless they were working at least twenty hours a work. The House bill contained even more stringent requirements that essentially prohibited able-bodied adults who did not hold a job from getting food stamps. Senator Kent Conrad (D-ND) convinced his colleagues to be more lenient. He suggested that states be able to exempt 20 percent of adult food stamp recipients from the work requirement if it would cause them hardship. His motion passed on a voice vote.[88]

The third issue involved the fate of people in families cut off from the welfare rolls because they had reached the five-year lifetime limit. The President favored, but failed to get, a provision that would have allowed states to provide vouchers or other forms of noncash assistance to needy families no longer eligible for cash assistance. The vouchers would have enabled these families to obtain necessary baby supplies such a diapers, cribs, clothing, and medicine as well as school supplies for older children. Families with dependent children who were cut off from the welfare rolls could still, if they were poor enough, qualify for Medicaid, food stamps, and housing assistance.[89]

The conference committee on the welfare reform bill began to meet on July 25, as speculation over whether Clinton would veto the final bill mounted. One analyst reported that the President had "almost no cards left to play" in pressuring the House and Senate negotiators. Newt Gingrich believed that the President "has an absolute moral obligation to sign this bill," but Senator Moynihan suggested signing the bill would put a blot on the President's eternal soul. "This is just a bad bill that will hurt all the wrong people and should be vetoed, period," one Democratic expert on welfare said. "They've got a 20-point lead. What good is it if they don't use it?" A politically tough veto in an election year might even strengthen the public's view of Clinton's character.[90]

Final Moves in 1996

On July 29 the House and Senate negotiators announced that they had reached agreements on most of the issues that divided them. The ban on legal immigrants who were not citizens would stand, as would the provision that families dropped from welfare would not be eligible for vouchers that would enable them to buy supplies for their children. The tough new work requirements for Food Stamp recipients would also remain in the bill.[91]

Republicans confidently predicted that they had the votes to pass the measure over the President's veto. As word about the conference committee's decisions reached the general public, however, labor unions, the Urban League, the Children's Defense Fund, the National Conference of Catholic Bishops, and the Union of American Hebrew Congregations all announced their firm opposition to the bill and mobilized for a campaign to persuade the President to veto it and for Congress to sustain the veto. Reasserting his organization's traditional commitment to social reform, John J. Sweeney, the President of the AFL-CIO, said the bill was "bad for the country" and "harmful to poor families. I'm hopeful that the president has the compassion and courage to veto it." White House staffers remained noncommittal, saying only that they were analyzing the conference agreement and, in the words of White House staffer (and future Chicago mayor) Rahm Emanuel "seeing if Congress has made steps toward the president's goals."[92]

The drama reached its climax on the last day of July when President Clinton announced that he would sign the latest version of welfare reform once it reached his desk. The date marked an important moment in the welfare state. A Democratic president, who fancied himself the heir of Franklin Roosevelt and John F. Kennedy, broke with a policy that went back to the progressive era in the states and to the New Deal at the federal level. This policy had evolved into the notion that the families of dependent children who were in need could receive assistance from a federal- and state-funded program that paid cash benefits to anyone who met its terms, regardless of the total cost of the benefits. The President had hinted at his feelings many times before as he painted himself as a new Democrat who wanted to end welfare as we know it and as he encouraged the Republican Congress to keep working on a bill that he could sign. The two previous times a welfare bill reached his desk, the President managed to find something in them that justified a veto. He never attacked the most radical elements of the plan, such as time-limited welfare benefits and block grants to the states that would end the AFDC program as an entitlement. Instead he attacked the bill around its edges: it did not provide enough for child support; it disrupted the Food Stamp and Medicaid programs that were a vital part of America's safety net. In other words, unlike the Republicans who had come to power in 1995, the President did not want to dismantle the entire welfare state but rather to change one of its defective components. He relied on the intertwined pieces of the welfare state—the ones that had made it so hard to enact the Family Assistance Plan—to prevent social catastrophe.

When a welfare bill came his way for a third time, many on the White House staff encouraged him to veto it. For all of the many changes that Congress made on the successive drafts of the bill, certain features, such as cutting off benefits to noncitizens, still bothered the President. From all accounts, Clinton agonized over the decision. He had been ridiculed on many occasions for his tendency to hold long and rambling meetings that bore a closer resemblance to college bull sessions than to crisp and disciplined White House policy discussions. Unlike participants in many such discussions, those involved in the welfare debate knew that they were addressing a matter of real consequence at a real moment of decision.

For over two hours, Clinton listened to the members of his staff who had assembled in the Cabinet Room, and then he brought Vice President Gore and chief of staff Panetta into the Oval Office to help him reach a final decision. These individuals represented the two sides in the White House debate. Gore, the politician, Clinton's 1996 running mate, and Clinton's heir apparent, urged the President to sign the bill. Panetta, also a politician and a former member of Congress with considerable Washington savvy, spoke on behalf of the many staff members who had counseled a veto. The inner office meeting lasted only fifteen minutes before Panetta came out of the room and told the waiting speech writers to prepare a draft of remarks announcing Clinton would sign the bill. Everyone involved in the process was careful to point out that the President had focused on policy, not politics, during the discussion.[93]

Announcing his decision to a television audience at 2:26 in the afternoon, the President said he would sign the bill because, although it contained flaws that he hoped to remedy through future congressional actions, the welfare system was broken and in need of repair. Clinton realized that the window for change was open in the same way it had been open for Medicare in 1965. This time Congress rather than the President took the lead and controlled the debate. On this issue, however, the President was more than a cheerleader who applauded Congress's actions, as Lyndon Johnson had been during the enactment phase of Medicare. Instead, the President had used the veto as a means of influencing the legislation. In the end he believed that "this is the best chance we will have for a long, long time of ending welfare as we know it, by moving people from welfare to work, demanding responsibility, and doing better by children."[94]

Liberals like Moynihan and Donna Shalala respected the President's decision to the extent that they recognized it was final. "The President has made his decision," said a doleful Senator Moynihan. "Let us hope that it is for the best." Moynihan, whose views were often difficult to categorize, believed that liberals deserved some of the blame for the outcome. "For years," lamented the creator of Nixon's Family Assistance Plan, "whenever the critics said, correctly, that the welfare system was doing more harm than good, and suggested that it be rethought, its defenders screamed 'racism' and 'slavefare.' They did that until there was no public support left at all. Now they are stunned at what they are getting." Always good at producing the arresting quotation, Moynihan said that the Republican bill "is not welfare reform, but welfare repeal." Senator Paul Wellstone (D-MN) held firm to the liberal line that the legislation "would create more poverty and hunger among American children."[95]

The Republicans pressed the point that it was they, rather than Bill Clinton, who had brought about welfare reform. Haley Barbour, the Chairman of the Republican National Committee, said the Republican Congress had made welfare reform happen and that the President agreed to sign the bill because he feared the political consequences of a veto. Speaker Gingrich gave credit to Senator Dole for restarting the process in a way that permitted a successful conclusion. Candidate Dole commended the President "for finally climbing aboard the Dole welfare reform proposal."[96]

This view of Clinton as an opportunistic and calculating politician did the President a disservice. Beyond his political skills, he had a real knowledge of the details of the policy process and had on other occasions been referred to as a policy wonk. The President made a considered case for his actions, relying upon the anachronistic failure argument. He brought the discussion back to Senator Moynihan and noted that the Senator had often made the point that "when welfare was created, the typical welfare recipient was a miner's widow with no education, small children, husband dies in the mine, no expectation that . . . there was a job for the widow to do . . . and very few out of wedlock pregnancies and births." The President argued that "the whole dynamics were different then. . . . A system that was in place 60 years ago, that worked for the poverty population then, is not the one we need now." Since the nature of the poverty population had changed, the President said, "I am convinced that we have to be willing to experiment." State officials would soon discover, if they had not already, that they needed to "invest something" to move welfare recipients into jobs. Coming back to Senator Moynihan, the President said, "I'll just have to hope that in this one case I'm right and he's wrong."[97]

Congress reacted to the President's remarks in the same giddy way that the stock market greeted a good earnings report from a blue chip stock. That same afternoon the House approved the measure by a vote of 328 to 101. Half of the Democrats voted in favor. A day later the Senate passed the bill by a wide margin of 78–21, with the Democrats dividing 25–21 in favor. Among the converts to the cause were Senators Mikulski and Graham. Even the reluctant Republican Lauch Faircloth, who had worried throughout the process that the bill was not tough enough on illegitimate children, voted in favor.[98]

The President signed the bill on August 22 in a Rose Garden ceremony. In the history of America's welfare state, the moment resembled President Reagan's signing of the Social Security rescue legislation in 1983. Both presidents accepted the products of a divided Congress, not under their party's control, on an issue that played to the strengths of the opposite party. Both hoped that their positive attitudes would remove the issue from the debit to the credit side of the ledger. Although Clinton and Reagan were masters of the moment—"Today we are taking a historic chance to make welfare what it was meant to be: a second chance, not a way of life," Clinton said—the two moments differed. Few people objected to the Social Security rescue legislation, even though it meant benefit cuts to the recipients, because Social Security's liberal defenders had prepared the public for the moment and endorsed the outcome. Although they did not like the way in which the bill raised the retirement age, they applauded the way that it kept the structure of the program intact and introduced diagnosis-related groups into Medicare.

Democrats, including Senator Daniel Moynihan making another appearance at a historic moment, took their place next to Republicans as Reagan signed the bill outdoors in the chilly April air. The welfare reform bill that Clinton signed in the August heat still attracted its share of criticism, and few Democrats, many of whom were home on their August recess, attended the ceremony. Marian Wright Edelman, who remained an unsparing critic of the measure, called the signing ceremony "a moment of shame." The Children's Defense Fund, the National Organization of Women, and the Feminist Majority staged a protest near the White House. Nor were the Republicans in a charitable mood. The Dole campaign issued the statement, "By selling out his own party, Bill Clinton has proven he is ideologically adrift." The President was unfazed. "After I sign my name to this bill, welfare will no longer be a political issue," he said.[99]

Aftermath

Fallout over the issue continued even after the bill had become law. On September 11, two top officials of the Department of Health and Human Services resigned in protest, a stark contrast to the manner in which the AMA and many Republicans endorsed Medicare after its passage. Assistant Secretary Peter Edelman told his staff that he had devoted his life to the project of reducing poverty in America. "I believe the recently enacted welfare bill goes in the opposite direction," he said. Assistant Secretary Mary Jo Bane, who had been involved with the Clinton administration's welfare reform efforts from the very beginning, wrote an email message to her departmental colleagues that her "deep concerns about the welfare bill have led me to conclude that I cannot continue to serve." Wendell Primus, who had done the analysis showing that the welfare bills would push a million or more children into poverty, had already resigned, as had welfare guru David Ellwood, who had decamped for Harvard.[100]

In what had become a Washington tradition that Daniel Patrick Moynihan had started with his account of Nixon's failed attempt to pass the Family Assistance Plan, Edelman wrote about his Clinton administration experiences in an article for the *Atlantic*. It ran in the March 1997 issue under the provocative title "The Worst Thing Clinton Has Done." It consisted of a lawyerly critique of the new welfare law arguing that Clinton could have vetoed the law and still won the election and that Clinton had brought about many of his own dilemmas by not being firmer with the Republicans as they passed successive versions of the bill. Edelman charged that Clinton abandoned the approach of the 1988 Family Support Act that workfare needed to be supported by social services and never attacked the core of the Republican bill. The President concentrated on things like the Medicaid entitlement, and when the Republicans yielded on that, he had no fallback position. The bill itself would harm children in welfare families and immigrants who had not become citizens. The block grants would take fundamental constitutional rights away from welfare recipients and leave them at the mercy of the state governments. The Republicans underestimated the costs of putting welfare recipients to work in terms of childcare, job training, and medical care and were overoptimistic about the success of job training and job placement efforts. The 1996 election provided little evidence that the law could be fixed in a meaningful way. Edelman reached the conclusion, "The best that can be said about this terrible legislation is that perhaps we will learn from it and eventually arrive at a better approach. I am afraid, though, that along the way we will do some serious injury to American children, who should not have had to suffer from our national backlash."[101]

Mary Jo Bane also wrote about her experiences, although in a less dramatic and more academic way. She hoped to draw lessons from the 1996 experience that policy analysts could employ in future welfare reform endeavors. Writing at the turn of the century, she reported that the law had turned out differently from what she expected. Caseload declines, employment gains for welfare mothers, and declines in the poverty levels for single-mother families all exceeded expectations. For a social scientist, the problem was to isolate the effects of the 1996 law on these gains. Many things happened simultaneously, such as a spectacularly good economy and increases in the earned income tax credit and child support enforcement. Bane was convinced that these things mattered and the new welfare law was not the "cause" of the better than expected results in any simple way. Her most vivid memories of her administration experience consisted of "moments of startling ugliness." One Republican congressman compared welfare recipients to alligators in the Everglades and advised his colleagues not to feed either of them. A Democrat compared the Republicans to Nazis and accused them of committing genocide. She remembered the "gratuitously punitive" aspects of the welfare bill such as the "cutoffs of benefits to immigrants" that played to some "not very pretty stereotypes." She noticed the way that politicians used welfare bashing as an electoral strategy and regretted the close attention that the President paid to the polls conducted by his advisor Dick Morris. A veto, counseled Morris, would result in a drop of fifteen points in the approval ratings and possibly lead to losing the election.[102]

Conclusion

The Personal Responsibility and Work Opportunity Act of 1996 marked the single biggest change in the welfare laws since 1935. Time limits, including requirements to join the labor force within two years and to receive no more than five years of benefits in total, became national policy. Unmarried teenage mothers qualified for benefits only if the mother stayed in school and lived with an adult. Future legal immigrants would be banned from receiving welfare for their first five years, and food stamps would be limited for adults not raising children.[103]

The outcome owed a great deal to a sequence of historical events. In 1935 the federal government attempted to shore up a state system of aid to dependent children. Congressmen envisioned deserving widows as the major beneficiaries of the program. The situation changed somewhat in 1939 when the federal government added survivors' benefits to Social Security. Presumably, the survivors caseload would include many deserving widows. As usual, Congress did not swap out programs and instead added survivors' benefits to the pile of federal social welfare benefits.

AFDC endured through two major events that changed its politics. The first was the rise of illegitimacy, and the second was the revolution in female labor force expectations, which made it the norm for mothers to hold jobs in the labor force. The results were a change in the AFDC caseload to include more illegitimate children and a change in the AFDC strategy to make putting welfare mothers to work a major program objective. Both of these things put the AFDC program at a disadvantage, since the unwed mothers enjoyed few of the political advantages of the deserving widows and the government lacked the policy skills to devise programs that were capable of moving people from welfare to work. AFDC, still considered necessary for people in need and promising in its potential to do good, changed from an accepted tool of social policy in 1962 to an unambiguous failure in need of major reform or even replacement in 1996. These dynamics, as filtered through the political institutions of the time, led to the Personal Responsibility Act.

Bill Clinton won the 1996 election handily. He gave a campaign speech in Daytona in which he lauded the new bill and referred to it as the fulfillment of a promise made in the 1992 campaign. The President recalled his 1992 promise to "end welfare as we know it." He hailed the new welfare bill as a step toward a welfare system that "promotes independence, good parenting and successful work." The fact that the well-vetted Clinton made such a speech indicated that he had no doubts of the popularity of the law he had signed in August. By the end of the year he had some data that seemed to indicate the success of the new welfare law. In September the welfare rolls were a million people below their level in January. In the longer run, analysts such as economist Rebecca Blank noted that welfare caseloads "plummeted from 1996 through 2000," so that by 2001 they "were at their lowest level in 30 years, despite a vastly larger single-mother population."[104]

But it was a complicated story in which, as Mary Jo Bane had noted, it was difficult to separate the effects of the new welfare law from other effects such as an improvement in the economy. Nor was the 1996 law simply put in place and carried forward into the future. Congress made adjustments from year to year that changed the law in significant ways. Cutting legal aliens from the welfare rolls, for example, met with extreme pushback in states with large immigrant populations such as California and New York. The result was the passage of a 1998 law that granted permanent eligibility to all aliens who had been on the rolls when the welfare reform bill was enacted in August 1996. Because of such laws, aliens on the SSI rolls dipped only gently from 11 percent in 1996 to 8.4 percent in 2009. The effort to cut disabled children from the SSI rolls yielded even less satisfactory results. Because of the way the executive branch administered the 1996 law and the way Congress monitored the law, the number of children on SSI decreased by 11 percent between 1996 and 2000, but three years later the number had reached its 1996 level and by 2009 the number had risen another 25 percent beyond its 1996 level. These statistics proved that technicians or politicians could not run social programs as though they were machines. Circumstances changed. The institutional structure that governed the programs changed.[105]

In a sense, the changes made to the 1996 welfare law reflected the pattern already developed in the Social Security Disability Insurance program. In 1958 and 1960, those who wanted to expand the program picked off the low-hanging fruit without changing the program's basic structure. Something similar happened in welfare. In both cases prosperity facilitated the expansion of the program but expansion within the programs' institutional structure. More people might qualify for welfare, but it would be welfare funded as a block grant, not an entitlement, and it would be welfare with strict time limits and work provisions.

And despite the undoubted importance of the 1996 law, it did not completely undermine the structure that had been put in place in 1935. Aid to Families of Dependent Children changed to Temporary Aid to Needy Families, but the states ran both generations of programs. The federal government provided financial assistance to the states before and after 1996, even if block grants were not the same as matching. Means tests remained in every welfare law in every state of the nation before and after 1996.

Still, some laws were more enduring than others. The 1996 welfare reform law marked a permanent change in the nation's approach to the problem of maintaining the income of families with dependent children. A generation after the passage of the law, few people believed that another major revision of the welfare law, such as had taken place in the Clinton administration, was on the horizon.

Conclusion

Histories by their very nature contain lots of details that make it difficult to see the big picture. This book has featured long accounts of the passage of disability insurance in 1956, Medicare in 1965, and the Personal Responsibility and Work Opportunity Act in 1996. It tries to portray the world as contemporary policy makers saw it in part by relying on the stories in the newspapers and other contemporary documents that the policy makers themselves would have seen. In every case, no one knew what would happen next. People creating laws in 1956, 1965, and 1996 had no better purchase on the future than we have today. They were unable to see around corners and had no assurances that their efforts to pass a law would be successful. The inevitable uncertainty caused them to be alert to challenges from their opponents such as the American Medical Association or the Health Insurance Association of America or the opposition political party. It made them receptive to compromises that, so far as they were able to determine in the always murky policy environment, furthered their basic objectives and increased the odds of passing their law. Particularly in the 1996 case but in the other two cases as well, policy makers put a great premium on producing a law, at least once the situation had reached a certain critical mass, rather than allowing the existing laws that did not accomplish the policy goals of the moment to remain in place. In all three cases, the process remained open right until the time that the law was passed. Any account of a law's passage therefore needs to underscore the fluidity of the legislative process. In accounts of what happened next, the historian needs to understand that laws are at their most malleable in the process of creation and much less flexible after that.

Since origins always matter, the process of creating a law is always important—hence the long narratives in this book. Developments in the creation of a program create permanent structures that eventually produce problems but are difficult for policy makers to alter in the years after passage. This conclusion takes a last look at the programs, makes some generalizations about change over time in the policy process, and finishes with an observation about how to write about the history of social policy.

Social Security Disability Insurance

One might reconsider the three cases presented here. In the case of Social Security Disability Insurance, with the two sides evenly matched, liberals tried to tighten the definition of disability so as to reassure more hesitant conservatives that the program would not be profligate or undermine the process of rehabilitation. Only people who were truly down and out—unable to do any job that existed in substantial numbers in the national economy because of a physical or mental impairment—qualified for benefits. As an added safeguard, the program paid benefits only to people fifty or older and, unlike the other parts of Social Security, did not award extra money to cover a disabled worker's dependents. Each of these things contributed to the very narrow Senate passage of the measure by a one-vote margin.

The effort to assure that benefits went only to people who deserved them had consequences in the long run. At first legislators readily expanded the program along incremental lines by providing benefits for dependents and making the benefits available to working people of all ages. Then rising rates of disability alarmed program managers and called for a new response. Perhaps people were cheating the system and should be removed from the rolls, but that was a difficult maneuver to bring off in a policy environment filled with rights-conscious lawyers who wanted to protect the due process of social welfare benefit recipients and caseworkers in congressional offices responding to constituent complaints. Perhaps the very fact of being on the disability rolls for a period of years was disabling in and of itself, which meant it was futile to remove people who had been on the rolls for any length of time. Or perhaps policy could assume a kinder face and more people who received benefits could be rehabilitated rather than receiving a pension for life. Although policy makers were receptive to this idea, the definition of disability that Congress put into the 1956 law emphasized permanent and total disability and not the potential for rehabilitation. Formal efforts to link SSDI and vocational rehabilitation all failed because of the long shadow of the 1956 law. Passage of the Americans with Disabilities Act in 1990, which outlawed discrimination in hiring and public accommodations on the basis of disability, failed to open up the labor force for the people on the disability rolls. The ADA had a negligible effect on Social Security Disability Insurance.

In 1956, in the midst of the intense political bargaining, policy makers looked with favor on solutions to problems that had already been reached. In 1952 an almost casual suggestion to put the states in charge of determining whether someone was disabled found acceptance in a deadlocked congressional conference committee. That suggestion continued into the next round of negotiations in 1954 before becoming part of the 1956 disability insurance law. Problems with the state disability determination system arose almost immediately. It made decisions too slowly, as needy people waited for their benefits. It lacked consistency from state to state, even though the benefits were paid at the federal level and Social Security, unlike welfare, was a federal program. It led to contentious hearings before administrative law judges and federal judges. Although the problems were visible for all to see, the administrative structure in the 1956 law—unlike such features as limiting benefits to people over fifty—proved highly durable. It exemplified the process of path dependency.

Medicare

In the case of Medicare, the two sides were not as evenly matched, since the Democrats had won the 1964 election by landslide. The interest-group configuration around the issue of national health insurance for the elderly nonetheless made for a close political contest that began in 1961 but did not conclude until 1965. Doctors, health insurers, and hospital administrators could all put pressure on their representatives, regardless of their representatives' political affiliations. In an added complication, the Democratic majority was never quite as large as it looked on paper, because southern Democrats did not always vote with their party. Virginia Senator Harry Byrd chaired the Senate Finance Committee in both 1956 and 1965 and openly opposed the Democratic leadership in both instances. All of these things meant that the same process of political bargaining that characterized SSDI also applied to Medicare and kept Medicare's passage in doubt until the end of 1964 and the final contents of the legislation in flux until nearly the last minute.

Before Congress was done with Medicare, it established a separate trust fund and payment collection for the program, ceded responsibility for paying benefits to local intermediaries and private insurance companies, and agreed that the federal government would pay "reasonable costs" to hospitals and doctors who participated in the program. Rejected alternatives included such things as allowing beneficiaries a choice among private plans to pay for doctors' bills or permitting people with private health insurance coverage to opt out of the public Medicare program. These alternatives received serious discussion and might have become law if, for example, Medicare had passed the Senate in 1964. If those alternatives had become realities, the Medicare program would have taken a different path. Hence historical contingencies embedded in the policy process had real consequences.

The most important congressional adjustment to the Medicare law, one that was not completed until the spring of 1965, involved the creation of what became Medicare Part B to cover payments for doctors' services. This feature of the law was not included in the administration's proposal as late as the beginning of 1965. Instead the administration endorsed a proposal from Senator Javits to cover doctors' bills by allowing private health insurance companies to sell low-cost policies to the elderly. In the final legislation, Medicare Part A covered hospital insurance much along the lines the Kennedy and Johnson administrations had proposed, although Part A went through the usual bargaining process that affected such things as the number of days in the hospital that the program covered or whether beneficiaries could choose among three different plans with three different deductible schemes. Part B stemmed from an obvious gap that Medicare's opponents rushed to fill, producing many different plans between 1961 and 1965. Ideas that emerged from the discussion included the notion that any Republican scheme should be voluntary, in contrast to the administration's compulsory Medicare proposal, and any Republican scheme should not add to the employer's payroll taxes but should depend upon premiums paid by the beneficiaries themselves and support from general revenues. That led to a final legislative bargain in which the administration allowed a version of the Republican proposal to cover doctors' bills, but not also hospital bills as the Republicans would have wished. The administration got Part A but at the cost of creating Part B, which might in fact have represented an improvement over the plans for covering doctors' bill that were in the administration bill. As an added feature of the law that received relatively little discussion but that stemmed from the administration's legislative plans, the Medicare bill also initiated Medicaid, which was understood as state-run medical care for welfare recipients and the medically indigent.

The structure of the Medicare bill had many long-term consequences. In the first place, it lasted from 1965 to the present day. In the second place, the financing schemes for Parts A and B meant that Part A received no money from general revenues. Instead, it depended on a trust fund similar to the ones already in operation for old-age and survivors insurance and disability insurance. Policy makers could track the balance in this trust fund from year to year. Since Part B depended on general revenue financing in addition to the premiums that beneficiaries paid, it could not go bankrupt or at least not in the same way. As a result, the discussion of Medicare financing and the politically loaded question of whether the program would go bankrupt centered on Part A and not Part B. Reform in Medicare therefore came more quickly than in Part A than it did for Part B. The 1983 creation of diagnosis-related groups applied to Part A, not Part B, although Part B eventually acquired its own prospective payment system and controversies over the cost of Part B premiums started almost as soon as Medicare was passed. In the third place, the diagnosis-related groups—internal tampering with the way Medicare reimbursed hospitals—established a pattern for Medicare reform. Congress could make major changes in the program that preserved the program's benefits and retained the way that beneficiaries interacted with the program. As a result Medicare reform continued beyond the easy incremental changes between 1965 and 1972 that expanded the program to include disability insurance beneficiaries and, in a particularly odd development that only history could explain, people with end stage renal disease.

In the 1980s Republicans gained the upper hand in the Senate and won all three of the presidential elections. A crucial breakthrough occurred in 1995 when, for the first time in two generations, the Republicans took over the House of Representatives. Although a Republican agenda for Medicare reform took time to form and needed to respect the popularity that Medicare had achieved, it eventually took shape in two key pieces of legislation passed in 1997 and 2003. The first of these laws introduced the notion of consumer choice to the program. A person could always choose his doctor and his hospital. Now the program expanded to allow the person to choose among different health care financing plans that offered the advantages of being more inclusive—they could, for example, include prescription drugs—and perhaps cheaper. Republicans believed they were bringing the program up to date in a responsible manner that respected changing fashions in health insurance. The basic program structure of Parts A and B remained durable, with the result that the Republicans had to place their new program, which became Part C, on top of the existing one. Republicans delivered the long-promised benefit of prescription drugs to Medicare beneficiaries in 2003 but in a different manner than the traditional Medicare program. Private insurers sold prescription drug plans to Medicare beneficiaries, preserving, at least in theory, the notion of consumer choice—you could choose the plan that met your medical needs and suited your pocketbook—and the dynamic of market competition. In this manner, Congress and the George W. Bush administration created Part D. Similar to the 1997 reform, it had to be stacked on top of Parts A, B, and C.

The Personal Responsibility and Work Opportunity Act

The debate over the Personal Responsibility and Work Opportunity Act began with a consensus that welfare benefits should be time limited and should substitute paid employment for continued dependence on welfare. The consensus stemmed from the same forces that had produced the changes in Medicare at roughly the same time. It represented a real change in outlook from the original Aid to Families with Dependent Children program that was included in the Social Security Act in 1935 and the Kennedy-era amendments in 1962. The original program provided what were essentially pensions, similar to the ones that the elderly and blind were also receiving, for needy widows raising dependent children. The Kennedy variation left the original program largely intact but added a feature that encouraged state authorities not only to give financial aid to single mothers raising children but also to provide services to "cure" dysfunctional families and supply the human capital to make welfare mothers ready for the labor force. This permissive policy gave rise by 1967 to a more restrictive policy aimed at deterring people from applying for welfare and requiring welfare recipients to work. In a final iteration, policy makers transformed their perception of welfare from something disagreeable but necessary to something that produced more harm than good.

President Bill Clinton and House Speaker Newt Gingrich entered the debate at this point. Clinton had made welfare reform an issue in the 1992 election and touted the achievements of his home state of Arkansas. Gingrich gave welfare reform a prominent place in his Contract for America. Although there was general agreement on welfare as an avenue toward work and as a temporary form of government aid, the competition between Clinton and Gingrich led to the same process of political bargaining that had characterized the creation of Social Security Disability Insurance and Medicare. If anything, the Personal Responsibility and Work Opportunity Act took a more twisted path toward final passage than did the other two laws. President Clinton vetoed the first two versions of the legislation he received from the Republican Congress because of an unusual situation in which Republicans in Congress passed two versions of a welfare reform law. One was a stand-alone bill, and the other was part of a much larger budget reconciliation package. It took a third iteration of welfare reform that appeared just before the 1996 election (just as disability insurance became enmeshed in the 1956 election) to gain President Clinton's assent and become law. The long process of enactment created the same sense of fluidity that characterized the other two laws. Issues like food stamps (or SNAP), Medicaid, the treatment of immigrants, and the substitution of block grants for the previous matching grants in aid arose and only came to rest in the final legislation.

The 1996 law ended the AFDC program and started something called Temporary Aid to Needy Families. Dependent children and their mothers who met the state standards for relative poverty no longer received an entitlement to aid. Instead, states enjoyed the freedom to spend their block grants and redesign their welfare programs so that they became workfare programs largely as they liked. Both former Governor Bill Clinton and Newt Gingrich encouraged states to take the lead on welfare reform. But each of them believed that certain conditions needed to be met. Clinton wanted to make sure that workfare came bundled with such things as Medicaid and childcare. Gingrich wanted to make sure that all states made concerted efforts to discourage and ultimately end illegitimacy. The issue of how stringent state governments should be on babies born out of wedlock—should they be denied aid or given reduced aid?—became a major point of contention within the Republican caucus. Some Republicans believed that the fight against illegitimacy represented the very essence of welfare reform because illegitimacy was creating social problems of immense scale. These internal disputes complicated the efforts of Majority Leader Robert Dole to craft a bill acceptable to conservatives. Conservatives who did not believe in federal mandates nevertheless felt that the law needed to contain explicit sanctions against illegitimacy. So the final law was a curious combination of permissive block grants and restrictive government mandates. Like all laws, it was very much a product of its times, as the provisions related to immigrants revealed. In 1935 and 1962, policy makers did not focus on immigrants who were, in any case, receding in numbers and importance because of earlier immigration restriction laws. In 1996 the rights of noncitizens, many of whom came to this country because of 1965 immigration legislation, became very much an issue.

Like the other laws, the 1996 law had some give. The rights of some noncitizens to welfare were restored by future Congresses. Still, the 1996 law proved to have a durable structure, similar to the other two laws.

The Three Programs in Motion

Each of the laws began with a pattern of largely invisible incremental reform, which, in all three cases, meant bringing new groups into the law's coverage. Then something, usually a large and unexpected increase in expenditures, brought the incremental expansions to a halt. The situation might be compared to a watch that no longer keeps the correct time. The first response is to reset the watch. If the problem persists, one might tinker with the watch's internal workings. If the watch cannot be repaired, it might be time to buy a new watch.

These three steps corresponded to what happened to the three programs chronicled here. The disability rolls grew at what policy makers regarded as an alarming rate. In response, policy makers tried to police the rolls in order to restore them to their proper size and function.

After this attempt at resetting the program failed, policy makers looked under the hood, so to speak, and began to fiddle with things like the formula for computing benefits, repairing the watch, in other words. At the same time, policy makers worked hard to make the program a vehicle for rehabilitation by adding new features to the program. When all of these measures failed, policy makers decided they needed to work around the problem by leaving the disability insurance program in place but surrounding it with other programs, such as the Americans with Disabilities Act.

Medicare also grew at what policy makers believed to be an alarming and unsustainable rate. This time they skipped the step of resetting the program and moved directly to tinkering with its internal workings. Using sophisticated tools, they devised the prospective payment system and hoped that would fix the problem. Tinkering with Medicare proved to be more complicated than tinkering with disability insurance, since there was not one Medicare program but two. A prospective payment system for hospitals needed to be supplemented with a prospective payment system for doctors. Eventually policy makers decided that they needed to change Medicare's basic structure, but the program proved too popular, with too many people depending on it, for that. In response, policy makers decided to place new programs on top of the old ones, preserving the old while creating something new.

Finally, in the case of welfare reform, policy makers also ran into the problem of caseloads that were expanding well beyond their expectations and appeared to indicate that the program was breaking down. At first they tried to adjust the inner workings of the program by adding a rehabilitation component. When that strategy failed, they decided to replace the program altogether—to buy a new watch in other words. The new watch had all the modern features, such as time limits for welfare recipients and a new orientation—toward work and away from income maintenance.

What decided the basic fates of the three programs? Disability insurance and Medicare quickly acquired enough political heft to make them resistant to fundamental change, and any changes that policy makers attempted needed to respect that fact. The changes were either invisible to beneficiaries or added as a supplement to the basic program. The structure of disability insurance had fewer levers for policy makers to pull than did Medicare and hence the need to work outside of the program in order to effect change. Medicare was always a heterogeneous program with different approaches to insurance for hospital stays and doctor's visits. It fit the basic historical pattern to stack new programs on top of the old ones and include all of the programs in one legislative package. Welfare had a much weaker political following than the other two programs, but even then policy makers went to great lengths to improve the program before finally deciding to jettison it altogether in 1996.

In this manner, three of the most important programs in the American welfare state had different policy outcomes. Because of the processes of path dependency and policy feedback, to revert to the political science terms, the founding legislation of 1956, 1965, and 1935 respectively laid the foundations for the subsequent outcomes. It was as though the laws contained the programs' DNA, the genetic code that would govern the programs' subsequent development.

Comparing the Three Programs

At the same time, historical contingencies mattered at every turn of the programs' development. The original legislation might be the most important, but subsequent legislative rounds also mattered, and nothing about the outcomes of those subsequent rounds was preordained. Although the range of choices might narrow over time, choices still existed.

No two of the programs followed the same path. For example, changes in disability insurance were more cyclical than the changes in the other programs. When the headlines called attention to an alarming rise in the disability rolls, policy makers responded by making it harder to get benefits. Common devices included examining people on the rolls to see if they still belonged there or making technical changes in the benefit formula that policy makers hoped would be invisible to the general public and make the benefits less desirable. These devices altered the signals that the program's central office sent to the state agencies that admitted people to the rolls. Then, when the headlines called attention to the tragedy of worthy people being denied benefits, policy makers took their feet off the brakes and began to make it easier to get disability benefits. In Medicare, by way of contrast, the cost increases that arrested the pattern of incremental expansion tended to be more persistent than cyclical. The cost increases accelerated with the passage of time, in step with more general increases in health care expenses that caused the nation to devote a higher percentage of its growing national product to health care over time.

Hence Medicare, more consistently under discussion than the other programs, was more susceptible to the long-run changes in policy styles that marked the period from the Great Society to the Contract with America. Early on, a political consensus in the program developed around the notion of controlling costs even though people differed over what should be done with the savings. For conservatives cost control was an end in itself. For liberals cost controls were a means of having the financial resources to reach national health insurance and other ambitious social goals. The powerful interest groups that followed these discussions, such as representatives of hospitals, physicians, and prescription drug companies, listened to these policy discussions in self-interested ways that complicated the politics.

Some of the policy developments in Medicare and in the other two programs as well took place in very public settings. Diagnosis-related groups and rehabilitation schemes were things that were developed well within the policy process and outside of public view. Searching for a solution to health care cost inflation in an effort to free funds for other endeavors, the Carter administration tried the rather crude approach of setting a cap on hospital cost increases that would apply to the entire health care system and not just the Medicare program. That set off a very public feud that engaged both political parties and nearly all of the medical interest groups.

The discussion initiated in the Carter years led to the passage of new legislation in 1983 that established the principle of prospective payment in hospital payments. In this instance as in many others, policy makers tried to develop formulas that would handle politically contentious issues automatically and keep them from erupting into political controversies. The DRGs might also have reflected a level of technical competence that was not yet available to policy makers in 1965. This newfound quantitative competence, facilitated by the use of computers to make complicated technical adjustments in the payments from the federal government to hospitals, gave policy makers new tools to solve policy problems. The 1983 Medicare reforms had the pleasing result of requiring no changes in the program's administrative structure or even its benefits.

In the 1990s Medicare once again became a political symbol. In the face of continuing fiscal crises, liberals hoped to preserve the program, and conservatives wanted to reform it. At stake was the issue of whether America could afford entitlement programs or whether the government would ever be able to bring its deficits under control. Medicare was therefore at the center of domestic politics once again from 1993 to 1997 before an improving economy and the political needs of the moment produced new legislation. Policy makers have no assurance that the issue will not flare up again in future years particularly with Medicare's Part A trust fund keeping Medicare's financial status in constant view and providing an early warning system of future problems.

In place only since 1996, the Personal Responsibility and Work Opportunity Act has had less time to develop long-term trends. It marked the end of a reform process as much as a beginning, although such things are relative and highly dependent on one's vantage point. A historical perspective permits us to see that this law did not come from nowhere. As early as 1967 policy makers expressed dissatisfaction with a previous law they had enthusiastically put in place five years earlier. The problem related to the growing cost of the program, as with disability insurance and Medicare, but it involved more than that. Policy makers feared that welfare had become a way of life, particularly in cities that were undergoing a visible deterioration and producing riots that many Americans viewed with alarm. No one questioned whether medical care should be a way of life or whether there should be protection against the risk of disability. There was also a visible change in the caseload as the rising percentage of people of color on the welfare rolls and the increasing number of single mothers receiving benefits indicated.

The program responded to these changes in its environment, but it took more time than one might have expected. The first iterations of welfare reform were positive rather than negative or punitive. In 1962 the Kennedy administration created a program meant to cure the problems of dysfunctional families and make them better able to cope with the demands of the midcentury American labor force. The Nixon administration experimented with fundamental reform, eliminating the Aid to Families of Dependent Children program and replacing it with a guaranteed annual income that allowed "intact" families to receive welfare and that encouraged work. By 1974 the perception arose that the situation required something different, something more fundamental and something more punitive. That encouraged Governor Reagan and other policy makers who now called themselves conservatives to propose that welfare recipients be required to work in order to "pay off" their benefits and to eliminate some costly features of the program, such as subsidizing the cost of transportation and other expenses for working welfare recipients. In 1988 Reagan's approach led to a compromise measure that emphasized work for welfare recipients but, in the manner of Kennedy's earlier law, authorized social services, such as health care and childcare, that policy makers hoped would ease the transition from welfare to work. Then in 1996 came the law that brought many of the concerns that had developed since the 1960s to the fore and changed the very nature of the welfare program from a federal entitlement to a state manpower program that subsidized its beneficiaries for participating.

For all that it restarted the welfare program and treated single mothers and their children much more harshly than the others treated the elderly and people with disabilities, the 1996 legislation bore some similarities to the other two laws discussed in this book. For one thing it preserved much of what came before, despite the rhetoric around it proclaiming it as a fundamental, even revolutionary, reform. The bones of the New Deal and even earlier progressive era programs continued to show through. Welfare still offered benefits according to categories that had been established in the New Deal and in 1950. Dependent children were one of the original categories, and they remained the chief welfare clients after 1996. In other indicators of continuity, states continued to administer AFDC before and after the 1996 law, and before and after the law they depended on federal money to pay their expenses. If anything, their dependence on federal money increased in the Clinton/Gingrich era. Of course no one launched a campaign to end welfare dependency among the blind, nor did one hear much about the percentage of blind welfare recipients who were black. And for all that ending welfare as an entitlement constituted a major change, other programs, created in the New Deal and Great Society such as Medicaid and the Food Stamp Program, took up at least some of the slack. They could not be wiped away so easily as could Aid to Families with Dependent Children.

Despite this evidence of continuity, the fact that AFDC was transformed from an entitlement to a block grant represented a point of real change in social welfare policy. Behind this change lay the fact that the nation's governors had become an effective interest group in promoting welfare reform. When disability insurance and Medicare were created, many policy makers regarded the federal government as a superior level of government to administer social welfare policies. By the 1990s that appeared to change, and one result was the 1996 welfare law. Beyond that significant development, the 1996 law depended on policy analysis that was done in conservative think tanks, such as the Heritage Foundation, that took as an explicit goal a return to free market principles (which had never applied to welfare) and an end to federal government dominance in social policy (which was an undisputed fact in welfare policy). These conservative think tanks and other important organizations associated with the Christian right did not exist to nearly the same extent in 1956 or 1965.

In other words the policy environment changed over time to accommodate conservative goals and ideas more easily. Congressional subcommittees offered more avenues for conservatives to make their case, although liberals could also use the subcommittee system to their advantage. In the 1996 welfare reform, Senate and House subcommittees positioned themselves at the very center of the policy action. In the 1956 and 1965 pieces of legislation, these subcommittees were much less prominent, and in the House they were nonexistent. The legendary Wilbur Mills, for example, ran the Ways and Committee without permanent subcommittees, thus increasing his leverage over Medicare.

Another key change in the policy environment that arguably made it easier for conservatives to present their case related to changes in how the costs of prospective legislation were estimated. The old system put an emphasis on people within an agency, such as the Social Security or Medicare actuary, or on officials who worked in what became the Office of Management and Budget. An agency and a presidential administration had the power to issue cost estimates for bills that they wanted to pass and, within limits, to shape the policy environment to their advantage. The new system featured a nonpartisan Congressional Budget Office that reported to Congress and not the President. The Congressional Budget Office staffers benefited from the speed of computers, the presence of more data sources, and improvements in econometric methodology. All of these things tended to make the estimates more comprehensive or inclusive and thus higher than they might have been in an earlier era when, to a much greater extent, the government flew blind. Medicare and disability benefits were launched without a clear idea of its future costs. High cost estimates tended to favor conservatives over liberals.

The three case studies make it clear that social welfare politics is not a matter of being in favor of the expansion or contraction of the federal government. In each of the three cases here, the federal government played a leading role, but even when faith in the federal government's confidence to solve social problems was at its height, policy makers turned to the states (disability insurance) and the private sector (Medicare) to undertake difficult tasks. As a result, disability insurance represented a significant point of departure for the nation's Social Security program because it meant that, under the right conditions, retirement benefits were available at any age. But the crucially important task of determining which of the many applicants was disabled fell to the states, acting under contract to the federal government. State employees, not federal employees, reviewed disability files. In a similar sense, Medicare used private intermediaries and insurance carriers to administer the program. In both cases, critics questioned the legitimacy of the approach. Some people complained, for example, that it was easier to get disability benefits in Alaska than in Iowa or that the payment of Medicare claims operated differently in New Jersey than in Illinois. Regardless, the states and the private sector remained vital parts of the machinery.

As conservatives gained more control over Congress, they pushed the idea that the government should be smaller and more particularly less costly. At some fundamental level, they believed that states should have the freedom to follow their own predilections to reflect local preferences. Crucially, though, they also saw the point of using the federal government to set the central direction of social policy. Hence they favored a national welfare law that set national standards over such things as whether illegitimate children were entitled to welfare or whether Medicaid should fund abortions. They trusted the government when it spoke in their voice.

Thinking About the Process of Change over Time

So how then did America's welfare state change between the Great Society and Newt Gingrich's opportunity society? For a great portion of the time, Republicans replaced Democrats as the proprietors of this welfare state. The programs of the New Deal and the Great Society—disability insurance and Medicare in particular—nonetheless showed a great resistance to change that left them standing in the age of Donald Trump. And even when conservatives succeeded in creating new programs, these programs relied on the basic structures of the old programs. Changing conditions put pressures on social welfare programs to change. Women entered the labor force in large numbers and called into question some of the main assumptions of the old Aid to Families with Dependent Children program. People with disabilities became recognized as a minority group with their own civil rights law, making the equation of disability and the inability to work more problematic. Medicare reflected an old style of unmanaged care that did not create incentives for improved outcomes. It paid for services, as one former head of the administering agency put it, by the yard. Gradually it became outmoded with the result that Parts C and D of the program differed from the ones created in 1965.

Change does not come easily to the social welfare system. There is a reason that so much of America's welfare state dates from the great bursts of activity in 1935 and 1965 with much less happening in the years between 1935 and 1950 or between 1972 and 1996. The prognosis then is for a welfare state that grows incrementally to accommodate change and always lags behind current events. At the same time, the welfare state remains a site of incessant activity as policy makers try to adapt old programs to new conditions.

To cast the argument of this book in broader terms, one might begin with the proposition that all programs reflect the conventional wisdom of the era of their founding. In a sense that means that all social welfare laws are memos from the past. At the same time, however, all programs reflect the serendipitous events that arise in the legislative process. This book abounds with examples. Senator Walter George wants to leave behind a lasting legislative monument. The two leaders of the labor movement die at almost exactly the same time. Wilbur Mills agrees to a Republican proposal in order to reduce the burdens on the Social Security trust fund. Governor Tommy Thompson seeks to gain national exposure through the issue of welfare reform, just as Ronald Reagan and Bill Clinton had already done. Once put in place, all programs operate through "baked in" institutional structures that are inherited from previous laws. Disability insurance and Medicare utilized the payroll tax collection system of the Social Security program. Welfare reform needed to take into account that the states already ran their Aid to Families with Dependent Children programs.

The origins of a program launch it on a path that is guided by its original structure. At the same time, each of the programs eventually endures crises that put the program under stress and, depending on the magnitude of the stress, induce change. Examples of problems that a program might encounter include changes in the conventional wisdom, as in the fundamental reorientation of AFDC from a humanitarian program to a manpower program for single mothers. The institutional structure of a program might either create problems as the program grows, such as disparities among states in awarding disability benefits, or it might seem so anachronistic that it requires substantial repair to respond to modern conditions, such as whether Medicare would be compatible with a national health insurance program. External forces such as the state of the economy (a recession makes it hard to fund Medicare or disability insurance) or demographic pressures (the birth rate declines below expectations or the immigration rate increases) might also reopen the legislative process and create a new path for the program. The clearest example of that among the three case studies is what happened to the AFDC program in the Clinton-Gingrich era.

One should be suspicious of the generalizations in the previous paragraph because historical particulars that are different from program to program and year to year shape policy outcomes. I would suggest, however, that the three programs discussed in this book are important not only as instructive studies of the policy process but in and of themselves. The Social Security Disability Insurance program demands attention because it set the terms for the nation's disability policy as fundamentally a problem of income maintenance rather than a source of rehabilitation or a vehicle for civil rights. The importance of Medicare needs little defense. The program has become the most influential of America's medical programs because it is the largest single source of payments that hospitals receive. The history of the provision of medical care after 1965, a history that comes up often in political discussions, would be impossible without including Medicare. Finally, AFDC and welfare reform hold an important place in how the United States treats poverty and influence how Americans wish to treat minorities and women.

Most of the historical literature about each of these programs puts historians in the role of social critics. Disability insurance unfairly equates a physical handicap and the ability to work. Medicare perpetuates the mistakes of an inefficient, inequitable, and needlessly expensive medical system. Temporary Aid to Needy Families places unfair burdens on African Americans and single mothers who live in the inner cities. In the role of social critic, historians illuminate much about what is wrong with

US social policy and even, although somewhat cautiously, indicate ways it could be improved.

I suggest another lens for the history of social policy, and that is to concentrate on the administrative structure of important social programs and to chronicle the politics that those structures make. Whether that approach helps us understand social welfare policy is for the reader to decide.

Notes

Introduction

1. Paul A. David, "Clio and the Economics of QWERTY," *Economic History*, May 1985, pp. 332–337; Paul Pierson, "Review: When Effect Becomes Cause: Policy Feedback and Political Change," *World Politics* 45 (July 1993): pp. 595–628; Paul Pierson, "Increasing Returns, Path Dependence and the Study of Politics," *American Political Review* 94 (June 2000): pp. 251–267; Elizabeth Clemens and James M. Cooke, "Politics and Institutionalism: Explaining Durability and Change," *American Review of Sociology* 23 (August 1999): pp. 441–466; James Mahoney, "Path Dependence in Historical Sociology," *Theory and Society* 29 (August 2000): pp. 507–548.

2. "The law of 1956 bore many marks from its long and intensely political passage." Martha Derthick, *Policymaking for Social Security* (Washington, DC: Brookings Institution, 1979), p. 308.

3. Andrea Louise Campbell, "Policy Feedback," in *Oxford Bibliographies* (2018), http://www.oxfordbibliographies.com/view/document/obo-9780199756223/obo-9780199756223-0235.xml; Daniel Béland, "Reconsidering Policy Feedback: How Policies Affect Politics," *Administration and Society* 42 (2010): pp. 568–590; Suzanne Mettler, "The Policyscape and the Challenges of Contemporary Politics to Policy Maintenance," *Perspectives on Politics* 14 (2016): pp. 369–390.

4. David Brooks, "'Medicare for All': The Impossible Dream," *New York Times*, March 5, 2019; "Medicare for All: Being Cost Efficient Gets Incredible Results," http://www.medicareforall.org/pages/Home.

5. Jeffrey A. Jenkins and Eric M. Patashnik, "Living Legislation and American Politics," in *Living Legislation: Durability, Change, and the Politics of American Lawmaking*, ed. Jenkins and Patashnik, (Chicago: University of Chicago Press, 2012), pp. 5–6; Patashnik, *Reforms at Risk: What Happens after Major Policy Changes Are Enacted* (Princeton, NJ: Princeton University Press, 2008).

6. Robert C. Lieberman, *Shifting the Color Line: Race and the American Welfare State* (Cambridge, MA: Harvard University Press, 1998); Gareth Davies and Martha Derthick, "Race and Social Welfare Policy: The Social Security Act of 1935," *Political Science Quarterly* 112 (Summer 1997): pp. 217–235.

7. Deborah Stone, *The Disabled State* (Philadelphia: Temple University Press, 1984); Robert Haveman, Victor Halberstadt, and Richard Burkhauser, *Public Policy toward Disabled Workers: Cross-National Analyses of Economic Impacts* (Ithaca, NY: Cornell University Press, 1984); Jennifer L. Erkulwater, *Disability Rights and the American Social Safety Net* (Ithaca, NY: Cornell University Press, 2006); Erkulwater, "Constructive Welfare: The Social Security Act, the Blind, and the Origins of Political Identity among People with Disabilities, 1935–1950," *Studies in American Political Development* 33 (April 2019): pp. 110–138; Erkulwater, "How the Nation's Largest Minority Became White: Race Politics and the Disability Rights Movement," *Policy History* 30 (2018): pp. 367–369; Felicia Kornbluh, "Disability, Antiprofessionalism, and Civil Rights: The National Federation of the Blind and the 'Right to Organize' in the 1950s," *Journal of American History* 97 (2011): pp. 1023–1047; Richard Scotch, *From Good Will to Civil Rights: Transforming Federal Disability Policy*, 2nd ed. (Philadelphia: Temple University Press, 2001).

8. See for example Institute of Medicine, *Medicare: A Strategy for Quality Assurance*, ed. Kathy Lohr (Washington, DC: National Academy Press, 1990).

9. Christy Ford Chapin, *Ensuring America's Health: The Public Creation of the Corporate Health Care System* (New York: Cambridge University Press, 2015), pp. 1, 3, 7–8.

10. Larry DeWitt and Edward D. Berkowitz, "Health Care," in *A Companion to Lyndon B. Johnson*, ed. Mitchell R. Lerner (Malden, MA: Wiley-Blackwell, 2012), pp. 163–186; Eugene Feingold, *Medicare: Policy and Politics; A Case Study and Policy Analysis* (San Francisco: Chandler, 1966); Richard Harris, *A Sacred Trust* (New York: New American Library, 1966); Theodore Marmor, *The Politics of Medicare* (Hawthorne, NY: Aldine De Gruyter, 1973); Herman Somers and Ann Somers, *Medicare and the Hospitals: Issues and Prospects* (Washington, DC: Brookings Institution, 1967); Sheri David, *With Dignity: The Search for Medicare and Medicaid* (Westport, CT: Greenwood, 1983); Allen Matusow, *The Unraveling of America: A History of Liberalism in the 1960s* (New York: Harper and Row, 1984), p. 228; Jonathan Oberlander, *The Political Life of Medicare* (Chicago: University of Chicago Press, 2003).

11. Beatrix Hoffman, *Health Care for Some: Rights and Rationing in the United States since 1930* (Chicago: University of Chicago Press, 2012), pp. xii, 127–128.

12. Martin Gilens, *Why Americans Hate Welfare: Race, Media, and the Politics of Antipoverty Policy* (Chicago: University of Chicago Press, 1999); Mimi Abramowitz, *Regulating the Lives of Women: Social Welfare Policy from Co-*

lonial Times to the Present (Boston: South End, 1996); Martha Davis, "Welfare Rights and Women's Rights in the1960s," *Journal of Policy History* 8 (1996): pp. 144–165; Joanne Goodwin, "'Employable Mothers' and 'Suitable Work': A Reevaluation of Welfare and Wage-Earning for Women in the Twentieth-Century United States," *Journal of Social History* 29 (1993): pp. 253–274; Linda Gordon, *Pitied but Not Entitled: Single Mothers and the History of Welfare* (New York: Free Press, 1994); Alice Kessler-Harris, *In Pursuit of Equity: Women, Men, and the Quest for Economic Citizenship in Twentieth-Century America* (New York: Oxford University Press, 2001); Premilla Nadsen, "Expanding the Boundaries of the Women's Movement and the Struggle for Welfare Rights," *Feminist Studies* 28 (2002): pp. 271–301; Barbara Nelson, The Origins of the Two-Channel Welfare State: Workmen's Compensation and Mothers' Aid," in *Women, the State, and Welfare*, ed. Linda Gordon (Madison: University of Wisconsin Press, 1990), pp. 123–151; Jill Quadagno, *The Color of Welfare: How Racism Undermined the War on Poverty* (New York: Oxford University Press, 1994); Rickie Solinger, *Wake Up Little Susie: Race and Single Pregnancy before* Roe v. Wade (New York: Routledge, 1993).

13. Jennifer Mittelstadt, *From Welfare to Workfare: The Unintended Consequences of Liberal Reform, 1945–1965* (Chapel Hill: University of North Carolina Press, 2005), p. 13.

14. Joe Soss, "The Racial Biases of the Welfare System," Spotlight on Poverty and Opportunity, https://spotlightonpoverty.org/spotlight-exclusives/the-racial-biases-of-the-welfare-system/; Sanford F. Schram, Joe Soss, and Richard C. Fording, eds., *Race and the Politics of Welfare Reform* (Ann Arbor: University of Michigan Press, 2003). Another key book is Gilens, *Why Americans Hate Welfare*.

15. Derthick, *Policymaking for Social Security*; Derthick, *Agency under Stress: The Social Security Administration in American Government* (Washington, DC: Brookings Institution, 1990).

Chapter One

1. I should note at the outset that the same 1956 legislation that included disability insurance also made special provisions for women that also lowered the age at which they could collect Social Security benefits. The new law permitted women to retire and receive other benefits at age sixty-two (see Wilbur Cohen, *Retirement Policies under Social Security: A Legislative History of Retirement Ages, the Retirement Test, and Disability Benefits* [Berkeley: University of California Press, 1957]). Although I focus on disability insurance, legislators considered disability benefits and early retirement for women in tandem. Early retirement for women was a less controversial measure than the creation of disability

benefits, complicating historical formulations about the relationship between gender and social welfare policy (see Alice Kessler-Harris, *In Pursuit of Equity: Women, Men, and the Quest for Economic Citizenship in 20th-Century America* [New York: Oxford University Press, 2003]). Social Security Commissioner Charles Schottland regarded the early retirement benefits as "sweeteners" in the legislation (Charles Schottland, interview by Edward Berkowitz, Waltham, MA, September 20, 1978).

2. Derthick, *Policymaking for Social Security.*

3. Richard Verville, *War, Politics, and Philanthropy: The History of Rehabilitation Medicine in America* (Lanham, MD: University Press of America, 2009); Glenn Gritzer and Arnold Arluke, *The Making of Rehabilitation: A Political Economy of Medical Specialization, 1890–1980* (Berkeley: University of California Press, 1985).

4. James Patterson, *Grand Expectations: The United States, 1945–1974* (New York: Oxford University Press, 1996); Simon Hall, *1956: The World in Revolt* (London: Pegasus Books, 2017).

5. Edward D. Berkowitz, *Disabled Policy: America's Programs for the Handicapped* (New York: Cambridge University Press, 1987), pp. 41–78.

6. Berkowitz, *Disabled Policy*, pp. 41–78.

7. John D. Morris, "Democrats Speed Pension Revisions," *New York Times*, June 22, 1955, p. 1.

8. Sanford Jacoby, *Modern Manors: Welfare Capitalism since the New Deal* (Princeton, NJ: Princeton University Press, 1997), Jill Quadagno, *The Transformation of Old Age Security: Class and Politics* (Chicago: University of Chicago Press, 1988).

9. Oliver Garceau, *The Political Life of the American Medical Association* (Cambridge, MA: Harvard University Press, 1941); James Gordon Burrow, *AMA: Voice of American Medicine* (Baltimore: Johns Hopkins University Press, 1963).

10. Eve Edstrom, "Changes Forecast in Social Insurance," *Washington Post*, January 4, 1956, p. 44; Rodney Crowther, "Controversial Issues Await Early Congressional Action," *Baltimore Sun*, January 3, 1956, p. 6.

11. House Ways and Means Committee, *Report 1189*, July 14, 1955, p. 3.

12. C. Esco Obermann, *A History of Vocational Rehabilitation in America* (Minneapolis: T. S. Denison, 1965); Mary E. MacDonald, *Federal Grants for Vocational Rehabilitation* (Chicago: University of Chicago Press, 1944).

13. Edward D. Berkowitz, *Rehabilitation: The Federal Government's Response to Disability, 1935–1954* (New York: Arno, 1980), pp. 262–289.

14. House Ways and Means Committee, *Report 1189*, July 14, 1955, pp. 6–8.

15. House Ways and Means Committee, *Report 1189*, July 14, 1955, p. 47.

16. "Additional Remarks of Hon. Noah M. Mason," in House Ways and Means Committee, *Report 1189*, July 14, 1955, pp. 68–71.

17. Edstrom, "Changes Forecast in Social Insurance."

18. *Congressional Record*, July 18, 1955, p. 10775.

19. Stanford M. Jacoby, "Employers and the Welfare State: The Role of Marion Folsom," *Journal of American History* 80 (September 1993): pp. 525–556.

20. Berkowitz, *Disabled Policy*, p. 67.

21. Edward D. Berkowitz, *Robert Ball and the Politics of Social Security* (Madison: University of Wisconsin Press, 2003), p. 98.

22. Berkowitz, *Robert Ball*, p. 98. Robert Ball of the Social Security Administration came at Folsom from the opposite direction. Ball was convinced that Folsom "favored a modest type of disability program" and might be persuaded to advocate the measure in public or persuade the administration not to oppose the measure too strenuously in private. Ball worked hard to soften the tone of the testimony that Folsom would give to the Senate Finance Committee and believed that Folsom wanted him to do so. Assistant Health, Education, and Welfare Secretary Roswell Perkins tried to make Folsom's testimony congruent with the administration's previous position on the matter. Even when it became clear that the administration would not support disability insurance, the struggle continued. Ball called it a "matter of degree of opposition." He wanted to preserve Folsom's flexibility. He and Perkins fought over every word of Folsom's testimony, "I arguing for the softer word and he for the harsher word each time."

23. Betty Pryor, "Earlier Retirement Opposed," *Washington Post*, March 23, 1956, p. 18; Joseph R. Slavin, "Liberalized Old-Age Is Opposed," *New York Herald Tribune*, March 23, 1956, p. 13; John D. Morris, "Folsom Opposes New Pension Bill," *New York Times*, March 23, 1956, p. 29.

24. Pryor, "Early Retirement Opposed."

25. John Van Camp, "Meany Urges Emphasis on US Defenses," *Baltimore Sun*, January 1, 1956, p. 3.

26. Robert Zieger, *American Workers, American Unions, 1920–1985* (Baltimore: Johns Hopkins University Press, 1986) provides a good background for the labor history recounted here.

27. Edward D. Berkowitz, "The First Social Security Crisis," *Prologue*, Fall 1983, pp. 132–149.

28. "New Merger Bid on Eve of A.F.L. Meeting," *New York Herald Tribune*, September 16, 1951, p. 21.

29. "William Green Is Dead at 82; Headed A.F.L. since 1924," *New York Times*, November 22, 1952, p. 1; "William Green Dies at 82; A.F.L. President 28 Years," *New York Herald Tribune*, November 22, 1952, p. 1; "William F. Green, AFL Leader, Dies," *Los Angeles Times*, November 22, 1952, p. 1.

30. Robert Levey, "Meany Is Likely to Succeed Green; Speculation Rises on Labor Unity," *New York Times*, November 22, 1952, p. 24. A. H. Raskin, "A.F.L. Picks Meany, Moves to Revive Merger with C.I.O.," *New York Times*, November 26, 1952, p. 1.

31. A. H. Raskin, "2 Big C.I.O. Unions Swing to Reuther, Assuring Election," *New York Times*, December 2, 1952, p. 1.

32. Nelson Lichtenstein, *Walter Reuther: The Most Dangerous Man in Detroit* (Urbana: University of Illinois Press, 1996); A. H. Raskin, "The New Labor Leaders—A Dual Portrait," *New York Times Sunday Magazine*, December 21, 1952, p. SM12.

33. A. H. Raskin, "Reuther Elected President of C.I.O.," *New York Times*, December 5, 1952, p. 1.

34. "Rusk and Meany Join in Pledge to Seek Unity of C.I.O.," *New York Times*, December 6, 1952, p. 1; Elie Abel, "C.I.O. Gives A.F.L. Terms for Merger," *New York Times*, March 23, 1953, p. 1; "CIO, AFL Mark Raid Agreement," *Baltimore Sun*, June 10, 1954, p. 1; Howard Norton, "Meany Sees Closer Labor Political Tie," *Baltimore Sun*, May 20, 1954, p. 8; Howard Norton, "AFL and CIO to Sign No-Raid Pact June 9," *Baltimore Sun*, May 15, 1954, p. 1; "Pact Signing," *Baltimore Sun*, June 30, 1954, p. 4.

35. Howard Norton, "CIO's Greeting First Since '35," *Baltimore Sun*, September 22, 1954, p. 1; Howard Norton, "15 AFL, CIO Leaders Vote for Merger Plan," *Baltimore Sun*, October 16, 1954, p. 1.

36. George Meany, "Merger and the National Welfare," *Industrial and Labor Relations Review* 9 (April 1956): pp. 349–351; Howard Norton, "20 Labor Chiefs Sign Pact, See Organization of 15,000,000 Members," *Baltimore Sun*, February 10, 1955, p. 1.

37. Howard Norton, "AFL and CIO Clear Road for Merger," *Baltimore Sun*, July 20, 1955, p. 1; Howard Norton, "AFL's Final Convention O.K.'s Merger," *Baltimore Sun*, December 2, 1955, p. 1; Peter J. Kumpa, "New 16,000,000 Group Will Open Its First Meeting Monday," *Baltimore Sun*, December 3, 1955, p. 1.

38. Arthur J. Altmeyer, *The Formative Years of Social Security* (Madison: University of Wisconsin Press, 1968), p. vii. The advocates of Social Security went to great lengths to highlight the differences between labor legislation—such as workers' compensation, unemployment compensation, and old-age insurance—and poor law legislation, such as welfare payments to the indigent elderly, the blind, or dependent children. The Social Security program did not deal with paupers or others outside of the margins of American life but rather workers and their families whether poor or rich. The program encompassed many but not all of those at the lower end of the income scale. Although it helped to solve social problems, it was not in itself a vehicle of racial equality, gender equality, or slum clearance.

39. Edward D. Berkowitz, *Mr. Social Security: The Life of Wilbur J. Cohen* (Lawrence: University Press of Kansas, 1995), pp. 1–25.

40. Berkowitz, *Robert Ball*, pp. 23–73.

41. Berkowitz, *Mr. Social Security*, pp. 54–55.

42. Edward D. Berkowitz, *America's Welfare State from Roosevelt to Reagan* (Baltimore: Johns Hopkins University Press, 1991), pp. 39–65.

43. Ronald L. Heinemann, *Harry Byrd of Virginia* (Charlottesville: University Press of Virginia, 1996).

44. Anthony Badger, "The South Confronts the Courts: The Southern Manifesto of 1956," *Journal of Policy History* 20 (2008): pp. 126–142.

45. Derthick, *Policymaking for Social Security*, pp. 55–58.

46. Rodney Crowther, "Benefits Rise Cost Scanned at Hearings," *Baltimore Sun*, January 26, 1956, p. 4.

47. "Farm Changes Sought," *New York Times*, January 28, 1956, p. 24; "Boost in Aid for Nation's Blind Urged," *Baltimore Sun*, February 3, 1956, p. 2.

48. "Doctors Open Fight against Disabled Pay," *Baltimore Sun*, February 10, 1956, p. 6.

49. "Senate Urged Not to Alter Security Law," *Los Angeles Times*, February 15, 1956, p. 39; Rodney Crowther, "Old-Age Pay Shift Fought," *Baltimore Sun*, February 22, 1956, p. 6.

50. "Reuther Backs Bill Providing Disability Pay," *Chicago Tribune*, February 21, 1956, p. 3.

51. Rodney Crowther, "Units Hit Bill on Disability," *Baltimore Sun*, February 23, 1956, p. 6.

52. "Death Seen for Social Security Bill," *Washington Post*, March 5, 1956, p. 18.

53. "Payne Backs Plan for Women to Get Social Security at 62," *Baltimore Sun*, April 3, 1956, p. 5; Rodney Crowther, "Senate Showdown Vote Near on Social Security Changes," *Baltimore Sun*, April 26, 1956, p. 2.

54. Joseph R. Slevin, "Rejects Old Age Pay Revisions," *New York Herald Tribune*, May 11, 1956, p. 3; Betty Prior, "Senators Reject Benefits for Disabled at Age 50," *Washington Post*, May 11, 1956, p. 2; John D. Morris, "Senators Strip Pension Plan of Major Benefit Increases," *New York Times*, May 11. 1956, p. 1.

55. Senate Finance Committee, "Social Security Amendments of 1956," *Report 213*, June 5, 1956, pp. 1–28.

56. Rodney Crowther, "Highway Bill, Social Security Changes Advanced in Senate," *Baltimore Sun*, May 26, 1956, p. 5; "Pension Bill OK'd; Tailored to Ike Wishes," *Chicago Tribune*, May 26, 1956, p. 14.

57. Senate Finance Committee, *Report 213*, pp. 127–134.

58. Luther Harmon Zeigler Jr., "Senator Walter George's 1938 Campaign," *Georgia Historical Quarterly* 43 (December 1959): pp. 333–352.

59. "Dean of the Senate: Walter Franklin George," *New York Times*, May 10, 1956, 18; James Reston, "The Decline of Eloquence in the Congress," *New York Times*, January 31, 1954, p. E8.

60. "Senator George Steps Down," *Washington Post*, May 10, 1956, p. 12.

61. Berkowitz, *Mr. Social Security*, p. 116.

62. Wilbur Cohen to Elizabeth Wickenden, March 4, 1956, Elizabeth Wickenden Papers, Wisconsin Historical Society, Madison.

63. Wilbur Cohen, "The Situation in Social Security," February 16, 1956, Box 70, Wilbur Cohen Papers, Wisconsin Historical Society, Madison.

64. Berkowitz, *Disabled Policy*, pp. 75–76.

65. Paul Douglas, *In the Fullness of Time: The Memoirs of Paul Douglas* (New York: Harcourt, Brace, Jovanovich, 1972), pp. 391–392.

66. "Douglas Predicts O.K. on Disability Payments," *Chicago Tribune*, June 23, 1956, p. 16; John Morris, "Senate Approval of Benefits Near," *New York Times*, July 4, 1956, p. 17; "New Social Security Plan for Women Set," *Los Angeles Times*, July 8, 1956, p. A9; "Fight Looms on Social Security Law," *Los Angeles Times*, July 15, 1956, p. B30.

67. *Congressional Record*, July 16, 1956, pp. 12885 (Lehman).

68. *Congressional Record*, July 17, 1956, pp. 13023 (Jackson), 13039 (Gore).

69. *Congressional Record*, July 17, 1956, pp. 13026–13038; Dominick Pratico, *Eisenhower and Social Security: The Origins of the Disability Program* (New York: Writers Club Press, 2001) provides a useful overview of this debate and of the history detailed in this chapter. I read the Kindle edition.

70. Clarence B. Lasby, *Heart Attack: How Ike Beat Heart Disease and Held on to the Presidency* (Lawrence: University Press of Kansas, 1997).

71. Robert Caro, *Master of the Senate: The Years of Lyndon Johnson* (New York: Alfred A. Knopf, 2002), pp. 640–657.

72. *Congressional Record*, July 17, 1956, p. 13046; Henry Viscardi Jr., *A Man's Stature* (Rutland, VT: Paul S. Eriksson, 1987); Howard Rusk and Eugene Taylor, *New Hope for the Handicapped: The Rehabilitation of the Disabled from Bed to Job* (New York: Harper and Brothers, 1949).

73. Caro, *Master of the Senate*, p. 677.

74. Caro, *Master of the Senate*, p. 678.

75. "Roll-Call of Senate Votes on Pension Amendment," *New York Times*, July 18, 1956, p. 16.

76. Victor Christgau, "Director's Bulletin 239,"July 18, 1956, Social Security Administration History Archives, Baltimore.

77. "Fast Accord Seen on Pension Bill," *New York Times*, July 19, 1956, p. 18; "Social Security Conferees Agree," *Chicago Tribune*, July 21, 1956, p. 3; Joe Hall, "Social Security Bill Goes to White House," *Washington Post*, July 28, 1956, p. 13.

78. "Urges Ike Veto of Changes in Pension Law," *Chicago Tribune*, July 31, 1956, p. 3.

79. Charles E. Egan, "President Signs Pension Measure," *New York Times*, August 2, 1956, p. 1.

80. Dwight D. Eisenhower to Edward F. Hutton, October 7, 1953, Central

Files, Box 848, File 156-C, Dwight D. Eisenhower Library, Abilene, KS; "Social Security Hit," *New York Times*, December 2, 1956, p. 65.

81. Expanding the welfare state did not necessarily mean a straightforward victory of the public sector over the private sector. Instead public Social Security and private fringe benefits expanded together, if not for small businesses then for large employers. Over the previous thirty years, roughly analogous to the life span of Social Security, the General Motors Corporation had paid out more than $357 million in fringe benefits. These included increases in life insurance protection (which complemented Social Security old-age and survivors insurance), benefits for absences due to disability, and hospital and surgical insurance. Carroll E. Williams, "Workers Gain New Benefits in Industry," *Baltimore Sun*, December 7, 1956, p. 38; Jennifer Klein, *For All These Rights: Business, Labor, and the Shaping of the American Public-Private Welfare State* (Princeton, NJ: Princeton University Press, 2003).

82. "Folsom Says Stevenson Ignores Welfare Facts," *New York Herald Tribune*, November 3, 1956, p. 12.

83. "Ike's Health Seen as Definite Issue," *Baltimore Sun*, August 28, 1956, p. 4.

Chapter Two

1. *Congressional Record*, July 17, 1956, p. 13046.

2. The White House, "Social Security Disability Insurance: A Lifeline for American Workers and Families," July 2015, pp. 2, 5.

3. The White House, "Social Security Disability Insurance," pp. 5, 10, 11.

4. The White House, "Social Security Disability Insurance," p. 5.

5. Tad DeHaven, "The Rising Cost of Social Security Disability Insurance," *Policy Analysis* (Cato Institute), August 6, 2013, pp. 2, 7.

6. Congressional Budget Office, "Social Security Disability Insurance: Participation and Spending," June 2016, p. 1.

7. The White House, "Social Security Disability Insurance," p. 2; *Annual Statistical Report on the Disability Insurance Program 2015*, SSA Publication 13–11826, October 2016, unpaginated prefatory material.

8. *Annual Statistical Report*, p. 131, table 50; Congressional Budget Office, "Social Security Disability Insurance," p. 5.

9. DeHaven, "The Rising Cost of Social Security Disability Insurance," p. 8.

10. Martha Derthick, *Policymaking for Social Security* (Washington, DC: Brookings Institution, 1979), pp. 308–315.

11. Daniel Beland, *Social Security: History and Politics from the New Deal to the Privatization Debate* (Lawrence: University Press of Kansas, 2005).

12. Daniel Béland, "Reconsidering Policy Feedback: How Policies Affect Politics." *Administration and Society* 42 (2010): 568–590; Andrea Louise

Campbell, "Policies Make Mass Publics," *Annual Review of Political Science* 15 (2012): 333–351; Suzanne Mettler, "The Policyscape and the Challenges of Contemporary Politics to Policy Maintenance," *Perspectives on Politics* 14 (2016): 369–390.

13. Remarks of Carl Perkins, *Congressional Record*, July 31, 1958, p. 15764.

14. Edward D. Berkowitz, *Disabled Policy: America's Program for the Handicapped* (New York: Cambridge University Press, 1987), p. 80.

15. Berkowitz, *Disabled Policy*, p. 109.

16. George K. Wyman to William Mitchell, November 5, 1959, Records of the Social Security Administration, RG 47, File 326.102, Box 70, Accession 64A-751, Washington National Records Center, Suitland, MD.

17. Statement of William L. Mitchell, December 7, 1959, RG 47, File Identical Memorandum, Box 22, Accession 67-270, RG 47; Statement of Arthur Flemming before House Committee on Ways and Means, March 1960, Social Security Legislative Archives, Social Security Library, Baltimore. Much of this material has been moved from the Library to the Office of the Social Security Historian, Baltimore.

18. See Edward D. Berkowitz and Larry DeWitt, *The Other Welfare: Supplemental Security Income and U.S. Policy* (Ithaca, NY: Cornell University Press: 2013), chapter 1.

19. Berkowitz, *Disabled Policy*, p. 83.

20. Berkowitz, *Disabled Policy*, p. 83; Congressional Budget Office, "Social Security Disability Insurance," p. 3.

21. Congressional Budget Office, "Social Security Disability Insurance," p. 3.

22. Berkowitz, *Disabled Policy*, p. 90.

23. Congressional Budget Office, "Social Security Disability Insurance," p. 4.

24. DeHaven, "The Rising Cost of Social Security Disability Insurance," p. 12.

25. DeHaven, "The Rising Cost of Social Security Disability Insurance," p. 12.

26. *Annual Statistical Report*, p. 17, table 1; Berkowitz and DeWitt, *The Other Welfare*, p. 100.

27. Berkowitz, *Disabled Policy*, p. 111.

28. Berkowitz, *Disabled Policy*, pp. 83–87.

29. Berkowitz and DeWitt, *The Other Welfare*, pp. 102–103.

30. Berkowitz and DeWitt, *The Other Welfare*, p. 119.

31. Berkowitz, *Disabled Policy*, p. 128.

32. Berkowitz, *Disabled Policy*, pp. 115–120.

33. Berkowitz, *Disabled Policy*, p. 115.

34. Berkowitz, *Disabled Policy*, p. 119.

35. Jon Ward, *Camelot's End: Kennedy vs. Carter and the Fight that Broke the Democratic Party* (New York: Hatchette Books, 2019); Timothy Stanley,

Kennedy vs. Carter: The 1980 Battle for the Democratic Party's Soul (Lawrence: University Press of Kansas, 2010).

36. Edward D. Berkowitz, *Robert Ball and the Politics of Social Security* (Madison: University of Wisconsin Press, 2003), p. 273.

37. Berkowitz, *Disabled Policy*, pp. 124–125.

38. Berkowitz, *Disabled Policy*, p. 127.

39. Berkowitz and DeWitt, *The Other Welfare*, p. 131.

40. Berkowitz, *Disabled Policy*, pp. 131–132.

41. Berkowitz, *Disabled Policy*, p. 126.

42. Berkowitz, *Disabled Policy*, pp. 133–134.

43. Berkowitz, *Disabled Policy*, p. 127.

44. Berkowitz, *Disabled Policy*, p. 132.

45. Berkowitz and DeWitt, *The Other Welfare*, p. 131.

46. Ted DeHaven, "The Rising Cost of Social Security Disability Insurance," p. 6.

47. *Annual Statistical Report*, p. 95, chart 10, pp. 106–108, table 40.

48. Edward D. Berkowitz and David Dean, "Lessons from the Vocational Rehabilitation / Social Security Administration Experience," in *Disability, Work, and Cash Benefits*, ed. Jerry L. Mashaw et al. (Kalamazoo, MI: Upjohn Institute, 1996), p. 224.

49. Berkowitz and Dean, "Lessons," p. 225.

50. Edward D. Berkowitz, "The Federal Government and the Emergence of Rehabilitation Medicine," *Historian* 11 (August 181): pp. 530–545.

51. Berkowitz and Dean, "Lessons," p. 225; Arthur Altmeyer to Wilbur Cohen, October 8, 1956, Arthur Altmeyer Papers, Wisconsin Historical Society, Madison.

52. Berkowitz and Dean, "Lessons," p. 225.

53. Berkowitz and Dean, "Lessons," p. 226; Martha Lentz Walker, *Beyond Bureaucracy: Mary Elizabeth Switzer and Rehabilitation* (Lanham, MD: University Press of America, 1985).

54. Roswell Perkins, interview by Peter Corning, Columbia University Oral History Collections, New York.

55. Berkowitz and Dean, "Lessons," pp. 227–228.

56. Berkowitz and Dean, "Lessons," p. 229.

57. Berkowitz and Dean, "Lessons," p. 229.

58. Berkowitz and Dean, "Lessons," p. 235.

59. Berkowitz and Dean, "Lessons," p. 236.

60. Personal observations of the author. My father was one of the people involved in the creation of Tickets to Work, and he attended the Clinton signing ceremony.

61. Edward D. Berkowitz, "George Bush and the Americans with Disabilities Act," in *Principle over Politics? The Domestic Policy of the George H. W.*

Bush Administration, ed. Richard Himelfarb and Rosanna Perotti (Westport, CT: Praeger, 2004), pp. 143–155. I delivered this paper at a conference at Hofstra University on the George H. W. Bush presidency. The President attended the session, which also included remarks from Bush administration officials and leaders of the disability rights movement.

62. Edward D. Berkowitz, "A Historical Preface to the Americans with Disabilities Act," *Journal of Policy History* 6 (1994): pp. 96–119.

63. Berkowitz, "George Bush and the Americans with Disabilities Act," p. 145.

64. Berkowitz, "A Historical Preface to the Americans with Disabilities Act," p. 112.

Chapter Three

1. For the ways that the conventional wisdom shifted over time see Beatrix Hoffman, *The Wages of Sickness: The Politics of Health Insurance in Progressive America* (Chapel Hill: University of North Carolina Press, 2001); Hoffman, *Health Care for Some: Rights and Rationing in the United States since 1930* (Chicago: University of Chicago Press, 2012); Monte M. Poen, *Harry S. Truman versus the Medical Lobby: The Genesis of Medicare* (Columbia: University of Missouri Press, 1979). I have written about the changing definition of health insurance over time in Edward D. Berkowitz, "Medicare and Medicaid: The Past as Prologue," *Health Care Financing Review* 29 (Spring 2008): pp. 81–93.

2. The legislative precedent for state regulation of insurance was the McCarran-Ferguson Act of 1945, which is a continuing subject of policy discussion. See, for example, Lawrence S. Powell, "The Assault on the McCarran-Ferguson Act and the Politics of Insurance in the Post-Katrina Era," *Issue Analysis*, September 2007, distributed by the National Association of Mutual Insurance Companies.

3. The facts and figures are readily available from the internet as, for example, William J. Clinton, "Remarks to the Convocation of the Church of God in Christ at Memphis, Tennessee," The American Presidency Project, http://www.presidency.ucsb.edu/showelection.php?year=1964; and History, Art & Archives, United States House of Representatives, "89th Congress (1965–1967)," http://history.house.gov/Congressional-Overview/Profiles/89th/.

4. Wilbur Cohen to the Secretary (Celebrezze), June 9, 1964, Wilbur Cohen Papers, Wisconsin Historical Society, Madison.

5. Wilbur Cohen to Clinton Anderson, November 18, 1964, Chronological Files, Cohen Papers.

6. Wilbur Cohen to Clinton Anderson, November 19, 1964, Cohen Papers;

Cohen to Clinton Anderson, December 8, 1964, Cohen Papers; Cohen to Larry O'Brien, May 6, 1965, Cohen Papers.

7. Joe R. Sweeney, "Harry Byrd: Vanished Policies and Enduring Principles," *Virginia Quarterly Review* 52, no. 4 (Autumn 1976), pp. 596–612; *History of the Committee on Finance*, Senate Document 97-5 (Washington, DC: Government Printing Office, 1981), pp. 111–166.

8. Julian E. Zelizer, *Taxing America: Wilbur D. Mills, Congress, and the State, 1945–1975* (New York: Cambridge University Press, 1998).

9. Sheri I. David, *With Dignity: The Search for Medicare and Medicaid* (Westport, CT: Greenwood, 1985); Stephen George Anastos Jr., "Selling Medicare, Forgetting Medicaid, 1960–1967" (undergraduate honors thesis, Harvard University, 2011); Edward D. Berkowitz, *Mr. Social Security: The Life of Wilbur J. Cohen* (Lawrence: University Press of Kansas, 1995), pp. 166–168.

10. Wilbur Cohen to Douglas Brown, May 26, 1969, and Douglas Brown to Wilbur Cohen, May 31, 1960, Cohen Papers; William Reynolds, interview by Peter Corning, Columbia Oral History Collection, p. 26, annotated notes available in Box 94, Wilbur Cohen Papers, Lyndon Baines Johnson Presidential Library, Austin; Rosemary Stevens, *Welfare Medicine in America: A Case Study of Medicaid* (New York: Free Press, 1974).

11. "Analysis of Proposals for Optional Features in Health Insurance Plan for the Aged under Social Security," February 15, 1961, Box 140, Cohen Papers.

12. Berkowitz, *Mr. Social Security*, pp. 171–172.

13. "Proposals to Modify Anderson-King," June 12, 1963, Subject Files 1961–1964, June 2, 1962–June 13, 1963, Box 36, Theodore Sorensen Papers, John F. Kennedy Library, Boston.

14. Wilbur Cohen to Ted Sorensen, July 6, 1962, Box 76, Cohen Papers.

15. Berkowitz, *Mr. Social Security*, pp. 171–174.

16. Wilbur Cohen to the Secretary, October 29, 1963, Box 146, Cohen Papers; David, *With Dignity*, chapter 6.

17. Edward D. Berkowitz, *Robert Ball and the Politics of Social Security* (Madison: University of Wisconsin Press, 2003), pp. 128–131.

18. Berkowitz, *Mr. Social Security*, pp. 183–187.

19. Daniel F. Kelly, "6 GOP Senators Offer Alternative Medicare Bill," *Washington Post*, January 17, 1964, p. A2.

20. Wilbur Cohen to the Secretary, January 19, 1964, Cohen Papers.

21. Wilbur Cohen, "Background Briefing on President's Message on Health," in the Fish Room in the White House, February 10, 1964, Box 278, Cohen Papers.

22. Berkowitz, *Robert Ball*, p. 130; Wilbur Cohen to I. S. Falk, April 8, 1964, Cohen Papers.

23. Wilbur Cohen to Ted Sorensen, May 5, 1966, Cohen Papers; Cohen to the Secretary, May 5, 1964, Cohen Papers.

24. Wilbur Cohen to the Secretary, May 15, 1964, Cohen Papers.

25. Wilbur Cohen to the Secretary, May 25, 1964, Cohen Papers; Cohen to Arthur Altmeyer, May 26, 1964, Cohen Papers.

26. "Postpone Vote on Medicare," *Chicago Tribune*, June 24, 1964, p. 25; Rowland Evans and Robert Novak, "The Fruitless Courtship," newspaper clipping in Cohen Papers.

27. Wilbur Cohen to Social Security Experts, July 2, 1964, Cohen Papers.

28. Richard L. Lyons, "House Ups Social Security Pay," *Washington Post*, July 30, 1964, p. A1; Wilbur Cohen to the Secretary, July 8, 1964, Cohen Papers; Cohen to the Secretary, July 13, 1964, Cohen Papers.

29. "Attack Social Security Bill at Hearings, Fear Boost in Benefits Would Kill Medicare," *Chicago Tribune*, August 7, 1964, p. B13; Mary Pakenham, "Senate Given Optional Plan on Medicare," *Chicago Tribune*, August 15, 1964, p. 4; Eve Edstrom, "Medicare Option Plan Would Give Health Aid, Cash," *Washington Post*, August 15, 1964, p. A1.

30. Eve Edstrom, "Celebrezze's Reply on Medicare Hit," *Washington Post*, August 7, 1964, p. A2.

31. Mary Pakenham, "Social Security Rise OK'd; Medicare Fails," *Chicago Tribune*, August 18, 1964, p. 1; Eve Edstrom, "Medicare Cast Aside by Senate Committee," *Washington Post*, August 18, 1964, p. A1.

32. William Moore, "Open Debate over Social Security Bill," *Chicago Tribune*, September 1, 1964, p. 21; Richard L. Lyons, "Shifts Made in Medicare by Backers," *Washington Post*, September 1, 1964, p. A1.

33. Joseph Hearst, "Senate Will Act Today on Medical Care," *Chicago Tribune*, September 2, 1964, p. 3.

34. Robert C. Albright, "Medicare Is Approved by Senate, 49–44," *Washington Post*, September 3, 1964, p. A1.

35. "Goldwater, Johnson on Medicare," *Washington Post*, September 3, 1964, p. A15.

36. "Report on a Hospital Insurance Plan Discussed with the Conference Committee on H.R. 11865," in Cohen to Clinton Anderson, November 3, 1964, Cohen Papers.

37. Eve Edstrom, "Medicare Hopes Soar on Rumors, Then Plunge," *Washington Post*, September 25, 1964, p. A1.

38. Eve Edstrom, "Medicare, All but Dead, Comes Up Again Today," *Washington Post*, October 2, 1964, p. A1.

39. Wilbur Cohen, "November 15, 1964, State Department Building," Cohen Papers; "Discussion with President Johnson," November 17, 1964, Cohen Papers.

40. Eve Edstrom, "Separate Medicare Tax Studied," *Washington Post*, November 6, 1964, p. A2.

41. Eve Edstrom, "Mills Describes Health Plan He'd Back," *Washington Post*, December 4, 1964, p. A15.

42. Austin C. Wehrwein, "A.M.A. Head Urges Renewed Fight against Administration Medicare Bill," *New York Times*, December 1, 1964, p. 28.

43. "Summary of Major Provisions of Hospital Insurance and Social Security Amendments of 1965," November 24, 1964, in Secretary to the President, November 24, 1964, Cohen Papers.

44. Wilbur Cohen to Clinton Anderson, November 18, 1964, Chronological Files, Cohen Papers.

45. Wilbur Cohen to Clint Anderson, December 11, 1964, Cohen Papers.

46. Wilbur Cohen to Clinton Anderson, November 18, 1964, Cohen Papers.

47. Wilbur Cohen to Clinton Anderson, December 1, 1964, Cohen Papers.

48. "The Child Health Act," December 10, 1964, in Wilbur Cohen to the Secretary, December 10, 1964, Cohen Papers.

49. Wilbur Cohen to the Secretary, December 17, 1964, Cohen Papers; Cohen to Secretary, September 10, 1964, Cohen Papers.

50. Wilbur Cohen to the Secretary, December 17, 1964, Cohen Papers.

51. Wilbur Cohen to Cecil King, December 31, 1964, Cohen Papers; Cohen to Abraham Ribicoff, December 31, 1964, Cohen Papers; Marjorie Hunter, "Medicare Plan to Be Expanded," *New York Times*, January 3, 1965, p. 1.

52. Eve Edstrom, "Medicare Wins Strength, 3 Republicans Vow to Help," *Washington Post*, January 6, 1965, p. A2; Edstrom, "Early Passage of Medicare Seen by Mills," *Washington Post*, January 8, 1965, p. A1.

53. Philip Warden, "House Dems Add Power; Remove Medicare Block," *Chicago Tribune*, January 8, 1965, p. 1.

54. Philip Warden, "Early Action on Medicare Is Predicted," *Chicago Tribune*, January 8, 1965, p. 7.

55. Austin Wehrwein, "New Health Plan Offered by AMA," *New York Times*, January 10, 1965, p. 1.

56. "6 in GOP Prepare Wide Medicare Plan," *New York Times*, January 12, 1965, p. 16.

57. "Byrnes Asks 3-Billion Year Health Plan," *Chicago Tribune*, January 29, 1965, p. A10; Eve Edstrom, "GOP Offers National, Voluntary Health Plan," *Washington Post*, January 29, 1965, p. A2; John D. Morris, "G.O.P. Offers a Medicare Plan Based on Voluntary Premiums," *New York Times*, January 29, 1965, p. 13.

58. Memorandum from Wilbur J. Cohen to the President, January 29, 1965, Records of the Department of Health, Education, and Welfare, RG 235, Accession 69A-1793, File LL, Box 16, National Archives.

59. Eve Edstrom, "Early Medicare Bill Writing Seen," *Washington Post*, January 24, 1965, p. A2; Joseph A. Loftus, "Medicare Action Begins Tomorrow," *New York Times*, January 26, 1965, p. 14.

60. John D. Morris, "House Hearings Open on Medicare," *New York Times*, January 28, 1965, p. 14.

61. Wilbur Cohen to the Secretary, February 4, 1965, 5:00 p.m., Cohen Papers; Wilbur Cohen to the Secretary, February 8, 1965, RG 235, Accession 69A-1793, File LL, Box 16, National Archives; Cohen to the Secretary, February 4, 1965, Cohen Papers.

62. Charles Mohr, "President Urges Public to Press Medicare Action," *New York Times*, February 17, 1965, p. 1.

63. Wilbur Cohen to the President, March 2, 1965, Cohen Papers. Just how spontaneous Mills's action was remains an area of scholarly contention. Some people argue that Mills had arranged the matter in advance and consulted with President Johnson. I can only add that in conversations I had with Wilbur Cohen, Robert Ball, and Fred Arner, a staffer from the Congressional Research Service, each assured me that Mills came up with the idea on the spot and astounded each of them. See David Blumenthal and James A. Morone, *The Heart of Power: Health and Politics in the Oval Office* (Berkeley: University of California Press, 2009).

64. Wilbur Cohen to the President, March 2, 1965, Cohen Papers.

65. Blumenthal and Morone, *The Heart of Power*, p. 189; Rowland Evans and Robert Novak, "Inside Report: Mills the Miracle Worker," *Washington Post*, April 6, 1965, p. A17; Berkowitz, *Mr. Social Security*, pp. 231–232; Berkowitz, *Robert Ball*, pp. 128–133.

66. Robert Dallek, *Flawed Giant: Lyndon Johnson and His Times, 1961–1973* (New York: Oxford University Press, 1998), pp. 206–208; John D. Morris, "Mills to Support Revised Social Security," *New York Times*, March 11, 1965, p. 18.

67. Wilbur Cohen to Jack Valenti, March 4, 1965, Cohen Papers; John D. Morris, "Mills and Byrnes Debate Medicare," *New York Times*, April 7, 1965, p. 13.

68. John D. Morris, "Medicare Vote Held Up in House for a Draft of Latest Revisions," *New York Times*, March 20, 1965, p. 15.

69. Wilbur Cohen to Larry O'Brien, March 11, 1965, Cohen Papers.

70. Wilbur Cohen to Larry O'Brien, March 17, 1965, White House Central Files, Lyndon Baines Johnson Presidential Library, Austin.

71. Wilbur Cohen to Larry O'Brien, March 11, 1965, Cohen Papers; Lawrence O'Brien to the President, March 17, 1965, White House Central Files.

72. Jack Valenti to the President, April 22, 1965, White House Central Files, LE/IS 1, Box 75; Bill Moyers to the President, April 26, 1965, White House Central Files.

73. Jack Valenti to the President, April 22, 1965; President Johnson scribbled a note on this memorandum saying, "Please ask Ackley and Fowler to ask their friends to pipe down." Cohen to Lawrence O'Brien, RG 235, Accession 69A-1793, File LL, Box 16, National Archives.

74. Lee White to the President, April 26, 1965, White House Central Files.

75. For example, Part B included 80 percent payment of physicians' and surgeons' fees after an annual deductible of fifty dollars; 80 percent payment, after a fifty-dollar deductible, of care in a mental hospital with a lifetime maximum of 180 days; and 80 percent payment of home nursing care, again with a fifty-dollar deductible, for up to 100 days each year (with no prior hospital stay required). John D. Morris, "Medicare: The Prospects and the Politics," *New York Times*, March 25, 1965, p. E7.

76. John D. Morris, "Expanded Medicare Bill Is Voted by House Panel," *New York Times*, May 24, 1965, p. 1.

77. "Byrd Promises LBJ Action on Medicare," *Washington Post*, March 27, 1965, p. A2.

78. White House Tapes, March 1965, number 11, Social Security Administration website, https://www.ssa.gov/history/LBJ/lbj.html.

79. Wilbur Mills, *Congressional Record*, April 7, 1965, p. 6956.

80. Wilbur Mills, *Congressional Record*, April 7, 1965, p. 6957.

81. Wilbur Mills, *Congressional Record*, April 7, 1965, p. 6958.

82. Wilbur Mills, *Congressional Record*, April 7, 1965, p. 6958.

83. John D. Morris, "Mills and Byrnes Debate Medicare," *New York Times*, April 18, 1965, p. 13.

84. Philip Warden, "Medicare OK'd by House," *Chicago Tribune*, April 9, 1965, p. 1 (for vote totals); Richard L. Lyons, "Medicare Passed by House, 313–115," *Washington Post*, April 9, 1965, p. A1 (for Celebrezze quote and votes by party); John D. Morris, "House Approves Medicare, 313–115; G.O.P. Plan Loses," *New York Times*, April 9, 1965, p. 1 (for LBJ statement).

85. "A Boycott of Medicare by Doctors in Several States Called a Possibility," *New York Times*, May 13, 1965, p. 27.

86. Austin C. Wehrwein, "Doctors Pressed to Defy Medicare," *New York Times*, June 19, 1965, p. 30.

87. Delos Smith, "AMA Faces Crisis on Medicare," *Washington Post*, June 20, 1965, p. A5.

88. Austin C. Wehrwein, "New A.M.A. Chief Warns against Medicare Boycott," *New York Times*, June 21, 1965, p. 1.

89. Ronald Kotulak, "Doctors Battle Over Boycott of Medicare," *Chicago Tribune*, June 22, 1965, p. 1.

90. Wilbur Cohen to Dr. Jack Schrieber, May 11, 1965, Cohen Papers.

91. "Medicare Revised by Senate Group," *New York Times*, June 4, 1965, p. 22; Wilbur Cohen to Larry O'Brien, March 16, 1965, Cohen Papers.

92. Eve Edstrom, "Senator Long Charges Medicare Lacks Key Benefit," *Washington Post*, May 1, 1965, p. A5.

93. Wilbur Cohen to Larry O'Brien, May 6, 1965, Cohen Papers.

94. John D. Morris, "Long Bids Senate Widen Medicare," *New York Times*, May 1, 1965, p. 11; Eve Edstrom, "Sen. Long Presents Medicare Bill on Cata-

strophic Ills," *Washington Post*, May 19, 1965, p. A6; John D. Morris, "Medicare Revised to Help the Poor," *New York Times*, June 18, 1965, p. 1.

95. Wilbur Cohen to the President, June 17, 1965, Cohen Papers; Morris, "Medicare Revised to Help the Poor."

96. Hartke's amendment also upped the number of days in a nursing home to one hundred with a charge of five dollars daily after the twentieth day. He also persuaded his colleagues to add seventy extra home nursing visits at no extra charge to the patient. The committee accepted all of these things by a voice vote. Eve Edstrom, "Medicare Bill Approved by Senate Group," *Washington Post*, June 24, 1965, p. A1; John D. Morris, "Senate Unit Kills Medicare Change," *New York Times*, June 24, 1965, p. 1.

97. Clinton Anderson to the President, July 1, 1965, White House Central Files; Eve Edstrom, "Medicare Program Passes Senate Finance Committee," *Washington Post*, June 25, 1965, p. A1; John D. Morris, "Medicare Voted by Senate Panel," *New York Times*, June 25, 1955, p. 25.

98. Philip Warden, "Senate Opens Debate on Medicare Bill," *Chicago Tribune*, July 7, 1965, p. A1.

99. Robert C. Albright, "Senate Votes Security Pay Option at 60," *Washington Post*, July 8, 1965, p. A1; Cohen to the President, July 12, 1965, Cohen Papers.

100. Albright, "Senate Votes Security Pay Option at 60."

101. John D. Morris, "Medicare Nears Senate Passage," *New York Times*, July 9, 1965, p. 9.

102. Philip Warden, "Senate Passes Medicare," *Chicago Tribune*, July 10, 1965, p. N1; John D. Morris, "Senate Passes Medicare Bill by Vote of 68–21," *New York Times*, July 10, 1965, p. 1; Robert C. Albright, "Medicare Cleared by Conferees," *Washington Post*, July 22, 1965, p. A1.

103. A patient who had spent at least three days in the hospital would be eligible within fourteen days of his discharge for one hundred days of convalescence in a nursing home, with copays kicking in after twenty days. These results were complicated in the manner of any insurance policy but manageable in a political sense. Philip Warden, "O.K. 90 Days of Hospital Aid for Medicare," *Chicago Tribune*, July 15, 1965, p. A1; John D. Morris, "Medicare Panel Settles Key Item," *New York Times*, July 15, 1965, p. 13.

104. John D. Morris, "Conferees Agree on Medicare Bill; Report Due Today," *New York Times*, July 21, 1965, p. 1; Wilbur Cohen to Lawrence F. O'Brien, July 20, 1965, RG 235, Accession 69A-1793, File LL, Box 16, National Archives.

105. Robert C. Albright, "Medicare Cleared by Conferees," *Washington Post*, July 22, 1965 p. A1; John D. Morris, "Medical Aid Bill Voted by House," *New York Times*, July 28, 1965, p. 18; "Vote Tallies for Passage of Medicare in 1965—Actions in Congress," at Social Security Administration website, https://www.ssa.gov/history/tally65.html. One reason for moving fast was that the legis-

lation contained retroactive Social Security benefits that might be mailed out as early as September. That would give beneficiaries an immediate reward and perhaps make them more patient to wait for the Medicare benefits that would begin in July 1966.

106. "A.M.A. Chiefs Vow to Obey Medicare Bill," *Chicago Tribune*, July 30, 1965, p. A11; Wilbur Cohen to Douglas Cater, July 26, 1965, Cohen Papers.

107. I base this account of President Johnson's visit to Independence, Missouri, on the President's "Daily Diary" for Friday, July 30, 1965, Lyndon Baines Johnson Presidential Library, Austin, available online at the Social Security Administration website.

108. John D. Morris, "President Signs Medicare Bill; Praises Truman," New *York Times*, July 31, 1965, p. 1; Phillip Dodd, "Medicare Is Law of Land," *Chicago Tribune*, July 31, 1965, p. N1.

109. Horace Busby to Valenti, Cater, Moyers, and Watson, July 22, 1965, White House Central Files.

110. Edward T. Folliard, "Medicare Bill Signed by Johnson," *Washington Post*, July 31, 1965, p. A1.

111. "Social Security Agency Plans 6,000 New Jobs," *New York Times*, July 31, 1965, p. 9; "Medicare to Spark Nursing Home Rise," *Washington Post*, October 16, 1995, p. E15; "Medicare a Golden Chance, Hospital Officials Here Told," *Washington Post*, November 9, 1965, p. C24; "16 Are Named to Help Draft Medicare Rules," *Washington Post*, November 12, 1965, p. A2; "Continental Aid Considers Medicare an Opportunity," *Chicago Tribune*, December 13, 1965, p. E7.

112. Although, as we shall see, a major expansion of the American welfare state also occurred in 1972, proving that the Great Society influenced social welfare policy at least until then.

Chapter Four

1. Future developments might challenge this statement. In the 2020 campaign, for example, liberals expressed the hope that there would be "Medicare for all."

2. "CMS Program Data—Populations," CMS Fast Facts, July 2016.

3. "National Health Expenditures Calendar Year 2014," CMS Fast Facts, July 2016.

4. "Personal Health Care (PHC) Expenditures by Source of Funds Selected Calendar Years, 1960–2012," *Medicare and Medicaid Research Review, Annual Statistical Supplement 2013*, table 1.1.

5. "Medicare," *Medicare and Medicaid Research Review, Annual Statistical Supplement 2015*, p. 37.

6. Richard S. Foster, "Trends in Medicare Expenditures and Financial Status, 1966–2000," *Health Care Financing Review*, Fall 2000, p. 39.

7. "National Health Expenditures Calendar Year 2014," CMS Fast Facts, July 2016.

8. Edward D. Berkowitz, *Robert Ball and the Politics of Social Security* (Madison: University of Wisconsin Press, 2003), pp. 133–142.

9. Lyndon B. Johnson, "Special Message to the Congress Proposing Programs for Older Americans," January 23, 1967, in *Public Papers of the Presidents of the United States, 1967* (Washington, DC: Government Printing Office), p. 32; the quotation is from Richard Rettig, "Origins of the Medicare Kidney Disease Entitlement: The Social Security Amendments of 1972," in *Biomedical Politics*, ed. Kathi E. Hanna (Washington, DC: National Academy Press, 1991), p. 186.

10. Robert M. Ball, "Social Security Amendments of 1972: Summary and Legislative History," *Social Security Bulletin*, March 1973, pp. 18–19.

11. My account of the End Stage Renal Disease Program follows that of Richard Rettig, "Origins of the Medicare Kidney Disease Entitlement." This article contains all of the quotations.

12. Edward D. Berkowitz, *Something Happened: A Political and Cultural Overview of the Seventies* (New York: Columbia University Press, 2006), pp. 85–87.

13. Joseph L. Falkson, *HMOs and the Politics of Health System Reform* (Chicago: American Hospital Association: 1980), pp. 67–87; Lawrence Brown, *Politics and Health Care Organization: HMOs as Federal Policy* (Washington, DC: Brookings Institution, 1983), pp. 296–297.

14. Harold S. Luft, *Health Maintenance Organizations: Dimensions of Performance* (New York: John Wiley and Sons, 1981); Luft, "Assessing the Evidence on HMO Performance," *Milbank Memorial Fund Quarterly* 58 (Winter 1980): pp. 501–536.

15. As a means of boosting the effort, the federal government authorized loans and grants to HMOs that met the federal requirements. In typical fashion, these requirements combined liberal desires for such things as community rating in which rates could vary only by family size and the conservative encouragement of market forces to reduce health care cost. Poor people would be charged the same rate as rich people; the patient's copayments were limited. Brown, *Politics and Health Care Organization.*

16. This was the idea behind Part C of Medicare created in 1997 and discussed in the next chapter.

17. Jimmy Carter, "Remarks at the Dedication of the John F. Kennedy Library," October 20, 1979, available on the Kennedy Library's website, https://www.jfklibrary.org/About-Us/About-the-JFK-Library/History/1979-Dedication-Remarks-by-President-Carter.aspx.

18. Karen Davis, telephone interview by Edward Berkowitz, September 7, 1995, CMS Oral History Project, p. 278.

19. Davis, interview, pp. 280–281.

20. Benjamin Heineman, telephone interview by Edward Berkowitz, October 24, 1995, CMS Oral History Project, p. 346; Joseph Onek, interview by Berkowitz, August 10, 1995, Washington, DC, CMS Oral History Project, p. 437.

21. "Excerpts from President's Statement on Measures to Reduce Inflation," *New York Times*, April 16, 1977, p. 11; "Hospital Cost Limit Proposed," *Los Angeles Times*, p. A1.

22. Richard D. Lyons, "Carter to Propose Limit on Increases in Hospitals' Fees," *New York Times*, April 23, 1977, p. 1; Lyons, "Carter Proposes Law for Tough Controls on Hospital Charges," *New York Times*, April 26, 1977, p. 1.

23. Lyons, "Carter Proposes Law for Tough Controls on Hospital Changes."

24. Frank Swoboda, "Carter Asks Hospital Cost Curbs," *Baltimore Sun*, April 26, 1977, p. A1.

25. Philip Shabecoff, "HEW Orders Steps to Control Rise in Medical Costs," *New York Times*, April 13, 1978, p. A15.

26. Steven V. Roberts, "Hospital Costs Bill Dead for the Year," *New York Times*, November 6, 1977, p. 24.

27. Dan Rostenkowski, "A Challenge to the AMA," letter to the editor, *Chicago Tribune*, December 24, 1977, p. 6.

28. Roberts, "Hospital Costs Bill Dead for the Year"; Roberts, "The Making of a Congressional Bill: Aides Taking Larger Role in Legislative Process," *New York Times*, March 17, 1978, p. A9.

29. "Medicare Plan B to Cost 50 Cents a Month More in July," *Baltimore Sun*, January 4, 1978, p. A6.

30. Philip Shabecoff, "Health Industry Forms a Voluntary Program to Control Hospital Costs," *New York Times*, January 31, 1978, p. 9.

31. "Blow Dealt to Health Care Bill," *Los Angeles Times*, February 2, 1978, p. B6.

32. Philip Shabecoff, "Hospital Cost Plan in Peril in Congress," *New York Times*, February 13, 1978, p. A13.

33. Shabecoff, "Hospital Cost Plan in Peril in Congress."

34. Martin Tolchin, "Hospital Cost Plan Periled by Dispute," *New York Times*, February 11, 1978, p. 24; Joseph A. Califano Jr., *Governing America: An Insider's Report from the White House and the Cabinet* (New York: Simon and Schuster, 1981), pp. 148–149.

35. Philip Shabecoff, "Health Lobby, Picture of Health," *New York Times*, April 16, 1978, p. 163.

36. "Hospital Cost Bills Get Congress Priority," *Baltimore Sun*, April 26, 1978, p. A8.

37. Harry Kelly, "Russo 'Stabbed Me in the Back': Carter," *Chicago Tribune*, July 26, 1978, p. 2.

38. "Hospital Panel Keeps Alive Bill on Hospital Costs," *New York Times*, June 8, 1978, p. D19; 'Hospital Panel Rejects Carter Hospital Plan," *Chicago Tribune*, July 19, 1978, p. 1.

39. "Push to Curb Hospital Costs Loses," *Chicago Tribune*, August 4, 1978, p. 2.

40. "Administration Backs Compromise to Curb Hospital Costs," *Baltimore Sun*, August 17, 1978, p. A9; "Carter Renews Battle against Hospital Costs," *Los Angeles Times*, September 25, 1978. P. A2; Alice Bonner, "Unit Approves Hospital Cost Curb Bill," *Washington Post*, July 22, 1978, https://www.washingtonpost.com/archive/politics/1978/07/22/unit-approves-hospital-cost-curb-bill/8fd461bf-bc7f-41d8-9a10-355b8773ac4d; "Hospital Cost Control Legislation Dies," *Congressional Quarterly Almanac 1978*, https://library.cqpress.com/cqalmanac/document.php?id=cqal78-1239720.

41. "Congress Fails to Adopt Curbs on Medical Bills," *Baltimore Sun*, October 15, 1978, p. A8.

42. Martin Tolchin, "White House Maps Hospital Cost Plan," *New York Times*, February 25, 1979, p. 43.

43. Lynne Olson, "To Save His Bill, Carter May Soften His Demand for Hospital Cost Controls," *Baltimore Sun*, January 18, 1979, p. A1.

44. Jimmy Carter, "The State of the Union," January 25, 1979, *Public Papers of the Presidents of the United States, 1979*, book 1 (Washington, DC: Government Printing Office), pp. 123–124.

45. Martin Tolchin, "Carter Asks Action on Hospitals' Costs," *New York Times*, May 2, 1979, p. A14.

46. Bill Neikirk, "New Fight Shaping Up on Hospital Cost Plan," *Chicago Tribune*, February 4, 1979, p. 5.

47. Tolchin, "Carter Asks Action on Hospitals' Costs."

48. Mary Russell, "Hospital Cost Control Bill Clears First Hill Hurdle," *Washington Post*, April 26, 1979, p. A3.

49. Philip Shabecoff, "Kennedy Offers Broad Health Plan and Challenges Carter to Support It," *New York Times*, May 15, 1979, p. A1. The situation forced the President to present his own health insurance plan on June 12. He made the passage of this plan, which he unveiled in a personal White House appearance with Senators Russell Long and Abraham Ribicoff standing behind him, contingent upon the prior passage of hospital cost containment. Kennedy held his own news conference on Capitol Hill. With liberal groups such as members of the National Council of Senior Citizens in attendance, Senator Kennedy said of Carter's plan that "this step is a regressive one, inconsistent with the goal of a truly single-class health care system." Martin Tolchin, "Carter and Kennedy Press Rival Efforts on Health Program," *New York Times*, June 13, 1979, p. A1.

50. "Panel Votes Hospital Cost Curb," *Washington Post*, July 18, 1979, p. A13; Thomas B. Edsall, "House Cost Bill Faces Tough Subcommittee Fight, " *Baltimore Sun*, March 6, 1979, p. 8.

51. The Commerce Committee bill included a feature that allowed either house of Congress to veto the imposition of mandatory controls for the next year, regardless of whether the voluntary limits had been exceeded, at the end of September. Spencer Rich, "Hill Panel Defeats Moves to 'Gut' Hospital Cost Containment Bill," *Washington Post*, September 26, 1979, p. A4; Rich, "House Commerce Committee Clears Hospital Cost Bill," *Washington Post*, September 27, 1979. p. A9.

52. Thomas B. Edsall, "Hospital Cost-Control Bill Apparently in Real Danger," *Baltimore Sun*, November 13, 1979, p. A8.

53. Steven V. Roberts, "Mandatory Limits on Hospital Costs Rejected by House," *New York Times*, November 16, 1979, p. A1; Spencer Rich, "President's Plan on Hospital Costs Killed in House," *Washington Post*, November 16, 1979, p. A1.

54. Spencer Rich, "Panel Presses HEW on Ways to Cut Waste in Health Care," *Washington Post*, May 22, 1980, p. A2.

55. Schweiker was a former Senator from Pennsylvania and the person who agreed to be on Ronald Reagan's ticket in Reagan's unsuccessful 1976 run for president. "Cut in Medicare Eyed in Long Hospital Stays," *Chicago Tribune*, January 9, 1982, p. 3; "Medicare Patients May Be Forced to Pay 10% of Hospital Charges," *New York Times*, January 9, 1982, p. 11.

56. In addition, the administration wanted to increase the out-of-pocket charges for Medicare and to make it clear that private insurance, rather than Medicare, should become the first payer for people who remained employed after age sixty-five. It also did not want to give Medicaid patients a free ride and insisted they pay at least something each time they saw a doctor. Paul Houston, "Deep Cuts in Health Aid to Be Asked," *Los Angeles Times*, January 23, 1982, p. 1. Reagan also proposed a swap of functions with the states. The federal government would run Medicaid and pay for it, and the states would run their AFDC programs. The swap never advanced very far in Congress.

57. Robert Pear, "Reagan Reported Asking Benefit Cut," *New York Times*, February 5, 1992, p. A18.

58. Dr. Robert Rubin, interview by Edward Berkowitz, Fairfax, VA, August 16, 1995, CMS Oral History Project, pp. 484–485; Robert Reinhold, "Health Care Plan Gets Final Review," *New York Times*, February 14, 1982, p. 22.

59. Robert Pear, "Critics Say Reagan Medicare Cuts Would Only Shift Hospital Costs," *New York Times*, March 3, 1982, p. A21.

60. Michael Millenson, "Hospitals Face Threat of U.S. Price Controls," *Chicago Tribune*, March 13, 1982, p. C17; Robert Reinhold, "Reagan Changing Health Care Plan," N*ew York Times*, March 14, 1982, p. 1.

61. Michael J. Millenson, "Medicare Plan May Slash Costs," *Chicago Tribune*, April 19, 1982, p. 1; Robert Pear, "Hospital Industry Proposes Fixed Payments for Medicare Patients," *New York Times*, April 20, 1982, p. B6.

62. Robert Reinhold, "Reagan Changing Health Cost Plan," *New York Times*, March 14, 1982, p. 1.

63. Reinhold, "Reagan Changing Health Cost Plan"; Rick Mayes, "The Origins, Development and Passage of Medicare's Prospective Payment System," *Journal of the History of Medicine and Allied Sciences* 62, no. 1 (January 2006): 21–55.

64. Reinhold, "Reagan Changing Health Cost Plan"; Millenson, "Medicare Plan May Slash Costs."

65. Houston, "Deep Cuts in Health Aid to Be Asked"; Michael deCourcy Hinds, "President Appeals for GOP Budget," *New York Times*, May 23, 1982, p. 9; Howell Raines, "Reagan Assails O'Neill on Pension Issues," *New York Times*, May 25, 1982, p. D21.

66. "Created by the Congressional Budget Act of 1974, reconciliation allows for expedited consideration of certain tax, spending, and debt limit legislation. In the Senate, reconciliation bills aren't subject to filibuster and the scope of amendments is limited, giving this process real advantages for enacting controversial budget and tax measures." David Reich and Richard Kogan, "Introduction to Budget 'Reconciliation,'," updated November 9, 2016, Center on Budget and Policy Priorities, https://www.cbpp.org/research/federal-budget/introduction-to-budget-reconciliation.

67. Paul Houston, "Senators Ask Cuts in Medicare, Medicaid," *Los Angeles Times*, June 25, 1982, p. 16.

68. Spencer Rich, "Insurers, Elderly Defend Medicare," *Washington Post*, June 26, 1982, p. A5.

69. As always, though, there were politically induced exceptions to the proposed rule. Public hospitals, such as the large health and hospital system in Representative Rangel's New York City district, treated many indigent patients and therefore had less opportunity than other hospitals to shift its costs to paying customers. The system received an exemption. So did small hospitals with less than fifty beds, thus accommodating rural hospitals. Spencer Rich, "House Panel Approves Cuts in Medicare," *Washington Post*, July 14, 1982, p. A2.

70. Spencer Rich, "Conferees Reach Accord on $12.5 Billion Cut in Health, Welfare Plans," *Washington Post*, August 11, 1982, p. A3.

71. The details, as always in congressional funding formulas, were complicated. Researchers in the Social Security Administration explained that "the target rate is set using the previous year's allowable cost per case (or after the first year, the previous year's target amount) increased by the percentage increase in the hospital wage and price index, plus 1 percentage point. For the first

two years, hospitals with operating costs above the target rates would be reimbursed up to 25 percent of those excess costs; none of the excess would be reimbursed in the third year." Hospitals that kept their costs below the target rate of increase received "a bonus of 50 percent of the savings (not to exceed 5 percent of the target rate.)" "Summary of 1982 Legislation Affecting SSI, OASDI, and Medicare," *Social Security Bulletin*, July 1983, pp. 49–57.

72. Spencer Rich, "Schweiker Approves the Framework of Medicare Prospective Payment Plan," *Washington Post*, September 10, 1982, p. A4.

73. HCFA was a bureaucratic creation of the Carter administration and placed Medicare and Medicaid in one administrative entity. Califano, *Governing America*, pp. 43–45; I have conducted a series of interviews on the creation of the HCFA that are contained in the CMS Oral History Project transcripts.

74. I base my discussion of Carolyne Davis's life and career on my interview with her in Washington, DC, on November 8, 1995, CMS Oral History Project, pp. 108–129.

75. States that received waivers had to follow a certain format such as having a plan that was statewide. "U.S. Acts to Revise Medicare Pay Plan," *Chicago Tribune*, October 7, 1982, p. 2.

76. "U.S. Proposes New Medicare Payment Plan," *Los Angeles Times*, October 7, 1982, p.A1.

77. Robert Pear, "Lawmakers Challenge Planned Medicare Shift," *New York Times*, November 23, 1982, p. A25.

78. "Major Changes in Medicare Sent Congress," *Los Angeles Times*, December 28, 1982, p. A1.

79. "Plan Sets Limits on Fees Medicare Pays Hospitals," *Chicago Tribune*, December 29, 1982, p. 12; Robert Pear, "Top Health Official Urges Per-Illness Medicare Fees," *New York Times*, January 1, 1983, p. 6.

80. Pear, "Top Health Official Urges Per-Illness Medicare Fees."

81. For more on the resulting 1983 Social Security amendments see W. Andrew Achenbaum, *Social Security: Visions and Revisions* (New York: Cambridge University Press, 1986); Berkowitz, *Robert Ball*, pp. 270–333.

82. Robert Rubin, interview by Edward Berkowitz, August 16, 1995, Fairfax, VA, CMS Oral History Project, p. 488.

83. In a look toward the future, the committee ordered that a study be made to determine if a prospective payment system could also be developed for physicians (under Medicare Part B) and required the Secretary of HHS to submit recommendations for incorporating capital-related costs and return on net equity into the prospective payment system. "House Panel OKs Medicare Ceilings," *Chicago Tribune*, February 15, 1983, p. 9; Spencer Rich, "Fixed Payments in Advance Backed for Medicare Services by Hospitals," *Washington Post*, February 25, 1983, p. A4.

84. John A. Svahn and Mary Ross, "Social Security Amendments of 1983: Legislative Provision and Summary of Provisions," *Social Security Bulletin*, July 1983, p. 9.

85. For a good account of the legislative history of the measure see Svahn and Ross, "Social Security Amendments of 1983"; for journalistic accounts see Spencer Rich, "Social Security Bailout Expands, Advances," *Washington Post*, March 3, 1983, p. A6; "Social Security Bill Clears House Panel with a Few Extras," *Chicago Tribune*, March 3, 1983, p. 3.

86. The best account of the Senate's actions is Svahn and Ross, "Social Security Amendments of 1983."

87. See Svahn and Ross, "Social Security Amendments of 1983," pp. 35–40.

88. To be sure, a six-month delay in the cost of living adjustments meant a permanent reduction in a person's Social Security benefits. The situation was similar to that of a bank that skipped a periodic interest payment to its customers—that money would never be made up. Still, the depositors in both the bank and the Social Security system were better off than if either institution had gone out of business.

89. John Iglehart, "Medicare Begins Prospective Payment of Hospitals," *New England Journal of Medicine* 308 (June 9, 1983): pp. 1428–1432; Iglehart, "The New Era of Prospective Payment for Hospitals," *New England Journal of Medicine* 307 (November 11, 1982): pp. 1288–1292.

90. Rick Mayes and Robert A. Berenson, *Medicare Prospective Payment and the Shaping of U.S. Health Policy* (Baltimore: Johns Hopkins University Press, 2006), pp. 56, 82.

Chapter Five

1. Steven M. Gillon, *The Pact: Bill Clinton, Newt Gingrich, and the Rivalry that Defined a Generation* (New York: Oxford University Press, 2008).

2. Michael Boskin, *Too Many Promises: The Uncertain Future of Social Security* (Homewood, IL: Dow Jones Irwin, 1986); A. Haeworth Robertson, *The Big Lie: What Every Baby Boomer Should Know about Social Security and Medicare* (Washington, DC: Retirement Policy Institute, 1997); Peter Ferrara and Michael Tanner, *A New Deal for Social Security* (Washington, DC: Cato Institute, 1998).

3. Lawrence Mead, *Beyond Entitlement: The Social Obligations of Citizenship* (New York: Free Press, 2008).

4. Testimony of Newt Gingrich, January 5, 10, 11, and 12, 1995, in *Contract with America: Overview, Hearings before the Committee on Ways and Means*, (Washington, DC: Government Printing Office, 1995), p. 15; Robin Toner, "Gin-

grich Vows Total Review of Medicare for Cost Savings," *New York Times*, January 31, 1995, p. A1.

5. Haynes Johnson and David S. Broder, *The System: The American Way of Politics at the Breaking Point* (New York: Hatchette Book Group, 1997).

6. Michael Wines, "Democrats Strongly Attack G.O.P. Budget Plan," *New York Times*, January 7, 1995, p. 1.

7. Spencer Rich, "Tougher Debate on Medicare Looming," *Washington Post*, February 6, 1996, p. A13.

8. "Managed care" was a nebulous term, but it implied that health insurance payers would take a more active role in case management, not simply paying bills but making sure that a person's medical care was effective and efficient.

9. Milt Freudenheim, "Health Care Costs by Employers Drop for First Time in a Decade," *New York Times*, February 14, 1995, p. A1; Spencer Rich, "Trustees Warn of Medicare Collapse," *Washington Post*, April 4, 1995, p. A4.

10. Carlos Zarabozo, "Milestones in Medicare Managed Care," *Health Care Financing Review* 22, no. 1(Fall 2000): pp. 61–67.

11. Robin Toner, "Hunt for Savings Turns to Higher Costs for Affluent Beneficiaries of Medicare," *New York Times*, February 18, 1995, p. A16.

12. A good scholarly source on the Medicare battles of the 1990s and on Medicare more generally is Jonathan Oberlander, *The Political Life of Medicare* (Chicago: University of Chicago Press, 2003).

13. Ann Devroy, "GOP Would Slash Medicare to Fund Tax Cuts for Rich, Clinton Warns," *Washington Post*, May 4, 1995, p. A5; Michael Wines, "Gingrich Promises Big Medicare Cut with Little Pain," *New York Times*, May 8, 1995, p. A1.

14. Eric Pianin, "Senate Passes Balanced Budget Plan," *Washington Post*, May 26, 1995, p. A1.

15. Robin Toner, "In Budget Battle, a Side Skirmish over Medicare," *New York Times*, May 29, 1995, p. 10.

16. Robin Toner, "Anger and Suspicion Pervade Hearings on Medicare Cuts," *New York Times*, June 7, 1995, p. A25; Spencer Rich and Judith Havemann, "House GOP Medicare Plans Would Raise Copayments, Deductibles," *Washington Post*, July 18, 1995, p. A4.

17. Rich and Havemann, "House GOP Medicare Plans Would Raise Copayments, Deductibles."

18. Robin Toner and Robert Pear, "Medicare, Turning 30, Won't Be What It Was," *New York Times*, July 23, 1995, p. 1.

19. Adam Clymer, "2 Political Parties Turn to Airwaves for Medicare Debate," *New York Times*, August 16, 1995, p. B10; Eric Pianin, "Medicare Proposal Projected to Save $270 Billion Is Submitted by Packwood," *New York Times*, September 6, 1995, p. A13.

20. Robert Pear, "G.O.P. Puts Friendlier Face on Its Plans to Overhaul Medicare," *New York Times*, September 7, 1995, p. A25.

21. Robert Pear, "Democrats Vow to Slow G.O.P. Plan for Medicare," *New York Times*, September 14, 1995, p. B12.

22. Robert Pear, "G.O.P.'s Plan to Cut Medicare Faces a Veto, Clinton Promises," *New York Times*, September 16, 1995, p. 1.

23. David E. Rosenbaum, "Vote is 227 to 203," *New York Times*, October 27, 1995, p. A1; "Excerpts from House Debate on G.O.P. Plan to Overhaul Medicare System," *New York Times*, October 20, 1995, p. A26.

24. Under this arrangement, beneficiaries would purchase a high deductible / low premium plan to cover their catastrophic expenses. One could think of it as a cheap form of health insurance that protected an individual from unlikely catastrophes but did not provide coverage for most routine medical expenses (because the high deductible would get in the way). Since these plans would cost far less than a standard Medicare benefit, there would, in effect, be money left over for the individual to use, which he or she could use to establish an individual Medical Savings Account. Beneficiaries could use the money in this account to pay for their health care, with the withdrawals being nontaxable.

25. Adam Clymer, "Major Fight Looms, "*New York Times*, October 20, 1995, p. A1.

26. Jerry Gray, "Senate Softens Some Edges in Passing 52–47, Its Version of Vast Budget Cutbacks," *New York Times*, October 28, 1995, p. 1.

27. Todd S. Purdum, "President Warns Congress to Drop Some Budget Cuts," *New York Times*, October 29, 1995, p. 1.

28. Adam Clymer, "Of Touching Third Rails and Tackling Medicare," *New York Times*, October 27, 1995, p. D21.

29. Rene Sanchez, "Medicare Beneficiaries' Premium Is Central Issue in Feud over Budget," *Washington Post*, November 13, 1995, p. A9.

30. Adam Clymer, "Late Meeting Fails," *New York Times*, November 14, 1995, p. A1.

31. Robin Toner, "House Republican Freshmen Heed a Call to 'Shut It Down,'" *New York Times*, November 16, 1995, p. A1.

32. Jerry Gray, "Feuding Goes On as G.O.P. Presents Its Budget Plan," *New York Times*, November 17, 1995, p. A1; Todd S. Purdum, "A Washington Potboiler Steals Budget's Thunder," *New York Times*, November 17, 1995, p. A1.

33. The passenger was Peter Edelman, an Assistant Secretary at HHS. I spoke with him about this matter during a taping for the Clinton presidency project at the Miller Center, University of Virginia.

34. David Rosenbaum, "As Standoff Ends, Clinton Is Seeking the High Ground," *New York Times*, November 21, 1995, p. A1.

35. Michael Wines, "President, Yielding to G.O.P., Will Offer Plan Erasing Deficit," *New York Times*, December 6, 1995, p. 1.

36. Todd S. Purdum, "As Long Promised, President Vetoes the G.O.P. Budget," *New York Times*, December 7, 1995, p. A1.

37. Ann Devroy and Eric Pianin, "Partial Closing To Idle 280,000," *Washington Post*, December 16, 1995, p. A1.

38. Robin Toner, "Health Care's New Victim," *New York Times*, December 17, 1995, p. E4.

39. Spencer Rich, "Rivals in Medicare Reform Caught in Numbers Game," *Washington Post*, December 25, 1995, p. A4.

40. Eric Pianin and John Harris, "Clinton Signs Measures to Halt Shutdown," *Washington Post*, January 6, 1996, p. 1.

41. Adam Clymer, "A 3-Week Respite," *New York Times*, January 7, 1996, p. 1.

42. Robert Pear, "Shortfall Posted by Medicare Fund Two Years Early," *New York Times*, February 5, 1996, p. A1.

43. Eric M. Patashnik, *Putting Trust in the US Budget: Federal Trust Funds and the Politics of Commitment* (New York: Cambridge University Press, 2000), pp. 94–112.

44. Michael Wines, "Political Stakes Increase in Fight to Save Medicare," *New York Times*, June 3, 1996, p. A1.

45. Wines, "Political Stakes Increase in Fight to Save Medicare"; David E. Rosenbaum, "Gloomy Forecast Touches Off Feud on Medicare Fund," *New York Times*, June 5, 1996, p. A1.

46. Steven Pearlstein and Clay Chandler, "Medicare: After the Rhetoric, a Reality Check," *Washington Post*, November 3, 1996, p. H1.

47. Clay Chandler and Peter Baker, "Clinton Ponders Concessions on Medicare, Taxes," *Washington Post*, June 9, 1997, p. A4.

48. Clay Chandler, "Medicare Accounting Dispute Could Threaten Early Budget Accord," *Washington Post*, January 10, 1997, p. A12.

49. Robert Pear, "Medicare Panel Advises a Freeze on Hospital Pay," January 19, 1997, p. 1.

50. Robert Pear, "Medicare's Hospital Fund Going Insolvent, Trustees Affirm," *New York Times*, April 25, 1997, p. A16. In fact, though, conditions were improving. The economy's improved performance triggered higher estimates for the federal government's future revenues. More money in the treasury meant that more of the political sting could be taken out of the budget agreement.

51. Alison Mitchell, "President Offers Medicare Savings," *New York Times*, January 22, 1997, p. A1.

52. Eric Pianin and John Harris, "President, GOP Agree on Balanced Budget Plan," *Washington Post*, May 3, 1997, p. A1.

53. Robert Pear, "Battle Lines Form in Medicare Fight," *New York Times*, May 27, 1997, p. A1.

54. Robert Pear, "Seeking Bipartisan Support, Republicans Offer Medicare Plans," June 4, 1997, *New York Times*, June 4, 1997, p. A20.

55. Pear, "Seeking Bipartisan Support, Republicans Offer Medicare Plans."

56. Adam Clymer, "House Is Critical of Medicare Plan of Senate Panel," *New York Times*, June 20, 1997, p. A1; Robert Pear, "House and Senate Pass Legislation to Balance Budget," *New York Times*, June 26, 1997, p. D27.

57. Eric Pianin and Clay Chandler, "White House, GOP Reach Budget Agreement," *New York Times*, July 29, 1997, p. A1.

58. An arrangement in which patients would choose their doctors and hospitals, Medicare would make fixed monthly payments to the plan, and the plan would be free to charge whatever premiums it wished.

59. Jennifer O'Sullivan et al., *Medicare Provisions in the Balanced Budget Act of 1997*, Report 97-802 (Washington, DC: Congressional Research Service, 1997)–.

60. Andy Schneider, "Overview of Medicaid Provisions in the Balanced Budget Act of 1997, P.L. 105-33," https://www.cbpp.org/archives/908mcaid.htm; "Significant Changes Made in Children's Health, Welfare, Medicaid, and Medicare," National Association of Social Workers, http://www.naswdc.org/archives/advocacy/updates/1997/grbudget.htm.

61. Wilbur Cohen to Joseph Califano, January 19, 1968, Box 95, Wilbur Cohen Papers, Wisconsin Historical Society, Madison; Robert Ball, "Is Medicare Worth the Price?" *U.S. News & World Report*, July 21, 1969, copy available in Ball Papers, Wisconsin Historical Society, Madison.

62. Mark Santangelo, "Historical Perspective on Adding Drugs to Medicare," *Health Care Financing Review* 27, no. 2 (Winter 2005): pp. 25–33.

63. Richard Himmelfarb, *Catastrophic Politics: The Rise and Fall of the Medicare Catastrophic Coverage Act of 1988* (University Park: Pennsylvania State University Press, 1995), p. 21. Himmelfarb remains the best source on this topic, and I have relied on this source heavily.

64. Himmelfarb, *Catastrophic Politics*, pp. 25, 29–30.

65. In addition to Himmelfarb, see Thomas Oliver, Philip R. Lee, and Helene L. Lipton, "A Political History of Prescription Drug Coverage," *Milbank Quarterly* 82, no. 2 (2004): pp. 2–83–354; I have relied heavily on this article in my discussion of the Medicare Modernization Act of 2003.

66. Dan Rostenkowski, interview by Edward Berkowitz, Washington, DC, December 4, 2002, CMS Oral History Project, pp. 695–709.

67. Oliver, Lee, and Lipton, "A Political History of Prescription Drug Coverage," p. 304.

68. Daniel Beland, *Social Security: History and Politics from the New Deal to the Privatization Debate* (Lawrence: University Press of Kansas, 2005), pp. 164–185; Oliver, Lee, and Lipton, "A Political History of Prescription Drug Coverage," p. 339.

69. Thomas Scully, telephone interview by Edward Berkowitz, May 19, 2015, CMS Oral History Project, p. 28. I have based much of my account of this in-

cident and taken all of the quotations from this interview. The chapter on the Medicare Modernization Act in David Blumenthal and James A. Morone, *The Heart of Power: Health and Politics in the Oval Office* (Berkeley: University of California Press, 2009), pp. 385–408, is also useful, as is Kimberly J. Morgan and Andrea Campbell, *The Delegated Welfare State: Medicare, Markets, and the Governance of Social Policy* (New York: Oxford University Press, 2011).

70. Oliver, Lee, and Lipton, "A Political History of Prescription Drug Coverage," pp. 321–322.

71. Prescription drug plans could also be offered through the various health plans in Part C, which was renamed Medicare Advantage.

72. Oliver, Lee, and Lipton, "A Political History of Prescription Drug Coverage," pp. 316–318.

73. Information obtained by a relative on Medicare who subscribed to Part D. The company is called SilverScript, one of the largest in the Part D prescription drug program.

74. The information is from "Important Notice from George Washington University about Your Prescription Drug Coverage and Medicare," September 6, 2016.

75. Robert J. Myers with Richard L. Vernaci, *Within the System: My Half Century in Social Security* (Winsted, CT: Actes, 1992).

76. Joseph A. Califano Jr., *Governing America: An Insiders Report from the White House and the Cabinet* (New York: Simon and Schuster, 1981), pp. 43–45.

77. James Sundquist, *The Decline and Resurgence of Congress* (Washington, DC: Brookings Institution, 1980); Julian E. Zelizer, *On Capitol Hill: The Struggle to Reform Congress and Its Consequences* (New York: Cambridge University Press, 2004), p. 154.

78. Scully, interview, p. 31.

79. Mary Agnes Carey, "Retiring Medicare Actuary Reflects on the Politics of Health Care," *Kaiser Health News*, January 28, 2013; "The Foster Affair," editorial, *New York Times*, July 13, 2004; "Mysterious Fax Adds to Intrigue over Drug Bill," *New York Times*, March 17, 2004; "Inquiry Confirms Top Medicare Official Threatens Actuary over Drug Benefits," *New York Times*, July 6, 2004; "Senate Democrats Claim Medicare Chief Broke Law," *New York Times*, March 18, 2004; "Requesting the President and Directing the Secretary of Health and Human Services Provide Certain Documents to the House of Representatives Relating to Estimates and Analysis of the Cost of the Medicare Drug Legislation," House Report 108-754, October 7, 2004.

80. Louis Hays, interview by Edward Berkowitz, Washington, DC, April 22, 2015, CMS Oral History Project, p. 6.

81. "Patient Protection and Affordable Care Act," Public Law 111-148, March 23, 2010. Of course, many components of this law became controversial and invited the subsequent administration to make changes.

82. David Smith and Judith Moore, *Medicaid Politics and Policy*, 2nd ed., New Brunswick, NJ: Transaction Publishers, 2015), Kindle edition, location 996.; Derthick, *Policymaking for Social Security*.

83. Michael McMullan, telephone interview by Edward Berkowitz, May 29, 2015, CMS Oral History Project, p. 6; Kerry Weems, telephone interview by Berkowitz, May 27, 2015, CMS Oral History Project, p. 17; William Toby, interview by Edward Berkowitz, June 26, 2015, CMS Oral History Project, p. 9.

84. McMullan, interview, p. 29.

85. John D. Klemm, "Medicaid Spending: A Brief History," *Health Care Financing Review* 22 (2000): p. 105.

86. One such provision required states to use their Medicaid programs to pay Medicare deductibles and coinsurance for people with incomes below the poverty line. T. Rice, K. Desmond, and J. Gabel, "The Medicare Catastrophic Coverage Act: A Post-Mortem," *Health Affairs* 9 (1990): p. 77.

87. Beatrix Hoffman, *Health Care for Some: Rights and Rationing in the United States since 1930* (Chicago: University of Chicago Press, 2012), p. 188; Laura Katz Olson, *The Politics of Medicaid: Stakeholders and Welfare Medicine* (New York: Columbia University Press), pp. 69–70.

88. Klemm, "Medicaid Spending," p. 108; Olson, *The Politics of Medicaid*, p. 73.

89. Judith Feder, "The Missing Piece: Medicaid, Medicare, and Long-Term Care," in *Medicare and Medicaid at 50: America's Entitlement Programs in the Age of Affordable Care*, ed. Alan B. Cohen et al. (New York: Oxford University Press 2015), p. 57; Rashi Fein, "The Early Days of Medicare and Medicaid," in *Medicare and Medicaid at 50*, p. 49; Olson, *The Politics of Medicaid*, pp. 133–134, 26.

90. The creation of intermediate care facilities, which offered fewer services than so-called skilled nursing facilities, also facilitated both the growth of Medicaid and the growth of nursing homes. Feder, "The Missing Piece," p. 255.

91. Olson, *The Politics of Medicaid*, p. 5.

92. "Waxman, Henry Arnold," History, Art & Archives, United States House of Representatives, http://history.house.gov/People/Listing/W/WAXMAN,-Henry-Arnold-%28W000215%29/.

93. Rick Mayes, *Universal Coverage: The Elusive Quest for National Health Insurance* (Ann Arbor: University of Michigan Press, 2004), pp. 31–40; David Smith and Judith Moore, *Medicaid Politics and Policy*, Kindle edition, location 3775.

94. Michael Hash, interview by Edward Berkowitz, Washington, DC, May 11, 2015, CMS Oral History Project, p. 8; Herbert Kuhn, telephone interview by Edward Berkowitz, May 6, 2015, CMS Oral History Project, p. 2; Frank J. Thompson, "Medicaid Rising: The Perils and Pitfalls of Federalism," in *Medicare and Medicaid at 50*, ed. Cohen et al., p. 195; Paul Starr, *Remedy and Reaction: The*

Peculiar American Struggle over Health Care (New Haven, CT: Yale University Press, 2013), p. 71.

Chapter Six

1. Edwin Witte, *The Development of the Social Security Act* (Madison: University of Wisconsin Press, 1963), pp. 162–170.

2. Arthur J. Altmeyer, *The Formative Years of Social Security* (Madison: University of Wisconsin Press, 1968), pp. 43–73; Charles McKinley and Robert W. Frase, *Launching Social Security: A Capture-and-Record Account, 1935–1937* (Madison: University of Wisconsin Press, 1970).

3. Jill Quadagno and Madonna Harrington Meyer, "Organized Labor, State Structures, and Social Policy Development," *Social Problems* 36 (April 1989): pp. 181–196.

4. Karen M. Tani, *State of Dependency: Welfare, Rights, and American Governance, 1935–1972* (New York: Cambridge University Press, 2016).

5. Jerry R. Cates, *Insuring Inequality: Administrative Leadership in Social Security, 1935–54* (Ann Arbor: University of Michigan Press, 1983).

6. Edward D. Berkowitz, *Disabled Policy: America's Programs for the Handicapped* (New York: Cambridge University Press, 1987), p. 70.

7. Robert Ball, interview by Blanche Coll, Washington, DC, February 2, 1988; Gilbert Steiner, *The State of Welfare* (Washington: Brookings Institution, 1971); Blanche D. Coll, *Safety Net: Welfare and Social Security, 1929–1979* (New Brunswick, NJ: Rutgers University Press, 1995); Joseph A. Califano Jr., *Governing America: An Insider's Report from the White House and the Cabinet* (New York: Simon and Schuster, 1981), p. 43.

8. Edward D. Berkowitz, *America's Welfare State: From Roosevelt to Reagan* (Baltimore: Johns Hopkins University Press, 1991), pp. 100–111; Jennifer Mittelstadt, *From Welfare to Workfare: The Unintended Consequences of Liberal Reform, 1945–1965* (Chapel Hill: University of North Carolina Press, 2005).

9. Robert A. Moffitt and Peter T. Gottschalk, "Ethnic and Racial Differences in Welfare Receipt in the United States," in *America Becoming: Racial Trends and Their Consequences*, ed. Neil J. Smelser, William Julius Wilson, and Faith Mitchel (Washington, DC: National Academy Press, 2001), 2:152–173; Pamela J. Lopreset, "How Has the TANF Caseload Changed over Time," brief 8, March 2012 (Washington, DC: Urban Institute); Sanford S. Schram, "Putting a Black Face on Welfare: The Good and the Bad," in *Race and the Politics of Welfare Reform*, ed. Schram, Joe Soss, and Richard Fielding (Ann Arbor: University of Michigan Press, 2003), pp. 196–221.

10. Nate Hazeltine, "Ike's 8-Point Health Plan Asks for More Federal Aid," *Washington Post*, February 1, 1966, p. 1.

11. Wilbur Cohen to Myer Feldman, January 4, 1962,, Box 165, Wilbur Cohen Papers, Wisconsin Historical Society, Madison; Cohen to James H. McCarthy, February 27, 1962, Cohen Papers.

12. Wilbur Cohen, interview by Blanche Coll, Washington, DC, February 2, 1988.

13. Abraham Ribicoff, memorandum for the President, November 1, 1961, Box 137, Folder 2, Cohen Papers.

14. Memorandum for Mrs. Eleanor Roosevelt, December 19 1961, Box 136, Folder 2, Cohen Papers.

15. Edward D. Berkowitz, *Mr. Social Security: The Life of Wilbur J. Cohen* (Lawrence: University Press of Kansas, 1995), pp. 145–153.

16. "Caseload Data 1960 (AFDC Total)," "Caseload Data 1967 (AFDC Total)," "Caseload Data 1975 (AFDC Total)," all in Office of Family Assistance, Office of the Administration for Children and Families, Department of Health and Human Services, December 18, 2004; C. Peter Rydell et al., "Welfare Caseload Dynamics in New York City," New York City Rand Institute, October 1974, p. viii; Steiner, *The State of Welfare*, p. 296.

17. Wilbur Cohen to the President, July 14, 1967, Cohen to Elizabeth Wickenden, both in Cohen Papers, Box 93.

18. "House Unit Prepares Welfare Aid Changes Forcing Many Able-Bodied Adults Off Rolls," *Wall Street Journal*, July 27, 1967, p. 9; "Way Sought to Cut Down on Child Relief," *Washington Post*, July 26, 1967, p. 11; Leo Irwin to Marvin Watson, December 16, 1967, Joseph Califano Papers, Lyndon Baines Johnson Presidential Library, Austin, Box 51.

19. Molly C. Michelmore, *Tax and Spend: The Welfare State, Tax Politics, and the Limits of American Liberalism* (Philadelphia: University of Pennsylvania Press, 2012), pp. 70–81; "Social Security-Welfare Bill Comes before House Today," *Washington Star*, August 16, 1967, p. 3; William Seif, "7.6 Million on Welfare in U.S.," *Washington Daily News*, August 16, 1967, p. 25; "House GOP Unit Backs Raising Social Security Benefits," *New York Times*, August 17, 1967, p. 4.

20. Wilbur Cohen to the President, December 11, 1967, Cohen Papers; Secretary John Gardner to the President, December 11, 1967, Califano Papers, Box 51; Lyndon Johnson, material in EXLE/WE, Box 164, January 2, 1968, White House Central Files, Lyndon Baines Johnson Presidential Library, Austin; Cohen to the Secretary, November 20, 1962, Chronological Files, 1962, Cohen Papers.

21. Wilbur Cohen to Ellen Winston, February 23, 1967, Chronological Files, Cohen Papers; Martha Lentz Walker, *Beyond Bureaucracy: Mary Elizabeth Switzer and Rehabilitation* (Lanham, MD: University Press of America, 1985); Berkowitz, *Mr. Social Security*, pp. 151–152.

22. Felicia Kornbluh, *The Battle for Welfare Rights: Politics and Poverty in Modern America* (Philadelphia: University of Pennsylvania Press), p. 207.

23. Kornbluh, *The Battle for Welfare Rights*, p. 99.

24. Betty James, "Welfare Rally Threatens Riots," *Washington Star*, August 29, 1967, p. 1; Eve Edstrom, "Blistering Attacks on Welfare Curbs Fail to Sway Long," *Washington Post*, September 1, 1967, p. 4; Barry Kalb, "Angry Welfare Group Holds Hill Sit-In," *Washington Star*, September 3, 1967, p. 3; Eve Edstrom, "Irate Mothers Hold Wait-In," *Washington Post*, September 20, 1967, p. 1.

25. William Chapman, "Public Welfare System a Failure, Reagan Says," *Washington Post*, September 20, 1967, p. 6; Edmund Morris, *Dutch* (New York: Random House, 1999), pp. 368–369; Ronald Reagan, "Second Inaugural Address," January 4, 1971.

26. President's Commission on Income Maintenance Programs, *From Poverty Amid Plenty: The American Paradox* (Washington, DC: Government Printing Office, 1969).

27. The calculation worked as follows: the family received the $1,600 guarantee, plus the $720 disregard, plus an after-tax income of $1,140, which was half of $2,280, or $3,000 minus $720, for an "entitled" income of $3,460. Since the family already earned $3,000 from working, it would receive a government check for $460 plus coupons or "stamps" that it could use to purchase food. Vincent J. Burke and Vee Burke, *Nixon's Good Deed: Welfare Reform* (New York: Columbia University Press, 1974); Daniel Patrick Moynihan, *The Politics of a Guaranteed Annual Income: The Nixon Administration and the Family Assistance Plan* (New York: Vintage Books, 1973).

28. Berkowitz, *America's Welfare State*, pp. 127–130.

29. "Social Security Amendments of 1972," Senate Report 92-1230, September 26, 1972.

30. Brian Steensland, *The Failed Welfare Revolution: America's Struggle over Guaranteed Income Policy* (Princeton, NJ: Princeton University Press, 2017), chapter 4; Martin Anderson, *Welfare: The Political Economy of Welfare Reform in the United States* (Palo Alto, CA: Hoover Institution, 1978), pp. 135–148.

31. Tani, *State of Dependency*, p. 72; "Briefing Paper: The Work Incentive Program," April 25, 1975–, in Spencer Johnson Papers, Box 12, WIN File, Gerald R. Ford Library, Ann Arbor, MI, pp. 2–4.

32. Edward D. Berkowitz and Larry DeWitt, *The Other Welfare: Supplemental Security Income and U.S. Social Policy* (Ithaca, NY: Cornell University Press, 2013).

33. Edward D. Berkowitz, "Changing the Meaning of Welfare Reform," in *Maintaining the Safety Net: Income Distribution Programs in the Reagan Administration*, ed. John Weicher (Washington, DC: American Enterprise Institute: 1984), p. 31.

34. Berkowitz, "Changing the Meaning of Welfare Reform," p. 31; Kornbluh, *The Battle for Welfare Rights*, p. 92; Berkowitz, *America's Welfare State*, p. 134.

35. Judith M. Gueron and Richard P. Nathan, "The MDRC Work/Welfare

Project: Objectives, Status, Significance," paper presented at the Fifth Annual Research Conference of the Association for Public Policy, Analysis and Management, October 20–22, 1983, pp. 11–13.

36. John Svahn, interview by Edward Berkowitz, Washington, DC, November 17, 1983.

37. Robert Carleson, interview by Edward Berkowitz, Washington, DC, November 22, 1983.

38. James V. Saturno, "The Congressional Budget Process: A Brief Overview," Congressional Research Service, Report 7-5700, August 22, 2011.

39. Vee Burke, "Budget Cuts in AFDC," Issue Brief 81051, Congressional Research Service, 1981.

40. House Ways and Means Committee, *Background Material and Data on Major Programs within the Jurisdiction of the Committee on Ways and Means*, WMCP 98-1 (Washington, DC: Government Printing Office, 1983), pp. 3–12.

41. Berkowitz, "Changing the Meaning of Welfare Reform," p. 36.

42. Lawrence Mead, "Prospects for Welfare Reform," *Policy Forum*, November 1986; see also George Gilder, "Welfare Spurs Family Breakdown," *Insight*, June 23, 1986, pp. 68–69.

43. See for example, Edward D. Berkowitz, *Robert Ball and the Politics of Social Security* (Madison: University of Wisconsin Press, 2003), pp. 258–259.

44. Berkowitz, *America's Welfare State*, pp. 145–146; Julie Rovner, "Governors Jump-Start Welfare Reform Drive," *Congressional Quarterly*, February 28, 1987, pp. 376–378.

45. Berkowitz, *America's Welfare State*, p. 145.

46. Family Support Act, summary by the Institute for Research on Poverty at https://www.irp.wisc.edu/publications/focus/pdfs/foc114e.pdf; my discussion of this act derives from this summary.

47. Genetic testing also aided government authorities in establishing paternity.

48. States' matching funds could be cut in half unless 55 percent of the caseload fell into one of three prescribed categories: families with parents under the age of twenty-four with no high school diploma, families who had been on the rolls for more than three of the preceding five years, and families in which the youngest child was within two years of losing AFDC coverage because he or she had reached the age limit. The law also contained penalties for states that did not have enough people in JOBS to meet a federal standard.

Chapter Seven

1. Testimony of Sam Griswold, Donna Shalala, and Kweisi Mfume, *Welfare Reform Proposals*, Committee on Ways and Means, Subcommittee on Human

Resources, Serial 103-01 (Washington, DC: Government Printing Office:1995) (hereafter 1994 Ways and Means), pp. 672, 32, 795. Examples of similar testimony include William Goodling, Introductory Statement, and testimony of Robert Rector, *Contract with America: Hearing on Welfare Reform*, Committee on Economic and Educational Opportunities, Serial 104-10 (Washington, DC: Government Printing Office, 1995), p. 16.

2. Statement of Harold Ford, 1994 Ways and Means, p. 469; Statement of Charlie Rangel, *Contract with America: Welfare Reform*, Committee on Ways and Means, Subcommittee on Human Resources, Serial 104-43 (Washington, DC: Government Printing Office, 1996) (hereafter 1995 Ways and Means), p. 374; statement of Cardiss Collins, 1995 Ways and Means, p. 374; Statement of Lynne Woolsey, 1994 Ways and Means, p. 535; Testimony of Mrs. White, 1995 Ways and Means, p. 189.

3. Tom Gabe and Ruth Wasem, Congressional Research Service, to Clay Shaw, January 13, 1995, in 1995 Ways and Means, p. 233; testimony of David Ellwood, Committee on Finance, Subcommittee on Social Security and Family Policy, *Welfare Reform*, (Washington, DC: Government Printing Office, 1994), p. 10.

4. Jason Deparle, "The 1992 Campaign: Issues—Welfare; Talk of Cutting Welfare Rolls Sounds Good, but Progress Is Far from Sure," *New York Times*, October 17, 1992, p. 9. One of the more revealing biographies of Bill Clinton is David Maraniss, *First in His Class: The Biography of Bill Clinton* (New York: Simon and Schuster, 2008).

5. Richard L. Berke, "The 1992 Campaign: The Ad Campaign; Clinton: Getting People off Welfare," *New York Times*, September 10, 1992. A video of this ad is available on YouTube.

6. Mary Jo Bane, testimony in Committee on Finance, Subcommittee on Social Security, *Welfare Reform* (Washington, DC: Government Printing Office, 1994), pp. 5, 7, 11–13.

7. Ron Haskins, *Work over Welfare: The Inside Story of the 1996 Welfare Reform Law* (Washington, DC: Brookings Institution, 2006) provides a good introduction to the legislative process of producing the law; Clay Shaw, testimony in 1994 Subcommittee on Social Security hearings, pp. 23–24.

8. Testimony of Donna Shala in Subcommittee on Social Security and Family Policy, 1994, p. 88; testimony of Mary Jo Bane in Subcommittee on Social Security and Family Policy, 1994, p. 386.

9. Testimony of Clay Shaw in Subcommittee on Social Security and Family Policy, 1994, p. 396–397; testimony of Jane Meyers in Subcommittee on Social Security and Family Policy, 1994, p. 440.

10. Testimony of Mickey Kaus, Subcommittee on Human Resources, Committee on Ways and Means, *Contract with America: Welfare Reform* (Washington, DC: Government Printing Office, 1996), p. 1107; Testimony of Glenn

Luoury, *Contract with America: Welfare Reform*, p. 142; Testimony of Tim Hutchinson in Subcommittee on Social Security and Family Policy, 1994, p. 556.

11. Testimony of Rebecca Blank, Subcommittee on Human Resources, *Contract with America: Welfare Reform*, p. 197; Testimony of Mike Kopetski, in Subcommittee on Social Security and Family Policy, 1994, pp. 872–873.

12. I take this discussion of child disability benefits from Edward D. Berkowitz and Larry DeWitt, *The Other Welfare: Supplemental Security Income and U.S. Social Policy* (Ithaca, NY: Cornell University Press, 2013), pp. 32–35, 185–188.

13. Bob Woodward and Benjamin Weiser, "Costs Soar for Children's Disability Program, " *Washington Post*, February 4, 1994, p. A1.

14. See Ken Silverstein and Alexander Cockburn, "How Rich Journalists Stole Crutches from Crippled Children," *Counterpunch*, July 15, 1995, pp. 1–3.

15. Testimony of Wayne Parker, Subcommittee on Human Resources, *Welfare Reform*, January 13, 1995, p. 378.

16. Testimony of Jim McCrery, Subcommittee on Human Resources, *Welfare Reform*, January 13, 1995, p. 364; Testimony of Congressman Kleczka, Subcommittee on Human Resources, *Welfare Reform*, January 13, 1995, p. 367; Testimony of Rick Santorum, 1994, Subcommittee on Social Security and Family Policy, 1994, pp. 444–445.

17. Testimony of James B. Gardner, Subcommittee on Human Resources, *Welfare Reform*, January 13, 1995, p. 384.

18. I take this discussion of noncitizens on the SSI rolls and the reference to the *Washington Post* from Berkowitz and DeWitt, *The Other Welfare*, pp. 191–194.

19. By welfare Santorum meant some sixty programs, including free childhood immunizations and subsidized school lunches. The Clinton administration took a more tempered view and decided that a person should become a citizen or at least reside in the country for five years before claiming benefits. The Republicans were willing to consider exemptions for people over seventy-five. Testimony of Rick Santorum, Subcommittee on Social Security and Family Policy, *Welfare Reform*, 1994, pp. 928, 966; Statement of Clay Shaw, Subcommittee on Human Resources, *Welfare Reform*, January 13, 1995, 360.

20. "Tax Dollars Aiding and Abetting Addiction: Social Security Disability and SSI Cash Benefits to Drug Addicts and Alcoholics," *Investigative Staff Report of Senator William S. Cohen*, February 7, 1994, "Executive Summary" and pp. 1–7; William S. Cohen, "Playing Social Security for a Sucker," *Washington Post*, February 23, 1994, p. A17.

21. Berkowitz and DeWitt, *The Other Welfare*, pp. 194–197.

22. Berkowitz and DeWitt, *The Other Welfare*, pp. 213–214.

23. Michael Wiseman, "State Strategies for Welfare Reform: The Wisconsin

Story," Institute for Research on Poverty, Discussion Paper 1066-95, revised December 1995, p. 3; Rebecca G. Barrett, "From Welfare to Work: The Precursors, Politics, and Policies of Wisconsin and Federal Work-Based Welfare Reform" (PhD diss., Ohio State University, 2012), p. 90.

24. Norman Atkins, "Tommy Thompson," *New York Times Sunday Magazine*, January 15, 1995, p. SM22; Barrett, "From Welfare to Work," pp. 85–86; Wiseman, "State Strategies for Welfare Reform," p. 15.

25. Barrett, "From Welfare to Work," p. 114.

26. Barrett, "From Welfare to Work," p. 121; Wiseman, "State Strategies for Welfare Reform," p. 16.

27. Wiseman, "State Strategies for Welfare Reform," pp. 22–25.

28. Wiseman, State Strategies for Welfare Reform," p. 22.

29. Statement of Gene E. Kussart, Senate Finance Committee, Hearings on Welfare Reform, *Welfare Reform*, January 18–February 25, 1994," p. 37.

30. Wiseman, "State Strategies for Welfare Reform," n.p., table 5, "Change in Total AFDC Caseload in Wisconsin."

31. Jerry Gray, "G.O.P. Governors Make Their Pitch," *New York Times*, January 7, 1995, p. 8.

32. Robert Pear, "Governors Propose a Limit to U.S. Control of Welfare," *New York Times*, January 28, 1995, p. A5.

33. Pear, "Governors Propose a Limit to U.S. Control of Welfare.".

34. Robert Pear, "Governors Deadlocked on Replacing Welfare Programs with Grants to States," *New York Times*, January 31, 1995, p. A14.

35. Pear, "Governors Deadlocked on Replacing Welfare Programs with Grants to States."

36. Robin Toner, "War over an Overhaul Appears to Be No Contest," *New York Times*, January 13, 1995, p. A-22; Robert Pear, "Democrats Call Republicans Too Lenient on Welfare," *New York Times*, February 11, 1995, p. 7.

37. "Opening Prepared Statement," Chairman Clay Shaw, Subcommittee on Human Resources, January 13, 1995, in Subcommittee on Human Resources, *Contract with America*, p. 7; Newt Gingrich, "Beyond the 100 Days," *New York Times*, February 22, 1995, p. A19.

38. Robert Pear, "House Backs Bill Undoing Decades of Welfare Policy," *New York Times*, March 24, 1995, p. 1.

39. Robert Pear, "Clinton Objects to Key Elements of Welfare Bill," *New York Times*, March 26, 1995, p. 1.

40. Steven A. Holmes, "Clinton Says He May Veto Welfare Bill," *New York Times*, April 9, 1995, p. 23.

41. Robert Pear, "G.O.P. Governors Urge Big Changes for Welfare Bill," *New York Times*, April 13, 1995, p. A1.

42. Robert Pear, "Senate Committee Approves a Vast Overhaul of Welfare," *New York Times*, May 7, 1995, p. 1.

43. Todd S. Purdum, "Republicans' Welfare Bill Is Again Attacked by Clinton," *New York Times*, June 7, 1995, p. A25.

44. Robert Pear, "Republican Squabble Delays Welfare Debate," *New York Times*, June 16, 1995, p. A19.

45. Richard L. Berke, "Dole and Gramm Clash on Revising Laws on Welfare," *New York Times*, July 16, 1995, p. 1.

46. Robert Pear, "Clinton and Dole Bidding to Break Welfare Impasse," *New York Times*, July 30, 1995, p. 1.

47. Robert Pear, "Senate Committee Approves a Vast Overhaul of Welfare," *New York Times*, May 27, 1995, p. 1; Pear, "Republican Squabble Delays Welfare Debate."

48. Pear, "Republican Squabble Delays Welfare Debate."

49. Berke, "Dole and Gramm Clash on Revising Laws on Welfare."

50. Robert Pear, "Dole Offers Welfare Bill, but Conservatives Reject It," *New York Times*, August 5, 1995, p. 8; John H. Cushman Jr., "Rivals Criticize Bill on Welfare Offered by Dole," *New York Times*, August 7, 1995, p. A1; Robert Pear, "Dole Courts Conservatives with Changes on Welfare," *New York Times*, August 10, 1995, p. B6.

51. Robert Pear, "White House Seeks Area of Welfare Accord with G.O.P.," *New York Times*, August 6, 1995, p. 24.

52. Robert Pear, "Senators Start Debate on Changes in Welfare," *New York Times*, August 8, 1995, p. B6.

53. Robert Pear, "Dole Postpones Further Debate on Welfare Bill," *New York Times*, August 9, 1995, p. A1.

54. Robin Toner, "New Senate Push on Welfare Revives Tensions in Both Parties," *New York Times*, September 9, 1995, p. 9; Ian Fisher, "Moynihan Stands Alone in Welfare Debate," *New York Times*, September 27, 1995, p. B1.

55. Robert Pear, "Dole Courts Conservatives with Changes on Welfare," *New York Times*, August 10, 1995, p. B6.

56. Alison Mitchell, "Clinton Prods Senate on the Welfare Overhaul," *New York Times*, September 10, 1995, p. 28.

57. Robin Toner, "Senators Gain on Welfare Bill but Delay Vote," *New York Times*, September 14, 1995, p. A1.

58. Alison Mitchell, "President Voices Optimism on Hopes for Welfare Bill," *New York Times*, September 17, 1995, p. 1.

59. Robin Toner, "A Landmark Shift," *New York Times*, September 20, 1995, p. A1; David E. Rosenbaum, "A Tough Bill to Say No To," *New York Times*, September 20, 1995, p. A1; "Clinton in Awkward Role in the Debate on Welfare," *New York Times*, September 21, 1995, p. B11.

60. Robert Pear, "President Draws Line on Welfare," *New York Times*, October 10, 1995, p. A18.

61. Ron Haskins, *Work over Welfare: The Inside Story of the 1996 Welfare Reform Law* (Washington, DC: Brookings Institution Press, 1996), Kindle positions 190, 229; Robert Pear, "G.O.P. Seeks Compromise on Welfare Bill," *New York Times*, October 25, 1995, p. B7. I should note that Charles Murray appeared in nearly all of the congressional committee hearings on welfare reform in 1994 and 1995, making his message very prominent among welfare reformers. Indeed, one part of the Republican plan was commonly referred to as "Murray light."

62. Haskins, *Work over Welfare*, Kindle position 3997.

63. Haskins, *Work over Welfare*, Kindle position 4050. The big budget reconciliation bill, HR 2401, was introduced by Representative John Kasich on October 17. It acquired the short title of "Balanced Budget Act of 1995."

64. "Steps in Budget Reconciliation Process," *New York Times*, October 27, 1995, p. D21; Jerry Gray, "Senate Softens Some Edges in Passing, 52–47, Its Version of Vast Budget Cutbacks," *New York Times*, October 28, 1995, p. 1.

65. Alison Mitchell, "White House Held On to Study of Senate Bill's Harm," *New York Times*, October 28, 1995, p. 9.

66. Alison Mitchell, "Greater Poverty Toll Is Seen in Welfare Bill," *New York Times*, November 10, 1995, p. A27.

67. Robert Pear, "House and Senate Leaders Compromise to Soften Welfare Bill," *New York Times*, November 11, 1995, p. 11; Pear, "Republicans in Accord on Welfare Bill," *New York Times*, November 15, 1995, p. B10.

68. Pear, "House and Senate Leaders Compromise to Soften Welfare Bill."

69. Pear, "Republicans in Accord on Welfare Bill."

70. Robert Pear, "Officials Assure Democrats of a Veto of the Welfare Bill," *New York Times*, November 30, 1995, p. B14.

71. Robert Pear, "As Welfare Compromise Emerges, Clinton Aide Says Veto Is Certain," *New York Times*, November 13, 1995, p. A1.

72. Pear, "Officials Assure Democrats of a Veto of the Welfare Bill."

73. Todd S. Purdum, "As Long Promised, President Vetoes the G.O.P. Budget," *New York Times*, December 7, 1995, p. A1.

74. Robert Pear, "School Lunch Discord Stalls the Welfare Bill," *New York Times*, December 6, 1995, p. B10.

75. Robert Pear, "House Sends Senate an Overhaul of the Welfare System," *New York Times*, December 22, 1995, p. A37.

76. Pear, "House Sends Senate an Overhaul of the Welfare System"; Pear, "Bill Would Sever Medicaid Benefits from Welfare Aid," *New York Times*, December 12, 1995, p. A1.

77. Robert Pear, "Welfare Bill Cleared by Congress and Now Awaits Clinton's Veto," *New York Times*, December 23, 1995, p. 1.

78. Robert Pear, "Clinton Vetoes G.O.P. Plan to Change Welfare System," *New York Times*, January 10, 1996, p. B7; Michael Wines, "Talks on Budget Are Put on Hold amid Uncertainty," *New York Times*, January 10, 1996, p. A1.

79. Robert Pear, "G.O.P. May Revive a Welfare Plan to Snare Clinton," *New York Times*, January 30, 1996, p. A1.

80. Robert Pear, "Governors' Welfare Plan Seeks to Close Gap on Bill," *New York Times*, February 7, 1996, p. A14; "On Social Policy, Governors Quietly Split the Difference," *New York Times*, February 8, 1996, p. A1.

81. Robert Pear, "House Democrats Assail Welfare Plan Backed by Governors," *New York Times*, February 21, 1996, p. A16.

82. Jerry Gray, "No Details on Deal," *New York Times*, April 24, 1996, p. A1.

83. Kenneth B. Noble, "Welfare Revamp, Halted in Capital, Proceeds Anyway," *New York Times*, March 10, 1996, p. 1.

84. Dirk Johnson, "Wisconsin Acts to End Welfare Entirely," *New York Times*, April 26, 1996, p. A26; Robert Pear, "Clinton Announces Steps to Find Parents Who Owe Child Support," *New York Times*, June 19, 1996, p. A14; Pear, "Clinton Wavers after Backing Welfare Plan," *New York Times*, June 15, 1996, p. 1; Alison Mitchell, "Clinton Tells of Plans to Keep Mothers on Welfare in School," *New York Times*, May 5, 1996, p. 22; Pear, "Clinton Endorses the Most Radical of Welfare Trials," *New York Times*, May 19, 1996, p. 1.

85. Adam Clymer, "Republicans Shift Strategy in Bid to Avoid Welfare Bill Veto," *New York Times*, July 12, 1996, p. A18; Robert Pear, "White House Is Optimistic about Chances of Welfare Bill with New G.O.P. Moves," *New York Times*, July 13, 1996, p. 10.

86. Robert Pear, "House Approves Shift on Welfare," *New York Times*, July 19, 1996, p. A1; Pear, "Big Role to States," *New York Times*, July 24, 1996, p. A1.

87. Robert Pear, "Senators Vote to Cut Off Benefits for Legal Aliens," *New York Times*, July 20, 1996, p. 7; Pear, "Gore Says He Expects an Accord on Welfare," *New York Times*, July 22, 1996, p. A13.

88. Robert Pear, "Senate Votes to Ease Work Requirements in Welfare Overhaul Bill, "*New York Times*, July 23, 1996, p. A11.

89. Pear, "Big Role to States."

90. Todd S. Purdum, "Clinton in a Box as a Welfare Bill Edges Closer," *New York Times*, July 26, 1996, p. A1.

91. Robert Pear, "Agreement Struck on Most Elements for Welfare Bill," *New York Times*, July 30, 1996, p. A1.

92. Robert Pear, "Republicans Finish Writing Welfare Measure, Clinton May Announce Position Today," *New York Times*, July 31, 1996, p. A11.

93. Todd S. Purdum, "Clinton Recalls His Promise, Weighs History, and Decides," *New York Times*, August 1, 1996, p. A1.

94. "Text of President Clinton's Announcement on Welfare Legislation," *New York Times*, August 1, 1996, p. A24.

95. Robert Pear, "Millions Affected," *New York Times*, August 1, 1996,

p. A1; "Excerpts from Debate in the Senate on the Welfare Measure," *New York Times*, August 2, 1996, p. 16.

96. Pear, "Millions Affected"; "Remarks by Gingrich and Other G.O.P. Supporters," *New York Times*, August 1, 1996, p. A25; Richard L. Berke, "Fulfilling '92's Promise, Capturing a '96 Issue," *New York Times*, August 1, 1996, p. A25.

97. "Text of President Clinton's Announcement on Welfare Legislation."

98. Pear, "Millions Affected"; Pear, "Senate Passes Welfare Measure, Sending It for Clinton's Signature," *New York Times*, August 2, 1996, p. A1.

99. Frances X. Clines, "Clinton Signs Bill Cutting Welfare; States in New Role," *New York Times*, August 23, 1996, p. A1; Neil A. Lewis, "A Friendship in Tatters over Policy," *New York Times*, September 13, 1996, p. A26. On the 1983 Social Security Amendments, see Edward D. Berkowitz, *Robert Ball and the Politics of Social Security* (Madison: University of Wisconsin Press, 2003), p. 323.

100. Alison Mitchell, "Two Clinton Aides Resign to Protest New Welfare Law," *New York Times*, September 12, 1996, p. A1.

101. Peter Edelman, "The Worst Thing Clinton Has Done," *Atlantic*, March 1997, available online at https://www.theatlantic.com/magazine/archive/1997/03/the-worst-thing-bill-clinton-has-done/376797/.

102. Mary Jo Bane, "Presidential Address: Expertise, Advocacy and Deliberation; Lessons from Welfare Reform," *Journal of Policy Analysis and Management* 20 (2001): pp. 191–197. Bane cites Kent Weaver's seminal book on the 1996 welfare reform, on which I have also relied in this chapter: R. Kent Weaver, *Ending Welfare as We Know It* (Washington, DC: Brookings Institution Press, 2000). Also useful is Weaver, "Deficits and Devolution in the 104th Congress," *Publius* 26 (Summer 1996): pp. 45–85.

103. "Spelling the End of Welfare as We Know It," *New York Times*, August 4, 1996, p. E3; Vee Burke, "The 1996 Welfare Reform Law," in Congressional Research Service, *Welfare Reform Briefing Book* (2003).

104. Alison Mitchell, "Congress Praises Welfare Bill in a Conservative Region," *New York Times*, October 24, 1996, p. B10; Robert Pear, "Clinton Cites Welfare Gains and Defends Overhaul Plan," *New York Times*, December 8, 1996, p. 35; Rebecca M. Blank, "Was Welfare Reform Successful?," *Economists' Voice* 3, no. 4 (September 2006): p. 2.

105. See Berkowitz and DeWitt, *The Other Welfare*, pp. 221–226.

Index

Aaron, Henry, 132
abortion, 240, 276
administrative law judges (ALJs), 56–58, 64–65, 264
Affordable Care Act, 185–88, 311n81
African Americans: Aid to Families with Dependent Children (AFDC) and, 7, 13, 197, 221, 274; Americans with Disabilities Act (ADA) and, 72; illegitimacy and, 13; Moyers and, 217; National Welfare Rights Organization (NWRO) and, 205; participation rates and, 197; racial issues and, 9, 12–13, 107, 197, 207, 222, 255; responsibility and, 13; riots and, 205, 217; stereotypes of, 13; Temporary Aid to Needy Families (TANF) and, 278; voting and, 30; welfare reform and, 197, 204–5, 217, 221, 225, 231
age limits, 15, 53, 60, 94, 161, 175, 316n48
Agricultural Adjustment Act, 35
AIDS, 177
Aid to Families with Dependent Children (AFDC): African Americans and, 7, 13, 197, 221, 274; as anachronistic failure, 191, 208, 221, 278; block grants and, 7, 187, 254, 268, 274; caseloads of, 13, 197, 202, 209–10, 221–22, 233, 259, 314n16; cash benefits and, 191, 199–200, 233; civil rights and, 8, 277; Clinton and, 6, 221, 268, 274, 278; Congress and, 6–8, 13; conservatives and, 7, 191, 199, 206, 219, 275; cost of, 196, 200–202; eligibility and, 213; end of, 14, 268; Family Assistance Plan (FAP) and, 206–12, 216, 219, 254; fathers and, 6, 196–97, 202, 207; food stamps and, 209, 233, 254, 274; Gingrich and, 6, 8, 190–91, 221, 268, 274, 278; guaranteed annual income and, 208; illegitimacy and, 7; institutional issues and, 191; interest groups and, 274; Kennedy and, 6, 199, 267–68; Learnfare and, 232; as manpower program, 278; means tests and, 12; Medicare and, 8; Mills and, 6, 202–3, 208, 214; mothers and, 6–7, 13, 199, 202, 205, 208–11, 214, 222, 232, 259, 268, 278; National Welfare Rights Organization (NWRO) and, 204–8; New Deal and, 274; Nixon and, 6, 207, 212, 273; opposition to, 202–6; origins of, 192–96; Personal Responsibility and Work Opportunity Act and, 267–68; political unpopularity of, 14; poverty and, 203, 206, 221, 268, 278; program comparisons and, 271–76; Public Welfare Amendments and, 200; questioning main assumptions of, 277; race and, 12–13; Reagan and, 6, 206, 211–14, 273, 303n56; rehabilitation and, 196–202; Republicans and, 159; Ribicoff and, 199; single mothers and, 7, 13, 278; Social Security Act and, 191; stigma and, 7, 12–13, 210; Temporary Aid to Needy Families (TANF) and, 7–8, 13, 261, 268, 278; unemployment and, 12, 202, 211, 214; welfare reform and, ix–x, 6–7, 13, 191, 196–214, 218–22, 232–33,

Aid to Families with Dependent Children (AFDC) (*continued*)
254, 259, 268, 274, 278, 316n48; widows and, 6–7, 12–13; workfare programs and, 191, 268; Work Incentive Program (WIN) and, 209; Work Not Welfare and, 233
Aid to the Permanently and Totally Disabled, 21
Albert, Carl, 82, 109
alcohol, 32–33, 50, 229–30
Altman, Stuart, 171
American Academy for the Study of Alcoholism, 32
American Academy of General Practice, 32
American Academy of Orthopedic Surgeons, 32
American Academy of Physical Medicine, 32
American Association of Retired Persons (AARP), 147, 164, 171, 179, 182
American Federation of Labor-Congress of Industrial Organizations (AFL-CIO), 61; Ball and, 27–28; Biemiller and, 37, 81, 118; Civil Rights Leadership Conference and, 107; Cohen and, 27–28, 36–37, 45, 81, 94, 118; Cruikshank and, 28, 36–37, 45, 81, 94; lobbying and, 25, 28, 37, 45, 81; Meany and, 23, 25–26, 37, 133; Social Security Administration (SSA) and, 45; Sweeney and, 253
American Hospital Association, 88, 112, 114, 133, 136, 141, 146–47, 150, 162
American Medical Association (AMA): disability insurance and, 18–19, 38, 43; doctors and, 18–19, 43, 83, 95, 101, 111–12, 117; George and, 38; Medicare and, 83, 95–104, 111–12, 117–20, 138, 156, 257; Personal Responsibility and Work Opportunity Act and, 262
American Public Welfare Association, 36
Americans with Disabilities Act (ADA), 8, 14, 72–75, 264, 270
Anderson, Clinton, 30–31, 81–82, 86, 93, 98, 114–15
Appel, James Z., 112
Arc, 228–29
Archer, Bill, 175, 248
Ashcroft, John, 240
autism, 66

Balanced Budget Act, 172–76, 180, 189
Ball, Robert: Anderson and, 81; Cohen and, 81; disability insurance and, 22, 27–28, 53, 81, 285n22; Folsom and, 22, 285n22; Kennedy and, 81; lengthy answers of, 53; Medicare and, 81, 83–84, 87–89, 94, 98, 102, 114, 118, 177, 296n63; prescription drugs and, 177; Social Security Administration (SSA) and, 53, 81, 285n22
Bane, Mary Jo, 224, 257–60, 323n102
Barbour, Haley, 255
Barkley, Alben, 30, 33–34
Barrett, Rebecca, 232
behavioral disorders, 227–28
Beneficiary Rehabilitation Program (BRP), 71–72
Bennett, Wallace, 33–41, 115
Bentsen, Lloyd, 179
Bettercare, 100
Biemiller, Andrew, 37, 81–82, 114, 118
Black Caucus, 221, 225
black lung, 59
Blank, Rebecca, 226–27
blindness, 7, 13, 59, 69, 72, 127, 193–94, 196, 198, 210, 267, 274–75, 286n38
block grants: Aid to Families with Dependent Children (AFDC) and, 7, 187, 254, 268, 274; Balanced Budget Act and, 176; Medicare and, 161, 176, 187–88; welfare reform and, 233–40, 246, 249, 254, 258, 261, 268–69
Blue Cross, 80, 85, 88–89, 95, 99, 105, 111, 126, 144, 150
Blue Shield, 80, 99, 105, 111
Boggs, Hale, 117
Bowen, Otis, 178–79
Brady, James, 73–74
Braun, Carol Mosely, 237–38
Breaux, John, 240, 248
Briggs, Philip, 145
Bromberg, Michael, 136, 146, 150–51, 153
Brookings Institution, 132
Brown v. Board of Education, 205
Broyhill, James, 138
Bureau of Old Age and Survivors Benefits, 22

Bureau of Public Assistance, 193–95
Bush, George H. W., 73–74, 162, 171, 223, 290n61
Bush, George W., 5, 51, 92, 162, 180–84, 189, 267
Byrd, Harry: background of, 29; cash benefits and, 40–41, 48, 50; Curtis' reform and, 43; disability insurance and, 28–37, 40–44, 47–50, 58, 265; Eisenhower and, 30; Johnson and, 33, 41, 44, 82–83, 113; Medicare and, 82–83, 90, 93, 95, 107–9, 113–16, 121, 137; Myers and, 31–32; Senate Finance Committee and, 28–36, 82, 90, 107–9, 113–14, 116, 265; Social Security Disability Insurance (SSDI) and, 47, 265; Viscardi and, 40–41; waning power of, 82–83; welfare reform and, 245
Byrnes, John, 93, 100–103, 105, 111

Califano, Joseph, 59–60, 134, 136–39, 141–43, 204
Camp, Dave, 226
Campbell, Andrea Louise, 4
cancer, 31, 84, 141, 155
Carleson, Robert, 212–13
Carlson, Frank, 115
Caro, Robert, 41
Carter, Jimmy: Americans with Disabilities Act (ADA) and, 73; Califano and, 59, 134, 136–39, 141–43; Democratic Congress and, 136–37; disability insurance and, 59–62, 73; HCFA and, 305n73; hospital cost containment and, 131–45, 149, 153, 302n49; inflation and, 131–33, 138–40, 142–43, 145, 148–49; Kennedy and, 135–43; Medicaid and, 133–34; Medicare and, 123, 131–49, 153, 186, 272, 302n49; New Deal and, 62; Reagan and, 62, 143–44, 149, 212; Russo and, 137–38, 140; State of the Union address and, 140; unions and, 137; welfare reform and, 131, 203, 212
Case, Clifford, 99
cash benefits, 89–90; Aid to Families with Dependent Children (AFDC) and, 191, 199–200, 233; disability insurance and, 16, 20, 34–35, 39–41, 48, 50, 58, 67, 69–70, 75; rehabilitation and, 2, 16, 35, 40, 69–70, 75, 78, 199–200, 204; Social Security and, 16, 50, 75, 77, 79, 84, 111, 191, 198, 228; welfare reform and, 191, 199, 209, 227–29, 233, 252–53
Celebrezze, Anthony, 107
Centers for Medicare and Medicaid Services (CMS), 181, 183–86, 188
Chafee, John, 236–37
Chapin, Christy Ford, 11
Chicago Medical Society, 112
childcare: day care and, 202, 220; illegitimacy and, 269, 276; welfare reform and, 209, 213, 216, 218, 223, 233, 238, 241–42, 247, 251, 258
Child Health Act, 97–98, 102
children, 286n38; abortion and, 240, 276; AFDC and, 6 (*see also* Aid to Families with Dependent Children [AFDC]); behavioral disorders and, 227–28; disability insurance and, 50, 53, 64, 67; disabled, 67, 103, 227–29, 243, 247, 260; fathers and, 6, 135, 149, 196, 200, 202, 207, 210–11, 217, 228, 231–32, 250, 291n60; food stamps and, 236 (*see also* food stamps); illegitimacy and, 13 (*see also* illegitimacy); juvenile delinquency and, 198, 219; Learnfare and, 232; Medicare and, 97, 103, 126–27, 141, 159, 171, 174, 176, 185, 187–88; misfortunes of parents and, 194; single-parent families and, 7, 13, 67, 191, 223, 226, 244, 258, 268, 273–74, 278; Special Supplemental Nutrition Program for Women, Infants, and Children and, 236; State Children's Health Insurance Program and, 187; stigma and, 227; welfare reform and, 190–206, 209–11, 214–29, 234–49, 252–61
Children's Defense Fund, 236, 253, 257
child support, 217, 232, 250, 254, 258
cirrhosis, 59
civil rights: Aid to Families with Dependent Children (AFDC) and, 8, 277; Americans with Disabilities Act (ADA) and, 72; disabilities and, 16, 72; Douglas and, 30; George and, 35; Medicare and, 90, 107–8, 119; Social Security Disability Insurance (SSDI) and, 10, 75, 278; welfare reform and, 204
Civil Rights Act, 90
Clements, Earle, 41

Cleveland, Grover, 23–24
Cleveland Clinic, 141
Clinton, Bill: Aid to Families with Dependent Children (AFDC) and, 6, 221, 268, 274, 278; Balanced Budget Act and, 172–76, 180, 189; Dole and, 165, 167, 172, 240–43, 246, 255, 257, 269; Family Support Act and, 223; Gingrich and, 6–7, 159–62, 165–68, 176, 221, 224–25, 234–36, 239, 241, 243, 246–48, 252, 255, 268–69, 274, 278; government shutdowns and, 152, 164–69; immigrants and, 268; interest groups and, 162; Kennedy and, 253; Medicare and, 159–76, 180–81, 184, 189, 269; Mills and, 6, 223, 277; National Governors Association and, 223, 234; New Deal and, 242; prescription drugs and, 180–81, 184; President's Working Group on Welfare Reform, Family Support and Independence and, 223–24; Roosevelt and, 253; second term of, 225; Social Security Disability Insurance (SSDI) and, 6, 230, 268; State of the Union address of, 249; Temporary Aid to Needy Families (TANF) and, 7, 261, 268; Ticket to Work and, 72, 291n60; welfare reform and, 6–7, 164, 172, 216, 221, 223–25, 230–61, 268–69, 274, 277–78, 318n19
Clinton, Hillary, 246
Cohen, Chris, 137
Cohen, Wilbur, ix, 9; AFL-CIO and, 27–28, 36–37, 45, 81, 94, 118; Ball and, 27–28, 81; Cruikshank and, 36–37, 81; Department of Health, Education, and Welfare and, 81, 198, 204; disability insurance and, 27–28, 36–37, 45, 64, 69; George and, 36–37, 45; Government Affairs Committee and, 64; Johnson and, 37, 45, 81, 89, 94, 118, 204, 296n63; Kennedy and, 81; Medicare and, 81–84, 87–89, 94, 98, 102–3, 106, 113–18, 121, 137, 296n63; pensions and, 198–99; promotions of, 81; Senate Finance Committee and, 36–37; "Tax Dollars Aiding and Abetting Addiction" report of, 229–30; welfare reform and, 198–99, 204
Cohen, William, 64, 229–30
Collins, Cardiss, 222
Commerce Committee, 135–42, 156, 188, 303n51
Commons, John R., 27
Community Work Experience Program (CWEP), 211–12, 214
Complementary Private Health Insurance for Individuals Aged 65 or Over, 88
Congress: adult welfare programs and, 13; Aid to Families with Dependent Children (AFDC) and, 6; conservatives and, 276 (*see also* conservatives); disability insurance and, 15–38, 42–45, 48, 51–55, 59–65, 68–76, 263–65, 285n22; House Ways and Means Committee and, 15, 83, 108, 120 (*see also* House Ways and Means Committee); liberals and, 24 (*see also* liberals); lobbying and, 2, 19, 25, 28, 37, 45, 81, 83, 122, 137, 139, 142, 147, 149, 163, 172, 216, 228; Medicare and, 4–5, 77–88, 91, 94–122, 126–59, 162–70, 173–89, 265–67, 275–76, 303n51, 303n56, 304n71; Personal Responsibility and Work Opportunity Act and, 268–69; political bargaining and, 2–4, 7, 14–15, 45, 77, 94, 116, 120, 125, 179, 235, 264–68; Senate Finance Committee and, 15, 23, 28–34, 36, 59, 82, 91, 107–9, 112–16, 120, 126, 129, 136, 138, 154, 162, 179, 205, 209, 211, 215, 222, 233, 236–40, 265, 285n22; Social Security Disability Insurance (SSDI) and, 2, 6, 48, 51, 60, 70–71, 127, 264; strict disability standards of, 53; unions and, 80–81; welfare reform and, 192–205, 208–17, 220–30, 233–40, 243–45, 248–60, 321n61
Congressional Budget Office (CBO), 48, 150, 173, 184, 275
Congressional Research Service, 83, 296n63, 317n3
Conrad, Kent, 252
conservatives: Aid to Families with Dependent Children (AFDC) and, 7, 191, 199, 206, 219, 275; Christian right and, 238–42, 275; disability insurance and, 16–17, 22–23, 28–30, 36, 38, 42, 48, 59, 74–75, 263; Heritage Foundation and, 242, 275; Medicare and, 84, 87, 90, 107, 112–15, 123, 135, 141, 144, 159, 163, 181–82, 269, 272–73, 275–76, 300n15; pen-

sions and, 16, 30, 163; Social Security and, 7, 17, 28, 38, 42, 75, 84, 87, 163, 181, 191, 220, 263, 275; welfare reform and, 191, 199, 206, 208, 212, 214, 219–22, 226, 233, 236–48
Constantine, Jay, 136
Continental Casualty Company, 119
Contract with America, 158–62, 176, 230, 236, 272
Cooper, Jere, 18, 83
cost of living adjustments, 76, 97, 153, 306n88
Cranston, Alan, 128
Cruikshank, Nelson: AFL-CIO and, 81; Biemiller and, 81–82; Cohen and, 37, 81; disability insurance and, 28, 36–37, 41, 45; George and, 36, 41–42; Johnson and, 41; labor and, 28, 37, 41, 81; Medicare and, 81–83, 85, 87, 89, 94, 98, 102, 114, 119; Mills and, 81
Curtis, Carl, 42–43, 116
Curtis, Thomas, 84, 93

Daley, Richard, 99, 135, 137
Daly, Sharon M., 249–50
Davis, Carolyne, 149
Davis, Karen, 132–33
deductibles: Medicare and, 87, 92, 95, 98, 100, 114–15, 134, 147, 179, 265, 297n75, 308n24, 312n86; one day, 98; uniform, 114; variable, 114–15, 265; Wagner and, 87
Democrats: Congressional majority of, 5, 16, 18; disability insurance and, 2, 17–24, 29–30, 33–38, 41–45, 62–63, 276; government shutdowns and, 152, 164–69; landslides of, 5, 80, 82, 264; Medicare and, 79–85, 90–94, 99, 101, 105, 111–16, 120, 129–31, 136–47, 150–52, 160, 162–71, 174–75, 178–85, 264–65; National Committee and, 163; northern vs. southern, 30; Social Security Disability Insurance (SSDI) and, 2; unions and, 2, 24, 30, 41, 44, 111, 225; welfare reform and, 208, 215–16, 220, 223–26, 232, 235–53, 256–58. *See also specific politicians*
Department of Health, Education, and Welfare: Califano and, 59–60; Cohen and, 81, 198, 204; disability insurance and, 18, 21–22, 54, 59–60, 68, 70–71, 285n22; Ellwood and, 222–24, 257, 317n3; Gardner and, 203; lack of leadership and, 137; Medicare and, 81, 87–88, 95, 97, 105, 107, 119, 129, 132, 134, 137, 140, 143, 178; Ribicoff and, 199; Weinberger and, 212; Welfare Administration and, 97–98, 195, 204–5, 215; welfare reform and, 198–99, 203–4, 209, 212
Department of Health and Human Services (HHS): Bane and, 224; Medicare and, 143–46, 148, 155, 163, 173, 178, 182, 305n83, 308n33; protesting resignations at, 247; welfare reform and, 221–24, 233, 245–46, 257
Derthick, Martha, ix, 3, 13–14
diagnosis-related groups, 148–56, 272
Dingell, John, 135, 164
Dirksen, Everett, 92, 115
disabilities: Americans with Disabilities Act (ADA) and, 8, 14, 72–75, 264, 270; civil rights and, 16; frozen wages and, 17; rehabilitation and, 2 (*see also* rehabilitation); SSDI and, 1 (*see also* Social Security Disability Insurance [SSDI]); unemployment and, 19, 50–51
"Disability, Antiprofessionalism and Civil Rights" (Kornbluh), 10
Disability Benefits Reform Act, 65
disability insurance: administrative law judges (ALJs) and, 56–58, 64–65, 264; Affordable Care Act and, 185–88, 311n81; age limits and, 15, 53, 60; American Medical Association (AMA) and, 18–19, 38, 43; approval rates for, 55; Ball and, 22, 27–28, 53, 81, 285n22; Byrd and, 28–37, 40–44, 47–50, 58, 265; Carter and, 59–62, 73; caseloads of, 62, 66, 70–71; cash benefits and, 16, 20, 34–35, 39–41, 48, 50, 58, 67, 69–70, 75; children and, 50, 53, 64, 67; Cohen and, 27–28, 36–37, 45, 64, 69; Congress and, 15–38, 42–45, 48, 51–55, 59–65, 68–76, 263–65, 285n22; conservatives and, 16–17, 22–23, 28–30, 36, 38, 42, 48, 59, 74–75, 263; Cruikshank and, 28, 36–37, 41, 45; Curtis and, 42–43; Democrats and, 2, 17–24, 29–30, 33–38, 41–45, 62–63, 276; determination services and, 62–

disability insurance (*continued*)
64; difficulty in passing bill, 1–3; disease and, 19, 40, 50, 54, 66–67, 75; doctors and, 2, 18–19, 28, 30–33, 40–43, 53, 55, 68; Eisenhower and, 18, 20–21, 25, 30, 35, 39–45, 53, 74; eligibility and, 35, 55, 62; employers and, 16–18, 30–32, 43, 71–74, 289n81; expansion of, 50–58; Folsom and, 21–24, 32–33, 36, 41, 44–45, 48, 50, 54, 285n22; George and, 34–39, 41, 45, 79; hospitals and, 19, 72–73, 289n81; House passage of, 16–21; House Ways and Means Committee and, 15, 18–20, 29, 31, 53, 60, 64, 69; inflation and, 54, 61; interest groups and, 15, 23–26; Johnson and, 29–30, 33, 37–45; labor and, 10, 12, 15–19, 23–34, 37, 39–53, 58, 60–61, 67, 70, 264, 285n26, 286n38; liberals and, 16, 20, 24, 26, 28–30, 34–37, 42, 44, 51, 61–62, 64, 72, 75, 263; locked-in policy and, 3–4; Medicare and, 6, 77 (*see also* Medicare); Mills and, 202–3; national health insurance and, 19, 30; New Deal and, 24–25, 62, 276; Nixon and, 41; patients and, 32, 40; payroll taxes and, 23, 32, 52, 55; pensions and, 30, 52; permanent and totally disabled and, 13, 21, 32, 35, 195–96; policy feedback and, 3–5, 13, 52, 271; poverty and, 47; program comparisons and, 271–76; program structure of, 54–58; Reagan and, 62–63, 65–66, 71–74; rejection rates and, 56; Republicans and, 2, 17–21, 25, 29–38, 44, 63–64, 69–74; retirement and, 15, 17, 22, 29, 31–32, 35–38, 42–45, 50–52, 56, 59; rise of rehabilitation and, 16–21; Roosevelt and, 24, 35, 37, 40; Senate Finance Committee and, 15, 23, 28–34, 36, 59, 285n22; Social Security Act and, 17, 24, 27, 32, 56, 69; standards for, 53, 62, 64; Supplemental Security Income (SSI) and, 59, 71, 73; suspension of, 62–66; Ticket to Work and, 72, 291n60; trust funds and, 3, 38, 42, 45, 52, 59–60, 70–71, 277; unemployment and, 17, 19, 24, 50–51, 286n38; welfare reform and, 6, 8, 16, 26–27, 42, 51–52, 55, 58–66, 75–76, 86, 127, 189–91, 202–3, 221–22, 225, 229, 266, 268, 273–74, 277; workers' compensation and, vii, 231, 286n38. *See also* Social Security Disability Insurance (SSDI)
Disability Rights and the American Social Safety Net (Erkulwater), 10
Disabled Policy (Berkowitz), ix
disease: AIDS, 177; cancer, 31, 84, 141, 155; disability insurance and, 19, 40, 50, 54, 66–67, 75; end stage renal, 5, 12, 54, 122, 127–29, 159, 189, 210, 266; environment of, 50, 58, 66–67, 75; heart, 40, 84; kidney, 8, 126–29; Medicare coverage and, 5, 8, 12, 122, 126–29, 150, 159, 177, 189, 266; welfare reform and, 210
Dixiecrats, 29
doctors: American Medical Association (AMA) and, 18–19, 43, 83, 95, 101, 111–12, 117; choice of, 310n58; disability insurance and, 2, 18–19, 28, 30–33, 40–43, 53, 55, 68; as government employees, 19, 78; Medicare and, 4–6, 12, 77–83, 88, 95–96, 101–6, 110–13, 117, 123, 126, 130, 144–45, 147, 150, 155–56, 169, 176–77, 180, 189, 265–67, 270–71, 303n56, 310n58; national health insurance and, 6, 19, 30, 176, 264; private health insurance and, 30, 77–81, 88, 130, 176, 265, 303n56; second opinions and, 135
Dodd, Christopher, 242
Dole, Robert: Clinton and, 165, 167, 172, 240–43, 246, 255, 257, 269; Medicare and, 147, 165, 167, 172; welfare reform and, 208, 234, 239–43, 246, 251, 255, 257, 269
Domenici, Pete, 167
Donaldson, Sam, 227–28
Doughton, Robert, 69
Douglas, Paul, 30, 34, 37–38, 40, 70, 82, 91, 113, 117
drug addicts, 229–30
Dukakis, Michael, 217
Dulles, John Foster, 35
Dunn, Loula, 36

Eastland, James, 42
Eastman Kodak, 21–22
Eberharter, Herman, 20–21
Edelman, Marian Wright, 236, 245–46, 257

Edelman, Peter, 257–58, 308n33
Eisenhower, Dwight D.: AFL-CIO and, 25; Byrd and, 30; cash benefits and, 41; Curtis and, 43; disability insurance and, 18, 20–21, 25, 30, 35, 39–45, 53, 74; George and, 35–36; heart attack of, 39; juvenile delinquency and, 198; rehabilitation and, 20; Social Security and, 2, 18, 20–21, 42–43, 45, 53, 225; welfare reform and, 198, 225
Eizenstat, Stuart, 142
elderly: AARP and, 147, 164, 171, 179, 182; Joint Committee on Aging and, 64; Medicare and, 4, 11, 77, 83–87, 92–94, 97–105, 110–11, 115, 118–19, 123, 126–27, 129, 144, 146, 150–55, 162–63, 165, 181, 187–88, 191, 210, 264–65, 267; National Committee on Health Care of the Aged and, 88; National Senior Citizens Council and, 81; nursing homes and, 77–78, 91, 99, 108, 114–20, 155–56, 179, 187–88, 238, 297n75, 298n96, 298n103, 312n90; old-age benefits and, 50, 53–54, 124, 193; Social Security and, 12–13, 77, 83–87, 93–94, 98–103, 110, 115, 119, 129, 153, 191–96, 267, 286n38; Supplemental Security Income (SSI) and, 59; welfare reform and, 191–96, 205, 210, 274
eligibility: Affordable Care Act and, 185–86; age limits and, 15, 53, 60, 94, 161, 175, 316n48; Aid to Families with Dependent Children (AFDC) and, 213; denial of, 55; determination services and, 62–64; Disability Benefits Reform Act and, 65; disability insurance and, 35, 55, 62; immigrants and, 260; Medicare and, 80, 94, 128, 161, 175, 185–86; Obama and, 185–86; Reagan and, 62–63, 65–66; roll purification and, 211; state flexibility in, 235; Supplemental Security Income (SSI) and, 228, 260; waiting periods and, 127–28; welfare reform and, 211, 213, 228, 235, 260
Ellender, Allen, 41, 99
Ellender, Joseph, 41
Ellwood, David, 222–24, 257, 317n3
Emanuel, Rahm, 253
employers: disability insurance and, 16–18, 30–32, 43, 71–74, 289n81; Medicare and, 101, 110, 129, 131, 158, 161, 176, 183, 189, 266; payroll taxes and, 12 (*see also* payroll taxes); welfare reform and, 192–93, 195
end stage renal disease, 5, 12, 54, 122, 127–29, 159, 189, 210, 266
Engler, John, 234–35, 239
Equitable Life Assurance Society, 101
Erkulwater, Jennifer, 10
Ervin, James, Jr., 41
Evans, Rowland, 103

Faircloth, Lauch, 238, 256
Falk, I. S., 67–68
Family Assistance Plan (FAP): Aid to Families with Dependent Children (AFDC) and, 206–12, 216, 219, 254; National Welfare Rights Organization (NWRO) and, 208; Nixon and, 127, 206–12, 216, 219, 254–55, 257; opposition to, 208; Reagan and, 211–12; welfare reform and, 127, 206–12, 216, 219, 254–55, 257
Family Support Act: Clinton and, 223; flexible format of, 218–19; Moyers documentary and, 228; Reagan and, 217; welfare reform and, 214–19, 223, 228, 230, 232, 258, 316n46
fathers, vii, 135, 149, 210, 231, 291n60; Aid to Families with Dependent Children (AFDC) and, 6, 196–97, 202, 207; child support and, 217, 232, 250, 254, 258; Moyers documentary and, 228; responsibility and, 211, 217, 227, 232, 250; unemployment and, 200, 202, 217
FDR Memorial, 72
Federation of American Hospitals, 136, 146–47, 150–51, 153, 162
Feminist Majority, 257
Fishbein, Morris, 112
Flemming, Arthur, 290n17
Fogarty, John, 204
Folsom, Marion: Ball and, 22, 285n22; cash benefits and, 41, 48; disability insurance and, 21–24, 32–33, 36, 41, 44–45, 48, 50, 54, 285n22; Myers and, 32; Social Security Administration (SSA) contacts and, 21–22; testimony of, 33

food stamps: Aid to Families with Dependent Children (AFDC) and, 209, 233, 254, 274; calculation of, 207, 315n27; expansion of, 207; illegitimacy and, 246; poverty and, 50, 207–9, 233, 236, 246, 249, 251–54, 259, 268, 274; SNAP and, 268; Social Security and, 50; as Special Supplemental Nutrition Program for Women, Infants, and Children, 236; welfare reform and, 207–9, 233, 236, 246, 249, 251–54, 259
Ford, Gerald, 100, 212
Ford, Harold, 141, 222, 317n2
Foreign Relations Committee, 35
Foster, Richard, 170
Fraser, Douglas, 137, 141
fraud, 32, 48, 143, 161, 222, 228
Frear, Allen, 34, 42
Fulbright, William, 41, 91
Fulton, Richard, 99

Gardner, John, 119, 178, 203
gender, 12, 283n1, 286n38
General Accounting Office (GAO), 62
George, Walter: AFL-CIO and, 37; American Medical Association (AMA) and, 38; civil rights and, 35; Cohen and, 36–37, 45; Cruikshank and, 36, 41–42; disability insurance and, 34–39, 41, 45, 79, 136, 277; Douglas and, 37–38; Eisenhower and, 35–36; Foreign Relations Committee and, 35; Johnson and, 37–38, 41, 45; retirement of, 45–46; Roosevelt and, 35, 37; Senate Finance Committee and, 38; Talmadge and, 35–36, 136
George Washington University Hospital, 130
Gephardt, Richard, 142, 160, 163–65
Gilens, Martin, 12
Gingrich, Newt: Aid to Families with Dependent Children (AFDC) and, 6, 8, 190–91, 221, 268, 274, 278; Balanced Budget Act and, 176; Clinton and, 6–7, 159–62, 165–68, 176, 221, 224–25, 234–36, 239, 241, 243, 246–48, 252, 255, 268–69, 274, 278; Contract with America and, 158–62, 176, 230, 236, 272; Dole and, 165, 167, 234, 239, 241, 243, 246, 255, 269; election victory of, 159; interest groups and, 162; Medicare and, 158–68, 176–77, 189–90, 269; opportunity society and, 236, 268, 276; Senate Finance Committee and, 239; Social Security Disability Insurance (SSDI) and, 6, 268; as Speaker of the House, 7–8, 159–60, 162, 166–67, 176, 221, 224, 234–36, 238, 243, 255, 268; Temporary Aid to Needy Families (TANF) and, 7, 268; welfare reform and, 6–7, 159, 221, 224–25, 234–36, 239, 241, 243, 246, 248, 252, 255, 268–69, 274, 276, 278
Goldbeck, Willis, 146
Goldwater, Barry, 80, 90, 92, 95, 120, 231
Gompers, Samuel, 23–26
Goodling, Bill, 246–47
Gore, Albert, 39, 82, 91, 93, 181, 254
Gottschalk, Peter, 197
Government Affairs Committee, 64–65
government shutdowns, 152, 164–69
Gradison, Willis, 147
Graham, Bob, 251, 256
Gramm, Phil, 239
Great Depression, 17, 31
Great Society: Ford and, 100; Goldwater and, 92; Johnson and, 89, 168, 207; liberalism and, 80; Medicare and, ix, 4, 80, 89, 92, 100, 119, 158, 168, 176, 180, 188, 272, 274, 299n12; New Deal and, 242, 274, 276; Republicans and, 92, 100, 158, 168, 180, 244, 276; Truman Library ceremony and, 119; welfare reform and, 203, 207, 210, 242, 244
Green, William, 24–25
Greyhound Bus Company, 73
Griffiths, Martha, 205
Griswold, Sam, 221
Gross, Julius, 118
guaranteed annual income, 206–9, 212, 220, 273

Harris, Patricia Roberts, 143
Harrison, Burr, 85
Hartke, Vance, 82, 90, 115–16, 128–29, 298n96
Hash, Michael, 188
Haskins, Ron, 224, 244–45
Health Care Financing Administration (HCFA), ix, 149, 184–85, 305n73

Health Care for All Americans Act, 141
Health Insurance Association of America, 119, 145, 147, 262
health maintenance organizations (HMOs), 130–31, 164, 176, 178, 187, 300n15
heart attacks, 25, 39–40, 45, 79, 150
heart disease, 40, 84
Heinz, John, 64, 179
Heller, Walter, 94
Heritage Foundation, 242, 275
Herlong, Sydney, 90
Hill, Lister, 204
Himmelbarb, Richard, 178
Hispanics, 7, 197–98
Hobby, Oveta Culp, 21
Hoffman, Beatrix, 11, 292n1
Holland, Spessard, 42
homelessness, 230, 236–37
Hoover, Herbert, 25
hospitals: Affordable Care Act and, 185–88, 311n81; American Hospital Association and, 88, 112, 114, 133, 136, 141, 146–47, 150, 162; capped charges of, 133–34; choice of, 310n58; cost containment and, 131–45, 149, 153, 159, 185, 302n49; disability insurance and, 19, 72–73, 289n81; Federation of American Hospitals and, 146–47, 150–51, 153, 162; inflationary costs of, 125–26, 130–33, 138–40, 148–49, 272; Medicare and, 5–6, 12, 77–80, 83–85, 88–116, 119–26, 130–62, 168–80, 183, 185, 187, 263–67, 270–72, 278, 297n75, 298n103, 302n49, 304n69, 304n71; private health insurance and, 77–78, 88, 99, 130, 133, 144, 151, 160, 176, 265; target rates and, 304n71
House Ways and Means Committee: disability insurance and, 15, 18–20, 29, 31, 53, 60, 64, 69; Kopetski and, 226; Medicare and, 4, 79, 83–86, 89–90, 94, 97–108, 116, 120, 127–28, 135, 139, 141–42, 145–48, 152–56, 161, 175, 179, 183–84; Pickle and, 64; Shaw and, 235–36; Subcommittee on Health and, 135; Subcommittee on Human Resources and, 228, 235; Subcommittee on Welfare Reform and, 236; welfare reform and, 202–3, 224, 226, 228, 235–36
human capital, 202, 214, 268
Human Resources Committee, 135, 144
Humphrey, Hubert, 81, 118
hunger, 191, 255
Hunter, Robert, 138
Hutchinson, Tim, 226
Hutchison, Kay Bailey, 240
Hutton, E. F., 43

illegitimacy: abortion and, 276; Aid to Families with Dependent Children (AFDC) and, 7; black children and, 13; childcare and, 269, 276; as major social issue, 244; Republicans and, 208, 226, 237–40, 244, 246, 249, 256, 269; Ribicoff on, 199–200; stigma and, 13, 227; straw man arguments and, 226; welfare reform and, 197, 199, 208, 226–27, 232, 237–49, 256, 259
immigrants: Clinton and, 268; denying benefits to, 252; eligibility and, 260; noncitizens and, 229, 237, 251, 254, 269, 318n18; Southern, 13; welfare reform and, 229–31, 236–37, 247, 251–53, 258–60, 268–69
inflation: Carter and, 131–33, 138–40, 142–43, 145, 148–49; disability insurance and, 54, 61; hospital costs and, 125–26, 130–33, 138–40, 148–49, 272; indexing benefits to, 210; Medicare and, 125–26, 129, 161, 189, 272; national health insurance and, 123, 129–32; Social Security and, 54; welfare reform and, 210, 240
interest groups: Aid to Families with Dependent Children (AFDC) and, 274; Clinton and, 162; disability insurance and, 15, 23–26; Gingrich and, 162; labor and, 23–26; Medicare and, 80–82, 122, 134, 147–48, 152, 162, 174, 264, 272; National Governors Association as, 234–35; National Welfare Rights Organization (NWRO) and, 205; welfare reform and, 205, 228, 230, 234–35, 238
intermediate care facilities, 312n90
Internal Revenue Code, 110
International Association of Machinists, 27
Iran-Contra scandal, 179, 215

Jackson, Henry "Scoop," 38–39
Jacobs, Andy, 152
Javits, Jacob, 84, 86, 88, 91–92, 98–102, 265
Jeffords, James, 240
Job Opportunities and Basic Skills Training (JOBS), 218, 232, 316n48
job training, 199, 217–18, 223, 231–32, 238, 258, 316n48
John F. Kennedy Library, 132
Johns Hopkins, 154
Johnson, Lyndon Baines, ix; Byrd and, 33, 41, 44, 82–83, 113; Califano and, 134; Cohen and, 37, 45, 81, 89, 94, 118, 204, 296n63; Cruikshank and, 41; disability insurance and, 29–30, 33, 37–45; George and, 37–38, 41, 45; heart attack of, 39–40; landslide victory of, 82, 94; Medicare and, 80–83, 88–89, 92, 94, 102–4, 107, 111–14, 117–18, 120, 127, 134, 142, 168, 178, 255, 265, 296n63; Mills and, 81, 88–89, 94, 103–4, 111, 118, 202–3, 296n63; Senate Finance Committee and, 29–30, 38, 81–82, 127; welfare reform and, 202–4, 207, 255
Johnson, Robert Wood, ix, 144
Johnson, Van, 25–26
Johnston, Olin D., 41
Joint Committee on Aging, 64
juvenile delinquency, 198, 219

Kage, Ethel, 65
Kasich, John, 160, 167, 175
Kaus, Mickey, 226
Kennedy, Edward, 61–62, 131, 135–43, 175, 302
Kennedy, John F.: Aid to Families with Dependent Children (AFDC) and, 6, 199, 267–68; assassination of, 86; Ball and, 81; Clinton and, 253; Cohen and, 81; John F. Kennedy Library and, 132; Medicare and, 81, 83–89, 103, 109, 119, 132, 265; Mills and, 198; New Frontier of, 132; O'Neil and, 147; Public Welfare Amendments and, 200; Social Security Act and, 267; Sorensen and, 89; welfare reform and, 198–200, 233, 273–74; widows and, 267
Kennedy, Robert, 203–4
Kerr, Robert, 36–38, 40, 84, 86, 90, 97, 103, 247
Kerrey, Bob, 247
Kerr-Mills program, 84, 90, 97, 103
kidney disease, 8, 126–29
King-Anderson bill, 86, 114
Kopetski, Mike, 226
Kornbluh, Felicia, 10
Kussart, Gene R., 233

labor: AFL-CIO and, 23, 25–28, 36–37, 45, 61, 81, 94, 107, 118, 133, 253; bargaining and, 37; Community Work Experience Program (CWEP) and, 211–12, 214; Cruikshank and, 28, 37, 41, 81; disability insurance and, 10, 12, 15–19, 23–31, 34, 37, 39–53, 58, 60–61, 67, 70, 264, 285n26, 286n38; employers and, 12 (*see also* employers); Gompers and, 23–26; Green and, 24–25; job training and, 199, 217–18, 223, 231–32, 238, 258; as key interest group, 23–26; Meany and, 23, 26, 37, 133, 137; Medicare and, 80–81, 86–87, 111, 119–20, 128–29, 135–38, 159, 164, 277; out-of-pocket expenses and, 84, 106, 126, 134, 146, 161, 183, 303n56; pensions and, 15–16, 30, 52, 159, 163, 198, 208, 264; *People's Press* and, 28; political power of, 2, 15–16, 24–25, 31, 52, 81, 129, 164, 206, 208, 222, 225, 259; retirement and, 1 (*see also* retirement); skilled, 24, 83, 92, 125, 155, 312n90; slavery and, 205, 255; Ticket to Work and, 72, 291n60; unemployment and, 12 (*see also* unemployment); unions and, 2, 19, 23–28, 32–37, 41, 44–45, 61, 80–81, 94, 107, 111, 118, 129, 133, 225, 253; welfare reform and, 199, 202, 206–8, 214, 220, 222–25, 250, 253, 259, 268, 273; women and, 7, 12, 32, 42–43, 47, 67, 268, 277; workfare programs and, 16, 191, 205, 210–14, 258, 268–69; Work Incentive Program (WIN) and, 209, 217; younger workers and, 53, 63, 161
Labor and Public Welfare Committee, 87
LaHood, Raymond, 166
Landrum, Philip, 99
Learnfare, 232
Lee, Philip, 178, 181
Legal Action of Wisconsin, 232
legal aid, 63–64, 205

Lehman, Herbert, 38
Levin, Carl, 64–65
Levin, Sander, 249
Lewis, John L., 24
liberals: disability insurance and, 16, 20, 24, 26, 28–30, 34–37, 42, 44, 51, 61–62, 64, 72, 75, 263; Medicare and, 79–91, 96, 99, 103, 107–8, 113–15, 119–20, 129, 131–36, 139–42, 159, 178, 189, 272, 275, 299n1, 300n15, 302n49; pensions and, 16; Social Security and, 24, 28, 30, 35, 61, 80, 84, 87–88, 91, 99, 191, 202, 256, 263; welfare reform and, 191, 198–204, 208, 212, 214, 220, 225, 228, 234, 237–46, 249, 255–56
libertarians, 240
Lindsay, John, 203
Linton, Albert, 24, 33
lobbying, 216, 228; AFL-CIO and, 25, 28, 37, 45, 81; disability insurance and, 2, 19, 25, 28, 37, 45; doctors and, 19; Medicare and, 81, 83, 122, 137, 139, 142, 147, 149, 163, 172
Long, Russell: Cohen and, 82; George and, 34, 39; Medicare and, 82, 91, 93, 113, 115–17, 126, 302n49; welfare reform and, 205, 208, 210–11
loss of hearing, 59
Lott, Trent, 172
Loury, Glenn, 226
Lugar, Richard, 246

Malone, George "Molly," 41, 45
managed care, 5, 123, 135, 160–62, 169, 180–81, 187, 189, 277, 307n8
Marxism, viii
Mason, Noah, 20
matching funds, 316n48
Matsui, Robert, 249
Matusow, Allen, 11
Mayo Clinic, 132
McCarran-Ferguson Act, 292n2
McCarthy, Eugene, 82
McCarty, Margaret, 205
McCormack, John, 81
McCrery, James, 163, 228
McCurry, Michael, 165
McMahon, John Alexander, 133–34, 141, 150
McMullen, Michael, 186
McNamara, Pat, 87
McNerney, Walter, 89
Meany, George, 23, 26, 37, 133, 137
Medicaid: abortion and, 276; all payer system and, 149; beginnings of, 98, 103; George W. Bush and, 181; Carter and, 133, 138–39, 305n73; Clinton and, 164–65, 168–70, 251–52, 254, 258, 268–69, 274; Commerce Committee and, 156; cost of, 103–4, 143, 147, 156–57, 184; cuts to, 148, 156–57, 161–62, 303n56; deductibles and, 312n86; expansion of, 124, 176, 185–88, 312n90; hospital cost containment and, 135, 139; immigrants and, 251–52; Obama and, 189; original benefits of, 108; Reagan and, 154–55, 213; State Children's Health Insurance Program and, 187; state government and, 149, 218, 266, 312n86; unanticipated rise of, 185–88; welfare reform and, 209, 213, 217–18, 249, 251
Medical Savings Accounts, 164–65, 174, 176, 308n24
Medicare: age limits and, 94, 161, 175; deductibles and, 87, 92, 95, 98, 100, 114–15, 134, 147, 179, 265, 297n75, 308n24, 312n86; defined benefits and, 162–63; disease coverage and, 5, 8, 12, 122, 126–29, 150, 159, 177, 189, 266; eligibility and, 80, 94, 128, 161, 175, 185–86; employers and, 101, 110, 129, 131, 158, 161, 176, 183, 189, 266; enactment of, 109–17; expansion of, 77, 123–29; managed care and, 5, 123, 135, 160–62, 169, 180–81, 187, 189, 277, 307n8; out-of-pocket expenses and, 84, 106, 126, 134, 146, 161, 183, 303n56; payroll taxes and, 83, 94–95, 98, 100–101, 103, 105, 110–11, 129, 156, 170, 266, 277; private insurance and, 4, 77–81, 86, 88, 99, 123–24, 130, 133, 144, 151, 160, 164, 176, 189, 265, 303n56; program comparisons and, 271–76; rehabilitation and, 78, 113, 127, 177, 186; rise of regulation and, 148–55; voluntary enrollment and, 5; W-2 forms and, 110; waiting periods and, 127–28
Medicare+Choice, 176
Medicare Catastrophic Coverage Act, 178, 185, 187
Medicare for All, 4, 6

Medicare Modernization Act, 183–85, 310n65, 310n69
MedicarePlus, 164
mental disorders, 59, 64–67, 70, 109, 228
Meyers, Jane, 226
Mfume, Kweisi, 221
Michelmore, Molly, 203
middle class, 47, 192, 231
Mikulski, Barbara, 243, 249, 256
Mills, Wilbur, 202; Aid to Families with Dependent Children (AFDC) and, 6, 202–3, 208, 214; Clinton and, 6, 223, 277; Cooper and, 83; Cruikshank and, 81; disability insurance and, 202–3; Johnson and, 81, 88–89, 94, 103–4, 111, 118, 202–3, 296n63; Kennedy and, 198; Kerr-Mills program and, 84, 90, 97, 103; Medicare and, 4–6, 81–118, 122, 128, 198, 200, 202, 275, 277, 296n63; Public Welfare Amendments and, 200; Social Security Administration (SSA) and, 109–10; welfare reform and, 198, 200, 202–3, 208, 214, 223, 277
Mitchell, William L., 53–54, 179
Mittelstadt, Jennifer, 13
Moffitt, Robert, 197
More Social Security, Less Take Home Pay (booklet), 43
Morris, Dick, 259
mothers: Aid to Families with Dependent Children (AFDC) and, 6–7, 13, 199, 202, 205, 208–11, 214, 222, 232, 259, 268, 278; day care and, 202, 220; illegitimacy and, 7 (*see also* illegitimacy); Learnfare and, 232; Medicare and, 159; Moyers documentary and, 228; National Welfare Rights Organization (NWRO) and, 205; Personal Responsibility and Work Opportunity Act and, 268; responsibility and, 216–17, 227, 237–38, 273; single, 13, 191, 258, 268, 273–74, 278; teenage, 232, 237–39, 259; Temporary Aid to Needy Families (TANF) and, 278; unmarried, 237–39, 259; welfare reform and, 190–91, 198–99, 202–11, 214, 216–17, 220, 222, 228–29, 232, 237–39, 250, 258–60; Work Incentive Program (WIN) and, 209. *See also* children
Moving Ahead: Initiatives for Expanding Opportunity in America (policy paper), 224
Moyers, Bill, 217, 228
Moynihan, Daniel, 147, 216, 236, 238, 240, 242–43, 245, 248, 252, 255–57
Mr. Social Security (Berkowitz), ix
Murray, Charles, 244, 321n61
Murray, Philip, 25
Myers, Robert J., 31–32, 83, 102, 106–7

Nader, Ralph, 133
National Academy of Sciences, 143
National Academy of Social Insurance, ix
National Association for Medical Equipment, 174
National Association of Patients, 128
National Committee on Health Care of the Aged, 88
National Committee to Preserve Social Security and Medicare, 179
National Economic Council, 172
National Governors Association, 216, 219, 223, 234–35, 249
national health insurance: cost of, 11; demise of, 129–31; disability insurance and, 19, 30; doctors and, 6, 19, 30, 176, 264; Health Care for All Americans Act and, 141; inflation and, 123, 129–32; Kennedy and, 139–41; Medicare and, 6, 11, 84, 111, 118–19, 123, 128–43, 156, 160, 176, 178, 180, 264, 272, 278; Nixon and, 129
National Industrial Recovery Act, 24
National Institutes of Health, 139
National Labor Relations Board, 27–28
National Libraries of Medicine, ix
National Organization of Women, 257
National Senior Citizens Council, 81
National Veterans Medical Society, 32
National Welfare Rights Organization (NWRO), 204–9, 217, 232
Nelson, Gaylord, 131, 138
Nestingen, Ivan, 87
New Deal, viii; Aid to Families with Dependent Children (AFDC) and, 274; Carter and, 62; Clinton and, 242; disability insurance and, 24–25, 62, 276; Great Society and, 242, 274, 276; Kennedy and, 62, 253; Medicare and, 276;

welfare reform and, 196, 231, 242, 253; worker's compensation and, 231
New Frontier, 132
Nickles, Don, 236
Nixon, Richard M.: Aid to Families with Dependent Children (AFDC) and, 6, 207, 212, 273; China and, 208; disability insurance and, 41; Family Assistance Plan (FAP) and, 127, 206–12, 216, 219, 254–55, 257; Medicare and, 123, 127–30, 178, 184; national health insurance and, 129; prescription drugs and, 178; welfare reform and, 207–12, 255, 257
noncitizens, 229, 237, 251, 254, 269, 318n18
North Atlantic Treaty Organization (NATO), 36
Novak, Robert, 103
nursing homes: American Medical Association (AMA) and, 99; Ball and, 114; Gore and, 91; government reimbursement and, 78; Gross and, 118; Medicare and, 77–78, 91, 99, 108, 114–20, 155–56, 179, 187–88, 238, 297n75, 298n96, 298n103, 312n90; Ribicoff and, 116

Obama, Barack, 47, 50–51, 185–86, 188–89
O'Brien, Larry, 82, 97, 106, 114
O'Donnell, Kenny, 87
Office of Child Support Enforcement, 217
Office of Vocational Rehabilitation, 68, 71
Ohio State Medical Association, 111
old-age assistance, 186, 194–96
old-age benefits, 50, 53–54, 124, 193
Olson, Laura, 188
Omnibus Budget Reconciliation Act (OBRA), 213–14, 218
O'Neill, Thomas P., 147
out-of-pocket expenses, 84, 106, 126, 134, 146, 161, 183, 303n56

Packwood, Robert, 241
Panetta, Leon, 167, 235, 247, 254
Parker, Wayne, 228
participation rates, 197–98
Patashnik, Eric, 9
path dependency, 3, 5–7, 11, 14, 264, 271
patients: Affordable Care Act and, 185–88, 311n81; choices of, 168, 310n58; diagnosis-related groups and, 148–56, 272; disability insurance and, 32, 40; drugs and, 176–83 (*see also* prescription drugs); managed care and, 5, 123, 135, 160–62, 169, 180–81, 187, 189, 277, 307n8; Medical Savings Accounts and, 164–65, 174, 176, 308n24; Medicare and, 11, 78, 83, 87, 101, 105–6, 110, 112–15, 127–32, 135, 138, 141–51, 154–55, 168, 177, 187, 298n96, 298n103, 298n105, 300n15, 303n56, 304n69, 310n58; National Association of Patients and, 128; out-of-pocket expenses and, 84, 106, 126, 134, 146, 161, 183, 303n56; private health insurance and, 11, 130, 138, 144, 151, 177, 303n56
payroll taxes: disability insurance and, 23, 32, 52, 55; Medicare and, 83, 94–95, 98, 100–101, 103, 105, 110–11, 129, 156, 170, 266, 277; Social Security and, 2, 5, 12, 23, 32, 52, 83, 95, 100–101, 103, 110–11, 156, 277; welfare reform and, 194–95
pensions: conservatives and, 16, 30, 163; disability insurance and, 30, 52; liberals and, 16; Medicare and, 159, 163, 198, 208; retirement and, 15–16, 30, 52, 159, 163, 198, 208, 264; Social Security Act and, 198–99
People's Press (labor newspaper), 28
Pepper, Claude, 61, 178
Perkins, Carl, 52–53
Perkins, Roswell, 22, 285n22
Perlman, Selig, 27
permanent and totally disabled, 13, 21, 32, 35, 195–96
Personal and Family Responsibility Initiative, 232
Personal Responsibility and Work Opportunity Act, 230, 236, 259–60, 262, 267–69, 273
Pickle, Jake, 60, 64
policy feedback, 3–5, 13, 52, 271
Policymaking for Social Security (Derthick), ix
political bargaining, 2–4, 7, 14–15, 45, 77, 94, 116, 120, 125, 179, 235, 264–68
Potetz, Lisa, 157
poverty: Aid to Families with Dependent Children (AFDC) and, 203, 206, 221, 268, 278; disability insurance and, 47; homeless and, 230, 236–37; hunger and, 191, 255; Medicare and, 84, 95, 97, 186,

poverty (*continued*)
312n86; slavery and, 205, 255; Social Security and, 2, 84, 192; War on Poverty and, 203, 205; welfare reform and, 191–92, 203–6, 221, 223–24, 226, 241, 245, 255–58
Powell, Jody, 142–43
preferred provider organizations (PPOs), 162, 164, 176
prescription drugs: George W. Bush and, 180–83; Clinton and, 180–81, 184; early morning vote on, 181–82; Medicare and, 5, 8, 11–12, 122–23, 126, 138, 143, 159, 177–87, 215, 267, 272, 311n71, 311n73; psychotropic, 64; welfare reform and, 215, 226, 229–30, 267
President's Commission on Income Maintenance Programs, 207
President's Working Group on Welfare Reform, Family Support and Independence, 223–24
Prime Time (TV show), 227–28
Primus, Wendell, 257
private health insurance: doctors and, 30, 77–81, 88, 130, 176, 265, 303n56; hospitals and, 77–78, 88, 99, 130, 133, 144, 151, 160, 176, 265; Medicare and, 4, 77–81, 86, 88, 99, 123–24, 130, 133, 144, 151, 160, 164, 176, 189, 265, 303n56; patients and, 11, 130, 138, 144, 151, 177, 303n56
Prospective Payment Assessment Commission, 155–57, 173
Public Citizen's Health Research Group, 133
Public Health Service, 68, 128
Public Welfare Amendments, 200, 202, 219

Rabin, Yitzhak, 167
race, 9, 12–13, 107, 197, 207, 222, 255, 286n38
Rader, Lloyd, 36–37
Rangel, Charles, 222, 304n69
Rayburn, Sam, 18
Reagan, Ronald: Aid to Families with Dependent Children (AFDC) and, 6, 206, 211–14, 273, 303n56; Americans with Disabilities Act (ADA) and, 73–74; assassination attempt on, 74, 212; Beneficiary Rehabilitation Program (BRP) and, 71–72, 149, 213; Brady and, 73–74; Carleson and, 212–13; Carter and, 62, 143–44, 149, 212; Community Work Experience Program (CWEP) and, 211–12, 214; Disability Benefits Reform Act and, 65; eligibility standards and, 62–63, 65–66; Family Assistance Plan (FAP) and, 211–12; Family Support Act and, 217; Goldwater and, 92; Iran-Contra scandal and, 215; Medicare and, 143–49, 152, 154, 171, 178, 180, 189, 303n56; National Governors Association and, 216, 219; National Welfare Rights Organization (NWRO) and, 206; Omnibus Budget Reconciliation Act (OBRA) and, 213–14, 218; Schweiker and, 303n55; Senate Finance Committee and, 211; State of the Unionaddress and, 178; Stockman and, 62; Tax Equity and Fiscal Responsibility Act (TEFRA) and, 143–48; Weinberger and, 212; welfare reform and, 62–63, 65–66, 71–74, 206, 210–17, 256–57, 273–74, 277; workfare and, 210–14
Rector, Robert, 242
Reed, Bruce, 224
Reed, Ralph, 242
Reedy, George, 41
rehabilitation: administrative law judges (ALJs) and, 57; Aid to Families with Dependent Children (AFDC) and, 196–202; American Academy of Physical Medicine and, 32; Beneficiary Rehabilitation Program and, 71–72; Byrd and, 48, 50; cash benefits and, 2, 16, 34–35, 40, 69–70, 75, 78, 199–200, 204; civil rights and, 8, 278; Doughton and, 69; Eisenhower and, 20, 43, 45; eligibility and, 35; Folsom and, 22–23, 48, 50; medical associations and, 32–33; Medicare and, 78, 113, 127, 177, 186; objective of, 8; Office of Vocational Rehabilition and, 68, 71; political debate over, 32–35, 38, 40; poor state record of, 19–20; Public Welfare Amendments and, 200; remedying issues of, 67–75, 270, 272; retirement and, 8, 22, 45, 50, 52;

rise of, 16–21; Social and Rehabilitation Service and, 204, 212, 215; Social Security Administration (SSA) and, 67, 70–71; Social Security Disability Insurance (SSDI) and, 59, 67–75, 263–64, 278; systemic imbalance and, 52, 55; theme of, 2; Ticket to Work and, 72, 291n60; veterans and, 20, 68; Viscardi and, 40–41; vocational, 19–23, 33, 38, 67–75, 204, 264; welfare reform and, 191, 196–202, 204, 212, 215, 219, 238; World War II era and, 68

Republicans: Aid to Families with Dependent Children (AFDC) and, 159; Balanced Budget Act and, 176; block grants and, 269; Contract with America and, 158–62, 176, 230, 236, 272; disability insurance and, 2, 17–21, 25, 29–38, 44, 63–64, 69–74; frozen wages and, 17; government shutdowns and, 152, 164–69; Great Society and, 92, 100, 158, 168, 180, 244, 276; illegitimacy and, 208, 226, 237–40, 244, 246, 249, 256, 269; Iran-Contra scandal and, 179, 215; landslides of, 44, 214–15, 252; Medical Savings Accounts and, 164–65, 174, 176, 308n24; Medicare and, 5, 79–85, 88–94, 98–105, 108, 111, 115–17, 130, 142, 147, 152, 158–75, 179–182, 185, 188, 257, 265–68, 276; Murray light and, 321n61; National Committee and, 163; Social Security Disability Insurance (SSDI) and, 2, 70, 73; unions and, 2, 41, 44, 111, 225, 253; welfare reform and, 208, 212, 215–16, 220, 224–28, 277, 318n19, 321n61. *See also specific politicians*

responsibility: administrative, 28, 44, 58–59, 61, 80, 106, 110, 126, 146, 148, 161, 174, 180, 192, 196, 198, 215–16, 229, 265, 267; African Americans and, 13; fathers and, 211, 217, 227, 232, 250; Medicare and, 80, 106, 110, 126, 146, 148, 161, 174, 180, 265; mothers and, 216–17, 227, 237–38, 273; national health insurance and, 19; Personal Responsibility and Work Opportunity Act and, 230, 236, 259–60, 262, 267–69, 273; welfare reform and, 192, 196, 198, 215–16, 229–30, 236–38, 250, 255, 259–60, 262, 265, 267–68, 273

Reston, Jimmy, 35

retirement: AARP and, 147, 164, 171, 179, 182; disability insurance and, 15, 17, 22, 29, 31–32, 35–38, 42–45, 50–52, 56, 59; early, 15, 36, 43, 146, 283n1; legal age for, 1; Medicare and, 77, 85–86, 93, 101, 116, 119, 122, 127, 139, 146–47, 158, 160–61, 276; pensions and, 15–16, 30, 52, 159, 163, 198, 208, 264; rehabilitation and, 8, 22, 45, 50, 52; Social Security and, 1–2, 22, 36, 38, 43, 45, 59, 77, 85, 93, 101, 127, 161, 192–93, 220, 256, 276, 283n1; welfare reform and, 192–93, 220, 256; women and, 32, 42–43, 283n1

Reuther, Walter, 25–26, 32

Ribicoff, Abraham, 82, 90–92, 115–16, 199–200, 302n49

Rich, Spencer, 148, 160

Richardson, Bill, 167

Richardson, Elliot, 129

riots, 203–5, 207, 217, 273

Rivlin, Alice, 150

Roberston, Absalom Willis, 42

Robert Wood Johnson Foundation, ix

Rockefeller, John D., 249

Rockefeller, Nelson, 22, 84, 88

Rogers, Paul, 136, 138–39

Roosevelt, Franklin D.: Clinton and, 253; court-packing plan of, 35; crippled legs of, 40; disability insurance and, 24, 35, 37, 40; FDR Memorial and, 72; George and, 35, 37; Social Security Act and, 24, 35, 192; welfare reform and, 192, 225, 249, 253

Rostenkowski, Dan, 99, 135–40, 145

Roth, William, 246

Rother, John, 171

Rubin, Robert, 144, 146, 149, 151–52

Rusk, Howard, 40

Russell, Richard, 35, 38, 41

Russo, Martin, 137–38, 140

Sain, Kenneth, 137

Sanders, Beulah, 205

Santorum, Rick, 228–29, 251–52, 318n19

Sarbanes, Paul, 243

Schreiber, Jack, 111–13
Schweiker, Richard, 143–45, 148–54, 303n55
Scully, Tom, 162
Senate Finance Committee: Anderson and, 81; Byrd and, 28–36, 82–83, 90, 107–9, 113–14, 116, 265; Chaffee and, 236; Cohen and, 36–37; Community Work Experience Program (CWEP) and, 211; disability insurance and, 15, 23, 28–34, 36, 59, 285n22; Family Assistance Plan (FAP) and, 208–9; George and, 35, 38; Gingrich and, 239; Gramm and, 239; Hartke and, 82; hospital cost containment and, 136; Johnson and, 29–30, 38, 81–82, 127; McCarthy and, 82; Medicare and, 82, 91, 107–9, 112–16, 120, 126, 129, 136, 138, 154, 162, 179, 265; National Welfare Rights Organization (NWRO) and, 205; Packwood and, 241; party division of, 29; Reagan and, 211; Ribicoff and, 82; Roth and, 246; style of, 29; welfare reform and, 59, 205, 209, 211, 215, 222, 233, 236–40
Shalala, Donna, 163, 173, 221, 234–35, 245, 247, 255, 317n8
Shaw, Clay, 224, 226, 229, 235–36
Shelby, Richard, 142
single mothers, 7, 12–13, 191
skilled nursing, 83, 92, 125, 155, 312n90
Skocpol, Theda, viii
slavery, 205, 255
Smathers, George, 42, 91–93, 117
SNAP, 268
Social and Rehabilitation Service, 204, 212, 215
social insurance: Falk on, 67–68; Medicare and, 6, 92, 95, 98, 106, 109, 186–87, 191; Mills and, 92; Social Security Act and, 12, 192–94; SSDI and, 6 (*see also* Social Security Disability Insurance [SSDI]); welfare reform and, 191–96. *See also* disability insurance
Social Security: administrative law judges (ALJs) and, 56–58, 64–65, 264; age limits and, 15, 53, 60, 283n1, 316n48; benefits level of, 12; cash benefits and, 16, 50, 75, 77, 79, 84, 111, 191, 198; conservatives and, 7, 17, 28, 38, 42, 75, 84, 87, 163, 181, 191, 220, 263, 275; cost of, 124; Curtis' reform and, 42–43; defined benefits and, 158; Eberharter on, 20–21; Eisenhower and, 18, 20–21, 42–43, 45, 53, 225; elderly and, 12–13, 77, 83–87, 93–94, 98–103, 110, 115, 119, 129, 153, 191–96, 267, 286n38; expansion of, 43–45, 50–59, 195, 225, 289n81; Folsom and, 21–23, 32, 36, 44–45, 285n22; food stamps and, 50; inflation and, 54, 210; liberals and, 24, 28, 30, 35, 61, 80, 84, 87–88, 91, 99, 191, 202, 256, 263; limitation of, 194–95; means test and, 193; Medicare and, 79 (*see also* Medicare); National Committee to Preserve Social Security and Medicare and, 179; old-age benefits and, 50, 53–54, 124, 193; omnibus law of, 54; path dependency and, 6–7; payroll taxes and, 2, 5, 12, 23, 32, 52, 83, 95, 100–101, 103, 110–11, 156, 277; political popularity of, 79; poverty and, 2, 84, 192; rejection rates and, 56; retirement and, 1–2, 22, 36, 38, 43, 45, 59, 77, 85, 93, 101, 127, 161, 192–93, 220, 256, 276, 283n1; retroactive benefits and, 96, 230, 298n105; success of, 192; unemployment and, 12, 24, 192, 286n38; W-2 forms and, 110; welfare reform and, 7, 27, 42, 58–66, 75–76, 85, 127, 155, 191, 212–13, 220–21, 225, 229–31, 268, 277
Social Security Act: Aid to Families with Dependent Children (AFDC) and, 191; Amendments to, 7, 69, 95, 127, 129, 195; categories of, 192–93; disability insurance and, 17, 24, 27, 32, 56, 69; Kennedy and, 267; Medicare and, 96, 111, 158; pension approach of, 198–99; Personal Responsibility and Work Opportunity Act and, 267; Roosevelt and, 24, 35, 192; social insurance and, 12, 192–94; welfare reform and, 191–95, 198, 213, 220
Social Security Administration (SSA), 168, 186; administrative law judges (ALJs) and, 56–57; AFL-CIO and, 45; Ball and, 53, 81, 285n22; benefit applications and, 3; Bureau of Public Assistance and, 193–95; Cohen and, 27–28; costs of elderly and, 93; expansion of, 118–19;

Falk and, 67–68; financing issues and, 93, 95; Folsom and, 21–22; increased hearings of, 57; Mills and, 109–10; Mitchell and, 53–54, 179; Office of the Actuary and, 183; Office of Vocational Rehabilitation and, 68, 71; Perkins and, 53; rehabilitation and, 67–71; Social Security Board and, 193; Social Security Disability Insurance (SSDI) and, 196; Svahn and, 212; Switzer and, 69–71, 204; target rates and, 304n71; Welfare Administration and, 97; welfare reform and, 193–94, 196, 212, 215
Social Security Advisory Council, 178
Social Security Board, 27–28, 31, 193
Social Security Disability Insurance (SSDI), viii–ix; abuse of, 227–29; administrative law judges (ALJs) and, 57; Byrd and, 47–48, 265; cash benefits of, 20, 39–40, 48, 50, 67, 69, 75; civil rights and, 10, 75, 278; Clinton and, 6, 268; Congress and, 2, 6, 48, 51, 60, 70–71, 127, 264; costs of, 48–50; defenders of, 6; Democrats and, 2; difficulty in passing bill for, 1–3; Eisenhower and, 2; expansion of, 50–54, 59; Gingrich and, 6, 268; importance of, 10; income maintenance and, 278; interfund borrowing and, 60; limitations on, 230; Medicare and, 127, 265; Obama and, 47; poverty and, 2; rehabilitation and, 59, 67–75, 263–64, 278; Republicans and, 2, 70, 73; retirement and, 1; Social Security Administration and, 196; stigma and, 227; waiting periods and, 127–28; welfare reform and, 58–66, 261
Sorensen, Ted, 89
Soss, Joe, 13
Special Supplemental Nutrition Program for Women, Infants, and Children, 236
Springer, Elizabeth, 36
Stark, Pete, 185
State Children's Health Insurance Program, 187
Stennis, John C., 42
stereotypes, 13, 225, 229–30, 259
Stevenson, Adlai, 25, 29, 44
stigma: Aid to Families with Dependent Children (AFDC) and, 210; illegitimacy and, 13, 227; single mothers and, 7, 12, 191; welfare reform and, 191, 195, 210, 227
St. Jude's Children's Hospital, 141
Stockman, David, 62, 71, 149, 213
straw man arguments, 225–30
strokes, 47, 65
Supplemental Security Income (SSI): disability insurance and, 59, 71, 73; elderly and, 59; eligibility and, 228, 260; Erkulwater on, 10; welfare reform and, 59, 210, 227–30, 246, 252, 260
Svahn, John, 212
Sweeney, John J., 253
Switzer, Mary, 69–71, 204

Taft-Harley bill, 225
Talent, Jim, 236, 244
Talmadge, Herman E., 35–36, 91, 126, 136–38, 209
tax cuts, 158, 161–62, 169, 173, 181, 238
"Tax Dollars Aiding and Abetting Addiction" (Cohen), 229–30
Tax Equity and Fiscal Responsibility Act (TEFRA), 143–48
Temporary Aid to Needy Families (TANF): African Americans and, 278; Aid to Families with Dependent Children (AFDC) and, 7–8, 13, 261, 268, 278; Clinton and, 7, 261, 268; Gingrich and, 7, 268; mothers and, 278
Thomas, Bill, 161, 175
Thompson, Tommy, 230–35, 239, 277
Thornburgh, Richard, 74
Ticket to Work, 72, 291n60
Truman, Harry S., 29, 117–19
Trump, Donald, 92, 231, 276
trust funds: disability insurance and, 3, 38, 42, 45, 52, 59–60, 70–71, 277; George and, 38, 45–46; Johnson and, 38; Medicare and, 5, 85, 93, 95, 110, 156, 160, 168, 170–73, 180, 265–66, 273; Mills and, 277; separate, 3, 38, 42, 45, 95, 110, 156, 265
Twentieth Century Fund, viii–ix

unemployment: Aid to Families with Dependent Children (AFDC) and, 12, 202, 211, 214; deadbeats and, 217; disability insurance and, 17, 19, 24, 50–51, 286n38; earned benefits and, 12; fathers

unemployment (*continued*)
and, 200, 202, 217; Great Depression and, 17; intact families and, 200; Social Security and, 12, 24, 192, 286n38; welfare reform and, 192, 200, 202, 211, 214, 217, 222, 231, 241
unions: AFL-CIO and, 23, 25–28, 36–37, 45, 61, 81, 94, 107, 118, 133, 253; Carter and, 137; Congress and, 80–81; Democrats and, 2, 24, 30, 41, 44, 111, 225; disability insurance and, 19, 23–27, 32–34, 41, 44, 61; Gompers and, 23–26; Green and, 24–25; labor movement and, 2, 19, 23–27, 32–34, 41, 44, 61, 80–81, 111, 129, 225, 253; Republicans and, 2, 41, 44, 111, 225, 253
United Auto Workers, 24–25, 137, 141
United Mine Workers, 24
United Steelworkers, 24–25
Urban League, 253

Valenti, Jack, 107, 296n73
Vanik, Charles, 99, 141
Vanishing Family, The: Crisis in Black America (Moyers), 217
veterans, 20, 32, 68, 118, 128
Viscardi, Henry, 40–41
vocational rehabilitation (VR), 19–23, 33, 38, 67–75, 204, 264

W-2 forms, 110
Wagner, Robert, 87
Wagner Act, 24
waiting periods, 127–28
Wamp, Zach, 166
Ward, Donovan, 95
Ware, Norman, 27
War on Poverty, 203, 205
Washington Business Group on Health, 146
Watson, Tom, 35
Watts, John C., 90
Waxman, Henry, 139–43, 147, 150, 179, 188
Weinberger, Caspar, 212
Weld, William R., 235
Welfare Administration, 97–98, 195, 204–5, 215
welfare queens, 228
welfare reform: Disability Benefits Reform Act and, 65; eligibility and, 211, 213, 228, 235, 260; Family Assistance Plan (FAP) and, 127, 206–12, 216, 219, 254–55, 257; Family Support Act and, 214–19, 223, 228, 230, 232, 258, 316n46; food stamps and, 207–9, 233, 236, 246, 249, 251–54, 259; New Deal and, 196, 231, 242, 253; Personal Responsibility and Work Opportunity Act and, 230, 236, 259–60, 262, 267–69, 273; President's Working Group on Welfare Reform, Family Support and Independence and, 223–24; Public Welfare Amendments and, 200, 202, 219; workfare programs and, 16, 210–14
Wellstone, Paul, 255
Why Americans Hate Welfare (Gilens), 12
widows: Aid to Families with Dependent Children (AFDC) and, 6–7, 12–13; Kennedy and, 267; Medicare and, 96; welfare reform and, 191, 196–98, 208, 221, 256, 259
Wilbur Cohen Papers, 9
Wilensky, Gail, 171–72
Wiley, Alexander, 42
Wiley, George, 42, 205
Williams, John, 209
Wilson, Pete, 240
Wisconsin Works, 232–33
Witte, Edwin, 27
Wofford, Thomas A., 41
Wolfe, Sidney M., 133
women: AFDC and, 191 (*see also* Aid to Families with Dependent Children [AFDC]); age of for Social Security, 283n1; children and, 7 (*see also* children); food stamps and, 236 (*see also* food stamps); labor and, 7, 12, 32, 42–43, 47, 67, 268, 277; Medicare and, 188, 191; mothers, 6–7 (*see also* mothers); National Organization of Women and, 257; retirement and, 32, 42–43, 283n1; Special Supplemental Nutrition Program for Women, Infants, and Children and, 236; welfare reform and, 198, 221, 226, 228, 236–37, 239, 242, 257; widows, 6–7, 12–13, 96, 191, 196–98, 208, 221, 256, 259, 267
Woodward, Bob, 227–28

workers' compensation, vii, 231, 286n38
Work Experience and Training Program, 231–32
workfare programs, 16, 191, 205, 210–14, 258, 268–69
Work Incentive Program (WIN), 209, 217
Work Not Welfare, 233
World War II era, 16, 24–25, 40, 67–68
Wright, Jim, 179
Wyden, Ronald, 150, 174

Young, Milton, 42
younger workers, 53, 63, 161